THE HIGH COURT OF PARLIAMENT
AND ITS SUPREMACY

THE HIGH COURT OF PARLIAMENT
AND ITS SUPREMACY

AN HISTORICAL ESSAY ON THE BOUNDARIES
BETWEEN LEGISLATION AND ADJUDICATION
IN ENGLAND

BY

CHARLES HOWARD McILWAIN

THOMAS BRACKETT REED PROFESSOR OF HISTORY AND
POLITICAL SCIENCE IN BOWDOIN COLLEGE

NEW HAVEN : YALE UNIVERSITY PRESS
LONDON : HENRY FROWDE
OXFORD UNIVERSITY PRESS
MDCCCCX

COPYRIGHT, 1910, BY YALE UNIVERSITY PRESS

ENTERED AT STATIONERS' HALL, LONDON

PRINTED IN THE UNITED STATES.

TO THE MEMORY OF
MARY IRWIN McILWAIN

Preface

DR. Augustus Jessopp, in the Preface to his *Studies by a Recluse*, says: "Three years ago I published a collection of papers which I had the presumption to call Historic Essays, in which some of the critics discovered, as a matter of course, a bad blunder or two, and therefore proceeded to censure me for presumption. The fact is, that I was still possessed by the old-fashioned notion that the word 'essay' meant an *attempt* and nothing more." It is only in this old-fashioned sense that I have ventured to call this volume an "essay." In it I have concerned myself only in tracing the history of certain legal ideas. The conclusions that have seemed to me to be deducible from the facts met with in this historical survey may be summarized as follows:

(*a*) England after the Norman Conquest was a feudal state, *i. e.*, its political character is better expressed by the word feudal than by the word national. (*b*) As a consequence, her central assembly was a feudal assembly, with the general characteristics of feudal assemblies. (*c*) One of those characteristics was the absence of law-*making*. The law was declared rather than made. (*d*) The law which existed and was thus declared was a body of custom which in time grew to be looked upon as a law fundamental. Rules inconsistent with

PREFACE

this fundamental law were void. Such a law was recognized in England down to modern times. (*e*) Another characteristic of the times was the absence of a division of labour between different "departments" of government and the lack of any clear corresponding distinctions in governmental activity, as "legislative," "judicial," or "administrative." (*f*) Parliament, the highest "court" of the Realm, in common with the lower courts, participated in these general functions of government. It both "legislated" and "adjudicated," but until modern times no clear distinction was perceived between these two kinds of activity, and the former being for long relatively the less important, we may say roughly that Parliament was more a court than a legislature, while the ordinary courts had functions now properly called legislative as well as judicial. (*g*) "Acts" of Parliament were thus analogous to judgements in the inferior courts, and such acts were naturally not treated by the judges in these courts as inviolable rules *made* by an external omnipotent legislative assembly, but rather as judgements of another court, which might be, and were at times, treated as no modern statute would ever be treated by the courts to-day.

The "legislative" activity of our courts to-day in the United States is a fact that is rightly attracting great attention at the present time, as is shown by the number of recent monographs and articles upon it. It

PREFACE

is a subject of the utmost consequence. This legislative activity is no mere accident; it must have causes, and some of these must be historical causes. Some investigation of these is absolutely prerequisite to any thorough understanding of our judicial system, and to a perception of the kind of changes which would most likely tend toward its betterment. This essay is offered as an attempt to account on historical grounds for the growth of these great powers now exercised by our courts, greater here than in England, because the like tendency was there checked by the growth in the seventeenth century of a new doctrine of parliamentary omnipotence.

I entered upon this study without preconceptions. During the course of it I came to the conclusion that the weight of contemporary evidence was against some views held by men whom I have always looked up to, and shall always look up to, as my leaders and guides in this field. As these divergences of views were not on matters of detail, but concerned things which are the very marrow of the subject under discussion, this has unavoidably given to certain parts of the book a polemical cast, and might lead one to think that it was written from the beginning merely to bolster up a preconceived theory. Such is not the case. Accepting the fact of the great and far-reaching activity of our courts, I have here merely tried to trace the tendency

PREFACE

historically back to mediaeval England, where I believe it has its origin; with the later, or American part of the development, I have had nothing to do.

In my treatment of this subject I have tried to keep within the limits I set for myself at the beginning. Though I have argued against historical views which seemed insufficiently supported by evidence, I have done so without considering the bearing of those arguments upon controverted questions of to-day. Our legal institutions, in common with our other institutions, may be looked at in two ways. Even men's highest religious beliefs and aspirations may in all probability be rightly traced back to instincts which are so elemental and "low" that they are shared by animals far down in the scale of life. By demonstrating this humble origin, and the gradual development out of it, some scientists have supposed that they were disposing of the claims of religion upon the attention of men. They have assumed that a judgement—to use Professor William James's expression—which is purely "existential" has validity also as "a proposition of value." Thus to mistake the history of an institution for its rational justification seems to me a confusion of the worst sort.

In like manner, to say that the present attitude of our courts toward statutory enactment has an historical basis, to hold as I do that it is a judicial habit which

PREFACE

can be traced back to conditions in mediaeval England, is by no means to give it a clean bill of health. To say that this habit has precedent for it is not necessarily to say that it is wholly good. To show that it has marked resemblances to conditions in Tudor England is not enough to shield it from the criticism of the twentieth century. I have differed in some historical points from the excellent article of Professor Roscoe Pound on "Common Law and Legislation," in the *Harvard Law Review* of a year or two ago, but I do not feel that his views of the present relation of legislation and judicature are affected in any way by those differences, whichever of us should prove to be right. He says: "Our constitutional polity expressly contemplates a complete separation of legislative from judicial power.... Not only is a doctrine at variance with that polity inapplicable to American conditions, but if it ever was applicable, the reasons for it have ceased and it should be abandoned." If my study has shown that the present-day extension of judicial action in America has grown out of conditions in the England of an earlier day, it has shown another thing no less clearly — namely, that the government of Tudor England was a government of *fused* powers (while that of the United States to-day is a system of separated powers); and therefore, that the former activity of the judges in England was due to a *fusion* of governmental powers, not to a *division* of

PREFACE

those powers. The extent of "judicial" activity under such conditions is a very dangerous precedent, if it is to be followed slavishly and applied without discrimination to a system in which there is a balance between *divided* powers, where an encroachment of one department upon another may endanger the balance and threaten the whole. It is not fitting that the legal historian should follow precedent to such an extent as in all cases to justify the existence of legal rules merely because he finds for them an unbroken history or even a former usefulness. "The capital fact in the mechanism of modern states is the energy of legislatures."

The fact that I have not been able to follow in all points the masters of English historical jurisprudence has had another result which probably needs explanation. It has made necessary quotations from *pièces justicatives* longer and more frequent than is usual in a writing which makes no claim to be a treatise. The illustrations were intended originally as illustrations merely. In some places, where the points illustrated were at variance with writers of authority, I have felt, however, that it would be presumptuous not to give further proof, and in such places more examples have been given, even at the risk of tediousness. This might seem to give the book an appearance in some places of aiming at an exhaustive treatment of the subjects covered; an aim which the performance would not jus-

PREFACE

tify, and one which has been as far as possible from my thoughts.

Many essential points concerning the development of English central institutions in the middle ages must be made less obscure before generalizations can be formed concerning them in any but a tentative way. In the case of the Receivers and Triers of Petitions in Parliament and one or two other points, I hope in the future to be able to offer some conclusions resulting from a detailed examination of the unprinted records. The materials upon which this study is based are only such as may be found in print in the larger libraries of the United States.

I have tried, in the footnotes and the notes at the ends of the chapters, to indicate in all cases the authorities or sources on which my statements are based. I have also at times placed in them discussions which the general reader might consider too technical. These footnotes will show how much I owe to writers such as Professor Dicey, Sir Frederick Pollock, Mr. Pike, and others. But no specific references can indicate the general debt I owe to the writings of the greatest English historian of our day. It is enough to say that this volume grew out of a paper which I had the honour to read, at a meeting of my colleagues, on the life and writings of Frederick William Maitland.

Hitherto I have spoken mainly of the United States.

PREFACE

But after all, the subject I have taken up in this volume bears even more directly upon the past and present of England and the British Empire than it does upon the United States. The principles and tendencies I have here tried to present and illustrate have been to me a clue which seemed to lead through many a part of English history which before appeared a well-nigh hopeless labyrinth. If I have succeeded in making plain what those tendencies and principles are, I am not without hope that they may be found in some degree helpful to others as well as to myself.

Recent important events in the British Empire, it seems to me, have strengthened some conclusions I had set down in the text. The federation of South Africa and other events of less importance have given encouragement to us who believe in and hope for the future of the British Empire. In England itself it is becoming evident that the long reign of Edmund Burke is about over. For more than a century the political principles which his unrivalled genius distilled from the Whig system of aristocratic rule have been accepted as the ultimate type of free government. These principles, however, predicated a legislative body representative indeed, but sovereign. Burke's candid declaration to his constituents at Bristol, that their candidate when elected was "not a member of Bristol," but "a member of Parliament," admirable as it is, would

PREFACE

lead to certain defeat to-day. "Authoritative instructions" may still be unknown to the laws of the land, but they are a commonplace of democratic rule which no man can now in practice ignore. Mr. Bryce and Professor Dicey have invented a distinction between legal and practical sovereignty to meet this change, the legal sovereign being the Parliament, the practical sovereign, the electors. In the eighteenth century no such distinction was necessary, for Parliament was to all intents and purposes sovereign practically as well as legally. But it may well be doubted whether the doctrine of parliamentary sovereignty in any form that means much can long survive the triumph of democracy. In England democracy has but recently begun to put forth the power that has been legally hers for half a century, but already we find the House of Lords itself justifying its rejection even of a government revenue measure, on the ground that it must be submitted to the people for ratification. Such doctrines, from whatever source they come, are subversive of the old Whig doctrine of a Parliament of "representatives." When the referendum really comes, the sovereign Parliament must go. But whether for good or for evil, the referendum, in principle at least, seems to be coming.

Along with the aristocratic sovereign Parliament, it seems likely, will go also the ancient party lines. The

PREFACE

principle of the referendum and of authoritative instructions is a solvent not only of parliamentary sovereignty, but of the old two-party system as well. That system was the creature of aristocratic government: it would seem that it cannot long survive its creator. One is tempted to doubt whether it still survives. "Parliamentary government," Bagehot thought, "is, in its essence, a sectarian government, and is possible only when sects are cohesive." But in the chaos of groups and coalitions, of conflicting and confusing issues in England to-day, it requires good eyes to see what Burke in the eighteenth century so clearly saw and so elegantly described,—"a body of men united, for promoting by their joint endeavours the national interest, upon some particular principle in which they are all agreed." On the Continent it has never really existed. In the United States it may be doubted whether it has ever existed in the form meant by Burke. Before the Civil War in America a permanent two-party system would have been hard to find; since the war, and largely as a consequence of it, one party has been able to retain almost unbroken power. But now that the results of the war are becoming generally accepted, the growth of independent voting, the scramble for "issues," and the appearance of organized disaffection within party lines, all point to the passing of a phase whose continuance has been due mainly to circumstances that were excep-

PREFACE

tional and not inherent in our political being. Bolingbroke and Washington as political philosophers must be considered far below the level of Burke, and they no more anticipated our modern democracy than he did, but some of their ideas of government seem more in accord with the phase we are now entering than were those of Burke. More than formerly—I am not expressing opinions; only describing conditions—men are heeding Bolingbroke's advice: "Whatever ministers may govern, whatever factions may arise, let the friends of liberty lay aside the groundless distinctions, which are employed to amuse and betray them; let them continue to coalite,"—and Washington's warning: "The common and continual mischiefs of the spirit of party are sufficient to make it the interest and duty of a wise people to discourage and restrain it."

Whatever the future of democracy may be, the main problems to be worked out are the same in America and England, and no thoughtful American can be blind to the immense importance for him of England's solution of these problems; no candid American, whatever his ancestry, can help feeling the deepest interest in them, touched with gratitude for the nation to which we all owe our institutions, our laws, and our political ideals; and many of us so much more.

I hardly dare hope that my work will be found free from errors, even errors of a serious character. It is

PREFACE

scarcely necessary to say that for all such and for all untenable views, I alone am responsible. How many more errors I have escaped through the kindness of friends, no one can know so well as myself. Among those to whom I am indebted for many valuable suggestions are Mr. W. La Roe, Jr.; Professor Edward S. Corwin, whose forthcoming book on the Growth of Judicial Review deals with tendencies in the United States whose prior development in England I am here endeavouring to trace; Professor Morris W. Croll; Professor George Burton Adams; President A. Lawrence Lowell, who was kind enough to spare time to read over the manuscript and recommend alterations, which I have endeavoured to make, though I am afraid I have not in all cases succeeded; Professor Edward Channing, to whose encouragement and suggestions at many stages of the work and long before it began, I owe more than I can well express; my friend Mr. Walter L. Whittlesey, on whose advice and assistance I have depended constantly from the beginning to the end of the undertaking; and finally, Professor Winthrop M. Daniels, at whose suggestion this book was first undertaken, and to whose interest, counsel, and help, above all others, its existence is due. One other name I regret that I cannot include among these, but I must acknowledge the heavy debt I owe to his teaching and to the example of his unrivalled scholarship, though

PREFACE

his death deprived me of the aid he would have given so gladly and I should have prized so highly in the preparation of this book. I mean Professor Charles Gross. My thanks are due also to Mr. Byrne Hackett and the Yale University Press for much help and unvarying courtesy and consideration.

I cannot close this preface without referring to one whose interest in the fortunes of this volume and unselfish gratification at any favour it may ever chance to win would have been far deeper than any like feelings of my own. It would have been my highest privilege to dedicate this book to her: now I can only inscribe it with gratitude and love to her memory.

Princeton University
  Princeton, New Jersey
    June, 1910

Table of Contents

CHAPTER I

	PAGE
Introduction	3
Note A: The Judges in Council	39

CHAPTER II

The Fundamental Law	42
Note A: The Fundamental Law in Bracton	101
Note B: The Beginning of Practical Legislative Sovereignty by Parliament	103
Note C: The Law of Nature in the Dialogue of the Doctor and Student	105

CHAPTER III

Parliament as a Court	109
Note A: Judicial Interpretation of Edward III's Statute of Treason	247
Note B: Early Cases Determined in Parliament	248
Note C: The Relations of Chancery and Parliament	250
Note D: The *Auditores* or Triers of Petitions in Parliament	251

CHAPTER IV

The Relations of "Judiciary" and "Legislature"	257
Note A: Parliamentary Omnipotence and International Law	329
Note B: Parliament as an Advisory Council	330

[xxi]

TABLE OF CONTENTS

Note C: The Delegation of Power by Parliament — 331

Note D: Secondary Legislation in England — 334

CHAPTER V

The Political History of Parliamentary Supremacy — 336

Note A: Parliament's Formal Assertion of Sovereignty — the Declaration of May 27, 1642 — 389

Note B: Parliamentary Sovereignty and the British Empire — 390

Index — 395

THE HIGH COURT OF PARLIAMENT
AND ITS SUPREMACY

"*We must not be in a hurry to get to the beginning of the long history of our law. Very slowly we are making our way towards it. The history of law must be a history of ideas. It must represent, not merely what men have done and said, but what men have thought in bygone ages. The task of reconstructing ancient ideas is hazardous, and can only be accomplished little by little. If we are in a hurry to get to the beginning we shall miss the path. Against many kinds of anachronism we now guard ourselves. We are careful of costume, of armour and architecture, of words and forms of speech. But it is far easier to be careful of these things than to prevent the intrusion of untimely ideas. In particular there lies a besetting danger for us in the barbarian's use of a language which is too good for his thought. Mistakes then are easy, and when committed they will be fatal and fundamental mistakes. If, for example, we introduce the* persona ficta *too soon, we shall be doing worse than if we armed Hengest and Horsa with machine guns or pictured the Venerable Bede correcting proofs for the press; we shall have built upon a crumbling foundation. The most efficient method of protecting ourselves against such errors is that of reading our history backwards as well as forwards, of making sure of our middle ages before we talk about the 'archaic,' of accustoming our eyes to the twilight before we go out into the night."*

F. W. MAITLAND: DOMESDAY BOOK AND BEYOND

CHAPTER I

Introduction

ONE of the most remarkable generalizations in Professor Dicey's brilliant book, *The Law of the Constitution*, is the statement that "federalism substitutes litigation for legislation."[1] This statement has a peculiar importance in countries—of which there are so many on the continent of Europe—whose central institutions have in large part been consciously modelled in recent times upon those of England. Its importance is greater still in a country like our own, where not only central but local institutions as well stand to the English Constitution in the infinitely closer and more intimate relationship of parent and child.

That there is an extraordinary amount of litigation here—that we are a "litigious people"—may be admitted at once. It is true that constitutional matters of the highest concern to the people are commonly settled in the United States by private actions between individuals,—matters often that would never in the ordinary course come before an English court of law.

This is so well understood that illustration is unnecessary, and so noticeable a part of our system that it has probably attracted more attention among foreign observers than any other of our institutions. De Tocqueville was struck with awe at the power of a

[1] Page 175 (7th ed.).

court that could summon "sovereign powers to its bar."[1] Our Supreme Court, and—it should not be forgotten—others of our courts as well, do adjudicate matters of supreme constitutional importance; but, to an American and to an English eye, "there is nothing strange or mysterious" in this.[2] For, after all, the only material difference between the activity of our federal courts and that of an English court lies in the fact that our courts have a constituent law to interpret; the English courts have none. In organization and functions they are essentially alike.

It may be said, then, that our surplus litigation must be due to that constituent law,—to our written constitution. It will be readily admitted that a written and a "rigid" constitution is a practical necessity in a modern federal state.[3] The complex machinery of such a composite state as the United States would be unworkable without it. Does it follow, however, that the deflection of constitutional questions toward the courts, here so noticeable, is the result wholly, or even in part, of our having a written and a "rigid" constitution? To put the question concretely: May we say that the power or duty of our federal courts by virtue of which they submit acts of Congress to the test of a comparison with the higher constituent law, is a power due to our having a written constitution? Or must we

---

[1] *Democracy in America* (tr. by Reeve), 4th ed., vol. i. p. 160.
[2] Bryce, *American Commonwealth*, 3d ed., vol. i. pp. 250-6.
[3] Dicey, *Law of the Constitution*, p. 142.

INTRODUCTION

not say that it is due to something entirely different? An examination of the constitution of Switzerland or of the German Empire would seem to set that question at rest. In neither of these two great non-English federations is the interpretation of the acts of the legislature entrusted to the courts; though in one of them, namely, Switzerland, the constituent law is marked off from ordinary legislation almost if not entirely as definitely as is our own.

It seems not true, then, that a judicial interpretation is a necessary accompaniment to a written constitution. "So far as the grounds for this remarkable power are found in the mere fact of a constitution being in writing, or in judges being sworn to support it, they are quite inadequate."[1] If our federal judges have no powers not common to an English judge, save the power of interpreting laws by the light of a higher constitution, and if a higher constitution does not necessarily confer on the *courts* the power to interpret it; then it is very hard to see how federalism in itself has anything directly to do with constitutional interpretation, or with the settlement of constitutional questions by litigation rather than by legislation alone.

And yet, in the United States, where modern federalism has had the longest development, and in the greater self-governing colonies of England, where the federal principle is increasingly active, it is true that this idea of the judicial review of legislation, this liti-

[1] Thayer, *Legal Essays*, p. 2.

gious attitude toward constitutional questions, is deeply interwoven with the political thought of the people. If Professor Dicey had confined his statement to federations in English-speaking countries, it would be true; but true, because the countries are English-speaking, and not because they are organized under a federal system. In short, the idea of a judicial review of legislation, and of a constituent law as well, are in origin English ideas, and arise in no way from federalism itself. Their source is to be sought in English history rather than in the conditions of modern political life.

The origin and development of these ideas in England, and their transfer to America, where they have had a fuller growth than in the mother country, will make up the bulk of this essay.

The beginnings of that development are wrapped up with the beginnings of Parliament itself. It will be necessary, therefore, to preface our account of a judicial review of legislation with a summary statement of the character of the English central assemblies in the period following the Norman Conquest. The accuracy of any such description of the mediaeval English Parliament will depend mainly upon our understanding of the spirit and working of those political institutions which we generalize under the name of feudalism. Any general description of feudalism or discussion of the vexed question of its introduction into England would be out of place here, but no adequate idea of

INTRODUCTION

the nature and activity of the English central assemblies of the middle ages is possible without a brief consideration of the influence of feudalism upon the government of the Norman kings. We must, for example, inquire whether their rule should best be described as a monarchy practically absolute, or as a monarchy limited; if limited, whether the checks upon the royal power are to be looked for in a consciousness of nationality among the people, or merely in feudal immunity. These questions will naturally turn largely upon the constitution and powers of the early assemblies. The answers to them are of three principal kinds. Three general theories have been held at various times by historians as to the character of the English monarchy under the Norman kings, which may be roughly designated as the autocratic, the national, and the feudal.

Of these three, Gneist may probably be regarded as the chief exponent in recent times of the first, or autocratic theory. With Brady and Filmer, he regarded the Conqueror practically as an absolute despot; for him the curia, which the Conqueror used for convenience, was neither Saxon *Witenagemot* nor Norman *Cour de Baronie*, but only a number of individuals whom the King employed to carry out his commands. "These conventions were not 'feudal parliaments,' but only great councils of notables."[1] "The error lies in the pedantic interpretation which would create constitutional

[1] *Constitutional History* (Eng. trans. by Ashworth), vol. i. p. 292.

THE HIGH COURT OF PARLIAMENT

bodies out of a government with changing counsellors."[1]

The "national theory," or the rather exaggerated form it has sometimes taken, which might better be called the "insular theory," refuses to see any break of much consequence at the Conquest. It was the ancient Witenagemot that continued under the Norman kings; everything remained essentially English, with only a thin Norman or feudal veneer, most of which was put on not by the Conqueror, but later by such persons as Ranulf Flambard, of infamous memory. In the nature of things, this accretion must soon have worn away and the original, the ancient "English" constitution, have emerged, unchanged in any important respect by this temporary and foreign covering.[2]

The nature of the Curia, or central assembly, under this theory is definitely settled. "Our national Assembly has changed its name and its constitution, but its corporate identity has lived on unbroken."[3] "The

---

[1] *Const. Hist.*, vol. i. p. 271.

[2] "What was the real position of a landowner of Norman descent within a generation or two after the Conquest? He held English lands according to English law; in all but the highest rank, he lived on equal terms with other landowners of English birth; he was himself born on English soil, often of an English mother; he was called on in endless ways to learn, to obey, and to administer, the laws of England. Such a man soon became in feeling, and before long in speech also, as good an Englishman as if he had come of the male line of Hengest or Cerdic. There was nothing to hinder even one of the actual conquerors from thoroughly throwing in his lot with his new country and with its people. His tongue was French, but in truth he had far more in common with the Englishman than with the Frenchman." Freeman, *Growth of the English Constitution*, 4th ed., p. 73.

[3] *Ibid.*, p. 66.

INTRODUCTION

House of Lords not only springs out of, it actually is, the ancient Witenagemot. I can see no break between the two. King William summoned his Witan as King Eadward had summoned them before him."[1]

The feudal theory is based on the belief that in England, in the period of the Norman kings, feudalism was well established, that though those kings were stronger and more independent than their brothers of the Continent, yet they ruled under feudal conditions. Powerful they were, and could do things unheard of on the Continent, but this power in the Norman period was exercised under feudal forms and subject to most of the feudal limitations. With an army made up of feudal lords, the King may not have been their peer, but neither was he their absolute master. Their help he must have in war, and with this was involved their counsel in times of peace. But counsel was not command and advice was not compulsion. In our modern constitutional systems, as Professor Dicey has shown, assemblies are seldom truly consultative: their advice is a command. A sovereign who must consult an assembly must usually obey it. It is wrong to assume that such must have been the function of counsellors in mediaeval times; it is equally wrong to go to the other extreme and deny that the King was bound in any way or in any degree. Counsellors were a strength in peace because they were a necessity in war. Their advice may

[1] Freeman, *op. cit.*, p. 62. In describing this sort of history writing Professor Vinogradoff has used the apt expression "retrospective nationalism." *English Society in the Eleventh Century*, p. 5, note 2.

not always have been obligatory, but it was never negligible; and beyond doubt the general conditions of the feudal régime were felt by all, both King and lords, as binding upon them. "It was rather the King's privilege than his duty to receive counsel. . . . A feudal monarch had to dread the isolation, not the union of his liegemen. . . . It was only a weak or tyrannical king—a John or a Richard II—who neglected to ask counsel; for the ruler who acted without the advice of his great men distinctly outraged the moral feeling of his day."[1] Without such an understanding no state could have existed. The state thus depicted was far from an ideal one, but it was only obedience to such rules that prevented utter anarchy. Under then existing conditions an absolute despotism was as impossible as a constitutional government of the modern type. That peculiar thing which is neither of these was the feudal monarchy.

The solution of such a problem as the character of the English monarchy under the Norman kings cannot be an easy one, because in England, as elsewhere in western Europe, there were diverse precedents. In England, there was the monarchy before the Conquest with its Witan; on the Continent, there were the imperial traditions of Charles the Great.[2] There were in fact

[1] Dicey, *Privy Council*, pp. 2-5.
[2] "Consideré comme souverain d'institution divine, le roi est l'unique et suprême distributeur de la justice. Ses fonctionnaires ne doivent la rendre qu'en son nom. Tout pouvoir judiciare n'est qu'une émanation du sien. Cette théorie, réalisée déjà sous le gouvernement de Charlemagne, sera celle qui prévau-

INTRODUCTION

everywhere, or nearly everywhere, in the midst of feudal decentralization precedents for a strong monarchy and also germs of nationality. But as yet they were germs only, even in England. It is an anachronism of the worst sort to use the word "nation" or "national" in speaking of England in the eleventh and twelfth centuries, unless that word is to be deprived of most of its modern meaning. Such may be said to be the feudal theory.

Of the above theories, the autocratic has probably had the least influence. Filmer and Brady urged it against the claims of the parliamentary party in the seventeenth century; and Gneist in the nineteenth, if compared with Freeman, for example, seems to have had few followers.[1] The national theory has had a far greater effect. It may almost be called the traditional view of early English history. It is the theory that ap-

dra définitivement au déclin de la période féodale. Elle a toujours été pratiquée, d'une manière plus ou moins apparente, même pendent les premiers siècles capétiens. Mais comme, à cette époque, le roi joue aussi le rôle de suzerain, son pouvoir judiciare s'exerce en partie, suivant la forme féodale, par la réunion des vassaux ou des pairs qui constituent sa cour. Ainsi que toutes les institutions royales de la même période, l'histoire de la justice capétienne porte à la fois l'empreinte de la conception purement monarchique et celle de la coutume féodale. Au point de vue de ses attributions judiciaires, la *curia regis* est donc, dès l'origine, constituée de deux éléments de provenance très différente : des conseillers royaux chargés de juger au nom du souverain, et des vassaux réunis sous la direction du suzerain. Ces deux éléments ont coexisté de tout temps, bien que dans une proportion variable, et le progrès monarchique a précisément consisté à faire prédominer le premier." A. Luchaire, *Institutions Monarchiques*, vol. i. pp. 277, 278.

[1] Gneist of course admits that a feudal element was introduced later. It is only in the Norman period that he denies its influence. Becket's trial he considers the beginning of its influence on the Curia. *Const. Hist.*, vol. i. p. 288 and note.

peals to the national pride of Englishmen, and the one that most of them have held more or less strongly. It is to be expected that the later constitutional development in England, so entirely different from that on the Continent, should lead English historians to the quite natural, though entirely unnecessary, assumption that this difference had always existed. Such a view was by no means unwelcome to those who believed, for example, that their national church had had an organization separate from the rest of western Europe before the events of the sixteenth century. It is not so much a wider outlook (Freeman's certainly was wide enough) that has changed, or seems to be changing, all this; it is rather that a sounder method has taken the place of the older one. It is beginning to be seen that men have in the past really advanced the cause of liberty, though often entirely unconscious of any such intention, or even when their aims were entirely selfish. The Anglo-Saxon freeman, proud of his liberty, and consciously preserving for future nations those institutions which England was later to hand on to the civilized world, is harder to see than he was twenty-five years ago.[1] Ranulf Flambard even has found a defender, who shows that many of those "feudal abuses" Flambard has so long been charged with were really the work of the Conqueror himself.[2] Simon de Montfort would hardly be called by a sober historian of to-day "the hero and

[1] See, for example, Petit-Dutaillis, *Studies Supplementary to Stubbs's Constitutional History*, vol. i. p. 127 et seq.
[2] J. H. Round, *Feudal England*, p. 225 et seq.

INTRODUCTION

martyr of England."[1] Such a historian would scarcely take the view of a fairly recent biographer, that Thomas Becket was a great champion of the ancient laws and liberties of the realm of England;[2] or hold with Thierry that he spent his life fighting the cause of the Saxons against the Normans.[3] Even the Church has not escaped, and it is becoming evident that in ecclesiastical affairs, as in others, the England of the middle ages was not so very unlike the rest of Christendom.[4]

To attack the traditional view of Magna Charta would have been almost as bad as blasphemy not so very long ago. In 1667 even a Chief Justice of the King's Bench was called to the bar of the Commons and forced to a humble apology for a contemptuous expression let fall concerning it in a moment of anger;[5] but one of the leading English historians of to-day says clearly that in his opinion Magna Charta was

[1] Freeman, *Growth of the English Const.*, p. 69.
[2] R. A. Thompson, *Thomas Becket, Martyr Patriot*, London, 1889.
[3] A. Thierry, *History of the Conquest of England by the Normans.* (Translated by William Hazlitt, London, 1848.)
[4] See Maitland, *Roman Canon Law in the Church of England*, London, 1898, especially page 51 et seq. Referring to the famous statutes from Merton to the statutes of Praemunire, Maitland says: "Here, then, we may see a collision between the claims of the church and the claims of the state; but there was no collision between the law of the church of England and the law of the church of Rome." *Ibid.*, p. 54. Even Bishop Stubbs, who had presented the opposite view in the *Report of the Ecclesiastical Courts Commission* in 1883, admitted before his death that Maitland's position in this matter was unassailable. A. T. Carter, *A History of English Legal Institutions*, 3d ed., p. 233, note 1. Professor Pollard admirably sums up Maitland's contention respecting the English Church when he says: "But it is not so clear that the Church has always been anti-papal, as that the English laity have always been anti-clerical." *Henry VIII.*, edition of 1905, p. 233.
[5] *Grey's Debates*, vol. i. pp. 63, 64, 67.

merely a class document and not the work of the people; not a great landmark of constitutional progress, but even in certain important respects a hindrance to that progress.[1]

Such statements may seem too strong — in the opinion of the writer they are too strong; but the essential fact is forcing itself on men's minds that in 1215, and before, England was feudal much as the rest of Europe was feudal; that Magna Charta is first of all a feudal document and not a national one.[2]

But no formula can fully express the life of any period. To say that the epoch of the Norman kings was a feudal period is not to exclude all elements of nationality, nor to deny a tendency in the monarchy toward absolutism. It is a matter of emphasis, and the emphasis has in general been put far too strongly on these national elements, while there has been a danger

[1] Edward Jenks, *The Myth of Magna Carta: Independent Review*, vol. iv. p. 260 et seq.

[2] This view has never been stated with more force and clearness, and yet with caution, than by Professor George B. Adams, in an article from which the following is an extract: "Before 1215 in the history of English institutions, general as distinguished from local, lies nothing but the feudal system, modified only in the direction of a more absolute monarchy. The two fundamental principles of the constitution which Magna Carta declared were both fundamental principles of feudalism, and were drawn directly from it in 1215. The origin of the English limited monarchy is to be sought not in the primitive German state, nor in the idea of an elective monarchy or a coronation oath, nor in the survival of institutions of local freedom to exert increasing influence on the central government. Though all these were contributory, combined they could not alone have produced the result. The principle which moulds and shapes all elements into the great result came from feudalism." *American Historical Review*, vol. xiii. pp. 229-45, 713-30. The quotation is from page 245. See also Petit-Dutaillis, *Studies Supplementary to Stubbs's Constitutional History*, ch. xii.

INTRODUCTION

of forgetting that nationality in anything like its developed modern form existed nowhere in western Europe in the early middle ages, not even in England.

It is true also that the King in England was often able to make the Council more subservient by placing in it men who owed everything to him, and thus to lessen the power of the nobility. There is, in fact, no more prolific cause of friction between the King and his barons in the mediaeval period than this. It is noteworthy, however, that the continued opposition of the barons to this practice shows that it was regarded as an abuse.

Too much has often been made of the fact that the strongest protests against these royal favourites were against Gascons and other "foreigners." Native-born Englishmen who opposed the interests of the nobility were hated almost as much, and the nobility themselves were willing to follow the leadership of a "foreigner" at any time if he would champion their cause against the King, as appears in the case of Simon de Montfort. They were willing to follow the standard of a French prince if he would lead them, even against their own King. It was their class rather than their nation that attracted their loyalty. When it is really seen how much this long struggle between King and barons was a class struggle and not a national one, it becomes harder to be sure on which side the sympathies of a modern historian ought to be. When it was thought, for example, that Simon embodied simply the national spirit against the despotism of the King, it was easy to be on Simon's side; but when we see that it was feudal immunity rather than national wellbeing for which he was fighting, it is hard to avoid feeling that, after all, probably Edward, and possibly even Henry, was not so much in the wrong in fighting tendencies so anarchic. At the same time, we must always admit that these feudal immunities, the privileges of a class and not of the nation, and struggled for as such by the nobility, were a subtraction from the royal power which formed the most valuable precedent for the later exercise of national rights when the nation had finally become self-conscious enough to assert them. The history of that change from class feeling to national feeling is the most important and the least understood thing in early English history.[1]

The most striking fact about the Council in this feudal period is its varied functions. It was court of law, advisory council, and exchequer all in one. The assembly of Tacitus shows this same fusion of judicial functions with activities which we consider totally different. This absence of a division of labour is characteristic of the feudal period,[2] and England was no exception to the rule. It is utterly impossible in this period, with the

[1] Hatschek, *Englisches Staatsrecht*, vol. i. pp. 234, 237, 238.
[2] "Ce qui caractérise la justice capétienne durant les deux siècles qui ont immédiatement suivi la fondation de la dynastie, c'est l'absence d'une organisation spéciale. La cour du roi remplissait alors sa fonction judiciare avec la même personnel, dans les mêmes circonstances de temps et de lieu, que ses autres attributions de l'ordre politique ou administratif." Luchaire, *Institutions Monarchiques*, vol. i. p. 304.

INTRODUCTION

data that we have, safely to draw any definite line between *Parliamentum, Curia, concilium ordinarium, concilium privatum, magnum concilium, commune concilium.* Because all these names have come down to us, and because in a later period separate bodies of men did exist to correspond with some of these names, it has been assumed that there was at the time we are considering a series of councils, each with its legal powers definitely marked off and assigned to it. This is not borne out by any evidence that is contemporary; and the indiscriminate way in which contemporaries used these various terms indicates that they themselves drew no sharp lines of division.[1] Between these separate bodies that might be supposed to correspond to the different names, there seems to have existed no difference but a difference of function. Even this it is not always possible to find, and when found, it turns out to be a temporary or occasional difference arising from accident or convenience, not from legal definition. At some times more men seem to have attended the Council than at others. At such times it may be called the *Magnum Concilium.* That the *Magnum Concilium,* however, was a distinct body, separate in function, in organization, in rights, no contemporary description of it gives us the right to say.[2] This fusion, which we are tempted wrongly to call

[1] L. O. Pike, *Constitutional History of the House of Lords*, p. 40.
[2] Stubbs in his usual cautious manner seems to have discarded these distinctions. *Const. Hist.*, vol. i. (6th ed.), pp. 406, 407. Professor G. B. Adams is more outspoken: "These, then, are the two essential things to have clearly in mind in beginning to study the constitutional history of England : that all the functions of the state were exercised by a single institution, and that the institu-

a confusion of powers judicial and non-judicial, and the lack of demarcation between the larger and the smaller Council, are clearly indicated in the various official records, when we begin to have official records, and they furnish the best proof of the statements made above. Speaking of the highest court, which we should call the Parliament, Maitland says: "For a while this highest tribunal is hardly distinct from the king's bench. Every plea in the king's bench is in theory a plea *coram ipso domino rege*, and the rolls of the king's bench never cease to be *coram rege* rolls. The superior tribunal is rather, if we may so speak, an afforced, an intensified form of the inferior tribunal than a separate court; a plea that is put upon the parliament roll may be put upon the king's bench roll also; the justices of the king's bench are members of the council, and a case heard at a full meeting, a parliament, of the council, is heard by, among others, the justices of the king's bench. A plea may be adjourned from a parliament to the

tion existed under two forms which were distinguished from each other only by size and manner of meeting." *Am. Hist. Rev.*, vol. xiii. p. 13. Again he says: "The point of importance and difficulty is not the composition or the meeting of the smaller *curia*, but the fact that it was in rights, powers, and functions, the larger. It was not a committee of the larger, its powers were not vested in it by the larger, it was not responsible to the larger; it was the larger." *Ibid.*, p. 12. "A full meeting of the council is a full meeting of the king's bench, of the common bench, of the chancery, of the exchequer: it is this, and more than this." F. W. Maitland, *Records of the Parliament of 33 Edw. I.* (Rolls Series), Introduction, p. xlvii (hereafter cited as *Parl. Roll*). "I have not come upon any contemporary and official authority which shows that the king has more than one council, or which qualifies the term *consilium* with any such adjectives as *ordinarium*, *privatum*, or the like." *Ibid.*, p. xlvii, note 1. See also *ibid.*, p. lxxxviii, note 1; Hale, *Jurisdiction of the Lords House*, 52-4; Hatschek, *Englisches Staatsrecht*, vol. i. pp. 233, 234.

INTRODUCTION

king's bench or from the king's bench to a parliament without breach of continuity."[1]

What, then, were the true relations of "Council" and "Parliament"? Legally they were one. The Council could act in the name of Parliament,—in fact, to all intents and purposes was Parliament. And yet certain meetings of the Council—"parliaments of the council," Maitland calls them—were more largely attended than ordinary meetings, though this in no way altered the legal status of the Council, nor gave any additional validity to the acts of these extraordinary sessions.

The twelfth century had seen the beginning of the courts of the King's Bench and Common Pleas, or at least one of them. For the reasons given, these cannot be sharply separated from the Council; neither were they committees of the Council, nor distinct offshoots of it. And yet we can speak of them as existing, though we cannot find the exact line that legally divides them from the Council, and practically they were often merged with it.

Now apparently Bracton knew only two central law

[1] Maitland, *Parl. Roll*, Introd., pp. lxxx, lxxxi. See also Pollock and Maitland, *Hist. of Eng. Law*, 2d ed., vol. i. pp. 199, 200. The Parliament of 1305 was together three weeks. The Council stayed behind after the additional members were dismissed and did nearly all the business of the session, and yet it remained a "parliament" and was styled a "full" and a "general" Parliament. Maitland, *Parl. Roll*, Introd., pp. xxxv, xxxvi.

"The jurisdiction of the Council over the proceedings of the King's justices was exercised in a manner rather resembling the authority which a tribunal possesses over its members, than as resulting from the subjection of one court to another court, distinct in function, but superior in authority." Palgrave, *King's Council*, p. 118. See also Pike, *Const. Hist. of the House of Lords*, pp. 42, 43, and the cases there cited.

courts, the justices *de Banco* and those *Coram Rege*.[1] Half a century later the author of *Fleta* begins his chapter on the courts with the statement: "For the King has his court in his Council, in his Parliaments, in the presence of the counts, barons, great men and other learned men, where are determined the doubts of the judges; and when new injuries have arisen, new remedies are provided and justice is there meted out to each one according to his deserts."[2] What is this court which the King has "in his Council, in his Parliaments;" what is its jurisdiction, what is its relation to the judges *de Banco* and *Coram Rege*, and how and when and why did it come into existence? Maitland believes that here we have a new court above the courts known to Bracton. "A new tribunal is evolved, or rather, two tribunals become three."[3] "However ancient may be the roots whence the jurisdiction of 'the king in his council in his parliaments' draws its nourishment, it is a new thing that men should see three different tribunals rising one above the other; it is a new thing that they should see a yet higher court above that court

---

[1] He is apparently giving an exhaustive list of the courts, in which he mentions the following: (1) "quidam ... capitales, generales, perpetui et majores a latere Regis residentes ... (2) alii perpetui, certo loco residentes, sicut in banco ... (3) alii itinerantes de loco in locum ... (4) justitiarii constituti ad quasdam assisas." Lib. iii. fol. 108, par. 2.

[2] "Habet enim Rex cur[iam] suam in consilio suo, in Parliamentis suis, praesentibus praelatis, com[itibus], baron[ibus], proceribus, & aliis viris peritis, ubi terminatae sunt dubitationes judiciorum, & novis injuriis emersis nova constituuntur remedia, & unicuique justitia, prout meruit, retribuetur ibidem." Lib. ii. cap. 2, sec. 1.

[3] *Parl. Roll*, Introd., p. lxxxi.

INTRODUCTION

which is held in theory *coram ipso domino rege.*"[1] And yet, "to deny that it is the king in council is impossible; to deny that it is the king in parliament, or rather that its sessions are parliaments, is impossible."[2]

Probably the simplest explanation of this difficult problem is the best. It requires an effort to get rid of modern conceptions, but we must if we would understand these proceedings. Edward had called his great men together many times in the years before the Parliament of 1305. Occasionally he had summoned knights to meet with them; in 1295 he had summoned representatives from the towns also. It is well known that Edward shared his burdens with more classes of the people than his predecessors had done. The famous words quoted from Justinian's Code in the writs of 1295, though they have often been over-emphasized, were not entirely an accident,—"what touches all should be approved by all."[3] The writs of that year to the barons called them to treat with the prelates and other nobles "and other inhabitants of our realm."[4]

---

[1] *Parl. Roll*, Introd., pp. lxxxiv, lxxxv. Holdsworth agrees with this view, *History of English Law*, vol. i. pp. 170, 171. See also Pike, *op. cit.*, p. 43.

[2] Maitland, *Parl. Roll*, Introd., p. lxxxii.

[3] "Sicut lex justissima, provida circumspectione sacrorum principum stabilita ortatur et statuit, ut quod omnes tangit, ab omnibus approbetur, sic et innuit evidentur, ut communibus periculis pro remedia provisa communiter obvietur." *Parl. Writs*, vol. i. p. 30; *Lords' Report on the Dignity of a Peer*, vol. i. p. 212 et seq., vol. iii. pp. 66, 67 (edition of 1829); Parry, *Parliaments and Councils of England*, pp. 57, 58; Code 5, 59, 5; Stubbs, *C. H.*, vol. ii. (4th ed.), p. 133, note 4, and references there cited.

[4] "Ac aliis incolis regni nostri," etc. *Parl. Writs*, vol. i. p. 33; *Lords' Report*, vol. iii. p. 71.

THE HIGH COURT OF PARLIAMENT

The preamble of the Statute of Westminster the First in the third year of King Edward I (1275) mentions, in addition to the spiritual and temporal lords, "la Communaute de la tere ileokes somons."[1]

From such examples, which might be multiplied indefinitely, it seems clear that at times Edward felt the need of help, financial or otherwise, from new classes of the people. In such cases they were summoned to his "Parliament." But Parliament could exist equally well without them. Their presence was in no sense necessary in order to give legal validity to its acts. Petitions were, in fact, often granted before they came to the session,[2] ordinances were sometimes made after they had gone home,[3] cases were heard and determined in their absence; and yet these acts were all done in Parliament, in a "full" or "general" Parliament.[4] In other years the Parliament was a complete one, though these additional members never came at all. When they did come, however, they seem to have been a constituent part of Parliament.

And now we must make an attempt at an explanation of these seeming contradictions. In the years closely following the Conquest the administration of the law was not differentiated from other administra-

---

[1] *Statutes of the Realm*, vol. i. p. 26. There is a list of such statutes in Prynne, *Brief Register*, vol. i. p. 383 et seq.
[2] Maitland, *Parl. Roll*, Introd., p. lvii.
[3] *Ibid.*, pp. xxxv, xxxvi; *Lords' Report*, vol. i. p. 261.
[4] Maitland, *loc. cit.*; Parry, *Parliaments and Councils of England*, p. 65, note *h*.

INTRODUCTION

tion. The Council could attend to all. It was a council of notables not specially trained. Law was not technical enough yet to require that. The members of the Council were great nobles, except where the King was strong enough to add to their number a colleague of humble origin more subservient to himself.

Increase of business, with its routine, its formalities, and its consequent technicalities, in time made this no longer practical. A change was sure to come, and it was greatly accelerated by the reforms of Henry II. A division of labour was inevitable. Official routine and the growth of precedent would naturally follow; the officials would become permanent and men trained in their office. It was probably thus that the separate courts with their trained judges in time emerged.

But the old theory remained. These courts were still the Council, their acts were its acts, their judges were its members; and, on the other hand, *any* of the members of the Council might on occasion sit as judges in the courts. In practice, however, we find that the ordinary business of the courts was usually ended in the court where it originated and without outside assistance.

Therefore, though the old theory remained, though the Council was the court and the court was the Council, in practice the whole Council would probably be actually called in only in extraordinary cases,—in cases of difficulty where the judges felt the need of having their opinion strengthened by their fellow council-

THE HIGH COURT OF PARLIAMENT

lors,[1] or where there was no rule in existence to guide them in their decision.[2] This is no "court of appeal" in our sense. The idea of an appeal is too refined for those facts. About all we can say is that at times the judges of the Bench or *Coram Rege* felt the need of help in difficult or new cases. The whole Council in such cases would assist in the decision, and yet there was no sharp division in theory between the court alone and the court plus the Council sitting in this capacity. But such practices, long enough continued, actually change the theory itself, when men have forgotten the previous state of affairs. And it may well be that in the half century between Bracton and Fleta, the continuous practice had at length led to the feeling that in some way the Council was a separate and superior court to the judges *de Banco* and *Coram Rege*.[3] The line between them could not be accurately drawn, for in strict legal theory it did not exist, and hence Fleta is very vague in his description; but the theory was undergoing a change, nevertheless.

In all this, however, it must be kept in mind that the ultimate source of all these divisions and the basis of the authority of all—whether we mean the judges *de Banco Regis* or *Coram Rege*, or speak of the whole Council, now viewed in the new sense of a court of

[1] Fleta, as we have seen, describes the Curia as the place "ubi terminatae sunt dubitationes judiciorum." *Ante*, p. 20 and note.

[2] "& novis injuriis emersis nova constituuntur remedia." *Ante*, p. 20, note.

[3] On this subject see *The Beginning of the King's Council*, by Professor James F. Baldwin, in *Transactions of the Royal Historical Society* (New Series), vol. xix., especially sec. 3, p. 47 et seq.

INTRODUCTION

higher dignity and authority than these—lay in the ancient jurisdiction of the Council itself; and that the Council, in theory if not always in practice, was identical with every one of these bodies.

Then came the changes mentioned above. New classes were called in to assist the King with counsel or money. There was in existence, however, but one assembly, and, therefore, though these new classes might give their money as separate orders and might meet apart from the others in doing so, yet in obeying the King's summons they had to become a part, and they did become a real and a constituent part, of that one assembly, the Parliament; but the core of this assembly remained the Council,—"The King's Council in his Parliament."

The Rolls of Parliament show that a large part of the work of the "Parliament" was what we should call "judicial," consisting of those cases that had proved too hard or too novel for the judges in the separate courts. Obviously this would be no kind of business for the untrained "aliis incolis regni." So the cases were settled before these came to give their advice or their money, or were left until they had gone home again. As the bulk of early "legislation"—if we may use such a term—was only "novis injuriis emersis nova ... remedia," limited in amount and exceptional in character, most of the business of a session must have been of such a nature that it could be done only by "The King's Council in his Parliament." Thus the

"Commons," when we find a Commons, may have lent their authority to Parliament, but in practice at first had but little influence over much of its activity. This explanation, though in part conjectural, may serve in some degree to remove the apparent inconsistency resulting from the indiscriminate use by contemporary writers of such terms as *Consilium* and *Curia Regis* for so many different things.[1]

Undoubtedly one reason why we cannot get a clearer-cut picture of the great central courts at this time is the indefiniteness that we find in the names employed to designate these courts and their activities in contemporary accounts and records,—an indefiniteness in words which is only proof of the indefiniteness of the thought of the men of that day, and an indication of a corresponding absence of special organization in the institutions they described. It is next to impossible to define such institutions exactly without making the definition untrue to the facts. In a picture of the institutions of mediaeval times we must be satisfied with hazy outlines. If in such a picture we demand all the sharpness of figure and detail that we might reasonably expect when modern institutions are described, we deceive ourselves; for such details can be supplied at this late day only by giving words a sense definite it may be, but one that they never had in the minds of the men that used them. The result may be artistic:

---

[1] Stubbs, *C. H.*, vol. ii. pp. 260, 261; Pike, *Const. History of the House of Lords*, pp. 47, 48.

INTRODUCTION

it will not be truthful. This is but to paraphrase the words of the late Professor Maitland: "If we speak, we must speak with words; if we think, we must think with thoughts. We are moderns, and our words and thoughts can not but be modern. Perhaps, as Mr. Gilbert once suggested, it is too late for us to be early English. Every thought will be too sharp, every word will imply too many contrasts. We must, it is to be feared, use many words and qualify our every statement until we have almost contradicted it. The outcome will not be so graceful, so lucid, as Maine's Ancient Law."[1]

As an example of this indefiniteness in words, take the word *Parliament*, to which we attach such a definite meaning. It meant nothing more in the mouths of mediaeval Englishmen than any meeting for speech or conference.[2] This might be a conference held by

---

[1] *Township and Borough*, p. 22.

[2] See Barrington, *Observations on the Statutes*, 2d ed., pp. 58, 59; Brady, *Introduction*, pp. 71-3; Twysden, *Government of England* (Camden Society), p. 136. Twysden uses the word himself in this sense. "Who so observes the scope of this, the severall instructions given to the privy counsell and judges (for they went generally together as persons intrusted in the government of the state) by sundry parlyaments too long to bee heere repeated, may easily discerne a care taken to preserve the rights of monarchy," etc. (p. 114). Maitland sums it up in his usual incisive way in speaking of the early petitions in Parliament: "Parliament, or 'a parliament,' is not conceived as a body that can be petitioned. A parliament is rather an act than a body of persons. One cannot present a petition to a colloquy, to a debate. It is but slowly that this word is appropriated to colloquies of a particular kind, namely, those which the king has with the estates of his realm, and still more slowly that it is transferred from the colloquy to the body of men whom the king has summoned. As yet any meeting of the King's Council that has been solemnly summoned for general business seems to be a parliament." *Parl. Roll*, Introd., p. lxvii. "The personification of Parliament which enables us to say

the King of England with a foreign king or one with his own men. After it came into use, the word for a while was interchangeable with *colloquium*, which is usually found instead of it in the earlier records. When the full meaning of this is considered, it becomes evident what a host of modern ideas crowd upon us when we use the word *Parliament*. It is at once seen that the word can be used of the Council with no necessary implication of representation, or of legislation in the modern sense. Brady makes much of this point in his argument with Petyt, and his reasoning seems unanswerable. It is not strange, under these circumstances, that we have difficulty in determining the exact nature of the court that the King had "in his Council in his Parliaments."[1]

The first strictly contemporary mention of the word Parliament as a name for the common council of the realm seems to have been by Matthew Paris for the assembly of 1246;[2] while the first use of the word in

that laws are made by, and not merely in, parliament, is a slow and subtle process. . . . As to the word 'council,' it is important to remember that in the middle ages no distinction was or could be drawn between 'council' and 'counsel;' both were *consilium*." *Ibid.*, p. lxvii, note 1. Wykes, under the date of 1261, speaks of the King's fearing his barons, — "quod recusabant cum eo parliamentare" (*Annales Monastici*, Rolls Series, vol. iv. p. 129; Hody, *History of Convocation*, p. 357), — using the word in a general sense, as Chaucer does later:

"O cruel goddes, that governe
This world with binding of your word eterne,
And wryten in the table of athamaunt
Your parlement and your eterne graunt."

The Knighte's Tale, lines 445-8. Cf. *Troilus and Criseyde*, book iv. line 143.
[1] Pike, *Const. Hist. of the House of Lords*, pp. 47, 48.
[2] *Chron. Maj.* (Rolls Series), vol. iv. p. 518; *Hist. Anglorum* (Rolls Series),

INTRODUCTION

any act or statute was in the preamble of the Statute of Westminster the First (3 Edward I).[1] After this the use of the word gradually became general and in time it became the usual name for the estates of the realm, having a definite meaning as it has to-day.

An equally instructive example of the indistinctness of the meaning of words is the word *curia*, or its French and English equivalent, *court*, the most comprehensive of all the terms applied to the early councils. Originally a garden or enclosure,—a meaning that it still retains,—the word then came to mean the meeting of the lord's vassals that was habitually held in his enclosure, whether garden or hall. Any meeting of such a formal

---

vol. iii. p. 5; Hody, *History of Convocation*, pp. 326, 327; Stubbs, *C. H.*, vol. i. p. 611 and note 2. Parry (p. 33, note) mentions John of Brompton as using the word "long before," but as the chronicle bearing that name was probably not written before the middle of the fourteenth century, that case may be dismissed. Prynne notes the fact that though Matthew Paris uses the name five or six times for the years 1246-7, he never uses it anywhere else before or after. *Brief Register*, vol. i. p. 401. (This is the final chapter in volume i. of the *Register*, but the paging seems to be wrong.) See also Parry, p. 72, note v.

[1] *Statutes of the Realm*, vol. i. p. 26; Prynne, *Brief Register*, vol. i., final chapter. See also Stubbs, *C. H.*, vol. i. p. 611 and note 2; Gneist, *C. H.*, vol. i. p. 320, note; Hody, *Convocation*, pp. 326-8; Hearn, *Government of England*, pp. 261-3. The famous assembly that met at Oxford in 1258 is called by the King a "Parliament" in his letters of safe conduct to the envoys of Llewellyn (Rymer's *Foedera*, book i. part ii. p. 38, Hague edition); *Lords' Report*, vol. i. p. 99. Earlier still, in a writ of the 28th year of Henry III, directed to the sheriff of Northamptonshire, the word *Parliamentum* was used of the great meeting at Runnymede in 1215. Petyt, *Rights of the Commons Asserted*, p. 33; Brady, *Introduction*, p. 71; *Lords' Report*, vol. i. p. 461; Stubbs, *C. H.*, vol. i. p. 611. Prynne gives a very complete catalogue of the early mentions of the word, both officially and unofficially (*Brief Register*, vol. i., final chapter); see also his *Observations on Coke's Fourth Institute*, p. 2. The early uses of the word on the Continent are given by Du Cange, s. v. *Parliamentum*. Cf. also Stubbs, *C. H.*, vol. i. p. 611 and note 2; Luchaire, *Institutions Monarchiques*, vol. i. pp. 253, 254 and notes, p. 305 and note 3.

THE HIGH COURT OF PARLIAMENT

kind would be a "court," whatever the character of its business might be. "At first this body is not a judicial body at all, in the modern sense," says Professor Jenks; "it is the Court at St. James', rather than the Court at Temple Bar. It is merely the household of a great potentate, in which the affairs of interest to its master are discussed."[1] In fact, its business was both judicial and legislative, for it discussed questions of all kinds; and yet, strictly speaking, it was neither, for there was no clear distinction then made between "legislative" and "judicial." The absence of distinction is only another proof of the absence of special organization. To this day we retain the same indefiniteness of meaning noted by Professor Jenks, when speaking of the Court of St. James and the Courts at Temple Bar. We shall see what a part this vagueness of meaning played at a later stage in English history, when we find men asserting that the law of Westminster Hall is not the same as the law of the High Court of Parliament.[2]

---

[1] *Law and Politics in the Middle Ages*, p. 134.

[2] On the history of the word *court* see the dictionaries of Littré, s. v. *Cour;* Du Cange and Spelman, s. v. *Curia;* New Oxford Dictionary, s. v. *Court.* The "t" which is found at the end of the early French form of the word shows that it is derived from the low-Latin *cors* or *cortis*, which is nothing but a contracted form of *cohors*, a garden or enclosure, a word related possibly to *hortus*. Later men began to translate *cour* or *court* into *curia*, in their written documents. This change does not seem to have brought much alteration of meaning, except that it obscured the humble origin of the word and tended to bring into it some of the juristic ideas of Rome. Instances of the original meaning of the word *court* are to be found among English documents. Thus in a charter of King Stephen we find the expression, "Curia et Domus Regiae." Madox, *History of the Exchequer*, ch. i. sec. ii. (vol. i. p. 2, in edition of 1769).

The word *aula*, which was employed in mediaeval England along with *curia*, furnishes another instance of this same vagueness. *Aula*, like *cortis*, meant

INTRODUCTION

Two classes of men in the King's Court in his Council in his Parliaments need to be noted especially,—the barons, including the bishops, and the judges.

The distinction between the nobles and the judges, as we have seen, grew up gradually as the growing intricacy of the law slowly but surely substituted for untrained nobles in the King's courts men whose sole claim to the office was their knowledge of the law. For long, both classes deliberated together in the Council; but in time the disparity of rank made itself felt. The narrowly trained judges were, or were believed to be, unfit to counsel the King on great matters of policy, and we find at length that they have become mere advisers. They are still members of the Council, their technical knowledge is necessary especially for the judicial work, but the acts of the Council are no longer their acts. They give their advice, and the nobles follow it or not as they wish. The judges are still legally

---

an enclosure or hall, and was used of the meetings of the lord's men held there exactly in the same way that the word *court* was used. The barbarous *halla* was also manufactured from the Saxon *heall* to mean the same thing, but it was not applied to the central assembly. The promiscuous use of words such as *tractatus, colloquium, parliamentum*, etc., shows that there was as yet no official name for the central "court." Another word that proves the indefiniteness of the functions of the king's ministers is the word *justiciarius*. It is beyond question that the early *capitalis justiciarius* had functions of the most varied kind,—as varied, in fact, as those of the King himself. Even the other and lesser justiciars for a long time after the Conquest were general administrative officers rather than the "justices" which some of them in time became. It is evidently in this more general sense that Hoveden uses the word in reference to events of the year 1191: "Et eodem die comes Moretonii, et archiepiscopus Rothomagensis, et alii regis justitiarii, concesserunt civibus Londiniarum habere communam suam." Vol. iii. p. 141 (Rolls Series). See Spelman, *Glossary*, s. v. *Justitia;* Du Cange, *Justitiarius*.

summoned as members, but have become in reality very nearly the same as the Crown's legal advisers of modern times. The history of the change is very hard to trace. I cannot find that it has attracted much attention, and yet it seems to me a very important matter. For so long as the judges were a constituent part of the Council, so long as they had an equal right of deliberating with the barons, we can draw no line between the Council and the Parliament. But so soon as these men of the law are excluded from the decision of questions at issue and brought in merely as advisers, a line begins to appear between these two bodies. If we knew when the two classes of members ceased to have equal powers in the Council, we should have an approximate date for the separation of the Parliament and Council, and thus for the beginning of the jurisdiction of the House of Lords as such. For the most easily marked distinction between the House of Lords and the Council in these early days seems to be that in the Lords' House the judges advised only; in the early Council they both advised and voted. Of course when the division was once made, the difference between the Council and the Parliament increased, and yet even to the end of the Tudor period the difference is not so great as we are likely to think, as is attested by the activity of the Council in legislative as well as judicial matters throughout Elizabeth's reign. When the jurisdiction of the Council ended and that of the House of Lords began is one of the unsolved questions of early

INTRODUCTION

English history,[1] but we have not gone far enough even to state the problem correctly until we grasp the fact that it was the voting or not voting of the judges that made a great part of the difference.

Prynne argues elaborately that the councillors were "no essential members of the Parliaments or Great Councils of England."[2] Their functions as mere advisers he believes to be characteristic of them even from the beginning. Sir Matthew Hale, on the other hand, thinks that originally the judges had a voice.[3] Much has been made by Prynne and others of the difference between the form of summons to the judges and that to the barons. The writ to the judges summoned them to treat "cum ceteris de consilio nostro" or "cum proceribus," etc.; while in the case of the barons it was "cum *ceteris* praelatis, proceribus," etc. On account of the absence of the *ceteris* before *proceribus* in the writ to the

[1] The Lords Commissioners were unable to answer the question. "When this jurisdiction ceased to be exercised by the Sworn Council of the King, and the part of it which remains was transferred to the Lords Spiritual and Temporal in Parliament assembled, the Committee have been unable to discover." *Report on the Dignity of a Peer*, vol. i. p. 296. The commissioners here seem to think that an actual "transfer" of the jurisdiction must have taken place. If Parliament and the Council were originally one, it is hardly proper to speak of a "transfer." See also Parry, p. 92 and note *g*.

[2] *Brief Register*, vol. i. p. 361 et seq.

[3] "But as to their suffrages in point of judicature in the lords house, it should seem by the many instances *inter placita parliamenti tempore E. I.* some whereof are before mentioned, they had their voices and suffrages therein. But about the time of E. 3 they began to be but in nature of assistants or advisers, and the authoritative and judiciary power rested in the lords house, which what it was we shall hereafter see." *Jurisdiction of the Lords House*, p. 59; see also pp. 155,156. Apparently Lord Hale here refers to judicial matters exclusively. It will become apparent later, however, that in the earlier history of Parliament this line cannot be drawn definitely.

THE HIGH COURT OF PARLIAMENT

judges it has been argued that the judges were not a constituent part of the Council. But the writs varied from time to time, and their forms were hardly rigid enough, in the earlier period of which we are speaking, to bear so large an argument.[1] Aside from the writs there is little to give us any light on this important problem.[2]

To this statement, however, one important exception must be made. A study of the councillors' oath has brought out some facts which tend to bear out the conclusions of Lord Hale. The first mention of such an oath is found by Professor Baldwin, whom I am following here, in 1233, and references occur fairly frequently in the following years. Apparently the same oath was taken by the justices in common with the other members of the Council in the time of Edward I.

"Under Edward I," says Professor Baldwin, "probably most of the justices and barons of the exchequer were sworn as members of the Council. . . . From this time the justices and barons of the exchequer, while holding close advisory relations with the council, evidently became distinct and separate from it. The councillor's oath ceased to be taken by them, as oaths of

---

[1] An account of some of the changes in the writ is to be found in Hale, *Jurisdiction of the Lords House*, pp. 11-13. See Stubbs, *C. H.*, vol. iii. (5th ed.), p. 406. Filmer sees no essential difference between the writ to the barons and that to the judges. *Freeholders' Grand Inquest*, p. 56. There is a case in Parliament cited by Hale from the reign of Edward III, where the judges are spoken of together with "aliis proceribus et magnatibus de consilio domini regis." *Jurisdiction of the Lords House*, p. 53.

[2] See Note A at the end of this chapter (p. 39).

INTRODUCTION

their own offices were devised which were in large part germinations from the earlier one.... By the twentieth year of Edward III, therefore, the justices are clearly distinct from sworn members of the council, and from this time the settled relation to the council of the justices of both benches, the serjeants-at-law, and the barons of the exchequer was that of advisers or assessors, who were summoned on occasion by authority of the council. It was furthermore enjoined repeatedly by ordinances of parliament that the council should summon these advisers in all legal questions, and that the justices should not fail to attend and to render their services."[1]

Though the judges lost their right to consent, their advice continued to have great weight in the deliberations of Parliament down to the present day.[2]

"With the reign of Richard II," says Professor Dicey, "the Council's period of growth closes. Before he reached the throne, the character of English institutions had become permanently fixed."[3] But in the system so fixed, the Council was an important factor, and in the Council the judges always took a very important part. They were consulted by the judges in the lower courts on doubtful or difficult cases; in the great parliamentary trials they took a foremost part; they as-

---

[1] *Eng. Hist. Rev.*, vol. xxiii. pp. 3, 4. See the references there cited and the article as a whole; also another article by the same author (*ibid.*, vol. xxi. pp. 6, 7), with references cited.
[2] *Ibid.*, vol. xxiii. pp. 4, 5.
[3] *Privy Council*, pp. 23, 24.

sisted in all legislation; in fact, as we shall see, for a considerable time the houses of Parliament were content to lay down the bare principles they wished to embody in the statutes, and the drafting of the acts was entirely in the hands of the Council. It was one of these judges of the Council who had announced the deposition of Edward II; it was another who declared that Richard II had forfeited his right to the crown; and in 1401 one of the judicial members of the Council opened the Parliament instead of the Chancellor.[1] "And to say the truth," Lord Hale declares, "although much of the antient power, jurisdiction, and consistency of the *consilium regis* is altered by the process of time and several acts of parliament, . . . yet, in the great court of parliament, at least the figure and model of the *consilium regis* and the persons whereof it consisted is to this day preserved in the lords house in parliament,"[2]— a statement that is almost as true in our day as it was in Hale's, for the judges are still summoned to the House of Lords and are assigned places on the woolsacks. It was established in the case of Daniel O'Connell, in 1844, that upon all cases coming before the lords by appeal, the law lords only should take part, which, together with the legislation of recent years, restores a certain measure of the ancient judicial powers of the judges in "The King's Council in his Parliaments."

In 1593 the Queen through the Lord Keeper de-

[1] Stubbs, *C. H.*, ch. xx. sec. 431.
[2] *Jurisdiction of the Lords House*, p. 58.

INTRODUCTION

clared to the Parliament that "she misliked also that such irreverence was shewed towards privy counsellors, who were not to be accounted as common knights and burgesses of the house, that are counsellors only during the parliament; whereas the other are standing counsellors, and, for their wisdom and great service, are called to the council of the state."[1] The power of advice that resided in the Council had, as Lord Hale says, "a double respect: one to the lords, to assist and advise them in passing bills; another to the king, when the bill passed both houses, to give the king their opinion touching such questions as should be by him or for him moved in council touching the same."[2]

In the activity of the Council after it became a separate body, which probably occurred before the time of Richard II, in whose reign its separate records begin, we have no interest here save for its influence on Parliament. But it is sufficiently clear, after a study of the Tudor period, that both in and out of Parliament the Council was then one of the most important organs of the government, if not the most important. In fact, it was not overshadowed by Parliament until the unwonted activity of the latter under the Stuarts. It was by no means an accident that one of the first acts of the Long Parliament was the abolition of the Court of Star Chamber.[3]

---

[1] *Parl. Hist.*, vol. i. p. 891.
[2] *Jurisdiction of the Lords House*, p. 80.
[3] For the importance of the Council in Parliament from Edward III to the present time see, generally, Hale, *Jurisdiction of the Lords House*, chs. ix.,

THE HIGH COURT OF PARLIAMENT

By the fourteenth century, then, we may say that the machinery of the English government was practically complete,—separate courts of law, a court of chancery, a council with important functions separate from Parliament, the House of Lords the highest judicial body in the state, an elective commons whose assent was necessary to legislation, etc.; though of course great changes were yet to occur within nearly all of these and in their relations to each other.

It remains to look back over this period and note some characteristics of the *work* of the Council and of the Parliament.

---

xiii., xxvii.; Prynne, *Brief Register*, part i. p. 383 et seq.; Holdsworth, *H. E. L.*, vol. i. ch. vi.; Stubbs, *C. H.*, vol. iii. pp. 461, 462; Dicey, *Privy Council*, parts ii. and iii.; May, *Parliamentary Practice*, 9th ed., pp. 56, 57, 253 et seq. (the ninth edition is the last one which appeared in the author's lifetime); Macqueen, *House of Lords and Privy Council Practice*, chs. iii. and xxii.; Lowell, *Government of England*, vol. ii. pp. 464, 465; *The Privy Council under the Tudors*, by Lord Eustace Percy (Oxford, 1907); *Proceedings of the Privy Council* (ed. by Sir Harris Nicolas); *Acts of the Privy Council* (ed. by J. R. Dasent).

INTRODUCTION

Note A. The Judges in Council
(*Page* 34)

The Lords Commissioners thought that possibly the second year of Edward III may have marked the beginning of the change by which the judges ceased to be equal with the other members in the Council, because in that year for the first time in the title of the placita they are declared to be "*in presentia domini regis procerum et magnatum regni in parliamento suo;*" thus seemingly indicating that the lords spiritual and temporal alone are meant. *Lords' Report*, vol. i. p. 296; Parry, p. 92, note *g*. The argument is based entirely on the supposition that the Council and the Parliament were separate in those early times and had been so before this date,—a view which I believe to be unsupported by the facts.

The famous case of Judge Tresilian, in the reign of Richard II, shows that at that time the judges had become mere advisers, but that the old order may have been recent enough to be remembered. Briefly stated the circumstances were as follows: In 1386 the "Lords Apellant" had impeached Michael de la Pole, Richard's Chancellor, for his support of the royal prerogative against them. In the next year the King summoned the judges and demanded their opinion of the legality of the Chancellor's condemnation of the year before. Tresilian and the other judges at that time gave it as their opinion that if the case were again before them, "the same justices and serjeant would not give the same judgment, because it seemed to them that the same is revocable as erroneous in every part." Then followed the period of the domination of the baronial party, during which Tresilian and others were condemned and executed. By the year 1398, however, the King was again in control, and in the Parliament of that year (21 Richard II) questions were again put to the judges concerning de la Pole's condemnation, whether he had really been guilty of treason, and whether the previous answers of Tresilian and his colleagues concerning the matter were proper answers or not. When asked what they thought of those answers, "Sir Thomas of Skelton learned in the law and William Hankeford and William Brenchley, the king's sergeants, being demanded by the king, of their advice in this behalf, said, That the answers were good and lawful. And that they would have given the same answers, if the said questions had been demanded of them. And my lord William Thirning, chief justice of the common bench, said, That the declaration of treason not declared, belongeth to the parliament; *but if he were a lord or a peer of parliament,* if he had been demanded, he would have said in the same manner. And in like manner, said my lord William Rikehyl, justice of the common place, and after the coming of my lord Walter Clopton, chief justice, he said in the like wise." On the strength of these opinions the Parliament adjudged the answer of Tresilian "juste bone & loiale," and the condemnation of de la Pole erroneous and revocable, and proceeded at once to reverse the sentence against him. (*Statutes of the Realm,* vol. ii. p. 104; *Rot. Parl.,* vol. iii. p. 358; Selden, *Judicature in Parliament: Works,* vol. iii. columns 1649, 1650.) The translation here given is Selden's, but the italics are not his.

In times of such disorder, too much reliance cannot be put on such proceedings as precedents, but Selden thinks that Tresilian was "much mistaken" because here he was expected to give his advice, not his consent, "and yet he saith, he gave his *consent.*" This questioning of the judges in the Parliament of 21 Richard II was a formal proceeding in Parliament, not a private consultation, for it is set down at length on the Parliament Roll, and as a result of it the condemnation of de la Pole was reversed by Parliament. There is no doubt that at this time the judges could properly advise, but could not consent. The cautious answer of the justices is evidence either that they knew this, or that they anticipated a possible return of the baronial party. The less cautious answer of the serjeants, while it may indicate nothing more than a desire on their part to ingratiate themselves with the King, may, on the other hand, have been induced, partially at least, by a recollection or a tradition of a time when the judicial members of the Council could consent as well as advise. The whole incident may be meaningless, for the times were revolutionary; but Selden, at least, did not consider it meaningless, and anything is welcome that will throw any light on the transformation of the jurisdiction of the Council into that of the House of Lords in Parliament. As to the judges in the Council in Parliament, see above all the valuable series of articles on the Council by Professor James F. Baldwin. *Royal Hist. Society Transactions,* N. S., vol. xix. p. 27; *Eng.*

INTRODUCTION

Hist. Rev., vol. xxi. p. 1; *Am. Hist. Rev.*, vol. xi. no. 1; also *The Court of Star Chamber*, by Cora L. Scofield, pp. xxvi, xxvii; Hatschek, *Englisches Staatsrecht*, vol. i. p. 239; and Note A at the end of chapter iii., on page 247 of this volume.

CHAPTER II

The Fundamental Law

LEGISLATION is distinguished from other sources of law mainly by the fact of its "deriving its authority from an external body or person."[1] Of lawmaking of this kind there was very little in mediaeval England. If we run through the various forms of law from the dooms of Ethelbert or Ine,[2] through the charter of the Normans, the assize of the earlier Angevins, through those great transitional documents such as Magna Charta or the Provisions of Oxford, through the statutes of Edward I, the petitions of the Commons, and finally the bills deriving their authority from their enactment "by the King our Sovereign Lord, with the Assent of the Lords and Commons in Parliament assembled,"—if we pass all these stages in review, it seems that the last stage appears only in times that are almost modern, and also that even after it has appeared, the activity of the legislature is greatly restricted up to comparatively recent times. In mediaeval England legislation in its proper sense was all but unknown. Laws in feudal times are in the main declarations of existing custom; they are, as Professor Jenks says, "not enactments, but records."[3] When on a feudal

---

[1] Maine, *Ancient Law* (Pollock's ed.), p. 28.
[2] These forms are summarized in Stubbs's *Lectures on Early English History*, pp. 297, 298.
[3] *Law and Politics in the Middle Ages*, p. 61.

THE FUNDAMENTAL LAW

manor there was doubt as to the existence or character of a custom of the manor, the question was settled by an inquest,—the *enquête par tourbe*. There was no declaration of a new law by the lord or by the suitors; the suitors on oath simply declared what the existing custom of the manor was.[1] Thus, to use Mr. Jenks's phrase, it was characteristic of all feudal law that it was "the law of a court."[2] So in England, as in the rest of feudal Europe, not only the laws of the local feudal units, but the laws of the King as well, were the laws of a *court*. Indeed it was mainly that which made the King's law "common;" for it could become so in those times only through the agency of courts whose jurisdiction extended over the whole kingdom or nearly so.[3] It was undoubtedly the procedure in these courts—called despotic, without a doubt, by the barons of the day—which must be considered as the most potent factor in the development of the English Common Law,—a procedure by which cases were drawn on one pretext or another from the lords' courts to the King's, by fiction of a failure of justice, by inducement of the Grand Assize or some other form of the inquest, or even without any fiction or inducement at all. Thus by force and by offering a justice that was quicker, surer, and more impartial, the King's courts through the various royal writs drew away from the

---

[1] Jenks, *op. cit.*, p. 23; Esmein, *Histoire du Droit Français*, 4th ed., pp. 720, 721; Brunner, *Die Entstehung der Schwurgerichte*, p. 385 et seq.
[2] *Op. cit.*, pp. 24, 25.
[3] *Ibid.*, pp. 35-7.

manorial and even from the old local courts the trial of the most important causes. What was most effective to make the law administered in the King's courts "common" was the uniformity of the procedure that thus prevailed throughout the kingdom. The substantive law was mainly custom, *declared*, not created, and not to be essentially altered; but now declared as the "common" custom of the realm by the King's judges. Most of the changes that were actually and consciously made were effected by means of instructions or "assizes" issued to the judges by the King, and were mainly alterations in procedure. Of the ordinance creating the Assize of *Novel Disseisin*, "which was in the long run to prove itself one of the most important laws ever issued in England, we have not the words;"[1] the exact dates of the ordinances for the Assize of *Darrein Presentment* and the Grand Assize—a corner-stone of early English real property law—are unknown.

Nevertheless, the "assizes" about exhaust the surviving "legislation" of the Norman and early Angevin period,—a period second to none in importance in the development of English law.

The Common Law was thus in the main the product of a court, not of a legislature, and its development was brought about through activities that are more accurately described as judicial than as legislative.

As in the local feudal courts we find the customs of

[1] Pollock and Maitland, *History of English Law*, 2d ed., vol. i. p. 146. For a general statement of this subject, see Pollock and Maitland, or Holdsworth, *History of English Law*, vol. i.

the manor, or the special customs of the district "declared," so likewise even in the great feudal central court of the King in his Council, the customs of the realm were "declared" also; on one occasion, it is said, by twelve men upon oath "nil pretermittentes, nil preuaricando commutantes,"[1] or, as it occurs in another text, "nil pretermittentes, *nil addentes*, nil preuaricando mutantes."[2]

Another famous instance, and this time a well attested one, of the use of what may be called an inquest, to declare the custom of the realm, is at Clarendon in 1164, when Henry II caused to be written down a "*recordatio vel recognitio* of a certain part of the customs and liberties and dignities of his ancestors."[3]

---

[1] This passage is so important that it should be quoted at length. It is the beginning of the so-called *Laws of Edward the Confessor:* "Post quartum annum adquisitionis regis Willelmi istius terre, consilio baronum suorum fecit submoniri per universos patrie comitatus Anglos nobiles, sapientes et lege sua eruditos ut eorum consuetudines ab ipsis audiret.

"Electis igitur de singulis totius patrie comitatibus duodecim, jurejurando inprimis coram eo sanxerunt, ut quoad possent, recto tramite incedentes, legum suarum ac consuetudinum sancita edicerent, nil pretermittentes, nil preuaricando commutantes." Liebermann, *Gesetze*, vol. i. p. 627. See Brunner, *Schwurgerichte*, p. 385. As to the authenticity of these laws, see Liebermann, *Ueber Leges Edwardi Confessoris*, Halle, 1896. See also Stubbs, *Lectures on Early English History*, pp. 48, 49, 82.

[2] Liebermann, *Gesetze*, vol. i. p. 627; Hoveden (Rolls Series), vol. ii. p. 219.

[3] Stubbs, *Select Charters*, p. 135 et seq. These famous "constitutions," the record declares, were drawn up in the presence of the archbishops and bishops and clergy, the counts and barons and great men of the realm, and attested "per archiepiscopos et episcopos et comites et barones et per nobiliores et antiquiores regni." Becket, whether he set his seal to the Constitutions or not,—there is some doubt of it (*Materials for the Life of Becket*, Rolls Series, vol. ii. pp. 382, 383; *Thomas Saga*, Rolls Series, vol. i. p. 169; Hoveden, Rolls Series, vol. i. p. 222),—afterwards refused to recognize their genuineness, but always referred to them as the customs "quas rex avitas vocabat." Hoveden,

THE HIGH COURT OF PARLIAMENT

Though all the instances are not so clear as these, the same principle runs through all: the "charters" of the Norman Kings profess always to secure rights already existing; the assizes, where they introduce new rules, do so in matters of procedure almost exclusively; Magna Charta corrects "abuses" that have grown up in violation of customary rules.[1]

The idea of "making" law is alien to then existing modes of thought, and when changes occur, as they must, if consciously made, they are usually only the correction of defects in the machinery for administering the ancient customs, or they purport to be the

vol. i. p. 222. Herbert of Bosham, hardly a very trustworthy authority for such matters, says the "customs" were the work of the archbishop's enemies, who had imposed on the King, who himself was ignorant of the customs. *Materials*, vol. iii. pp. 279, 280. William Fitz Stephen goes further, and says that "these constitutions had never been written before, and had not even existed at all in the realm of England." *Materials*, vol. iii. pp. 47, 48. These ecclesiastical writers are too much prejudiced and too ignorant of the laws of England to be witnesses of any value. I cannot find that Becket himself — whose knowledge at least must have been much greater — anywhere denies point-blank that the "so-called" constitutions of Henry's grandfather were real customs of the realm. He may have known too much law to do that, though he professed not to know it. *Materials*, vol. iii. p. 279. As a matter of fact, he cared little whether the constitutions were genuine or not. *Materials*, vol. iii. pp. 268, 269. He refused to recognize the constitutions because they were repugnant to a "higher law," above all Kings or their Councils.

[1] Other illustrations running back beyond Magna Charta could easily be given. For example: the so-called *Laws of William the Conqueror* purport to be the same as those of Edward the Confessor. Liebermann, *Gesetze*, vol. i. pp. 492, 493. The *Laws of Edward the Confessor* have already been referred to above. The Charter of Liberties of Henry I is mainly a promise to put away "the bad customs by which the realm of England was oppressed." Stubbs, *Select Charters*, p. 100. Stephen's first charter is an express confirmation of "all the liberties and good laws" of Henry I (Stubbs, *Select Charters*, p. 119), and in the second charter we find a promise to observe "*bonas leges et antiquas et justas consuetudines* in murders and pleas and other causes" (*ibid.*, p. 121).

THE FUNDAMENTAL LAW

restoration of these customs after a period of wrongful desuetude, or the abolishing of abuses that have contravened the ancient rules; or finally, if the changes cannot be brought conveniently under any of these, they are concealed under a fiction. Changes must inevitably occur in any system, and in a system of law and government which is developing as rapidly as was the case in mediaeval England, such changes must be great and fundamental. But the fact that these developments, great as they were, were so carefully covered up shows the attitude of men's minds towards "legislation." As Sidgwick says: "Law was to an important extent conceived by both governors and governed as a subject of science, capable of being learnt by special study, but not capable of being altered by the mere arbitrary will of government, any more than the principles or conclusions of mathematics."[1] Legislation, in fact, "was not the primary business of Parliament."[2] This is sufficiently evidenced by the small number of statutes that we find on the earlier rolls.

[1] *The Elements of Politics*, 2d ed., pp. 652, 653.
[2] Pollock, *First Book of Jurisprudence*, pp. 329, 330. See also A. L. Lowell, *Essays on Government*, pp. 195-7; Jenks, *Law and Politics*, pp. 59-61, 64; Pike, *Const. Hist. of the House of Lords*, pp. 310, 311. The feeling of the people against innovations in the law is expressed in a political song current in the reign of Henry III and written by some opponent of the baronial party. In the course of it the author says:

"Anglorum proceres legem fingendo novellam,
Ubere de regno terram fecere misellam.
. . . .
Conjurat populus fruiturus lege novella;
Fædere mox rupto consurgunt horrida bella."

Wright's *Political Songs* (Camden Society), p. 129. See also *post*, p. 67, note.

THE HIGH COURT OF PARLIAMENT

Even when changes were made in the legislative way, as we find in the remarkable and quite unusual legislative activity of Edward I's reign, the enactments, as we have seen, were generally restricted in scope and were evidently felt to be exceptional in character. This is shown in the preambles. To take only one example: the purpose of the King in having enacted the Statute of Gloucester, 6 Edw. I, is said to be, "*pur amendment de son roialme et pur plus pleiner exhibicion de droit*," — "two excellent ends of a Parliament," Coke says, "Regni melioratio, that is, for the common good of the Kingdom, the Parliament being Commune Concilium, and exhibitio Justiciae plenior, for nothing is more glorious and necessary, then full execution of Justice."[1] Of all the Parliaments of Edward I, we probably know most about that held in 1305. In that Parliament there was very little action we could call legislative,[2] there was no supply granted, and no evidence that any was asked.[3]

The Lords' Commissioners in 1820 were evidently under the impression that a Great Council of the Kingdom in the middle ages ought to be a "legislative" body. They are surprised that the Constitutions of Clarendon "do not expressly mention any obligation in these Ecclesiastics to attend in any Legislative Assembly."[4]

---

[1] 2 *Inst.*, 280. [2] Maitland, *Parl. Roll*, Introd., p. 1.
[3] *Ibid.*, p. liii. The famous reply of the barons at Merton in 1235 is here in point: "Et omnes Comites et Barones una voce responderunt, quod nolunt leges Anglie mutare, que usitate sunt, et approbate." 20 H. 3, c. 9.
[4] *Report*, vol. i. p. 46.

THE FUNDAMENTAL LAW

Speaking of the circumstances of the Great Charter, they say: "It has appeared to the Committee a striking Circumstance, that neither the King, nor the discontented Barons, nor the Barons who adhered to the King, at any Time appealed, for the Decision of their Differences, to a Legislative Assembly to be convened for that Purpose."[1] And again: "It is also remarkable that no Article in the Charter has Reference to the previous Existence of any Assembly convened for general Purposes of Legislation."[2] Still going on the assumption that Parliament was necessarily a "legislative" body, the Commissioners are nonplussed again by the proceedings in the year 1297 when the celebrated *Confirmatio Cartarum* was forced from Edward I. "These extraordinary Proceedings seem to demonstrate, that even in the 25th of Edward the First, the Constitution of the Legislative Assembly of the Kingdom was not definitely settled as now established, or that Edward did not acknowledge such a legal Establishment."[3] Although they call these proceedings "extraordinary," they are forced to admit that the English

---

[1] *Report*, vol. i. p. 63.
[2] *Ibid.* Speaking of Magna Charta, McKechnie says: "Not a word is said of any right inherent in the Council to share in legislation, to control or even to advise the Executive, or to concur in choosing the great ministers of the Crown. Neither deliberative, administrative, nor legislative powers are secured to it, while its control over taxation is strictly limited to the right to veto scutages and aids—that is to say, it only extends over that very narrow class of exactions which affected the military tenants of the Crown." *Magna Carta*, pp. 151, 152. See also Gneist, *C. H.*, vol. i. p. 309, note. See *Lords' Report* further, pp. 187, 188, 193, 194.
[3] *Lords' Report*, vol. i. pp. 224, 225.

THE HIGH COURT OF PARLIAMENT

Justinian "even at the Close of his Reign . . . took upon himself (to a certain Extent) to supersede the Authority of this Parliament, by qualifying the Execution of its Statute; which seems to shew, either that the Principles of a Constitutional Government were not then perfectly understood, or were not well settled by Practice; or that Edward assumed to himself a dispensing Power not consistent with *the Supremacy of a Legislative Assembly in Matters of Legislation.* Throughout his whole Reign, indeed, there appears a Mixture of Submission to the Controul of his Parliaments, and an Usurpation of Authority in Opposition to that Controul, which seem to demonstrate, not only his Unwillingness to submit to that Controul, but a Want of that Certainty as to the Extent of the Authority, both of the King and of his Parliaments, which Time and Practice have since produced."[1]

And though the commissioners were able to persuade themselves, notwithstanding these admissions, that by the reign of Edward I, "the Constitution of the Legislative Assemblies of England had . . . nearly approached the Form in which they have now been long established,"[2] a half century later, events in the Parliament of 14 Edw. III bring out again the familiar statement that "the Constitution of the Legislature in Parliament was not then definitely settled as it now is."[3]

[1] *Report*, vol. i. p. 253. The italics are not in the original.
[2] *Ibid.*, p. 254.   [3] *Ibid.*, p. 311.

THE FUNDAMENTAL LAW

To look at the Assemblies of Edward I, and before Edward I, with the expectation of finding "the Supremacy of a Legislative Assembly in Matters of Legislation," is surely to have a disappointing result. Too many things of that time must be described as "extraordinary," which from their frequency we should more truly call ordinary and normal. "We must read our history backwards as well as forwards," and by so doing the modern idea of legislation will almost disappear, Parliament will grow to seem, in so far as the growth of law is concerned, law-declaring rather than law-making. Edward I "created the most effective law-declaring machine in the Teutonic world of his day,"[1] but it cannot be described accurately as a "legislative Assembly."

With the reasons why this should be so in the middle ages, I am not here particularly interested: that it was so there can be no doubt; and it is further evident that such a conception of law, to whatever it may have been due, fitted in remarkably well with the other institutions and with the general political conceptions of the feudal time. Such customary laws as these, declared by inquest or by Council, hardly ever ostensibly altered, with no assignable beginning, must almost of necessity in process of time acquire a character of inviolability; and whether this inviolability be the result or the cause of the preservation of these customs, the feeling has somehow come into existence that there is

[1] Jenks, *Law and Politics in the Middle Ages*, p. 44.

a law fundamental and unalterable, and rights derived from it indefeasible and inalienable. The content of that law may not be definite,—in England it was always far from definite,—but the idea has lodged itself in men's minds as a formative principle, and once lodged it colours everything.

Furthermore, the rights guaranteed under these laws may be mainly the rights of a class. In feudal times they were almost exclusively so. But as time goes on, the basis of the state broadens. New classes "become of thegnright worthy,"—at the least, they become worthy to grant a share of the taxes. Through a process that is obscure in the extreme, but a process in which the decline of chivalry, the growth of the new learning, the increasing size of the known world, with the consequent shaking up of economic and social conditions, must have played a great part, there emerges finally an England where the loyalty to class has broadened out into a feeling of nationality, a solidarity to which the word "national" can properly be applied in describing its common institutions and ideas. In this process of development, the idea of the traditional law is never lost. At first it may be the privileges of the few that are treasured as inalienable and fundamental, but even these "liberties," though they may at first be actually licenses to oppress the mass of the people, are in a future time to prove the greatest inheritance of the nation. For these liberties are rights, and rights imply an immunity from arbitrary authority of which the

THE FUNDAMENTAL LAW

nation may avail itself when it has come into being. They carry with them the idea of government under law instead of limitless discretion,—"franchises," they are often called, and the word shows how negative was their early character and how narrow and exceptional they may have been in their origin.[1] But from such humble beginnings we may trace the great, if indefinite, body of rights which became the pride and boast of Sir John Fortescue and Sir Thomas Smith. The idea of a fundamental law in the sharpness of outline that it attained by the sixteenth century, of course we may not expect in mediaeval times, but that it existed as a controlling force is proved, for example, by such instances as have already been several times noted,—of William the Conqueror's professing to restore Edward's laws, or Henry I's promising to put away "omnes malas consuetudines,"[2] or Stephen's engaging to concede "all the good laws and good customs" of the time of Edward the Confessor.[3]

---

[1] No word better illustrates the change from feudalism to "nationalism"—if I may use such an expression—than this word *franchise*. "What a word is that franchise? The lord may tax his villain high or low, but it is against the franchises of the land, for freemen to be taxed, but by their consent in parliament. Franchise is a French word, and in Latin it is Libertas." Coke in debate on the supply in 1627 (*Parl. Hist.*, vol. ii. p. 237). Coke's ignoring the difference between feudal times and his own is here brought out in characteristic style. The passage is instructive in showing how in the seventeenth century men tried to fit feudal words to the facts of nationality. For examples of these liberties, see Madox, *Exchequer*, ch. xi.

[2] Stubbs, *Select Charters*, p. 100.

[3] *Ibid.*, p. 119. Twysden mentions the various expressions used in early times for these fundamental rights,—*antiquas libertates regni, rectum judicium terrae, lex terrae, jus regni, la franchise de la terre, le droit du royalme, the law of the land*, etc.,—"by all which various appellations are meant nothing else but those

THE HIGH COURT OF PARLIAMENT

Among the documents of feudal times Magna Charta, of course, stands preëminent. Whatever be the true character of that great document, whether it be really statute, treaty, private compact, or declaration of rights,[1] it is strictly true, as Stubbs says, that "the whole of the Constitutional History of England is a commentary on this charter."[2] The view maintained here is that Magna Charta is in the main a promise on the part of the King, in the usual form of a royal grant, that in future the customary privileges, franchises, and liberties of the barons shall not be infringed as they had been in the past. The "liberties" it protects are not quite all privileges of the barons, but the great preponderance of these over all others shows that the charter is a class document, the product of a period when as yet there are only two classes in the state strong enough to get their "rights" recognized,—the clergy and the nobility.[3] The claims arise mainly out of feudal conditions, the abuses are chiefly abuses of feudal customs,

immunities the subject hath ever enjoyed as his owne right, perteyning either to his person or his goods; and the grownd that hee doth so is, that they are allowed him by the law of the land, which the king alone can not at his owne will alter, and therefore can not take them from him, they beeing as aunctient as the kingdome itselfe, which the king is to protect.

"It is manyfest these 'liberties, franchises,' etc., are something did precede those writers or statutes which mention them, and were a rule or square to judge and condemne what is in them complayned of." *Government of England* (Camden Society), p. 82. See Gneist, *C. H.*, vol. i. p. 252.

[1] The various views are summarized in McKechnie, *Magna Carta*, pp. 123-7. Selden considered it a "statute." *Works*, vol. iii. col. 1993. For most points involved in this discussion of Magna Charta, see Petit-Dutaillis, *Studies Supplementary to Stubbs's Constitutional History*, vol. i. ch. xii.

[2] *Select Charters*, p. 296.

[3] See the summary in Petit-Dutaillis, *op. cit.*, p. 136 et seq.

the remedy is a typically feudal remedy.[1] Why, then, its great importance? Simply in this, that in it was embodied the principle of a fundamental law, a law with a penalty attached; and embodied in a more concrete and a more memorable form, if I may so say, than ever before,—a form that stuck in men's minds, that occurred to them as a concrete precedent when the same rights were infringed again, or as a powerful analogy when other rights of a similar character were violated. As Professor George B. Adams, whom I have followed here, says, in referring to the principle of a fundamental law binding even an unwilling king: "It was the work of Magna Carta to transfer this principle from the feudal to the modern state, and . . . in this fact we have the explanation of the influence and significance of the Great Charter in English history."[2]

Again the same author says: "It was not Magna Carta, but the circumstances of the future which gave to the fact that there was a body of law above the king creative power in English history. Magna Carta emphasized the fact and made the suggestion of the right of enforcement, in a way never to be forgotten, but this was all it did. Nor did feudal law furnish, except in a few particulars and these much transformed, the body of law by which the king was bound. The great work of Magna Carta was not done by its specific provisions;

---

[1] The Charter " was drawn up for the baronage and not for the nation as a whole." Petit-Dutaillis, *op. cit.*, p. 134. It was "essentially a document of feudal law." *Ibid.*, p. 140.

[2] *American Historical Review*, vol. xiii. p. 237.

the secret of its influence is to be found in its underlying idea."[1] It is one of the purposes of the brilliant article from which these quotations are taken to show that this idea of fundamental law, from which alone Magna Charta derived its immense importance, was the one formative idea in the English constitution whose development created the limited monarchy; that even Parliament itself, in its unintended development from the King's Council into the representative lawmaking organ of the state, is significant largely because in time it became the guardian of this great idea.[2] Thus it is not the circumstances surrounding its origin, but the "circumstances of the future;" not its true interpretation, but the glosses made on it by after generations that have given Magna Charta its place.

That wonderful and to us more or less mysterious change in England from a series of feudal ranks to an organic nation, which was complete in the reign of Elizabeth, made the feudal régime incomprehensible.[3] For whatever may be true socially, there is a wide gulf between a political society of ranks and classes, each acting and voting for itself, and a commonwealth as described by Sir Thomas Smith in the reign of Eliza-

[1] *Am. Hist. Rev.*, vol. xiii. p. 238, note 10.
[2] *Ibid.*, p. 233.
[3] It is true that Raleigh, in the dialogue, *The Prerogatives of Parliaments*, makes the Counsellor of State speak of the "Beginning of the Great Charter, which had first an obscure Birth from Usurpation, and was secondly fostered and shewed to the World by Rebellion" (*Harleian Misc.*, vol. v. p. 182, ed. of 1745), but in the dialogue there is no evidence that Raleigh had any conception of the feudal character of the document. See Filmer's *Patriarcha* (ed. by Morley), p. 64.

THE FUNDAMENTAL LAW

beth,—"a society or common doing of a multitude of free men collected together and united by common accord and covenauntes among themselves, for the conservation of themselves as well in peace as in warre."[1]

The great principle of Magna Charta was as important to the men of the seventeenth century in their constitutional struggles as it had been to the barons in 1215, and that principle was in essence unchanged, but the feudal setting was totally misunderstood. With the inevitable habit of reading later ideas into earlier institutions, they assumed that the circumstances surrounding the enunciating of the principle must have been the same in 1215 as they would be three centuries later, and so, to take the most notable example, the *judicium parium* becomes trial by jury. In short, the nation has at last come into existence, and the document which is strictly feudal is now interpreted in a new and a "national" sense. The baronial rights originally protected by the provisions of the charter have now become the rights of the "multitude of free men." But the principle is the same. There is a fundamental law which binds a king and beyond which he may not go. The principle has persisted through all changes. And Magna Charta is mainly important historically because men from feudal times onward centred their thought and their feeling on it, though in time they lost the comprehension of its details; and

[1] *De Republica Anglorum*, bk. i. ch. x.

because they felt for it the reverence that arose from the sacredness of the principle it preserved,—a reverence that men usually cannot feel for an abstract idea in itself, but find it necessary to concentrate upon some concrete statement or document. "There is scarcely one great principle of the English constitution of the present day, or indeed of any constitution of any day, calculated to secure national liberties, or otherwise to win the esteem of mankind, which has not been read by commentators into the provisions of Magna Carta."[1] What we mainly need, as Professor Vinogradoff says, is a history of the influence of the document.[2]

The importance of the principle contained in Magna Charta, and the difficulty of maintaining it, are both shown by the necessity for a reissue so soon as 1216, and the frequency of the reissues and confirmations thereafter.[3] Coke enumerates thirty-two of these in separate acts of Parliament. The significance of the underlying principle of Magna Charta, in contrast with

[1] McKechnie, p. 156. See also the same, pp. 147, 157, 158.
[2] *Law Quarterly Review*, vol. xxi. p. 257; McKechnie, p. 147; Jenks, in *Independent Review* for 1904, *The Myth of Magna Carta*. I am unable to go to the length the author does there in calling Coke the "inventor" of Magna Charta. The change from the feudal interpretation to the national one was gradual, and Coke was by no means the first man to adopt the national interpretation. Even before it had taken on this new idea, Magna Charta stood out as an exceptional and a "fundamental" document, as is evidenced by the frequent reissues and the numerous references made to it. Cf., for example, 5 Edw. III., cap. ix. A more moderate account, erring, if at all, on the other side, is to be found in Holdsworth, *H. E. L.*, vol. ii. pp. 168, 169.
[3] On this, see McKechnie, p. 164 et seq. For a valuable account of the reissues, see also Bémont, *Chartes*, Introd., p. xxvi et seq.; Coke, *2nd Inst.*, Proeme; Thomson, *Magna Charta*, p. 376 et seq., *passim;* Blackstone, *Great Charter*.

THE FUNDAMENTAL LAW

the specific provisions, is brought out more clearly by the importance of those provisions of the original charter which are entirely omitted in the reissues. The most noteworthy, of course, is the chapter which forbids the King to levy an aid without the consent of the commune concilium. This provision, in our eyes so important, does not appear in the first reissue in 1216, nor in the final form of the charter in 1225, and the principle of it was not successfully established until the great confirmation of 1297.

Among the confirmations of the Charter, that in 1368 is especially noteworthy. In the Parliament of that year it was "assented and accorded, That the Great Charter and the Charter of the Forest be holden and kept in all points; and if any Statute be made to the contrary, that shall be holden for none."[1] The meaning of these words seems clear. There is little doubt that when they were used, the intention of the men who drew them up was, exactly as stated, that thereafter Magna Charta should in its entirety be considered as nothing else than a fixed and unalterable law. Such an idea is to be expected at that time. It was only the habit of legislation, acquired later, and the consequent actual sovereignty of Parliament which arose

[1] "Est assentu et accorde qe la Grande Chartre et la Chartre de la Foreste soient tenez et gardez en touz pointz; et si nul estatut soit fait a contraire soit tenez pur nul." 42 Edw. III., cap. i. The great confirmation of 25 Edward I (S. R., vol. i. p. 123) had already declared void all contrary *jugementz* in future to be made. This may possibly include a statute, for, as we shall see, the word *judgement* in those days had a very inclusive meaning. Prynne seems to include a royal ordinance within the term. *Fundamental Liberties*, vol. i. p. 90.

in the seventeenth century, that altered men's ways of looking at this. The old idea kept cropping out again and again. Even when parliamentary sovereignty was attained, Parliaments are found every now and then using language inconsistent with its necessary corollary, the principle that no Parliament is bound by the acts of a prior Parliament. When the Parliament in 1706 passed the Act of Union with Scotland, they meant that it should be permanent and unchangeable if words ever mean what they seem to mean. This has been disregarded, of course, as was inevitable under the modern principle of parliamentary sovereignty when fully realized, but the fact that the men of 1706 used such language shows that even then at times Parliaments could fall back into the old manner of thinking.

The most striking instance of the exercise of parliamentary sovereignty is that of the Septennial Act in 1716, but surely the Parliament men of 1694 really meant what they said when they declared "That within three Years at the farthest, from and after the dissolution of this present Parliament, and so from time to time forever hereafter, within three Years at the farthest, from and after the Determination of every other Parliament, legal Writs under the Great Seal shall be issued by Directions of Your Majesties, Your Heirs and Successors, for calling, assembling and holding another new Parliament."[1]

Before the civil wars of the seventeenth century and

[1] 6 and 7 Wm. and Mary, cap. ii.

the familiarizing of the idea of a sovereign legislature, this idea of a fundamental law was normal and usual. This is not to say that Parliament never made innovations, nor is it to say even that enactments of Parliaments that contravened the principles of Magna Charta were never enforced. In a country such as England, where there is no formal distinction between a constituent law and ordinary legislation, it is hard to draw a line between these two kinds of law. If a constituent law ever existed in England it must be looked for mainly in the attitude of men toward the law, or, better, in the rules applied by judges in cases arising under the law. The fundamental law there may be contained in a document, or documents, as in the case of Magna Charta, but the validity of that law is not due to the form of the document or documents, but rather to the character of the principles. There is nothing in the documents themselves that claims superior respect over ordinary legislation; the documents purport to be only legislative acts of the ordinary character, if they be legislative at all. To look, then, in a country which has never permanently codified its constituent law, and in an age when such codification was as yet thought of by few or none, would be futile, if we were looking for a formal document which should contain the conscious expression of a "constitution."

But if we find in such a country, at such a time, that judges recognize certain rules, or to put it concretely some clauses of Magna Charta, as permanent and unchangeable, and avoid acts derogatory of them in the most palpable manner, whether by a thin fiction or otherwise, without arousing public opposition; if we find that legal commentators of accepted authority treat such derogatory acts as "infamous" or even as void; then it seems safe to conclude that there is in existence there, as an active living legal principle, the conception of a law superior in authority to the everyday enactments of a lawmaking body. When in addition it is borne in mind that in the England of that time, Parliament had not, as Seeley says, yet become an "organ of the commonwealth" in a very real sense; that its lawmaking was timid and sporadic; that it had little or no control over the frequency or infrequency of its sessions or over their duration; that it was only imperfectly representative in character, and that the actual lawmaking of the time was in great part effected outside its walls,—with such considerations in mind, the failure to find any written "constitution" will not blind us to the fact that even without it there is a profound difference between the theory and the practice in matters involving a "fundamental law" of the men of those times, and the doctrines and rules generally accepted in England to-day, when the principle of parliamentary omnipotence is a real and a practical force strong enough to reach the highest as well as the lowest, and inclusive enough to extend to matters no matter how minute.

If in the sixteenth century an act were passed con-

THE FUNDAMENTAL LAW

trary to the principles of Magna Charta, such an act might remain for a considerable time on the statute-book, and in all probability in most cases men would not dare openly to disobey it with impunity; but it is nevertheless true that they looked upon such an act, and judges acted with reference to it, in a way totally different from the disapproval that would be felt to-day if Parliament should pass an act which men felt would be harmful in operation or wrong in principle. If Parliament to-day should abolish trial by jury, the results may be imagined, but it is safe to say that no court would refuse to recognize the act as law. They would neither declare it void, nor interpret it in a sense palpably unintended by its makers, nor avoid it by a fiction. If its meaning was perfectly clear they would simply enforce it. I venture to believe that in the sixteenth century the case would have been wholly different. There was then, in a sense that has lost its vividness with the growth of Parliament's power, a true fundamental law. The general principle was more important than its specific content. Men may not always have been clear as to what particular rights or liberties were guaranteed by the fundamental law, but as to the existence of such a law there was no doubt, and any act that violated it was in a true sense felt to be no law.[1]

---

[1] "The Laws," says the Speaker of the House of Commons in 1604, "whereby the ark of this government hath ever been steered, are of three kinds; the 1st, the Common Law, grounded or drawn from the Law of God, the Law of Reason, and the Law of Nature, not mutable; the 2d, the positive Law, founded, changed, and altered by and through the occasions and policies of

THE HIGH COURT OF PARLIAMENT

Coke seldom states flatly that particular acts are not binding. Such a statement would hardly have been politic, but, to say the least, he habitually displays a feeling toward them as a lawyer that no judge of today would be tempted to express.[1]

Even Bacon agrees with Coke that Magna Charta is unalterable. In his *Brief Discourse upon the Commission of Bridewell* he says: "In the said great Charter of England, in the last chapter, amongst other things the King granteth for him and his heirs, that neither he nor his heirs shall procure to do anything whereby

---

times; the 3d, Customs and Usages, practised and allowed with time's approbation, without known beginnings." *Parl. Hist.*, vol. i. p. 1046. While this classification should be objected to, it is interesting to note the sharp division he makes between the common law and statute, only the second of which may be changed. See an expression of the same idea by James I in 1607 in describing the laws of Scotland. *Parl. Hist.*, vol. i. p. 1111.

[1] The statute of Henry VII, allowing justices to hear and determine alleged breaches of the statute law without presentment or verdict was his particular aversion. 11 Henry VII., cap. iii. "The Justices of Assise in their Sessions, and the Justices of Peace in every County, upon Information for the King, shall have Authority to hear and determine all Offences and Contempts (saving Treason, Murder, or Felony) committed by any Person against the Effect of any Statute made, and not repealed." This statute was repealed in the first year of Henry VIII (1 Henry VIII., cap. vi.). For Coke's opinion of this "unjust and injurious Act" of Henry VII, see 2 *Inst.*, 51; 4 *Inst.*, 41. The question of the interpretation of the confirmation of Magna Charta in the year 1368, quoted above, illustrates Coke's attitude. In regard to the so-called Statute *Praerogativa Regis* (17 Edw. II., st. 1, cap. xvi.), regarding forfeiture to the King of felons' lands and goods, Coke said: "If any Statute be made to the contrary of Magna Charta, it shall be holden for none. And therefore if *Praerogativa Regis*, anno 17 *E. 2 cap. ultima*, be contrary thereunto, it is repealed as to the Wast." 3 *Inst.*, 111; see also 2 *Inst.*, 37. Of course the confirmation of 1368 had occurred in the meantime, and notwithstanding it there was much difference of opinion on this particular point (*e. g.* see Jenkins's *Centuries*, p. 2, and the references there cited. Judge Jenkins himself believed that Magna Charta should stand only on points not altered by acts prior to 1368).

THE FUNDAMENTAL LAW

the liberties in the said Charter contained shall be infringed or broken; and if anything be procured or done by any person contrary to the premises it shall be had of no force or effect." He then cites some of the confirmations and adds: "It is assented and accorded that the great Charter of England and the Charter of the Forests shall be kept in all points, and if any statute be made to the contrary that shall be holden for none."[1]

Prynne quotes with approval Coke's views of Magna Charta expressed in the preface to his *Second Institute* as "a clear resolution, that the Principal Liberties, Customs, Laws, contained in these *great Charters*, and ratified by them, are both FUNDAMENTAL, PERPETUAL, & UNALTERABLE."[2]

Along the same lines Prynne argues in his *Soveraigne Power of Parliaments and Kingdoms*—a work that was printed by the order of the Commons in 1643 —against the King's right to withhold his assent to a bill that has passed the Houses of Parliament, "because it is point-blanke against the very letter of *Magna Charta* (the ancient fundamentall Law of the Realm, confirmed in at least 60 Parliaments) ch. 29. WE SHALL DENY, WE SHALL DEFERRE (both in the future tense) TO NO MAN (much lesse to the whole Parliament and Kingdome, in denying or deferring to passe such necessary publike Bills) JUSTICE OR RIGHT, A law which in

---
[1] *Bacon's Works* (edited by Spedding, Ellis, and Heath, Boston, 1861), vol. xv. p. 16. Mr. Heath thinks this was written in or before the year 1587, and considers it a genuine work of Bacon.
[2] *Fundamental Liberties*, pt. i. p. 11 (should be 10).

THE HIGH COURT OF PARLIAMENT

terminis takes cleane away the King's pretended absolute negative Voyce to these Bills we now dispute of."[1] The importance of the doctrine is manifest, when to bolster up the parliamentary party such sophistry as this can be gravely endorsed by the House of Commons. Such a statement serves also to show the influence of this principle upon the civil wars of the seventeenth century and its value in helping to explain them.

But it is not in Magna Charta alone that we must look for the fundamental law. Evidences of its controlling influence are frequent elsewhere, both in unofficial writings and public documents. In Bracton's day, it is clear that there is a body of law that the King cannot alter, or to put it another way, that there is in the state no "sovereign" freed from all obligations, whose will is law. It is true, there may have been no definite machinery in existence to punish a king who refused to recognize this fundamental principle, but nevertheless such action on his part outraged the feelings of the men of his day. He was acting lawlessly.[2]

In the troubled reign of Henry III, men felt that they were oppressed, but they express no desire for things revolutionary, nor even for new law. A sufficient remedy exists in the old law, and they ask only for a restatement and a better observance of it.[3]

---

[1] *Fundamental Liberties*, part ii. p. 74.

[2] Pollock and Maitland, *H. E. L.*, vol. i. pp. 181-3. See Note A at the end of this chapter (p. 101).

[3] This appears in the following extracts from a long political song, written soon after the battle of Lewes, and setting forth the principles of the barons in

THE FUNDAMENTAL LAW

In the next reign the doctrine of a fundamental law

their struggle with the King. It is printed in Wright's *Political Songs of England* (Camden Society).

"Igitur communitas regni consulatur;
Et quid universitas sentiat sciatur,
Cui leges propriae maxime sunt notae.
Nec cuncti provinciae sic sunt idiotae,
Quin sciant plus caeteris regni sui mores,
Quos relinquunt posteris hii qui sunt priores.
Qui reguntur legibus magis ipsas sciunt;
Quorum sunt in usibus plus periti fiunt;
Et quia res agitur sua, plus curabunt,
Et quo pax adquiritur sibi procurabunt." (pp. 110, 111.)

"Nam rex omnis regitur legibus quas legit;
Rex Saül repellitur, quia leges fregit;
Et punitus legitur David mox ut egit
Contra legem; igitur hinc sciat qui legit,
Quod non potest regere qui non servat legem:
Nec hunc debent facere ad quos spectat regem.
O Edwarde! fieri vis rex, sine lege,
Vere forent miseri recti tali rege!
Nam quid lege rectius qua cuncta reguntur,
Et quid jure verius quo res discernuntur?
Si regnum desideras, leges venerare;
Vias dabit asperas leges impugnare,
Asperas et invias quae te non perducent;
Leges si custodias ut lucerna lucent." (pp. 94, 95.)

"Praemio praeferimus universitatem;
Legem quoque dicimus regis dignitatem
Regere; nam credimus esse legem lucem,
Sine qua concludimus deviare ducem.
Lex qua mundus regitur atque regna mundi
Ignea describitur; quod sensus profundi
Continet mysterium, lucet, urit, calet;
Lucens vetat devium, contra frigus valet,
Purgat et incinerat quaedam, dura mollit,
Et quod crudum fuerat ignis coquit, tollit
Torporem, et alia multa facit bona.
Sancta lex similia p'rat (?) regi dona." (p. 115.)

One cannot help thinking that the writer of this must have been reading certain passages of Bracton's treatise, which had been completed a few years

THE HIGH COURT OF PARLIAMENT

is stated with the greatest clearness by Fleta.[1] The articles drawn up against Richard II also set forth the doctrine in many places. It is charged that the King, "not willing to keep or protect the just laws and customs of his kingdom, but according to his arbitrary will to do whatsoever should occur to his desires; sometimes, and very often, when the laws of his kingdom have been expounded and declared to him by the judges and others of his council, and that they have desired that he would do justice according to those laws, hath expressly, and with an angry and haughty countenance, said, 'that his laws were in his mouth;' and sometimes, 'that they were in his breast;' and that 'he himself alone could make and change the laws of his kingdom."[2] It may be said that this is no assertion of a fundamental law; it is nothing but a statement of the principle that laws should be made only in Parliament. By this time, it is true, Parliament

---

before. Cf. Bracton, fol. 107-107 B. This remarkable song also illustrates the fact, noted above, that legislation was not the rule in the middle ages—the communitas regni is to be consulted because it knows what the customs are, "quos relinquunt posteris hii qui sunt priores." It is not to make new law.

[1] "Parem autem non debet Rex in Regno suo habere, quo minus praecepta sua teneantur, cum par in parem imperium non habeat; nec superiorem habere debet in regno, nisi Deum et legem: Et quia per legem factus est Rex, dignum est quod dominatio et potestas legi attribuatur, et per ipsum tueatur cui lex honorem tribuit et potestatem." Lib. i. cap. 5.

"Temperent igitur Reges potentiam suam per legem, quae fraenum est potentiae, quod secundum leges vivant, quia hoc sanxit lex humana, quod leges suum ligent latorem, et alibi digna vox ex majestate regnantis est, legibus alligatum se Principem profiteri; praeterea nihil tam proprium imperio quam legibus vivere, et majus est imperio legibus submittere principatum," etc. Lib. i. cap. 17. See also Britton, folio 1.

[2] *Rot. Parl.*, vol. iii. p. 419. Translated in *Parl. Hist.*, vol. i. p. 259.

had acquired considerable power. A statement of the thirteenth century that the law is above the King will mean that it is above every one, for if one might correctly look for a "sovereign" power in the state in those times, that power would probably be said to reside in the King. A century later, it may be objected, there is doubt whether we should not say that Parliament is the real "sovereign;" and Richard's saying that "the laws are in his mouth" is therefore only a denial of "parliamentary sovereignty;" it has nothing to do with fundamental law. If such was the real ground of the indictment against Richard II, it is, however, very hard to understand such a statement as the following, which occurs in the arraignment of the King and refers to an article in his will: "By which article it may evidently enough appear, that the said king did obstinately strive to maintain and defend *those statutes and ordinances, which are erroneous and unjust and repugnant to all law and reason.*"[1] It is also charged that the King, "without any reasonable or lawful cause whatsoever, or any other process of law,"[2] "*in his Parliament*" banished Archbishop Arundel, "against the laws of his kingdom, so by him sworn to as aforesaid."[3] It seems clear from this that Richard's law-breaking here complained of was in part done by Act

[1] "Illa Statuta et Ordinationes, que sunt erronia et iniqua et omni juri et rationi repugnantia." *Rot. Parl.*, vol. iii. p. 421.
[2] "Absque Causa rationabili seu legitima quacumque, seu alio Juris processu." *Ibid.*
[3] "Contra Leges Regni sui, per ipsum ut prefertur juratas." *Ibid.*

of Parliament. The charge is against the "King in Parliament," if we may use a more modern expression. "Statuta" as well as "ordinationes"—if there be yet any essential difference between them[1]—may be "omni juri repugnantia."

It is to be noted also that the case of Archbishop Arundel was tried in Parliament, and though, as we shall see later, judgements of Parliament cannot in early times be distinguished from acts, but were proceedings fully as solemn and authoritative as statutes, yet the decision in this case was declared by the men of a subsequent Parliament to be "without lawful cause" and against the laws of the realm. The language in which Mr. Figgis so accurately describes the period following the Wars of the Roses is, except for a phrase or two, equally applicable here, and its aptness is my apology for quoting it at length: "Nor is it of the statute law that men are thinking; but of the Common Law, which, though containing much that may have originally been directly enacted, yet possesses that mysterious sanctity of prescription which no legislator can bestow. The Common Law is pictured invested with a halo of dignity, peculiar to the embodiment of the deepest principles and to the highest expression of human reason and of the law of nature implanted by God in the heart of man. As yet men are not clear that an Act of Parliament can do more than declare the Common Law. It is the Common Law which men set up as the object of

[1] For the distinction see *post*, p. 313 et seq.

worship. They regard it as the symbol of ordered life and disciplined activities, which are to replace the licence and violence of the evil times now passed away. Instead of local custom or special privilege one system shall be common to all. Instead of the caprice of the moment, or the changing principles of competing dynastic policies, or the pleasure of some great noble, or the cunning of a usurper, there shall rule in England a system, older than Kings and Parliaments, of immemorial majesty and almost Divine authority. 'Law is the breath of God; her voice the harmony of the world.' And the Common Law is the perfect ideal of law; for it is natural reason developed and expounded by the collective wisdom of many generations. By it kings reign and princes decree judgement. By it are fixed the relations of the estates of the realm, and the fundamental laws of the constitution. Based on long usage and almost supernatural wisdom its authority is above rather than below that of Acts of Parliament or Royal ordinances, which owe their fleeting existence to the caprice of the King or the pleasure of councillors, which have a merely material sanction and may be repealed at any moment."[1]

Though historians may have accepted such principles as historically true, they have frequently not applied them in specific cases, and have often spoken as though parliaments were practically as free in the thirteenth or fourteenth century to enact new laws as they are to-day. In the fifteenth, sixteenth, or even the seven-

[1] *The Theory of the Divine Right of Kings*, pp. 226-8.

teenth century, there is reason to believe that Englishmen—if their own words can be trusted—had not yet reached this modern point of view. Legislature and Parliament were not for them, as they are for us, practically convertible terms.

It is hardly necessary to refer to Fortescue's famous distinction between *Dominium Regale* and *Dominium Politicum et Regale,* which, along with the celebrated extract from Bracton, mentioned above, were quoted against the King by all parliamentary writers throughout the Stuart period.[1]

It requires conflict, even civil war, to bring out the strongest expressions of the principle of the supremacy of the law. There were practically no such struggles under the Tudor sovereigns, and the statements are fewer, but the doctrine was the same. The excellent old dialogue of the Doctor and Student, written early in the sixteenth century, declares that the sixth and last of the grounds of the law of England "standeth in divers statutes . . . in such cases where the law of reason, the law of God, customs, maxims, ne other grounds of the law seemed not to be sufficient to punish evil men and to reward good men."[2]

Sir Thomas More asserted the same principle in his own defence;[3] Manwood, in his treatise on the forest

[1] *De Laudibus,* cap. xxxiv., cap. ix.; *Governance of England,* chs. i.-iii.
[2] Dialogue I., ch. xi.
[3] When asked why judgement should not be given against him, he gave as one reason that the indictment was founded on a statute "contrarye both to the Lawes and Statuts of this Land, yete unrepealed, as they might evidently perceive in *Magna charta, Quod Ecclesia Anglicana libera sit et habeat*

THE FUNDAMENTAL LAW

laws, written in the reign of Elizabeth, quoted with approval the dictum that the King ought to be under God and the Law "because the law doth make him a King."[1] "Wherefore," says Hooker, "to define and determine, even of the Church's affairs by way of assent and approbation, as laws are defined in that right of power, which doth give them the force of laws; thus to define of our own Church's regiment, the Parliament of England hath competent authority."[2]

"New laws," says Lord Bacon, "are like the apothecaries' drugs: though they remedy the disease, yet, they trouble the body."[3] Coke refers to the repeal of the oppressive act of Parliament of 11 Henry VII., c. 3, as "A good caveat to Parliaments to leave all causes to

---

omnia jura sua integra, et libertates suas illaesas, and contrary to that sacred oath which the King's Heighnes himselfe, and every other Christian Prince at theire Coronations receaved." *The Life of Sir Thomas More*, by William Roper (Cambridge, 1888), p. 1.

[1] Edition of 1615, folio 25. See also Staundeford, *Pleas of the Crown: Introduction to the Reader;* Hearn, *Government of England*, 1st ed., p. 37.

[2] *Ecclesiastical Polity*, bk. viii., *Of the Authority of Making Laws*. This quotation may not seem very conclusive, but if it is compared with the power of Parliament as stated by Blackstone or De Lolme or Dicey, the great difference between it and them will become at once apparent. One reason why the Erastianism of Hooker was so much milder than that of Selden or Prynne, and therefore so much less objectionable to the great mass of Englishmen, lies in Hooker's conception of the powers of Parliament. To him it was not primarily a legislative body in our sense of the term; its power was rather a power to "define" and "determine," "by way of assent and approbation," existing laws and customs, save when changes were indispensable. The quotation here given comes from the suspected eighth book, but it sounds like Hooker.

[3] *Reading on the Statute of Uses*, *Bacon's Works* (ed. by Spedding, Ellis, and Heath), vol. xiv. p. 315 (Boston, 1861). "As the common law is more worthy than the statute law; so the law of nature is more worthy than them both." *Argument in the Case of the Postnati*, *Works* (Spedding, Ellis, and Heath's ed.), vol. xv. p. 202.

be measured by the golden and streight metwand of the Law, and not to the incertain and crooked cord of discretion."[1]

"Let your Lawes be looked into," James I declared to his Parliament in 1607; "for I desire not the abolishing of the Lawes, but onely the clearing and sweeping off the rust of them, and that by Parliament our Laws might be cleared and made knowen to all the Subjects."[2] "Where they [the statutes] have not altered the positive law," says Noy, "but have only increased or decreased the punishment thereof, they have done great good; but where they have altered the common law in substance, they have done great harm."[3]

[1] 4 *Inst.*, 41. "For any fundamental point of the ancient common laws and customs of the realm, it is a maxim in policy, and a trial by experience, that the alteration of any of them is most dangerous; for that which hath been refined and perfected by all the wisest men in former succession of ages, and proved and approved by continual experience to be good and profitable for the commonwealth, cannot without great hazard and danger be altered or changed. Infinite were the scruples, suits, and inconveniences that the statute of 13 E. I. *de donis conditionalibus* did introduce; . . . also, what suits and troubles arose by the statute of 34 Ed. 3 of *nonclaime*, enacted against a main point of the com. law, whereby ensued the universal trouble of the K's subjects, as it was resolved in parliament in 4. H. 7 cap. 24. is apparent to all of least understanding." 4 *Reports, To the Reader*. He also criticizes sharply the Statute of Wills, 32 and 34 H. 8, and comments on the famous declaration of the barons in the Statute of Merton, — "nolumus leges Angliae mutare." See also 2 *Inst.*, 210 (Commentary on West. I., c. 26): "It is a certain and true observation, that the alteration of any of those Maximes of the Common Law is most dangerous."

[2] *King James's Works*, pp. 509, 512.

[3] *A Dialogue and Treatise on the Law*, p. 29. "The Common Law excelleth the Statute Laws, and may controle Statutes." *For the Sacred Law of the Land*, by Francis Whyte (1652), p. 58. "For continual manners approved by the consent of those who use them, imitate Law: this is matter of fact, and consisteth in use and practice only, nor can it be created by charter or Parliament." *Ibid.*, p. 60.

THE FUNDAMENTAL LAW

Fundamental law played its greatest part in the great contest between the Parliament and the Stuarts, which was in its last analysis "a struggle of the common law against the king."[1] Fundamental law appears at its very outset, in the quarrel between King James and Chief Justice Coke. Up to this time the claims of kingship were not inconsistent with the existence of the fundamental law. In an organic state like Tudor England the King was looked upon still as an organ of the commonwealth, not as its master. The laws were the King's, but he ruled by them and could not rule without them. The King needed the support of law; it guaranteed him against disherison, it protected him against the encroachment of the Church. But the new learning, the break with Rome, and the beginnings of sectarianism, which resulted from the other two, with other causes more obscure, gradually wrought a change. Such deep-lying causes; a king like James, vain, weak, bullying and pedantic, but shrewd; and a royal title that was not the strongest possible,—all contributed to bring about the enunciation of the doctrine that the King was above the law. That doctrine, which James had already stated while under the power of the Lords of the Congregation, now that he was really a King he lost no occasion to din into the ears of his subjects. It is not wonderful that he met opposition. That opposition in its earlier stages centres about Coke. The wonderful amount of legal knowledge that he possessed,

[1] Maitland, *Constitutional History of England*, p. 271.

catalogued and uncatalogued, the narrowness of his outlook, the stubbornness of his character, which in the struggle with the King rises to a dignity worthy the name of courage,—all these, together with the necessity of finding a principle on which to ground opposition to the King's extravagant claims, contributed in one way or another to make Coke a marked man, and to raise his darling idea of a common law, fixed and immutable, to the dignity of a great constitutional principle; to make it the main base from which attacks were directed upon the theory of Divine Right. James's instinctive feeling towards lawyers was hostile. His Majesty had observed "that ever since his coming to the crown, the popular sort of lawyers have been the men, that most affrontedly in all parliaments have trodden upon his prerogative."[1]

The fundamentally legal character which was retained in a large measure to the very end by the great struggle of the seventeenth century in England clearly appears in the first skirmishes. So long as King and Parliament worked together, as Gardiner acutely remarks,[2] no question had arisen to affect the independence of the judges. But the Tudor times were gone, when Parliament and King were joint organs of the commonwealth. Plot and controversy had erected the King above the state and above all its other organs. Parliament was not yet sufficiently conscious of its powers to compete

[1] *Bacon's Works* (edited by Montagu), vol. ii. p. 494 (American ed.).
[2] *History of England*, vol. iii. pp. 1, 2.

THE FUNDAMENTAL LAW

for that commanding eminence, and so the negative check of the law was relied on alone as yet against the encroaching prerogative. Naturally it became the central principle in the strategy of both parties to capture the artillery of the law and turn it upon the forces of the enemy. The clause in the Act of Settlement which changes the tenure of judges[1] is justly regarded as one of the most important parts of the Revolution settlement. When the settlement of questions involving almost the very existence of the state depended upon the bare decision of the King's judges, and their own tenure of office upon the favour of the King, it is not strange that the oracles were sometimes suspected, nor is it strange that judges should be beaten down and cowed by the superior power of the King. When the King could descend to personal encounter with one of them, "looking and speaking fiercely with bended fist, offering to strike him," because that judge " humbly prayed the king to haue respect to the Common Lawes of his land," it is little wonder that even the inflexible Coke should fall "flatt on all fower" and humbly beg the King's pardon and compassion.[2]

As yet no subject could stand before the clenched fist of the King, but such expedients are dangerous. The struggle was thus early taking on the character of a personal breach between the King and a part of his

[1] Section iii.
[2] From a letter of Sir Rafe Boswell to Dr. Milborne, quoted by Roland G. Usher in *Eng. Hist. Rev.*, vol. xviii. pp. 669-70.

people, and the action of James, in heat of passion, thus putting aside the very dignity of which he was the most extravagant upholder, was no unimportant stage in the decline of respect for the kingly office which made possible the execution of Charles. The significance of the episode is that such a humiliating scene should be made merely because the King's judge begged him to have respect to the laws of the land. It serves to illustrate the true nature of the whole conflict that follows. It is unnecessary to follow the details of the controversy between the King and the Chief Justice which led to the removal of the latter: all were based on this fundamental antagonism between Coke's idea of a fundamental law, binding and protecting the King as well as his subjects, and the idea of the King, who "said that he was not defended by his laws, but by God."[1] It will be sufficient to look at some of the statements brought out on both sides by the controversy.

The idea of a King *legibus solutus* was not a new one to James. Long before he had laid down in no uncertain terms his idea of a "free" monarchy. In it the King was free of the laws,—"*Dominus omnium bonorum*, and *Dominus directus totius Dominii*, the whole subjects being but his vassals, and from him hold-

[1] Letter of John Hercy to the Earl of Shrewsbury, dated Nov. 25, 1608, printed in Lodge's *Illustrations*, vol. iii. p. 248. For the best and fullest account of the relations of James and Coke, see Gardiner's *History of England*, vol. ii. p. 35 et seq., and vol. iii. pp. 1-27; see also Coke's report of the Case of Prohibitions, 12 *Reports*, 63-5; Hearn, *Government of England*, pp. 297, 298; Homersham Cox, *Institutions*, p. 333 and note; Hallam, ch. vi. See also Mr. Usher's article mentioned above.

THE FUNDAMENTAL LAW

ing all their lands as their ouer-lord, who according to good seruices done vnto him, chaungeth their holdings from tacke to few, from ward to blanch, erecteth new Baronies, and vniteth old, without aduice or authoritie of either Parliament, or any other subalterin judiciall seate."[1] "As likewise, although I haue said, a good king will frame all his actions to be according to the Law; yet is hee not bound thereto but of his good will, and for good example-giuing to his subjects. ... And where he sees the lawe doubtsome or rigorous, hee may interpret or mitigate the same, lest otherwise *Summum jus* bee *summa injuria;* And therefore generall lawes, made publikely in Parliament, may upon knowen respects to the King by his authoritie bee mitigated, and suspended vpon causes onely knowen to him."[2] The idea of a fundamental law was not unknown to him, but it was a law to keep his people in subjection and his succession secure, nothing more.[3] In his later years he will hardly admit even

---

[1] *The Trew Law of free Monarchies: Works*, p. 202.
[2] *Ibid.*, p. 203.
[3] "And according to these fundamentall Lawes already alledged, we daily see that in the Parliament (which is nothing else but the head Court of the King and his vassals) the lawes are but craued by his subjects, and onely made by him at their rogation, and with their aduice: For albeit the king make daily statutes and ordinances, enjoyning such paines thereto as hee thinkes meet, without any aduice of Parliament or estates; yet it lies in the power of no Parliament, to make any kinde of Lawe or Statute, without his Scepter be to it, for giuing it the force of a law." *Ibid.*, p. 202. See also James's explanation of the meaning of the term "fundamental laws" used in Scotland, as "onely those Lawes whereby confusion is auoyded, and their Kings descent mainteined, and the heritage of the succession and Monarchie." *Speech before Parliament at Whitehall,* March, 1607: *Works*, p. 520.

that,—"He was not defended by his laws, but by God." "As for the absolute Prerogatiue of the Crowne, that is no Subject for the tongue of a Lawyer, nor is lawfull to be disputed."[1] In opposition to this theory, many of the lawyers "denied the necessity for there being any man or body of men above the law;"[2] it was "the golden met-wand and measure to try the causes of the subjects; and which protected his Majesty in safety and peace."[3]

To James's boast that "although we never studied the common law of England, yet are we not ignorant of any points which belong to a king to know,"[4] it was Coke's answer that causes concerning the life or property of the subject were not to be decided by natural reason, "but by the artificial reason and judgment of the law, which law is an act which requires long study and experience, before that a man can attain to the cognizance of it."[5] In opposition to the King and his claims, men set up the law itself as their sovereign by Divine Right, "For them law is the true sovereign, and they are not under the necessity of considering whether King or Lords or Commons or all three together are the ultimate authority in the State."[6] If,

[1] *Speech in the Star Chamber*, June 20, 1616: *Works*, p. 557. See other parts of this speech; also the remarkable speech made to the Lords and Commons on March 21, 1609, *Works*, p. 529.
[2] Maitland, *Const. Hist.*, p. 300.
[3] 12 *Reports*, 65.
[4] *Bacon's Works*, edited by Montagu (American ed.), vol. ii. p. 493.
[5] 12 *Reports*, 65.
[6] Figgis, *Divine Right of Kings*, p. 228.

however, the law was to be supreme, and at the same time a mystery open only to the initiated, it is clear that if the claim of the lawyers was to be admitted, the supreme authority would be their exclusive possession.[1] James's antipathy to the lawyers was founded in a true instinct, as was his opposition to the Presbyterians.

As the constitutional struggle grew more intense, the appeals to the fundamental law became more frequent. Gardiner thinks the term "fundamental law" originated among the courtiers of Queen Henrietta Maria, and first came into general use at the time of the agitation over the second ship-money writ in 1635.[2] The ship-money writ affected the people more directly than any prior acts of the King of a similar nature, the dissatisfaction that arose over it was more wide-spread and general, and the common use of the expression "fundamental law" probably dates from it. The idea of fundamental law, however, was, as we have seen, an old one, and the expression itself did not originate with the Queen's courtiers. "Fundamental law," which now became the common expression of a general dissatisfaction, had long been in use, at least among lawyers. In 1604, in the preamble to the Act of Parliament authorizing commissioners to treat with the Scotch commissioners concerning the Union, are men-

---

[1] Figgis, *Divine Right of Kings*, p. 229; Gooch, *English Democratic Ideas*, p. 63; Maitland, *Const. Hist. of England*, p. 301.
[2] *History of England*, vol. viii. pp. 84, 85.

tioned the "fundamentall and ancient Lawes, Priviledges and good Customes of this Kingdome."[1] In 1607, when the question of the Union again came up for debate, James, in a speech to both Houses of Parliament, was at great pains to point out that the Scots by the term "fundamental law" referred only to the royal succession, "not meaning it, as you doe, of their Common Law,"[2] thus showing that the expression had at that time, at least among English Parliament men, a definite and well-understood meaning. Coke, in his *Second Institute*, finished in 1628, speaks of Magna Charta as an "ancient and fundamental Law."[3]

In a conference between the houses in 1628, the Archbishop of Canterbury, on the part of the House of Lords, promised "to maintain and support the fundamental laws of the kingdom, and the fundamental Liberties of the Subject." Sir Dudley Digges in reply expressed the gratification of the Commons at the willingness of the Lords "to maintain and support the fundamental laws and liberties of England."[4]

The struggle over the Petition of Right and the question of Tonnage and Poundage did much to fa-

[1] 1 and 2 James I., ch. ii.
[2] *Works of King James I.*, p. 520. "Their meaning in the word of Fundamentall Lawes, you shall perceiue more fully hereafter, when I handle the objection of the difference of Lawes: For they intend thereby onely those Lawes whereby confusion is auoyded, and their King's descent maintained, and the heritage of the succession and Monarchie. . . . Not meaning as you doe, of their Common Law, for they haue none, but that which is called Jus Regis."
[3] Page 51. For date of Second Institute, see *Dictionary of National Biography*, s. v. *Coke*.
[4] *Parl. Hist.*, vol. ii. pp. 330, 331.

miliarize men still further with the idea of fundamental law. For example, when the Lords would have added to the Petition of Right the clause saving the "Sovereign Power" of the King, a storm of protest arose in the Commons. To acquiesce in this addition would be to "acknowledge a Regal as well as a Legal Power."[1] Pym recognizes clearly the sovereignty of the fundamental law, not only over the King, but over Parliament as well. "All our Petition is for the Laws of *England*, and this Power seems to be another distinct Power from the Power of the Law: I know how to add Sovereign to his Person, but not to his Power: And we cannot leave to him a Sovereign Power: *Also we never were possessed of it.*"[2] "These Laws are not acquainted with Sovereign Power," Wentworth declares. Coke's speech on this occasion is probably the most noteworthy of all. "I know," he says, "that Prerogative is part of the Law, but Sovereign Power is no Parliamentary word: In my opinion, it weakens *Magna Charta*, and all our Statutes; for they are absolute without any saving of Sovereign Power: And shall we now add it, we shall weaken the Foundation of Law, and then the Building must needs fall; take we heed what we yield unto, *Magna Charta is such a Fellow, that he will have no Sovereign.* I wonder this Sovereign was not in *Magna Charta*, or in the Confirmations of it: If we grant this, by implication we give

---

[1] *Rushworth*, vol. i. p. 562.
[2] *Ibid.*

a Sovereign Power above all these Laws."[1] Soon after, the receiving of Tonnage and Poundage without a grant was declared to be "a breach of the fundamental liberties of this kingdom."[2]

In 1641, in his argument against the Earl of Strafford, St. John declared: "In *England* there is the Common-Law, the Statutes, the Acts of Parliament, and Customs peculiar to certain places, differing from the Common-Law; If any question arise concerning either a Custom or an Act of Parliament, the Common-Law of *England*, the First, the Primitive and the General Law, that's the Rule and Expositor of them, and of their several extents."[3]

Once seized, the idea of fundamental law became the groundwork of most of the political writing of the time.

Prynne declares that "the people of England have both ancient and Fundamentall Rights, Liberties, Franchises, Laws, and a Fundamental Government, which like the Laws of the Medes and Persians, neither may nor ought to be altered, or innovated upon any pretence, but perpetually maintained, defended, with

---

[1] *Rushworth*, vol. i. p. 562. The italics are not in the original.
[2] Gardiner, *Documents*, p. 7.
[3] Rushworth, *Strafford's Trial*, p. 695. The great ship-money case had also brought out many fresh expressions of the old doctrine (*State Trials*, vol. iii. p. 825 et seq.); and from that time on, references in the debates of Parliament and in the documents drawn up there become so frequent that it is needless to follow them further. See, for example, in the Grand Remonstrance (Gardiner, *Documents*, p. 131), in the ordinance erecting a court to try the King (*ibid.*, p. 268), in the Agreement of the People (*ibid.*, pp. 281, 282).

greatest care, vigilancy, resolution, ... it being no lesse than a transcendent crime, and High Treason by our Laws, for any person or persons secretly or openly, to attempt the undermining or subversion of our fundamental laws, rights, Liberties, Government, especially by fraud, treachery, force or armed power and violence."[1] Selden, in his *Judicature in Parliament*, tries to prove that in early times judgements in Parliament were strictly guided per legem terrae, "which the parliament could not alter."[2]

Though the legislative activity of the Long Parliament was completing the creation of the sovereign legislature,[3] few leaders of the day saw it. Theoretically the sway of the fundamental law was unbroken and even extended. Between the meeting of the Long Parliament and the death of the King, the idea seems to have been gradually accepted by the majority of both parties, though they interpreted it differently. In 1647 the royalist Judge Jenkins wrote from his prison in the Tower: "The Law of this Land hath three grounds: First Custome, Secondly, Judiciall Records, Thirdly,

---

[1] *Good Old Fundamental Liberties*, pt. i. p. 27. In chapter i of the same work he sets about to prove that "the Kingdome and Freemen of England, have some ancient Hereditary Rights, Liberties, Priviledges, Franchises, Laws and Customs, properly called FUNDAMENTAL; and likewise a FUNDAMENTALL GOVERNMENT, no wayes to be altered, undermined, subverted, directly or indirectly, under pain of High Treason in those who shall attempt it: especially by fraud, force, or armed power" (pt. i. p. 9). He also enumerates the various statements by Parliament of the doctrine of a fundamental law (*ibid.*, pp. 9-27), and gives a list of what he considers the fundamentals (*ibid.*, p. 60 et seq.).
[2] *Works*, vol. iii. col. 1651.
[3] See Note B at the end of this chapter (p. 103).

THE HIGH COURT OF PARLIAMENT

Acts of Parliament. The two latter are but declarations of the Common-Law and Custome of the Realme, touching Royall Government. And this Law of Royall Government is a Law Fundamentall."[1]

Such royalists as adhered to the doctrine did so mainly because they looked on it as a safeguard of the kingship. When Cromwell became Protector, it is clear from his speeches that for him, as well, its principal value was as a protection from anarchy, or at least from extreme republicanism or the unchecked rule of the army. The writs of return to the Parliament, held under the Instrument of Government, contained the proviso that the persons elected "should not have power to alter the Government as now settled in one Single Person and a Parliament."[2]

In Cromwell's famous speech, provoked by this Parliament's refusal to be thus restricted, and by their "disowning" the Instrument, "contrary to the very fundamental things, yea against the very root itself of this Establishment," he sets forth his idea of the necessity for a fundamental law. "It is true," he says, "as there are some things in the Establishment which are Fundamental, so there are others which are not, but are Circumstantial. . . . But some things are Fundamentals! . . . These may *not* be parted with; but will, I trust, be delivered over to Posterity, as the fruits of our blood and travail. The Government by a single

---

[1] *The Works of Judge Jenkins* (1648), p. 5.
[2] *Cromwell's Speech of 12 September 1654*, Carlyle.

THE FUNDAMENTAL LAW

Person and a Parliament is a Fundamental! It is the *esse*, it is constitutive. . . . In every Government there must be Somewhat Fundamental, Somewhat like a *Magna Charta*, which should be standing, be unalterable. . . . That Parliaments should not make themselves perpetual is a Fundamental. Of what assurance is a *Law* to prevent so great an evil, if it lie in the same Legislature to *un*law it again? Is such a Law like to be lasting? It will be a rope of sand; it will give no security; for the same men may unbuild what they have built."[1]

The Levellers on their side at times avowed the same opinions.[2] "They assert it as Fundamental, that the Government of *England* ought to be by Laws, and not by Men," — a phrase that had lately been made famous by Harrington[3] and was destined to cross the sea and influence the constitutional thinking of the New World.[4]

---

[1] *Loc. cit.*

[2] *The Leveller*, an anonymous pamphlet published in 1659 and reprinted in the *Harleian Miscellany*. The quotation is from the latter (vol. iv. pp. 515, 516, edition of 1745); see also *ibid.*, p. 520.

[3] "Government (to define it *de jure*, or according to antient Prudence) is an Art whereby a Civil Society of Men is instituted and preserv'd upon the Foundation of common Right or Interest; or (to follow Aristotle and Livy) It is the Empire of Laws, and not of Men." *Oceana: Works*, p. 37.

[4] " In the government of this commonwealth, the legislative department shall never exercise the executive and judicial powers, or either of them; the executive shall never exercise the legislative and judicial powers, or either of them; the judicial shall never exercise the legislative and executive powers, or either of them; to the end it may be a government of laws and not of men." Pt. i. art. xxx., *Massachusetts Constitution of 1780*, Poore, *Charters and Constitutions*, vol. i. p. 960. For the influence of Harrington on the political thinking of the New World, see the article by Theodore W. Dwight in *Political Science Quarterly*, vol. ii. p. 1.

THE HIGH COURT OF PARLIAMENT

But events had moved so rapidly in England since the first session of the Long Parliament that men's views of the fundamental law had changed. The doctrine first emphasized by those who wished to keep the King within a legally defined prerogative, and opposed by the believers in Divine Right, had come to be used by both royalists and parliamentarians to a great extent. In the mouths of royalists, fundamental law meant royal government, and it was used to fend off the growing pretensions of Parliament. Parliament itself, on the other hand, as yet based its opposition to the King mainly on precedent; and the rights guaranteed by Magna Charta as then interpreted were looked on as their main protection against prerogative. Things could not stop there, however. As the contest became more bitter, and especially after the outbreak of hostilities, Parliament found itself doing acts of state quite unwarranted by any former or existing law. Drawing back was out of the question. The fundamental law was a weapon that might be turned against themselves, now that their own acts were clearly illegal. The execution of the King was a demonstration of that which the dullest man could understand. If fundamental law could be relied on by either party, the royalists had now violated it in a less startling manner than their opponents. But it was not the royalists alone that the parliamentarians found using the fundamental law to their disadvantage. The extreme republicans, of whatever name, found protection against

THE FUNDAMENTAL LAW

the tyranny of a legislature in the same old fundamental law. While their own views were as repugnant to that old law as they could well be, these men were acute enough to see that here was a weapon that could be used against the Parliament with great success. Parliament was still preserving such few forms of the constitution as were consistent with its own independent existence. It was peculiarly embarrassing to have its acts judged by the test of precedent and law, and it is an indication of the hold which the old idea still had upon Englishmen that the appeal to that idea should still have been so effective. The remarkable trial of Lilburne, in 1649, well illustrates this point. The popularity of Lilburne with the people, the reaction after the execution of the King, the evident timidity and almost terror displayed by the judges in that case, all serve to explain the acquittal of the accused; but it is none the less noteworthy that Lilburne depended almost entirely on his rights as a subject guaranteed by the ancient laws, and his iteration and reiteration of those laws is at once irritating, amusing, and instructive. Clarendon says that Cromwell looked upon Lilburne's acquittal "as a greater defeat than the loss of a battle would have been."[1] In the same year as his trial, Lilburne published his pamphlet on "The Legall Fundamentall Liberties of the People of England Revived, Asserted, and Vindicated." In it he asserts the illegality of Parliament's Acts, especially the Act for

[1] *Rebellion*, bk. xiv.

continuing their own existence, and cites Bonham's Case against the theory of parliamentary sovereignty. In a pamphlet published two years earlier—"The Peoples Prerogative and Priviledges, asserted and vindicated, (against all Tyranny whatsoever) By Law and Reason, Being a Collection of the Marrow and Soule of Magna Charta, and all the most principall Statutes made ever since to this present yeare, 1647. For the preservation of the peoples Liberties and Properties" —he attacks the same Act. "And for them [the Parliament] forever to shelter themselves from the lash and stroak of justice, or forever from being called to accompt, for all their Cheats, Robberies, and murthers, by getting the Kings hand to an Act to make them an everlasting Parliament, no more lyes in the King's power justly and legally to do, then to give them power to make us al absolute Vassals and Slaves, and to destroy all our Lawes, Libertys and propertys, and when they have so done, then to cut the throats of all the men in England besides themselves."

In reality, however, while the extreme republicans might make use of the idea of fundamental law on occasion,—especially as a protection when in danger, —there was nothing in the old law to which they could appeal as a basis for their constructive programme. It was only the negative aspect of the fundamental law that they accepted,—a limitation of the powers of a king or a parliament; their republicanism could find no precedent in the English constitution. Lilburne might talk of fundamental law at the time of his trial, but his real feeling is better expressed when he says: "The greatest mischief of all and the oppressing bondage of England ever since the Norman yoke is a law called the common law." And again: "Magna Charta itself being but a beggarly thing, containing many marks of intolerable bondage, and the laws that have been made since by Parliaments in very many particulars made our government more oppressive and intolerable."[1]

The feeling in the army was much the same way. Wildman gave voice to it in 1647 when he said: "I thinke [that] according to the letter of the law, if the King will [he may] kill mee by law. Aske any lawiers of itt; by the letter of the present law hee may kill mee, and 40 more, and noe law call him to account for itt."[2]

This double position of the republicans, while inconsistent, was not so inconsistent as it might seem at first sight. Though they rejected the common law, and regarded Magna Charta as "a beggarly thing,"—Cromwell himself only insisting on "Somewhat *like* a Magna Charta,"[3]—the pretensions of a virtually non-representative legislature had brought home to them the necessity of a check for it. The royalists could regard

[1] *Just Man's Justification*, quoted in *Clarke Papers* (Camden Society), vol. i. preface, p. lxi.
[2] *Clarke Papers*, vol. i. p. 406.
[3] For his contemptuous remarks concerning Magna Charta, quoted by Clarendon, see the *History of the Rebellion*, book xv.

the old fundamental law as such a check. That alternative was not open to the republicans. It was a double-edged weapon. The principles of the common law were as destructive of their own theories as they were of parliamentary sovereignty. A check on that sovereignty must be found, however, and the idea of a fundamental law supplied it. If an ancient fundamental law—if Magna Charta—could curb the King or the Parliament, why could not a new document be drawn embodying their own principles and free from the encumbrance of the old law, which should be binding upon and unalterable by the legislative power? Such a notion received the assent of the more extreme republicans because it restricted Parliament; it was favored by the more conservative, as Cromwell, because it offered a protection against the too sudden and sweeping changes which the radicals were clamouring for. And so we have the trial of a new thing in English history,—the written constitution.[1]

[1] It is no part of my purpose to trace the development of the idea of a written constitution except in so far as it appears to be an outgrowth of the older idea of a fundamental law. No doubt the English Puritans were influenced by earlier experiments of a like nature in New England. For the most complete account of the history of the written constitution, see W. Rothschild, *Der Gedanke der geschriebenen Verfassung in der Englischen Revolution*, Tübingen and Leipzig, 1903. Rothschild says comparatively little about the origin of the idea, but he traces it carefully through all the state papers from the *Heads of the Proposals* to the *Humble Petition and Advice*. Jellinek gives a short account, but traces the idea back to Fortescue, *Allgemeine Staatslehre*, 2d ed., p. 494 et seq. See Charles Borgeaud, *The Rise of Modern Democracy in New and Old England;* also *The Constitutional Experiments of the Commonwealth* (1649-60), by Edward Jenks. The texts of the various documents are given in convenient form in Gardiner's *Documents* of the Puritan Revolution; Ameri-

THE FUNDAMENTAL LAW

It would be wrong to think that the more extreme of the republicans were the only ones who regarded the common law as a "mischief." The work of the Long Parliament could not be undone. England had seen practically for the first time a legislative assembly of the modern type,—no longer a mere law-declaring, but a law-*making*, machine. The "High Court of Parliament" had not disappeared, but henceforth, as never before, lawmaking takes precedence of all other matters. The great phases of the English Parliament have been its history as a court, then as a legislature, and finally as a government-making organ. Parliament definitely passed out of the first of these stages at the first session of the Long Parliament.[1]

Men's political theories reflect the conditions about them. The English political thought of to-day and the speculation of the seventeenth century, from which it is directly derived, are no exception to this rule. Practical parliamentary omnipotence begat a theory of parliamentary sovereignty. After the parliamentary activity of the years following 1640, Parliament could never fall back into the place it had occupied under the Tudors and before, and men could never again think of it as

can constitutions are in Poore's *Charters and Constitutions*. The growth of the idea of putting restrictions on the Parliament may be traced in the *Clarke Papers*. See, for example, vol. i., preface, and pp. 386, 403, 406, 407-9, etc.

[1] This will not be misunderstood to mean that Parliament is not largely judicial or legislative to-day. It is only a question of emphasis, of precedence. It is one of the main purposes of this essay to prove the continued existence of Parliament's functions as a court, and to try to explain some of its modern characteristics by means of them.

they had formerly done. The strength of precedent might influence legal decisions for some time to come, but political philosophy henceforth strikes out in a new line. Milton in his zeal for the Parliament speaks of his opponents as "contesting for privileges, customs, forms, and that old entanglement of iniquity, their gibberish laws, though the badge of their ancient slavery."[1] Later he wrote: "But the parliament is above all positive law, whether civil or common, makes or unmakes them both." "For how," he asks, "could our forefathers bind us to any certain form of government more than we can bind our posterity?"[2]

The royalist writers are as much affected by the change as their opponents. For the future, there is little difference whether the writers be royalist or parliamentarian,—they both accept the new idea of *legislative sovereignty*. For the royalists this sovereignty lies in the King alone, for their opponents in the Parliament; but both reject the idea of a supremacy of law. To say with Hobbes and Filmer that the King is above the law, or with Milton that Parliament can make or unmake any law whatsoever, is to deny the traditional doctrine. The functions of King and Parliament are not *jus dicere*, as Coke thought, but *jus dare*. Judicial supremacy has given place to legislative sovereignty, whether the sovereign be the King or the Parliament. Speculators on both sides would have agreed with the

[1] *The Tenure of Kings and Magistrates* (published 1648-9).
[2] *Brief Notes on Dr. Griffith's Sermon* (published 1660).

admirable summary of Hobbes: "It is not wisdom, but authority that makes a law."[1]

In a nation's history, periods of civil war are usually followed by an acquiescence in strong government. The security of the Tudors on the throne after the Wars of the Roses was largely due to this fact, and out of it also in England of the seventeenth century grew the doctrine of legislative sovereignty which has had an unbroken history down to our time. The main source of the new theory was the actual exercise of legislative power after 1640, and the habituating of men's minds to it in those years. Hobbes makes his philosopher in the dialogue ask the lawyer: "When their new republic returned into monarchy by Oliver, who durst deny him money upon any pretence of *Magna Charta*, or of these other Acts of Parliament which you have cited? You may therefore think it good law, for all your books, that the King of England may at all times, that he thinks in his conscience it will be necessary for the defence of his people, levy as many soldiers and as much money as he please, and that himself is judge of the necessity."[2] "As for the common law contained in reports, they have no force but what the King gives them."[3] Filmer's

---

[1] *A Dialogue of the Common Laws: English Works* (Molesworth), vol. vi. p. 5. Hobbes's words here may be worth quoting a little more at length: "It is not wisdom, but authority that makes a law. Obscure also are the words *legal reason*. There is no reason in earthly creatures, but human reason. But I suppose that he [Coke] means, that the reason of a judge, or of all the judges together without the King, is that *summa ratio*, and the very law: which I deny, because none can make a law but he that hath the legislative power."
[2] *Ibid.*, p. 18.   [3] *Behemoth: English Works*, vol. vi. p. 210.

statements of this view have a more modern sound than those of Hobbes; his words might well have come from Austin himself: "It is not the being of a Custom that makes it lawful, for then all Customs, even evil Customs, would be lawful; but it is the Approbation of the supreme Power that gives a legality to the Custom: where there is no Supreme Power over many Nations, their Customs cannot be made legal."[1] "There never was, nor ever can be any People governed without a Power of making Laws, and every Power of making Laws must be arbitrary."[2] Such is the doctrine of the modern English constitution. Now and then, since the days of Filmer and Hobbes, the old doctrine has cropped out, especially in times of stress, but such times have been comparatively few and far between.[3]

From the foregoing account of the doctrine of fundamental law in England, it will be seen that the law declared by Parliament in the middle ages was a cus-

---

[1] *Observations upon H. Grotius De Jure Belli & Pacis.*
[2] *The Anarchy of a Limited or Mixed Monarchy*, preface; see also pp. 241, 242, 266-8 (edition of 1680); *Patriarcha*, ch. iii. sections 8, 9.
[3] For example, in 1688-9, *State Tracts*, vol. i. pp. 282, 423. Another such time was when the repeal of the American Stamp Act was under consideration in Parliament in 1766. Lord Camden, speaking of the Stamp Act, said: "In my opinion, my lords, the legislature had no right to make this law. The sovereign authority, the omnipotence of the legislature, my lords, is a favourite doctrine, but there are some things they cannot do," etc. *Parl. Hist.*, vol. xvi. p. 168. Lord Chancellor Northington answered: "My lords, I seek for the liberty and constitution of this Kingdom no farther back than the Revolution: there I make my stand." *Ibid.*, p. 171. Camden declared also that the Declaratory Act was "absolutely illegal," contrary to the laws of nature, "contrary to the fundamental laws of this constitution." *Ibid.*, p. 178. Again in 1775 Lord Camden returned to the same point in the debate on Lord Chatham's motion to withdraw the troops from Boston. *Parl. Hist.*, vol. xviii. pp. 164, 165.

tomary one. In no western country has precedent had such complete and unbroken sway as in England. The first fragmentary dooms we find, Ethelbert does not make, but, "*a sette.*"[1] From then till now, "the life and soul of English law has ever been precedent."[2] Absolutism has never been unchecked in England, and of a purely speculative basis of law there is no trace till times that are almost modern. The law of nature, or whatever that speculative basis may be called, appears remarkably late, and when it first appears it comes largely as an attempt, born of the curiosity of the Renaissance, to account for a body of customary law which has long been in existence, and whose binding character is unquestioned, though its beginnings are lost in antiquity. Indeed, one of the striking facts to be noted even as late as the seventeenth century is that political speculation in England cannot rid itself of this basis of a traditional, customary, fundamental law. Even Milton and Locke were not free from it, notwithstanding their contempt for the narrowness of the law; and it is a commonplace of the history of political thought, how Englishmen in their actions and their thinking on political matters have been bound by precedent rather than by abstract theories. "Of legalism there is much; of political science, none."[3] Rights are "asserted and maintained on the basis of ancient law and cus-

[1] Liebermann, *Gesetze der Angelsachsen*, vol. i. p. 3.
[2] Freeman, *Growth of the English Constitution*, p. 58. See also Dicey, *Law of the Constitution*, pp. 18, 19.
[3] Dunning, *Political Theories from Luther to Montesquieu*, p. 194.

THE HIGH COURT OF PARLIAMENT

tom,"[1] and for these rights, "a broader basis" than this one of customary law "enters into the consciousness of the English only very gradually."[2] "In all our great constitutional struggles," says Professor Hearn, "the question has been invariably argued on either side as a question of dry law."[3]

How preponderant in the idea of fundamental law custom was over *a priori* reasoning may easily be seen from the whole course of English legal history. The author of the *Doctor and Student* divides the law of reason into the "law of reason primary" and the "law of reason secondary." The distinction between them is in the fact that "reason secondary" "is grounded and derived of the general law." "And the law," he goes on to say, "is so full of such secondary reasons derived out of general customs and maxims of the realm, that some men have affirmed that all the law of the realm is the law of reason. But that cannot be proved, as me seemeth. . . . And it is not much used in the laws of England, to reason what law is grounded upon the law of the first reason primary, or on the law of reason secondary, for they be most commonly openly known of themselves; but for the knowledge of the law of reason secondary is greater difficulty, and therefore therein dependeth much the manner and form of arguments in the laws of Eng-

[1] Dunning, *Political Theories from Luther to Montesquieu*, p. 197.
[2] *Ibid.*
[3] *The Government of England*, 1st ed., p. 6; Lowell, *The Government of England*, vol. ii. p. 487.

THE FUNDAMENTAL LAW

land." This "law of reason secondary" seems to have much in common with that "artificial reason" which Coke set up in such exasperating fashion against the pretensions of James I as a judge.[1] "'Tis from the Statute-Book, not the Bible, that we must judg of the Power our Kings are invested withal, and also of our own Obligations, and the measures of our Subjection," said a pamphleteer of the Revolution;[2] and writers of that school could just as readily have substituted the "law of nature" for the Bible in this statement.

It is to be expected, of course, that this "artificial reason" would receive scant courtesy from writers like Hobbes, who had accepted the new theory of legislative sovereignty.[3]

Thus it appears that the law which we find enrolled among the records of the English mediaeval Parliament is in the main a body of custom of which the Parliament's enactments are only declaratory;

That certain great principles of this law were believed to be beyond the power of Parliament or of any other body of men to change;

That though this law was often identified with the law of nature, its inviolability was due in the first place to its universality as a custom.

If this be true, the Parliament where these customs

---
[1] See Note C at the end of the chapter (p. 105).
[2] *Reflections upon the Great Revolution: State Tracts*, vol. i. p. 253.
[3] For example, see Hobbes, *Dialogue of the Common Laws: English Works* (Molesworth), vol. vi. pp. 5, 6, 14, 15, 22.

were declared, affirmed, defined, and applied must have been a body with far different functions from those of our modern assemblies where laws are *made*.

THE FUNDAMENTAL LAW

Note A. The Fundamental Law in Bracton

(*Page* 66)

An attempt to keep the King within the bounds of the law seems to be indicated by the fact noted by Matthew Paris that at the coronation ceremony of Henry III the Earl of Chester carried the sword of St. Edward *"in signum quod comes est palatii et regem si oberret habeat de jure potestatem cohibendi."* Quoted in Pollock and Maitland, *H. E. L.*, vol. i. p. 182, note 5. Outside the Great Charter itself, no words have been cited so often in English constitutional crises as the famous words occurring in the text of Bracton: *"Rex autem habet superiorem, deum, s. Item legem, per quam factus est rex. Item curiam suam, videlicet Comites, Barones, quia Comites dicuntur quasi socii regis, et qui habet socium, habet magistrum, et ideo si rex fuerit sine fraeno, i. sine lege, debent ei fraenum ponere"* (folio 34). This wonderful passage, however, stands in glaring contradiction to several other passages in Bracton (*e.g.* folios 52 and 107), which state that the King has no peer upon earth, and no one who can coerce him. In folio 171 B Bracton says that the King cannot be punished by anyone save God himself, *"nisi sit qui dicat quod universitas regni et baronagium suum hoc facere debeat et possit in curia ipsius Regis."* Under this *nisi sit qui dicat* Maitland thinks "Bracton may well be stating his own opinion. Most undoubtedly he held that the King was bound by law, that God would exact of him a very strict account." The conclusion that Professor Maitland comes to after an exhaustive examination of the various MSS. of Bracton is that the famous sentence printed in folio 34 is not a part of the original text. Nevertheless, the sentence is of very ancient date. Professor Maitland thinks Bracton himself "may have written it in the margin of his manuscript, having learned and unlearned things since he wrote the body of the treatise." The statement is found in *Fleta,* which was written before the beginning of the fourteenth century, so it may be taken as a fair, if a strong, statement of the doctrine accepted in the latter part of the thirteenth century. The whole question of the authenticity of the passage is treated in a masterly manner by Professor Maitland, in *Bracton's Note Book,* vol i. pp. 29-33. See also G. B. Adams in *Am. Hist. Rev.*, vol. xiii. p. 730, note 31. Though the text of Bracton thus shows that the King has no superior and no peer on earth, the doctrine is not found there that the King is *princeps legibus solutus* (*Dig.* i. 3. 31). Bracton states very definitely a contrary doctrine (folio 107): "*Nihil enim aliud potest rex in terris, cum sit dei minister et vicarius, nisi id solum quod de jure potest, nec obstat quod dicitur, quod principi placet legis habet vigorem, quia sequitur in fine legis, cum lege regia quae de imperio eius lata est, i. non quicquid de voluntate regis temere praesumptum est sed animo condendi jura, sed quod consilio magistratuum suorum, rege autoritatem praestante, et habita super hoc deliberatione, & tractatu, recte fuerit definitum.*" The original of this is the famous statement of Ulpian (*Dig.* i. 4, 1; *Inst.* i. 2, 6): "*Quod principi placuit, legis habet vigorem: utpote cum lege regia quae de imperio ejus lata est, populus ei et in eum omne suum imperium et potestatem conferat.*" The importance of the principle enunciated here, its influence on later constitutional struggles in England, and the glaring discrepancy between Ulpian's statement and Bracton's version of it make it necessary to look more closely at this sentence.

This discrepancy was noticed "*non sine stupore*" and commented on at length by Selden (*Dissertatio ad Fletam*, cap. iii. 2). Bracton, it will be noted, omits entirely the last part of the original, beginning with the word *populus*, thus giving the sentence a wholly new meaning. The *cum*, which in the original introduces a clause that may be translated "*since* by the *lex regia*, which has been passed concerning his *imperium*, the people entrust to him all their imperium and power," is here made to do duty as a preposition instead of a causal conjunction, and the sentence ends with *lata est;* thus transforming the meaning into something like this: "For the King has no other power in the land, since he is the minister and vicar of God, except that alone which he derives from the law, and that is not to the contrary which says 'what pleases the prince has the force of law,' for there follows at the end of the law 'with the *lex regia* which has been passed concerning his imperium,'" etc. Such a garbling of the text might well excite the wonder of Selden, and the curious fact is that the changed form is given almost word for word by Fleta (lib. i. cap. 17, fol. 16, 17); and, according to Selden, also by the manuscript of Thornton, and in at least one manuscript of Britton (see Selden, *loc. cit.*, and Nichols's note to Britton, fol. 1). No explanation of this could keep us from surprise that these authors, who no doubt had the

THE FUNDAMENTAL LAW

whole text of this well-known sentence, should deliberately suppress a part of it and give it a sense entirely at variance with the interpretation of all other commentators and with its own plain meaning.

But the correct explanation, nevertheless, obviously is that in England, in Bracton's day and Thornton's, there was a law fundamental, not alterable by the King, under which he ruled, by which his action was circumscribed, and if Justinian's law-books were to be cited they must conform with the law of the land. In this connection see Holdsworth, *H. E. L.*, vol. ii. pp. 197-200.

Note B. The Beginning of Practical Legislative Sovereignty by Parliament
(Page 85)

It is not easy to fix with any exactness the date of the beginnings of the legislative activity which has become one of the main characteristics of modern Parliaments, nor to assign the causes of its growth. Jenks apparently regards the activity of Parliament in the separation of the Church of England from the Church of Rome as the culmination of the process. *Law and Politics*, pp. 44, 45.

Seeley thinks that the immediate cause of the "exceptional and strange" prominence of legislation in our own time "was the vast convulsions that followed the French Revolution." He believes that the "extreme and unprecedented prominence of legislation," due to these upheavals, was in turn the cause of the development of cabinet government in England in the nineteenth century. *Introduction to Political Science*, p. 288.

Maitland points out the fact that notwithstanding the bulk of the statute-book in the eighteenth century, comparatively few acts of real legislation were passed before the first reform act, which produced radical and sweeping changes in the laws, such, for example, as the Poor Law Reform Act of 1834. *Constitutional History of England*, pp. 382-4.

In tracing this development we must not overlook the importance of the activity of the Long Parliament and the Parliaments of the Protectorate,—an activity, notwithstanding the Major-Generals, that had become so much of a habit by 1660 that never again after the Restoration was it possible for a king to get along for years at a time without a parliament, as had been done so often before. The Restoration, Seeley thinks, marks the time when "the permanent Parliament takes its place ... among English institutions." *Political Science*, p. 258. It may be true, as Gneist says, that "legislation" really begins with the reign of Edward II. The only point insisted on here is that its growth was very gradual, and above all that the men of the day did not distinguish it with clearness from parliamentary action, now called judicial. A point has sometimes been made of the refusal of a petition in 18 Edward II, on the ground that the remedy asked for required a new law to which the *"comminaltie"* must assent. It must be remembered, however, that at the time *comminaltie* did not mean *Commons*. *Comminaltie de la terre*, in fact, meant the whole community in the time of Edward II,—a community that was not always "represented" as yet in the central assembly. There is difficulty, therefore, in connecting this statement with "legislation." In all probability a reply in this form was merely a mode of getting rid of the petition and little more. As Palgrave says, "It was a gracious way of giving a refusal." *Report on Public Petitions: Parliamentary Papers*, Session of 1833, vol. xii. p. 21.

Whatever dates we may set as the crises in this development, and to whatever causes we may ascribe these crises, it is clear that this legislative activity of Parliament has been a development, and a slow development. By the "logic of events" the new idea was slowly but surely borne in upon the minds of Englishmen that Parliament was a real lawmaking organ. Times of crisis, of course, hastened this process. Emergencies arose that required prompt action; existing laws were inadequate; no rule was in existence to be "determined;" there was no time for a fiction; a rule must be *made*. Such a crisis confronted the Long Parliament. It was met by an assumption of power wholly unusual. The acts of the Long Parliament, legal and illegal, justifiable and unjustifiable, did much to habituate the minds of Englishmen to a legislative assembly. Further back, the same could be said in a measure—though I think a much smaller measure—of the Reformation Parliament. After the Restoration the development was accelerated. It was, however, all one great movement, and the point chiefly to be emphasized here is the fact that the movement is essentially a modern one. Its result has been to transform

THE FUNDAMENTAL LAW

our practice in lawmaking and our conception of the lawmaking power, to alter our whole attitude toward changes in the existing frame of government. It is a far cry from the *Doctor and Student* to the *Principles of Morals and Legislation*. A long process of evolution was required to produce a Jeremy Bentham.

NOTE C. THE LAW OF NATURE IN THE DIALOGUE OF THE DOCTOR AND STUDENT
(*Page* 99)

THIS dialogue is probably the most valuable source of our knowledge concerning the relation of the law of nature to the law of England in the late mediaeval or early modern times. The first part was published in Latin in 1523. The author makes an elaborate division of laws into the Law Eternal, or the divine source from which are derived all laws known to men. These derivative laws, in turn, he divides into "the Law of God," *i.e.* revelation; "the Law of Man," *i.e.* positive law; and "the Law of Reason," "the which by the doctors is called the law of nature of reasonable creatures," — "the which, as I have heard say, is called by them that be learned in the law of England, the *law of reason*." As to the term "law of nature," he says, "it is not used among them that be learned in the laws of England to reason what thing is commanded or prohibited by the law of nature, and what not, but all the reasoning in that behalf is under this manner. As when anything is grounded upon the law of nature, they say, that reason will that such a thing be done; and if it be prohibited by the law of nature, they say it is against reason, or that reason will not suffer that to be done." It seems a rather interesting fact that the common lawyers rejected the term "law of nature," which was so familiar to the doctors of the civil law. If their "law of reason" were not in some respects different in its basis or its sanction or its substance from the law of nature, why should they go out of their way thus systematically to avoid the expression "law of nature"? The English "law of reason" seems to have had the same close relation to custom that the old law of nature had formerly borne to the *jus gentium;* "to discern the law of God and the law of reason from the law positive is very hard," says our author.

When the Student in the dialogue begins to enumerate the six grounds of the law of England, he subdivides the law of reason, as we have seen, into *the law of reason primary* and *the law of reason secondary*. The first of these seems to mean the rules by which a man is protected in what a modern jurist would call his personal rights; while the second deals with his property rights. The reason for this distinction appears in Dialogue II. (ch. iii.), where the author says "that the property of goods is not given to the owners directly by the law of reason, nor by the law of God, but by the law of man, and is suffered by the law of reason, and by the law of God so to be. For at the beginning all goods were in common.... But the law of reason secondary is again subdivided into *the law of reason secondary general* and *the law of reason secondary particular*. The first of these is the "law of property ... generally kept in all countries;" the second, our author says, "is derived of divers customs general and particular, and of divers maxims and statutes ordained in this realm."

One or two points are here interesting. In the first place, no purely personal rights depend upon the law of reason secondary particular, it is only property which may come under any other rules than the universal rules of nature; secondly, municipal laws relating to property, though laws of reason, are "derived of" customs, maxims, and statutes. It is in these laws of reason "derived of" customs, etc., that we can see that close relation between the positive law and the law of nature which has been such a marked characteristic of English legal speculation from the Renaissance to the present day. Thus the Student asks the Doctor who should be liable for beasts lawfully distrained and dying of hunger in pound overt. This question the Doctor answers correctly on the basis of the law of *reason*, but the Student asks, "Who hath taught thee to do so but reason derived of the said general custom?" (the custom "general" in England of impounding legally distrained cattle). This secondary particular reason is, then, clearly derived from customs, maxims, and statutes. Maxims are in turn derived from customs. These maxims are not a part of the law of reason; Saint Germain considers them an independent "ground" of the law of England. The law of reason is "derived of" them, but they are derived only of custom. "And they be of the same strength and effect in the law as statutes be. And though the general customs of the realm be the strength and warrant of the

THE FUNDAMENTAL LAW

said maxims, as they be of the general customs of the realm; yet because the said general customs be in a manner known through the realm, as well to them that be unlearned as learned, and may lightly be had and known, and that with little study, and the maxims be only known in the king's courts, or among them that take great study in the law of the realm, and among few other persons; therefore they be set in this writing, for several grounds, and he that listeth may so account them, or if he will, he may take them for no ground, after his pleasure." (Dialogue I., ch. viii.) Thus it is evident that the maxims are generalizations handed down by the oracles of the law and based upon the customary law. They consist of reasoning upon the customs, but they are not a part of the "law of reason." The law of reason may be based upon them, though they themselves are based only upon custom. This same particular reason may also be "derived of" a statute. Statutes and customs and maxims are in fact coördinate in authority, and a law of reason may be derived of all or any of the three, but when so derived it is of a higher authority than they. Thus a custom or maxim or statute against reason is void, even though the reason itself be derived from custom, maxim, or statute. A statute may change a custom, and apparently may even abrogate a maxim, but any custom or maxim or statute against reason is *ipso facto* void. In fact, the general test which Saint Germain usually employs to try whether anything in the law of England is based upon the law of reason or not, is whether it may be altered by statute or not (*e.g.* Dialogue I., ch. viii.).

As a piece of dialectics this division seemed to satisfy the Student and the Doctor, but when applied to the actual rules of law in England it is easy to see how hard it would be to decide whether a specific rule was in fact a law of reason "derived of" custom and unalterable by statute, or only the result of the judges' "reasoning" upon a custom,—a mere maxim which a statute might alter or entirely abrogate. The author confesses: "Moreover there be divers cases whereof I am in doubt whether they be only maxims of the law, or that they be grounded upon the law of reason," and he gives a long list of such maxims. In the end he gives up the attempt and leaves the question to the reader to decide: "And it is many times very hard and of great difficulty to know what cases of the law of

England be grounded upon the law of reason, and what upon custom of the realm; and though it be hard to discuss it, it is very necessary to be known, for the knowledge of the perfect reason of the law. And if any man think that these cases before rehearsed be grounded upon the law of reason, then he may refer them to the first ground of the law of England, which is the law of reason, whereof is made mention in the fifth chapter. And if any man think that they be grounded upon the law of custom, then he may refer them to the maxims of the law, which be assigned for the fourth ground of the law of England, whereof mention is made in the eighth chapter, as before appeareth." Thus though it is only the law of reason which can overcome a statute, it is easy to see how, in the hands of the common lawyers, this reason could become identified with the fundamentals of the common law, the "artificial reason" which might neither be known nor tampered with by the unlearned, even by a King.

Thus for Coke the greater principles of the common law, whether they were in origin customary or intuitive, could be looked upon in their entirety as sacred and unchangeable. That law was "the perfection of reason." However, it seems less probable that the practice of the common lawyers in subordinating enactment to custom was the result of such reasoning as Saint Germain's, than that his dialogue was an attempt to explain and justify, through the medium of the scholastic philosophy and the Civil Law, what had long been the actual practice of the judges of the common law. This subject is closely connected with the distinction made by lawyers between *malum in se* and *malum prohibitum*. See *Doctor and Student*, Dialogue I., especially ch. v. See also ch. vii.; Dialogue II., ch. xv.; *Reason and Conscience in Sixteenth Century Jurisprudence*, by Professor Vinogradoff, *L. Q. R.*, vol. xxiv. p. 373 et seq., especially pp. 376, 377; Finch's *Law* (1627), pp. 74, 75; *The History of the Law of Nature*, by Sir F. Pollock, *Journal of the Society of Comparative Legislation*, N. S., vol. ii. p. 418 et seq., and ch. iv. of his *Expansion of the Common Law;* Holdsworth, *H. E. L.*, vol. ii., appendix ii., *The Law of Nature and the Common Law*. On *malum prohibitum*, see 4 *Inst.*, 63; Blackstone, *Com.*, vol. i. pp. 54, 57; Amos's edition of Fortescue's *De Laudibus Legum Angliae*, p. 49, and references there cited.

CHAPTER III

Parliament as a Court

A. The Fusion of Legislation and Judicature

TO those who believed in a fundamental law immutable, the present-day doctrine of legislative sovereignty seemed new and contrary to the spirit of English institutions. In the constitutional struggle of Charles I's reign the doctrine of parliamentary sovereignty came to men, as Mr. Figgis truly says, "with all the force of a discovery."[1] It lent itself to the views of the more extreme on both the parliamentary and the royalist side, and its influence over men's minds since the days of Milton and Hobbes has become so complete that historians have well-nigh forgotten that any other theory ever existed.

The word *Parliament* has come to carry with it the idea of a lawmaking assembly of the type described by Blackstone. Men in time became so familiar with that idea that they were not conscious of the great and unwarranted assumption they were making when speaking of Tudor and pre-Tudor times; for Parliament, up to the time of the Tudors, was hardly thought of primarily or principally as a legislature: it was still in reality "The High Court of Parliament." That court then retained the varied functions of the old Curia, as Parliament now does; but the judicial functions bulked

[1] *Divine Right of Kings*, p. 232.

larger in men's minds than the legislative. Parliament still seemed primarily a law-declaring machine. So long as the law was a thing fundamental and immutable, "a subject of science, capable of being learnt by special study, but not capable of being altered by the mere will of government," Parliament's functions must have been conceived to be in large part merely the enforcing and applying of this law: Parliament must have been thought of first as a court rather than as a legislature. This I believe to have been the view prevailing, among lawyers at least, as late as the assembling of the Long Parliament. The statement of James I and Bacon, that a judge's functions were rather *jus dicere* than *jus dare*, would have seemed as properly applicable to the High Court of Parliament, if not so fully, as to the courts at Westminster Hall. The prominence of the judicial character of Parliament in the minds of men of the mediaeval period is the normal and natural consequence of the prevailing view that law was fixed; but it is at times surprising to find how late that idea has survived, how many of the characteristics even of the modern sovereign Parliament are due to it, and how many of the great parliamentary struggles of comparatively recent times have been influenced by the old conception of Parliament as a court.

"The function of a court of law," says Gneist, "was and remained the very kernel of every Germanic form of Constitution; judicial proceedings formed the current business of every national assembly."[1] Such a "national assembly" as England could be said to have had in the period of the Norman kings was "rather a court than an organized council."[2] The fact, already noted, of the frequent use of the word *curia* for such assemblies is a strong proof of this. Hoveden uses that word for the assembly in which the Constitutions of Clarendon were drawn up in 1164.[3]

Another proof, and a striking one, of the judicial character of the Council is afforded by the dispute between the kings of Castile and Navarre, which they agreed should be settled by a "judicium," "in curia ... regis Angliae," in 1177.[4]

---

[1] *Constitutional History*, vol. i. pp. 255, 256.
[2] Stubbs, *Constitutional History*, vol. i. p. 385; *Lords' Report*, vol. i. p. 21.
[3] Vol. i. (Rolls Series), pp. 222, 224, 225, cited by Pike, *Constitutional History of the House of Lords*, p. 29. "Et sic recessit archiepiscopus a curia." Hoveden, vol. i. p. 222. Hoveden, speaking of Becket's case in the Council of Northampton (which he calls a *magnum concilium*, vol. i. p. 224), says: "Et barones curiae regis judicaverunt eum esse in misericordia regis" (p. 225). See also Madox, *Exchequer*, ch. i. sec. iii.

The Lords' Commissioners in the *Report on the Dignity of a Peer* (vol. i. p. 46) noticed this and were much perplexed, concluding finally "that the Words 'Curia Regis,'" in the Constitutions of Clarendon, " were intended to include the 'Curia' when assembled for Legislative as well as when assembled for Judicial Purposes; and that the Words applicable to their Judicial Functions were inserted, because the Clergy declined attending any Lay Court of Justice in any Criminal Case in which Judgement was to be pronounced of Loss of Limb or Death."

[4] In this case, the "curia" to which it was referred consisted of the Archbishop of Canterbury, the bishops, counts, and barons, "and many others of the realm of England, clerics as well as laymen." Benedictus Abbas (Rolls Series), vol. i. p. 154). Benedict repeatedly uses the word *curia* (*ibid.*, p. 139), and so do the kings who were the parties in the suit (p. 140). Nothing brings out more clearly the judicial nature of the business of the Council on this occasion than the fact that each of the kings had sent a champion "ad suscipiendum duellum in curia

THE HIGH COURT OF PARLIAMENT

The Statute of Merton in 1235 is said in the preamble to be made "in Curia Domini Regis."[1] Under Edward I the same conditions remain: Parliament is still "pre-eminently intended to be a judicial assembly, to which the other functions are annexed."[2] An instance in this reign similar in some respects to that of the kings of Navarre and Castile under Henry II was the famous award in the case of the disputed Scotch succession in 1292.[3]

In 1322 the famous "Colloquium" met at York which revoked the ordinances made by the barons in 1310, and declared that in future such matters "shall be treated accorded and established in Parliaments by our Lord the King, and by the assent of the Prelates, Earls and Barons, and the Commonalty of the Realm." This has often been considered " the first express recognition of Parliament as a legislative assembly."[4]

Whether this be true or not, generations had yet to pass before the old "judicial" functions of Parliament

---

regis Angliae, si adjudicatum fuerit." *Ibid.*, p. 139. Another account of this case is to be found in Hoveden (Rolls Series, vol. ii. pp. 121-31). References to these passages are to be found in Pike, *Const. Hist. of the House of Lords*, p. 39, where a brief account of the case is also given. See also Madox, *Exchequer*, ch. i. sec. iii.

[1] *Statutes of the Realm*, vol. i. p. 1 (20 Henry III). See also Parry, *Parliaments*, p. 14, note.
[2] Gneist, *Const. Hist.*, vol. i. p. 415. See also Pike, *op. cit.*, pp. 43, 44; *Lords' Report*, vol. i. pp. 171, 174, 180, 182; Parry, pp. 49, 52, 53, 61, 69, and notes.
[3] Rymer (Hague ed.), vol. i. pt. iii. p. 93 et seq.; *Lords' Report*, vol. i. p. 206 et seq.
[4] Gneist, *Const. Hist.*, vol. ii. p. 21, note; Stubbs, *Const. Hist.*, vol. ii. p. 369; *Lords' Report*, vol. i. p. 282; Parry, pp. 85, 86; *Statutes of the Realm*, vol. i. p. 189.

gave way to the legislative. In fact, in the ordinances made in 1311 it is expressly stated that Parliament must be held once a year, or twice if necessary, for hearing pleas, including those "whereon the Justices are of divers Opinions."[1]

The oaths that were taken by the members of the Council show how much emphasis was placed upon matters judicial.[2] This judicial character of Parliament

[1] Ordinances 5th Edward II. (1311), article xxix., *Statutes of the Realm*, vol. i. p. 165. We find a case soon afterward of the enforcement of the ordinance; in it Judge Bereford declared: "And because the new Ordinances direct that when Justices are in doubt about their Judgment the cause shall be sent into Parliament, to Parliament you must sue." *Year Books* (Selden Society), vol. ii. p. 52. The *Year Book of 13 and 14 Edward III* reports a case which illustrates the close relations which still subsisted between Parliament and the other law courts under Edward III. See *Y. B. 13 and 14 Edward III.* (Rolls Series), p. 26 et seq. See also Mr. Pike's introduction to the same volume, p. xxxvi et seq., and also his *Constitutional History of the House of Lords*, p. 50 et seq. In the case in question there is a bewildering succession of hearings, but the significant fact is that apparently an appeal was taken to the King's Bench, though the case had already been in Parliament. Mr. Pike remarks in commenting on cases of this nature: "It was, indeed, a strange anomaly that although the aid of the King and Council might have been asked and obtained again and again before judgment was given, in the Court below, yet if error was after judgment alleged in proceedings before Justices of Assize or in the Court of Common Pleas, the Jurisdiction in Error was, in the reign of Edward III, as in later times, in the Court of King's Bench." Preface to *Y. B. 12 and 13 E. III.*, p. c.

[2] This is evident from the following part of the oath as it appears among the Statutes of Uncertain Date, printed in the *Statutes of the Realm*, vol. i. p. 248. "E qe vous ne lerrez pur nully, pur amur, ne haour, pur bon gre, ne pur mauveis gre, qe vous ne facez faire a chescun de quel estat ou condicion qil soit, droiture et reison, solunc votre poair et a votre escient, et qe de nully rien ne prendrez pur tort faire ne droit delaier.

"E qe en Jugement, ou droiture faire, la ou vous serrez assignez, vous nesparnierez nully, pur hautesce, ne pur poverte, ne pur richesce, qe droit ne soit fait."

See also *Eng. Hist. Rev.*, vol. xxi. pp. 2-4, where Professor Baldwin quotes from the *Annals of Burton* the Latin text of the oath taken in 1257, and compares it with the form given above.

also appears in many other ways. It appears in the practice of holding the Parliament on legal term days, which went back to the Saxon times.[1] To it may be attributed, in some degree at least, the exemption of peers from jury service.[2] There was, in fact, in feudal times no sharp line drawn between public and private rights.[3] Indeed, from one point of view, the very essence of feudalism was this fusion of public and private rights. And as with rights, so with their infringement and the manner of remedy. Wrongs against individuals were not clearly divided from crimes. This is probably the most characteristic feature common to the different *Leges Barbarorum*, and it survived to be a central fact of feudalism. Punishment of a private wrong in like manner is often indistinguishable from the punishment of an offence which we consider to be mainly against the state. Thus, as will be shown in greater detail later, there is no definite line that can be drawn between statute and ordinance, on the one hand, or even between an act and an "award" of Parliament. The determining of a suit between parties and the granting of a petition, whether the petition came from an individual, or a class, or the Commons, are alike "acts" of Parliament, and of equal force and dignity. A study of the controversial writings of the seventeenth century shows that even then, when an act of

[1] Stubbs, *C. H.*, vol. iii. pp. 390-3; Spelman, *The Original of the Four Terms of the Year* in *Reliquiae Spelmannianae*, p. 69 et seq.
[2] *Lords' Report*, vol. i. p. 69.
[3] Lowell, *Essays on Government*, pp. 184, 185.

PARLIAMENT AS A COURT

Parliament was passed overriding a judicial decision of the Lords, the whole Parliament was considered to be above the Lords,—an idea that does not occur to us to-day because we distinguish the judicial supremacy of the Lords from the legislative supremacy of Parliament. In the middle ages the boundary is indistinguishable between "acts" of Parliament that are particular and acts that are general, between acts that are private and acts that are public, between acts administrative, acts legislative, and acts judicial. Only gradually do these distinctions appear; and for a long period after they do, it is the judicial functions of the Assembly that dwarf the others. The Statute of Bigamy of 4 Edward I was in the character of a judicial interpretation of the words of a general council of the Church.[1]

A celebrated clause in the Statute of Westminster Second is significant: "And whensoever from henceforth it shall fortune in the Chancery, that in one Case a Writ is found, and in like Case falling under like Law, and requiring like Remedy, is found none, the Clerks of the Chancery shall agree in making the Writ; or the Plaintiffs may adjourn it until the next Parliament, and let the Cases be written in which they cannot agree, and let them refer themselves until the next Parliament, and let a writ be made by the advice of the learned in the law lest it should happen in future that the court should long time fail to minister Justice unto

[1] See 2 *Inst.*, 274.

complainants."[1] Evidently, in this case, as Mr. Holdsworth says, "it is not clear whether the clause refers to the judicial or to the legislative powers of Parliament, because at that time the line was not clearly drawn between these distinct powers."[2] A regular means of carrying this enactment into effect seems the object of the provision made at the Parliament of Lincoln in 1315, where the Chancellor, the Treasurer, and the judges of both benches are commanded to draw up a record of all cases pending before them "which cannot be determined outside of Parliament," and to refer the same to Parliament for adjudication.[3] Edward III's Statute of Treasons contains the following striking provision: "And because that many other like Cases of Treason may happen in Time to come, which a Man cannot think nor declare at this present

[1] 13 Edward I., Stat. 1, cap. xxiv. (1285).
[2] *H. E. L.*, vol. i. p. 188. A case in 3 Edward II brought out a remarkable statement from the Chief Justice that illustrates not merely the general judicial character of Parliament under the Angevins, as indicated in this and in other statutes, but also more specifically shows the lack of definition in the functions of the Council and the Chancellor. In that case Bereford, the Chief Justice, says that in the reign of Edward I a writ had issued from the Chancery to the Sheriff of Northumberland for the summons of Isabel, Countess of Albemarle, to the next Parliament to answer to the King touching what should be objected against her. "The lady came to the parliament and the King himself took his seat in the parliament." The lady's serjeant prayed judgement of the writ because it mentioned no certain article and she was arraigned of divers articles. Two of the justices were ready to uphold the writ, but Sir Ralph Hengham declared that "the law wills that no one be taken by surprise in the King's Court," and insisted that she should have notice. "Then arose the King, who was very wise, and said: 'I have nothing to do with your disputations, but, God's blood! *you shall give me a good writ before you arise hence.*'" *Year Books* (Selden Society), vol. iii. pp. 196-7.
[3] *Rot. Parl.*, vol. i. p. 350.

PARLIAMENT AS A COURT

Time; it is accorded, That if any other Case, Supposed treason, which is not above specified, doth happen before any Justices, the Justices shall tarry without any going to Judgement of the Treason, till the Cause be shewed and declared before the King and his Parliament whether it ought to be judged Treason or other Felony."[1]

In 1 Richard II, the Commons petitioned the King to hold a Parliament at least once a year for the hearing of cases where injustice had been done on account of delays in the King's Courts or where the judges could not agree.[2]

This fusion of functions, as may be expected, can be traced through abundant instances in legal records from Bracton's time on.[3] Such a view of Parliament, however, was not confined to lawyers in the later mediaeval period, as is indicated by the passage in the *Vision of Piers the Plowman*, where Peace is represented as coming into Parliament to "putte up a bylle" against Wrong, charging seduction and rape.[4] Parliament was called together in those times, as Palgrave says, "not only for the purposes of legislation or taxation, but to the intent that the complaints either of the commonwealth, or of individuals, might be discussed and heard. It was the King's great and extraordinary court of

---

[1] 25 Edward III., Stat. 5, cap. ii. See Note A at the end of this chapter (p. 247).
[2] *Rot. Parl.*, 1 Ric. II. (vol. iii. p. 23).
[3] See Note B at the end of this chapter (p. 248).
[4] Skeat's edition, Text C, passus v., line 45 and following.

THE HIGH COURT OF PARLIAMENT

justice, in which he was to grant redress when the ordinary tribunals were unable or unwilling to grant relief. Frequent Parliaments were required, because justice could not be administered without these assemblies. It was only in Parliament that the doubts of the learned in the law could be solved, and the obstacles impeding the due course of the law be removed.

"When the common-law became inefficient, the supreme remedial jurisdiction was vested in the High Court of Parliament. Here the people were invited to resort for the redress of all injuries and oppressions not cognizable elsewhere; and the inability of the petitioner to sue at common law, or to obtain a fair trial by jury, according to the ordinary process, is the most common allegation in the petitions."[1]

---

[1] *King's Council*, pp. 21, 22.

"Im Anfange, d. i. durch den grösseren Teil des Mittelalters hindurch, war das Gesetz nur ein Urteilsspruch (judgement), das sich vor andern Urteilssprüchen nur durch seine formelle Beweiskraft, weil es eben in die Statutenrolle eingetragen wurde, auszeichnete." Hatschek, *Englisches Staatsrecht*, vol. i. p. 97. "*Bis zum 17. Jahrhundert war das englische Gesetz nur eine Art Urteilsspruch, judicium, und selbst heute haften noch Ueberreste dieser Vorstellung dem englischen Gesetzbegriffe an.*" *Ibid.*, vol. i. p. 113.

"Unter den Normannenkönigen und den ersten Plantagenets dürfen wir uns die Gesetzgebung nur als Ausnahme, hingegen die Regelung der Lebensverhältnisse durch Common law als Norm vorstellen. Die ganze Masse des Rechts war *einheitlich*, denn selbst das Gesetz war von dem gewöhnlichen Urteilsspruch nicht verschieden, war Rechtssatz und zugleich Rechtsprechung, die im High court of parliament vor sich ging. Der mittelalterliche Richter kennt keine Rechts — oder Gesetzeslücken. Er findet entweder das angewandte Recht in dem ungeschriebenen Common law oder beschafft es vermöge seines richterlichen Arbitrium, wie *Bracton* nach unserer vorhergehenden Ausführung dies festgestellt hat." *Ibid.*

"Schon den Juristen der Tudors und Stuarts beginnt es einzuleuchten, dass ein Gesetz von einem Urteilsspruche wohl in seinem inneren Wesen ver-

PARLIAMENT AS A COURT

When we thus speak of Parliament as a "court of justice" and designate its actions as "judicial," it will be remembered that "court" and "judicial" are not to be used in their modern definite sense. We can never understand the institutions of mediaeval England if we consider Parliament as a "court of justice" which *in addition* exercised other distinct powers, or as a legislature with an addendum of other duties. It is the *fusion* of indefinite powers which is the most fundamental fact in English central institutions in the middle ages. It will be seen that this applies not to Parliament merely, but to all the other courts of the King as well, and it thus furnishes the key to the great problem which claims our main attention in this essay,— the relations existing between the King's High Court of Parliament and his other courts.

It must have been noticed that the instances cited above, many of them, refer to a period after the law courts and the Privy Council were definitely established as separate judicial tribunals. These bodies when they came into existence only shared with the Parliament in the "judicial" business; they did not supersede

scheiden sei. Das römische Recht, mit dem die Juristen der Tudors, wie wir oben gehört haben — sich besonders anfreundeten, hat sie inzwischen gelehrt, einen Unterschied zwischen Gesetz unt Urteilsspruch (judicium) zu machen. Daher finden wir denn auch in den Parlamentrollen des 31. Reg.-Jahres Heinrichs VIII. zuerst die Nomenklatur von 'Actes Publicke' im Gegensatz zu 'Actes Private,' was offenbar aus dem Bedürfnis entsprang, das wirkliche Gesetz, die allgemeine Normensetzung, von dem Urteilsspruch zu scheiden." *Ibid.*, vol. i. p. 119; see also p. 234. The beginning of a formal distinction between public and private acts in 31 Henry VIII as here pointed out is certainly of a great significance. See also Maitland, *Const. Hist. of England*, p. 105.

it. In fact, as we have seen, the line between the "jurisdiction" of Parliament and that of the other courts cannot be laid down, and that because it was not clearly perceived nor any necessity for it appreciated. Using "court" in the sense above noted, we may say, then, that the High Court of Parliament, though the greatest of the courts, was still a court; and if its higher dignity and representative character gave it the power to lay down a new rule when no old one could be found that was applicable, this power, though great and unique, was really only incidental, and neither new nor startling. It required time, a long time, and great changes in the state—the decline of class feeling, a wider distribution of wealth and culture and a widening political self-consciousness in consequence, a change in the conception of kingship, along with sharp controversies ecclesiastical and civil—to alter all this and subordinate the old idea of a court to the newer one of a legislature. It is the persistence of this old idea, notwithstanding the great changes, which is the important thing. Parliament has retained somewhat the character of a court while it has taken on the new duties of a legislature. Hardly anyone will deny the eminently judicial cast of Parliament in the middle ages; few have considered the importance of Parliament's retention of those judicial characteristics, after the other law courts grew into a separate existence, and fewer have reckoned with their influence upon the modern development and present form of parliamentary institutions,

PARLIAMENT AS A COURT

English and American. It is therefore this more modern phase of the history of the High Court which especially needs proof and illustration. It is believed that sufficient proofs do exist, and it is hoped that they can be here shown, to warrant the conviction expressed by Palgrave, that "the character of the English parliament as a supreme court of remedial jurisdiction has never altered, though many changes have taken place in its form."[1]

In Trewynard's Case, which involved the question of the privilege of a member of the Commons' House, it was declared that the "court of parliament is the most high court, and hath more privileges than any other court in the Kingdom."[2]

Cartwright in his first *Admonition* in 1572 offered to defend himself "in this High Court of Parliament."[3] "The Parliament," says Hooker, "is a Court, not so merely temporal as if it might meddle with nothing but only leather and wool."[4] "Of such courts as exercise the Queenes immediate autoritie," wrote Richard Cosin, one of Elizabeth's High Commission, "some haue no letters Patents of Commission to direct them; as, the *Parlement*, which is called, and sitteth by the

---

[1] *King's Council*, p. 125.
[2] 36-37 Henry VIII., *Dyer*, fol. 60 a. See also the case of the *Earl of Leicester v. Heydon* in 13 Elizabeth, *Plowden*, 384 et seq., where Parliament is spoken of as "a Court of the greatest Honour and Justice, of which none can imagine a dishonourable Thing" (p. 398).
[3] Extract in Prothero, *Documents*, p. 199.
[4] *Eccl. Pol.*, vol. viii., *Of the Authority of Making Laws.*

[121]

Queenes onely writ: the *Chauncerie*," etc.[1] Speaking of Parliament in the same reign, Judge Doddridge said: "So by looking back, it is easie to see the great antiquity of this high court, delivered, as you see, from before the Romans, but never so dignified, as since Queen Elizabeth's time. Now for the nature of a parliament, it is *consilium*, and it is *curia;* the power of it in matters hereditary and personal; the proceedings of it in causes criminal and civil."[2] "The tribunals or courts of justice in England," according to Camden, "are of three sorts: spiritual, temporal, and mixed, which last is the greatest and most honourable, called *Parliament*."[3] In 1589 the Speaker quieted a commotion in the Commons by putting them in remembrance "that every Member of this House is a Judge of this Court, being the highest Court of all other Courts, and the great Council also of this Realm, and so moveth them in regard thereof, that as in all other Courts, being each of them inferiour to this high Court, such confused courses either of contention, acclamations, or reciprocal bitter and sharp

[1] *An Apologie for Sundrie Proceedings by Jurisdiction Ecclesiasticall* (1593), part ii. p. 8.
[2] Hearne's *Curious Discourses*, vol. i. p. 289. Another anonymous writer of the same time has the same idea, though he is much impressed with the importance of the public business of Parliament. "The court of parliament," he says, "hath a double power; the one to consult by way of deliberation for the good government of the commonwealth, and so is *Consilium, non Curia;* another power it hath as a court, in administration of justice.

"The principal purpose of that assembly seemeth to be for consultation; for the writs are *ad Consultandum & deliberandum:* but being assembled, they may hold plea of causes." Hearne, *op. cit.*, vol. i. p. 294. This author seems to have a view more modern than most of his contemporaries.
[3] *Britannia* (Gough's edition), vol. i. p. cci.

PARLIAMENT AS A COURT

Speeches, terms or words are not any way either used or permitted amongst the Judges of the said Inferiour Courts, or the Chancellors admitted in the same Courts, so they would hereafter forbear to attempt the like disorders, as the honour and gravity of this House justly requireth."[1]

William Lambard in 1591 used the following words with reference to Parliament: "Hitherto of the *continuance* and *consent* of this our *chiefe and highest Court;* whereunto, after I shall have added a word or twaine of the *Iurisdiction* thereof, I will make an end.

"If all the *Iudgements*, as *Cicero* said, be *conversant*, either in *punishment* of *offences*, or in the *decision* of *Controversies;* then is the *judgement* of our *Parliament* of as ample *Authoritie*, as the *Sentence* of any, or all other *Courts* whatsoever: for it delivereth *Lawes*, that doe *binde* all *persons*, in all *causes*, as well *Ecclesiasticall*, as *Temporall*, whereof you may see a great many of *examples* in the *volume* of the old *Saxons Parliaments;* how strange a thing soever our *Popish Clergie* of latter times have thought that to be.

"It hath also *jurisdiction* in such *cases* which have need of *helpe*, and for which there is no *helpe* by any Law, already in *force;* And whereas the erronious *Iudgements* of any other *Courts* must be *reversed* by a *higher authority;* this *Court* doth not onely *reverse* the *errors* of the *Kings Bench*, which is *superiour* to all the *other;* but it may also *amend* the *errors* committed in the *Par-*

[1] D'Ewes, *Journals*, p. 434; see also pp. 514-16.

liament itselfe, if any such shall at any time appeare."[1]

This remarkable passage from the great antiquary and legal writer makes it evident not only that he regarded Parliament mainly as a court, but that he did not separate its legislative from its judicial functions. The making of new law is looked at as the decision of a new case, or as the reversal of an error of a preceding Parliament.

The testimony of a man like Lambard is of especial value. Among all the writers of Elizabeth's time, it is in importance second to none unless it be Sir Thomas Smith's. The long public career of Sir Thomas Smith, his ample training, the point of view adopted in his treatise, and its great popularity, all made the *Discourse on the Commonwealth of England* a book of the utmost importance. And no part of the book is of greater interest than the parts where he describes that "highest and most authenticall court of Englande, by vertue whereof all those things be established whereof I spake before, and no other meanes accounted vailable to make any new forfaiture of life, member, or landes of any English man, where there was no lawe ordayned for it before."[2]

"By order and usage of Englande," he says further, "there is three wayes and maners, whereby absolute and definite judgement is given, by parliament which

---

[1] *Archeion* (edition of 1635), pp. 272, 273. See also Crompton, *L'Authoritie et Jurisdiction des Courts*, ch. i., *De Treshault Court de Parliament*.
[2] *De Republica Anglorum*, book ii. ch. ii.

is the highest and most absolute, by battle and by the great assise.

"The matter of giving judgement by parliament betweene private and private man, or betweene the prince and any private man, be it in matters criminall or civill, for land or for heritage doth not differ from thorder which I have prescribed, but it proceedeth by bill thrise read in ech house and assented to as I have saide before, and at the last day confirmed and allowed by the prince. Howbeit such bils be seeldome receaved, because that great counsell being enough occupied with the publique affaires of the realme, will not gladly intermeddle it selfe with private quarels and questions. . . .

"The two first judgementes be absolute supreme and without appeale, and so is also the judgement by the great assise."[1] Here the prominence of the idea of a court is evident. The purely judicial functions of Parliament are the ones that should come in for a detailed description in a book on the English Commonwealth. Private bill "legislation" he also considers a judicial proceeding. The activity of the Parliament in public affairs which had been so great since Henry VIII's time, so acute an observer could not pass over, but he thinks of it as an instance of the old consultative power of the Council rather than as "legislation."

In the introduction to the latest edition of Smith's *Commonwealth*—an introduction which should be read by every one who wishes to understand the book itself

[1] *De Republica Anglorum*, book ii. chs. v.-viii.

THE HIGH COURT OF PARLIAMENT

—the editor, Mr. L. Alston, explains the object and point of view of the treatise. I shall quote him at some length.

"To Smith . . . the constitution of the commonwealth consists primarily of its courts and its various forms of law,—martial, ecclesiastical, and general. Nor is his book, though the treatment is intended to be comparative, greatly concerned with the contrast between 'constitutional' England and 'absolute' France, as we should expect if he were mainly interested in such questions as that of royal and parliamentary sovereignty. The regularly recurring contrast is that between England on the one hand and, on the other, those countries which 'doe followe the civill Law of the Romanes compiled by Justinian into his pandects and code.' . . .

"Why, then, does he devote those three lengthy chapters to the Prince and the Parliament? He does so because no account of the judicial system would be complete without them. . . .

"That word 'court' comes to our modern ears as a mere archaism when it is applied to Parliament. But to Smith the application seems a natural usage, expressive of a still living fact. He does not cut apart the legislative, judicial, and executive functions, and endeavour to assign each to a particular element in the constitution. Rather he tends to blur together the first two, and while of course clearly understanding the great practical difference between statutes and the sen-

PARLIAMENT AS A COURT

tences of lower courts, to treat them as being, for theoretical purposes, members of the same group. Both are the offspring of 'courts;' and though Parliament is the greatest among these, and has many functions which the others have not, it is not therefore an element in the constitution which is *sui generis*.[1] ...

"We, splitting across our institutions with the sharp hatchet of a theory, which declares one body to be properly legislative, and another properly judicial, find afterwards . . . that we have still to deal with legislature-made judicial sentences (such as bills of pains and penalties) and with judge-made law. Smith, not having so broken up his subject-matter, is not under any obligation to spend pains on reuniting the broken pieces."[2]

It may seem strange that such an observer as Sir Thomas Smith should fail to grasp the meaning of the growing legislative activity of Parliament, and should class it with trial by battle among the institutions of his country. This is no more surprising, however, than that Blackstone in 1758 should describe the English parliamentary system and leave out the Cabinet. The cases are an interesting parallel. In both, distance alone could give the perspective required. Smith was too near the events that were leading to legislative sovereignty to perceive their trend. For him Parliament was still primarily a court. It is easy enough for us to see the tendency, but the storm and stress of the Stuart period

---

[1] Introduction to the edition of 1906, pp. xxvii, xxviii.
[2] *Ibid.*, pp. xxxiii, xxxiv.

had to come before men could reach a realization of it. In like manner, it required the agitation over the Reform Bill before a Bagehot was likely to appear. Nevertheless, it must be admitted that some of Smith's statements go much further toward legislative sovereignty than those of any contemporary. In the beginning of his second book he says: "The most high and absolute power of the realme of Englande, consisteth in the Parliament." Then follows a long statement of the various powers of Parliament. He sums it up by saying: "And to be short, all that ever the people of Rome might do either in *Centuriatis comitijs* or *tributis*, the same may be doone by the parliament of Englande, which representeth and hath the power of the whole realme both the heade and the body."[1] Hallam seems to think this declaration too weak. He thinks Smith was shuffling because he did not want to abridge the latitude of royal proclamations.[2] Mr. Bryce believes that Smith here "set forth the legal supremacy of Parliament in words to whose clearness and amplitude nothing can be added to-day."[3] So do Professor Maitland[4] and Sir Frederick Pollock,[5] though the last-named writer admits that the lawyers of that day would not have concurred in such a view.[6]

[1] Book ii. ch. i.
[2] *Const. Hist.*, ch. v.
[3] *Studies in History and Jurisprudence*, p. 553.
[4] *Constitutional History of England*, pp. 254, 255 (written in 1888 or before).
[5] *History of the Science of Politics*, p. 54; *First Book of Jurisprudence*, p. 247 et seq.
[6] *First Book of Jurisprudence*, p. 250.

PARLIAMENT AS A COURT

On the other hand, Sir Thomas Smith's editor, Mr. Alston, is of the opinion that Smith "in declaring Parliament to be the most high and absolute power of the realm (in time of peace) is by no means bringing up for consideration the question of sovereignty in the modern sense, or making statements which have any direct bearing on the great controversy of the next century. . . . The contrast upon which Smith's attention is focused is not the contrast between the powers of the Prince and of the Parliament, but between the powers of Parliament and of those other courts which he describes in later chapters, and describes without any feeling of essential difference between them and this highest court. He is still, in this respect, under the influence of traditional theory."[1] Though Smith says Parliament is the "most absolute power" in England, the word "absolute" is here taken to mean "not subject to appeal."[2] There is good reason for this interpretation of the word. Smith himself elsewhere uses it thus, as is seen above.[3] Lambard also uses it in the same way.[4]

---

[1] Introduction, p. xxxiii.
[2] *Ibid.*, pp. xxxi, xxxii, and references there cited.
[3] E. g. *ante*, pp. 124, 125.
[4] *Archeion*, pp. 62, 63. "Then, I say, the King did commit to his *Chancellor* (together with the charge of the great *Seale*) his owne Regall, absolute, and extraordinarie preheminence of *Jurisdiction* in *Civill* Causes, as well for amendment as for supply of the *Common Law*." See also Nathaniel Bacon, *Discourse on the Government of England*, pt. ii. p. 162 (edition of 1682, first published in 1651); *New Oxford Dictionary*, s. v. *Absolute*. Lord Ellesmere, or the author of the tract attributed to him, while admitting that the Court of Chancery is below the Parliament, speaks of it as having two powers, *potentiam ordinatam* and *potentiam absolutam;* and *potentia absoluta*, he says, "is *lex naturae*,

The word was sometimes used in a somewhat different sense, namely, to indicate independence of any foreign power. So Milton says, "Whereas you cite out of Sir Edward Coke and others, 'that the kingdom of England is an absolute kingdom;' that is said with respect to any foreign prince, or the emperor."[1] But even in this sense the judicial idea of freedom from appeal is the central one. The authority is complete on the negative side, but not necessarily on the positive. It is this negative side of supremacy which is present in Locke's mind when he speaks of "even absolute power," as "not arbitrary by being absolute,"[2] and even Hobbes sometimes uses absolute in this sense.[3] No doubt Sir Thomas Smith, as a keen observer, was influenced by the altering political surroundings. It is not improper to say that Smith's was "the earliest definite statement" of the theory of parliamentary omnipotence; but it would be unwarrantable to conclude, therefore, that he made that statement, conscious of all its modern implications. That was reserved for a later generation. It was true of Smith, as it was of Coke, that he looked on Parliament primarily as the highest and

quae non habet certam ordinem, but useth all meanes to know the verity." *Observations on the Office of the Lord Chancellor*, p. 44.

[1] "Quod autem ex Edvardo Coco et aliis citas, 'Angliae regnum absolutum est imperium,' id est si ad ullum regem externum, aut Caesarem, respicias." *Pro Populo Anglicano Defensio* (1651), cap. ix.

[2] *Two Treatises of Government*, book ii. sec. 139.

[3] *Leviathan*, part ii. ch. xxii. See also Lowell, *Essays on Govt.*, pp. 202-5. For some uses of the word *absolute* in the other sense, see Prynne, *Soveraigne Power*, part iv. p. 15; Bacon, *Advice to Sir George Villiers; Speech on the Union of Laws.*

most honourable court, "absolute" and supreme, "the most authenticall" in the realm. The whole plan of his treatise shows this, and his frequent comparison of Parliament with the other courts, as well as his concrete statements.

To the same effect as Smith's *Commonwealth* is Harrison's *Description of England*, published with Holinshed's *Chronicle:* "The regiment that we haue therefore, after our owne ordinances, dependeth upon three lawes, to wit, Statute law, Common law, Customarie law, and Prescription, according to the triple maner of our trials and judgments, which is by parlement, verdict of twelve men at an assise, or wager of battell. . . .

"The first is deliuered unto us by parlement, which court, being for the most part holden at Westminster neere London, is the highest of all other, & consisteth of three seuerall sorts of people, that is to saie, the nobilitie, cleargie, and commons of this realme."[1]

Parliament under the Tudors was a legislature; its acts were many of them acts of real legislation, and these acts were not few in number. But it was not the unlimited legislature of more modern times. In Tudor times, it must also be admitted, the judicial functions of Parliament were to a great extent in abeyance. We have noticed one cause of it. The nobility were reduced to a powerlessness unknown before the Wars of the

[1] Edition of 1587, p. 179. For a discussion of Harrison's indebtedness to Smith for these views, see Mr. Alston's introduction to Smith's *Commonwealth*, p. xvi et seq.

Roses. The Parliament in which they had an hereditary right to sit could be dispensed with by the King for longer periods than would have been possible in earlier times. Much of the necessary business could be dispatched with much greater expedition and less friction by a smaller body which should include the King's judges. The business, of course, had to be done, and it was ever increasing in amount; but now the shortness of Parliament's sessions, and the long and varying intervals that might intervene between those sessions, made Parliament a very imperfect judicial instrument. The preamble of the Act of 1585 concerning appeals to the Court of Exchequer Chamber well illustrates this: "Forasmuch as erroneous Judgments given in the Court called the King's Bench, are only to be reformed by the High Court of Parliament: which Court of Parliament is not in these Days so often holden as in Ancient Time it hath been, neither yet (in respect of greater Affairs of this Realm) such erroneous Judgments can be well considered of and determined during the Time of the Parliament, whereby the Subjects of this Realm are greatly hindred and delayed of Justice in such Cases, Be it therefore enacted,"[1] etc.

Here we see the workings of the forces that were turning the Parliament into a legislature, and also the reasons for its decline as a court.

The Chancellor, the Council, and the Star Chamber

[1] 27 Eliz., ch. viii. See also *The Olde and Auncient Order of Keeping of the Parliament in England*, by John Vowell, *alias* Hooker, 1572, *Somers Tracts*, vol. i. p. 175 et seq., especially p. 179.

PARLIAMENT AS A COURT

had in fact long been "encroaching" on these judicial functions of Parliament. Parliament's loss of this kind of business is pretty accurately indicated by the growth of new courts. Palgrave has noted of the courts of equity that "in proportion as this channel enlarged, the number of Parliamentary Petitions decreased. Equity continued to gain rapidly upon Parliament, and about the time of Edward IV, when equity was fully established, the remedial jurisdiction of Parliament wholly ceased; and it does not appear to have been revived to any extent until the time of James I."[1] It may be doubted whether the cessation was entire as Palgrave thinks,—there is some evidence that it was not,—but judicial activity must have been vastly lessened. Hargrave, who is a strong upholder of the jurisdiction of Parliament, especially of the House of Commons, admits that "from the third of Henry the Fifth to the accession of James the First, there appears to have been little exercise of judicature in parliament civilly or indeed criminally; unless the cruel precedents of acts of attainder without hearing the accused, and the indulgent precedents of acts of restitution without assignment of errors, of both of which the number is great, are fit to be considered as judicial records."[2]

The extensive powers of the Council and the activity

---

[1] *Report on Public Petitions: Parl. Papers*, Session of 1833, vol. xii. p. 19. See Note C at the end of this chapter (p. 250).
[2] Preface to Hale's *Jurisdiction of the Lords House*, p. viii.

of bodies new and old, such as the Chancery, the Star Chamber, the Council of the North, the Council in the Marches of Wales, the courts of Requests, of Wards and Liveries, of Augmentations, of Exchequer Chamber, and of High Commission, to mention no others, show where this ever increasing business was handled. A consideration of these undoubted facts has too often led to the assumption that the Tudor Parliament was looked upon by contemporaries as the sovereign legislature of the kingdom in the same sense as to-day. This step would inevitably follow the altered conditions just so soon as men distinguished with sharpness and accuracy the spheres of legislation and judicature. It is the central thesis of this essay that the utterances of contemporaries show that in the Tudor and even in a large part of the Stuart period, men had not yet reached this clear distinction. It is admitted that most judicial business had by the end of the Tudor régime been transferred from Parliament to other bodies. It is not admitted that men perceived that Parliament had become a pure legislature, and nothing more. In addition to the testimony of contemporaries, one fact stands out to disprove it: if there is a clear distinction between legislation and judicature, if Parliament is a mere "legislature" and nothing more, then the courts will be mere courts and nothing more. Nothing is clearer from contemporary records, however, than the fact that some of these "courts" were, under the Tudors, almost as "legislative" in character as Parliament itself. "It is impossible," Professor Dicey says, "to draw any precise line between those offences which the Council punished, acting as a government, and those which it noticed in the character of a law court; and such a distinction, could it be made, would only mislead, for it would hide what is the characteristic feature of the period under review, the inseparable combination in the Council of political and judicial authority."[1] Professor Dicey had here in mind the administrative powers of the Council rather than its legislative capacity, but the latter cannot be excluded by anyone who will consider the things that were done by Henry and Elizabeth by mere proclamations issuing from the King in Council. A study of the records of the Court of Star Chamber discloses a similar fusion of powers, as might be expected from an offshoot of the Council, and justifies Hudson's description of the "Court,"— "it being composed . . . of all conditions of men, like another parliament, spiritual and temporal, nobles, and lawyers common and civil, and so fit to discern, order, and dispose of all things in the universal government."[2] "Through the medium of that Court," says Miss Scofield, "the Crown exercised legislative as well as judicial powers. The Star Chamber, although primarily a judicial tribunal, participated in the legislative powers usurped by the King and his Council. The Star Chamber not only expounded the laws, but even made laws.

[1] *Privy Council*, p. 106.
[2] *Collectanea Juridica*, vol. ii. p. 52.

It issued orders and decrees, often very comprehensive, and which in some cases are so closely analogous to orders in Council that they may not very incorrectly be regarded as such."[1]

Thus it appears that the loss by Parliament of its judicial functions under the Tudors was not accompanied, as we might expect on any theory of legislative sovereignty, by a corresponding gain in "legislative" business. We find, on the contrary, that the other "courts" were almost as serious rivals of Parliament in this sphere as in the sphere of judicature. Speaking of the period between 1485 and 1640, Dicey says: "To any one who reviews the history of the Council, these hundred and fifty years present a certain semblance of unity. They might be described as the age of 'government by Councils;' and exhibit, in the strongest colours, the merits and defects of a system nearly as different from the rule of Henry V as from the ministerial government of Victoria."[2]

It will be perceived that for the Tudor period at least I have been speaking of men's opinions rather than of Parliament's actions. Parliament had for a time failed to exercise most of its former judicial powers, and for a considerable time, no doubt, the greater bulk of its business had been what we should call legislative. That legislative action, however, does not imply a clear perception in Parliament, in the other courts, or out-

[1] *The Court of Star Chamber*, p. 49.
[2] *Privy Council*, p. 80.

PARLIAMENT AS A COURT

side of both, that Parliament's "acts" were different in nature from the "acts" of the other courts. And yet that clear perception was absolutely prerequisite to an understanding of the dogma of legislative sovereignty. It required the shock of civil war to teach men that the High Court of Parliament had become the Sovereign Legislature of the Kingdom.

When we pass from the Tudors to the reign of James I, a striking instance of the force of the idea of Parliament as a court is to be found in Lord Chancellor Ellesmere's speech in the Exchequer Chamber in the Case of the *Postnati*. During the course of the debate previously held in Parliament upon the Union, the judges had been asked their opinion on the status of the *postnati*, and had given an opinion, one only dissenting, in their favour. Parliament, however, had taken no formal action upon the question. Lord Ellesmere calls this opinion thus given by the judges in Parliament "the graue resolution of the judges in parliament, which (although some may tearme and accompt as bare opinions) I must alwayes valew, and esteeme as a reall and absolute judgement "[1] In other words, this bare opinion of the judges in Parliament, though not given upon an appeal, though there had been no hearing of the case in the House of Lords, though there was no formal parliamentary action of any kind based on the opinion, he apparently considers, nevertheless, as a statement of the law which should be treated by

[1] 2 *State Trials*, 667.

a judge as a binding precedent. This he could do only by assuming that Parliament was a court, and that the judges in stating their opinion there were doing exactly what they would do in handing down an opinion in the Court of King's Bench or Common Pleas. That this was actually his view he makes clear when he says: "Touching the opinion of the judges, some haue objected (yet modestly, and I suppose, according to their conscience and understanding) that there is not like regarde to be had of judges opinions giuen in parliament, as ought to bee of their judgements in their proper courts and seates of justice: for, in those places their oath bindeth them; but not so in the other. . . . 2. Their oath doth bind them as much in the court of parliament, as in their proper courts: for, that is the supreme court of all: and they are called thither by the king's writ, not to sit as tell-clockes, or idle hearers; but, 'quod personaliter intersitis nobiscum, ac cum cæteris de consilio nostro super dictis negotiis tractaturi, vestrumque consilium impensuri:' and those 'negotia' be 'ardua et vrgentia negotia regni, &c.' And their oath, amongest other thinges, is, that they shall counsell the king truely in his businesse.—3. This exception may serue against the judges, as well in cases when they sit and giue judgement, as justices of Assises, Nisi Prius, Oyer and Terminer, and Gaole Deliuerie, as in this case of parliament: for, there they haue none other oath but their generall oath."[1]

[1] 2 *St. Tr.*, 665. In the course of his argument he cites many interesting in-

PARLIAMENT AS A COURT

This view of Parliament also affected Coke's whole treatment of the Courts. In fact in his *Fourth Institute*, "Concerning the Jurisdiction of Courts," the first court treated of is "The High and most Honourable Court of Parliament." He speaks of the Parliament Rolls or "Records" of Parliament as valuable because "therein is set down in cases of difficulty, not only the judgment, or resolution, but the reason, and causes of the same by so great advice," and compares these "records" with the records of the King's other courts.[1] In like manner, he deals with the *lex parliamenti* and parliamentary privilege. The King cannot require the testimony of members of the House of Commons upon things done in the house itself, because "every Member of the Parliament hath a judicial place, and can be no witness." So cases of privilege should not be discussed in the other courts, for "every offence committed in any Court punishable by that Court, must be punished (proceeding criminally) in the same Court, or in some higher, and not in any inferiour Court and the Court of Parliament hath no higher."[2] "It is to be known, that the Lords in their House have power of Judicature, and the Commons in their House have power of Judicature, and both Houses together have power of Judicature."[3] He

---

stances of judges consulting the Council in difficult cases. Some of these occur among the cases already cited in this essay; many others, however, lack of space makes it impossible to mention here.

[1] 4 *Inst.*, 3, 4.
[2] *Ibid.*, 15.
[3] *Ibid.*, 23.

notes also that when a Parliament is dissolved without an act passed "*or judgment given*" it is no session of Parliament, but a Convention, and cites the Parliament of 18 Richard II, in which the petitions of the Commons were answered and judgement given in a case, but no act passed; "but it is no question but it was a Session of Parliament, for otherwise the Judgment should not be of force: and many times Judgments given in Parliament have been executed, the Parliament continuing before any Bill passed."[1] One of the most frequently cited passages from Coke is his statement: "Of the power and *jurisdiction* of the Parliament, for making of Laws in proceeding by Bill, it is so transcendent and absolute, as it cannot be confined either *for causes* or *persons* within any bounds. Of this Court it is truly said: Si antiquitatem spectes, est vetustissima, si dignitatem, est honoratissima, si jurisdictionem, est capacissima.

"Huic ego nec metas rerum, nec tempora pono.

"Yet some examples are desired, Daughters and Heirs apparent of a man or woman, may by Act of Parliament inherit during the life of the Ancestor.

"It may adjudge an Infant, or Minor of full age.

"To attaint a man of Treason after his death.

"To naturalize a meer Alien and make him a Subject born. It may bastard a child that by Law is legitimate, viz. begotten by an Adulterer, the husband being within the four Seas.

"To legitimate one that is illegitimate, and born be-

[1] *4 Inst.*, 28.

fore marriage absolutely. And to legitimate secundum quid, but not simpliciter."[1]

This is the passage cited to prove the legislative supremacy of Parliament. Blackstone quotes it in proof of that theory.[2] Professor Dicey remarks on the judicious choice of instances Coke has made in order to prove Parliament's omnipotence. Interference with public rights would be, Professor Dicey thinks, "a less striking exhibition of absolute power" than the interference with the rights of individuals shown in these instances.[3] To the same effect are the views of Sir Erskine May: "Many laws may be unjust, and contrary to sound principles of government: but Parliament is not controlled in its discretion, and when it errs, its errors can only be corrected by itself. To adopt the words of Sir Edward Coke, the power of Parliament 'is so transcendent and absolute, that it cannot be confined, either for causes or persons, within any bounds.'"[4] It is unnecessary to add any more of these, though there are many more such, for this is the prevailing interpretation of Coke's words. He is assumed to be speaking of the "Unlimited legislative authority of Parliament."[5]

And yet there are some striking differences between Coke's own statement and the glosses upon it. In the

[1] 4 *Inst.*, p. 36. The italics are not in the original.
[2] *Commentaries*, vol. i. pp. 160, 161.
[3] *Law of the Constitution*, p. 46.
[4] *Parliamentary Practice*, 9th ed., pp. 43, 44.
[5] Dicey, *op. cit.*, p. 39. See also, generally, Professor Maitland in *Social England*, vol. ii. (p. 476 et seq. in ed. of 1894).

first place, Coke's statement occurs in a treatise devoted exclusively to "the Judicature of Courts." This might naturally lead one to think that he might be speaking of the judicial side of Parliament. All these more modern writers, however, quote this passage in support of Parliament's legislative sovereignty. The words "for causes or persons" would hardly be used of legislative business,—not even of private bill legislation, if that were considered real "legislation." Coke is here certainly speaking of procedure by bill and he is also speaking of private bills. Does it follow that he considers such private bills as legislative in character? His statements about the "Court," its "jurisdiction," and the "causes" before it would render this highly improbable, even if the context and the character of the contents of the whole book were left out of account.

But, it may be asked, what practical difference does it make, whether Coke considered procedure by private bill legislative or judicial? In either case does he not speak of the power and jurisdiction as transcendent and absolute? Of the meaning of the word "absolute" we have seen something already. "Transcendent" is not unlike it. It surely will not be denied that when we speak to-day of the supreme legislature, *supreme* means something entirely different from the idea conveyed by the expression "supreme court." Take the latter expression as it is actually applied in the United States. We cannot properly speak here of our federal legislature as *supreme*, for in legislative matters that word

PARLIAMENT AS A COURT

has become practically synonymous with unlimited: a supreme legislature is now one that "is complete both on its positive and on its negative side. Parliament can legally legislate on any topic which, in the Judgment of Parliament, is a fit subject for legislation. There is no power which, under the English constitution, can come into rivalry with the legislative sovereignty of Parliament."[1] No such a legislature is known to our federal constitution. We do, however, use the term "supreme court." It occurs in the written constitution and is in everyday use, and we have no sense of impropriety in so using it. Is it true, therefore, that our highest court is unlimited, "complete," on its positive side as well as its negative? These very words, when applied to it, strike us at once as incongruous. Our highest federal court *is* supreme, but it cannot be said to be unlimited. Its limits are very definitely marked out, by the Constitution, by statute, and by usage, and yet it is "supreme." "Supreme" in the judicial sense, then, means without a superior, without an appeal, the *dernier resort:* it does not and never did imply the unfettered discretion which the modern idea of legislative supremacy unquestionably does convey. A supreme court may be complete on its negative side; it is not necessarily so on its positive side. The United States Supreme Court is not supreme in that sense; neither was the Court of Parliament of Coke's *Fourth Institute.*

[1] Dicey, *Law of the Constitution*, pp. 66-8.

The only ones who might object on theoretical grounds to this double use of the word supreme are the more extreme Austinians. They might indeed argue that the only limitation upon supremacy, be it the supremacy of the King, or of the courts, or of the legislature, is the limitation of law; and that, therefore, the body of men who ultimately lay down the law, be they King, or judges in a court, or the representatives in a sovereign Parliament, are, after all, unlimited in power,—in short, that "supremacy" *must* mean limitlessness. To such an argument I can only answer, first of all, that the distinction used above between positive completeness and negative completeness is used by so stanch an upholder of Parliament's legislative sovereignty as Professor Dicey. Secondly, I may point to the actual and well-nigh universal practice of to-day: "supreme" is, for example, actually applied generally throughout the United States to the courts; it is not used of the legislature. Lastly, I am unable to accept the dictum that the existence of a law always necessarily implies obedience to a political superior so "definite" as a rigid Austinian theory demands,—so definite as to require the invention of a distinction between "legal" and "practical" sovereignty to support it.[1]

---

[1] In using "supreme" in this limited sense to-day we are only following the accepted usage of the sixteenth and seventeenth centuries. "Supreme" as used in England then never meant *unlimited*, whether applied to a court or to a king. It implied rather the absence of a superior, and when, for example, it was used of the King of England, as it often was, this was done to emphasize his

PARLIAMENT AS A COURT

The events of the sixteenth and seventeenth centuries in England eventually did produce a theory of legislative sovereignty complete on both its negative and its positive side. Englishmen, after they had accepted the new theory, in their traditional manner

independence of Pope or Emperor or of any other power within the state, but never to imply that his power was without limits. See, for example, Lambard, *Archeion*, pp. 274, 275. So Hooker: "If the action which we have to perform be conversant about matters of mere religion, the power of performing of it is then spiritual; and if that power be such as hath not any other to overrule it, we term it dominion, or power supreme, so far as the bounds thereof extend. When therefore Christian Kings are said to have spiritual dominion or supreme power in ecclesiastical affairs and causes, the meaning is, that within their own precincts and territories they have an authority and power to command, even in matters of Christian Religion, and that there is no higher nor greater that can in those cases over-command them, where they are placed to reign as kings. But withal we must likewise note that their power is termed supremacy, as being the highest, not simply without exception of anything. . . . Supremacy is not otherwise intended or meant [than] to exclude, partly foreign powers, and partly the power which belongeth in several unto others, contained as parts in that politic body over which those kings have supremacy: *Where the King hath power of dominion, or supreme power, there no foreign state or potentate, no state or potentate domestical, whether it consisteth of one or many, can possibly have in the same affairs and causes authority higher than the king.*" Ecclesiastical Polity, book viii., " *What the power of Dominion is.*" Prynne habitually uses the word *supreme* in this sense, *e.g.*, *Soveraigne Power*, part i. pp. 34, 93; Twysden uses it in the same sense, *Government of England* (Camden Society), p. 18; also Algernon Sidney—speaking of "the name of *supreme* given to their magistrates" by nations, Sidney says: "It signifies no more, than that they do act sovereignly in the matters committed to their charge" (*Discourses concerning Government: Works*, p. 176). Hoadly argued in the same way against non-resistance: "Now to argue from any Person's being, by Title, *Supreme*, against *Equality* in any respect, is to abuse the *Reader* with Words, and to take the very thing for granted which is in dispute; and to lead him to think that *Supreme* and *Superior* are absolute Terms, and signify an absolute and unlimited *Supremacy* in all Cases: whereas he may find by daily Experience and Common *Sense* that the *words* in ordinary use never signify more than a limited *Superiority*, extending to *some Cases* only." *An Examination of the Patriarchal Scheme of Government* (2d ed., London, 1710), pp. 31, 32. See also the use of the word in Elizabeth's Act of Supremacy, 1 Eliz., cap. i., quoted below, p. 172.

began to search the records of their past to justify it. It was easy to fasten on such words as "absolute," "supreme," "transcendent," and interpret them in the new sense, and this was done with entire ingenuousness. In fact, it may be observed generally that this method of relying on precedents has been one of the mightiest factors in the development of the English constitution. Men cited as precedents for their actions or their views words and expressions that had grown up under different surroundings. The institutions had changed, the words had not. All unconscious of the change men still cited the old words, but to justify the new order. But for this, England would not have furnished the world the greatest example of the evolution of political institutions, coupled with a conservative temper in the people and a reliance upon precedent which is unexampled in European history. In the seventeenth century especially, the effect of this process upon England's development was very great. But what is admissible, it may be, in a judge, is not equally so in a critical historian. The stream of political thought in one sense is the converse of what we find in nature. As we follow it back toward its sources we find that instead of narrowing, it becomes ever wider. Institutions that are now narrow and definite become as we trace them back indistinguishable from others that we have always considered equally definite. To ignore this fact is fatal. To read the same definiteness into the earlier institutions is not necessarily to put words into men's mouths which they never uttered, but it is to put ideas into their heads that they never dreamed of. It is hardly going too far to say that the measure of our comprehension of the development of the institutions of central government in England in the seventeenth century is our ability to remake the historical "mistakes" of Sir Edward Coke. It is hardly necessary to add, however, that our attainments should not stop there.[1] Coke's words became in time of great service, when royal pretensions had to be met by parliamentary claims, and *vice versa;* but notwithstanding it all, Coke himself "had not really grasped the conception of sovereignty."[2] For him the High Court of Parliament was simply "absolute" and transcendent; it was nothing more.[3]

On any other interpretation it is impossible to reconcile Coke's words with his own statements made at other times. How, according to the prevailing interpretation, can Coke say that Parliament's power is absolute and transcendent, and at the same time hold, as he did in Dr. Bonham's Case, "that in many cases the common law will controul acts of Parliament and some-

---

[1] "Die englische Verfassungsgeschichte ist die Geschichte eines vom mittelalterlichen zum modernen umbildenden Staatswesens. Diese Umbildung ist natürlich begleitet von einer schärferen Ausprägung der Competenzgrenzen, die im Zwielicht des Mittelalters ineinanderflossen. Es geht aber nicht an, das heutige mittaghelle Recht künstlich wieder in die Beleuchtung der Morgendämmerung zu stellen." Jellinek, *Gesetz und Verordnung*, p. 26.
[2] Figgis, *Divine Right of Kings*, p. 230.
[3] Speaking of Coke, Dr. Hatschek says: "Der Gedanke, dass das Parlament Gerichtshof sei, wird von ihm der ganzen Interpretation der parlamentarischen Geschäftsordnung und der sog. Parlamentsprivilegien zugrunde gelegt." *Eng. Staatsrecht*, vol. i. p. 240.

times adjudge them to be utterly void"?[1] The truth is that these two statements are not really contradictory: for the one is not an assertion of the legislative supremacy of Parliament; the other is not a denial of it. Coke's actions may often have been capricious, as has been charged, but his legal and political theory was not so. Statements like the one in Bonham's Case were not, as has often been intimated, vagaries, due to caprice or temporary excitement, out of relation with his general teachings, isolated statements of a theory contrary to and incompatible with the generally accepted beliefs of the time. In reality, his statements were all of a piece and all easily reconcilable under the then prevalent theory of parliamentary "supremacy."

Evidence is found all through Coke's writings that the foregoing statements contain his true view of parliamentary institutions in England.[2] He never recognized the antithesis between legislation and adjudication by which the moderns have interpreted him.

As the conflict between King and Parliament grew closer, statements of Parliament's supremacy became more frequent, but on the very eve of Parliament's great practical demonstration of its legislative sovereignty, and in fact long after that, men kept on citing the old precedents for judicial supremacy, and it is often clear that they themselves did not notice that

---

[1] 8 *Reports*, 118.
[2] For example, see in addition to the references already given, 4 *Inst.*, 37-41, 43 (where he speaks of "Acts of Parliament enrolled in *other Courts*"), and 4 *Reports*, Introduction, p. v.

the legislative power they were actually advocating was anything different from the old powers of the High Court of Parliament.[1] The ship-money case is especially noteworthy in this respect. "I agree," said Sir Robert Berkley in that case, "the parliament to be a most ancient and supreme court, where the king and peers, as judges, are in person, and the whole body of the commons representatively."[2] Again: "I confess, that by the fundamental law of England, the parliament is 'commune concilium regis et regni,' that it is the greatest, the most honourable and supreme court in the kingdom; that no man ought to think any dishonourable thing of it: yet give me leave to say, that it is but a Concilium."[3] So also Sir William Jones, in an elaborate argument to justify the ship-money writs, urged that in the defence of the realm the King should be the judge of the means, even though his judgement might be expressed through his other judges: "We are judges cumulative, not primitive; so he is the supreme judge. In the parliament the king is the sole judge, the rest are but advisers. . . . So, as I have said before, he is the only supreme judge of the danger himself, and of the way of prevention, whether by his council or by his parliament."[4]

---

[1] See, for example, *Rushworth*, vol. i. p. 690; Sir J. Eliot's *Apology for Socrates*, in *Old South Leaflets*, p. 13. See also the trial of Sir J. Eliot and others for seditious speeches in Parliament, 3 *St. Tr.*, 296, 300, 309, 310 (1629).
[2] 3 *State Trials*, 1098.
[3] *Ibid.*, 1101.
[4] *Ibid.*, 1184.

The last of these instances is particularly interesting because it shows a characteristic lack of definition of judicial and legislative parliamentary acts. The King is the fountain of justice, and Parliament men are only his assistants in judicature; and for that reason he is to be the supreme "judge" of public measures for defence of the realm. It would be hard to find in the middle ages a better example of the fusion of the legislative and judicial; for it is to be noted that Sir William Jones is not talking about trial of peers, or parliamentary privilege, or hearings on appeal, or even private bill procedure. He is talking about something that would be to-day purely legislative.

These instances have come from the King's judges, who might be expected to have some leanings toward any doctrine that was opposed to parliamentary legislative sovereignty, but like opinions may be found on the other side as well. For example, St. John said: "If an erroneous Judgment was given before the statute of 27 Eliz. in the King's-bench, the King could not relieve his grieved subject any way but by Writ of Error in parliament: neither can he out of parliament alter the old laws, or make new, or make any Naturalizations or Legitimations, nor do some other things: and yet is the parliament his Majesty's Court too, as well as other his Courts of Justice,"[1] etc. In 1641 St. John, who was chosen by the Commons to present to the Lords their reasons for passing the Bill of Attain-

[1] 3 *St. Tr.*, 862.

der against the Earl of Strafford, made a statement which seems to mark the transition from the old idea to the new. After pointing out that there are two grounds for every judgement, either the law in being "or else the use of the same Power for making new Laws, whereby the old at first received life," and discussing briefly the first of these, he says, in regard to the second: "My Lords, in the other Consideration of using the Supream Power, the same Law gives Power to the Parliament to make New Lawes, that enables the Inferiour Court to Judge according to the Old. The Rules that guides the Conscience of the Inferiour Court is from without, the Prescripts of the Parliament, and of the Common Law; in the other, the Rule is from within, that *Salus populi* be concerned, that there be no wilful oppression of any of the Fellow-Members, that no more Blood be taken then what is necessary for the Cure, the Lawes and Customs of the Realm as well enable the Exercise of this, as of the Ordinary and Judicial Power.

"My Lords, What hath been said, is because that this proceeding of the Commons by way of Bill, implies the use of the meer Legislative Power, in respect new Laws are for the most part past by Bill.

"This, my Lords, though just and legal, and therefore not wholly excluded; yet it was not the only ground that put the Commons upon the Bill, they did not intend to make a new Treason, and to Condemn my Lord of *Strafford* for it; they had in it other considerations likewise, which were to this effect.

"*First*, The Commons knew, that in all former Ages, if doubts of Law arose of great and general Concernments, the Parliament was usually consulted withal for resolution, which is the reason that many Acts of Parliament are only Declarative of the Old Law, not Introductive of a New, as the Great *Charter* of our Liberties; the Statute of Five and twentieth year of *Edward* the Third of Treasons; The Statute of the Prerogative, and of late the Petition of Right; if the Law were doubtful in this Case, they perceived the Parliament (where the old way is altered, and new Laws made) the fittest Judge to clear this Doubt."[1]

We seem to see in this the old judicial idea jostled by the new conception of "meer Legislative Power." St. John evidently considers a bill of attainder essentially judicial in character, for he hastens to justify it by precedents that are judicial, and to explain that the Commons do not intend to make a new treason, nor to "decline your Lordships Justice in the Judicial way." He sees, however, a sharp contrast between judicial and legislative power, which he is under the necessity of trying to explain. Such a necessity would not have occurred to a lawyer half a century earlier. His explanation is vague, of course, but who can say with certainty, even to-day, whether a bill of attainder was really judicial or legislative? The new idea had, in fact, now to be reckoned with. It was expressed in the

[1] Rushworth, *Strafford's Trial*, p. 676.

PARLIAMENT AS A COURT

course of the same trial by Lord Digby with reference to bills of attainder, in words that can hardly be improved upon: "I know, Mr. Speaker, there is in Parliament a double Power of Life and Death by Bill, a Judicial Power, and a Legislative; the measure of the one, is what's legally just; of the other, what is Prudentially and Politickly fit for the good and preservation of the whole. But these two, under favour, are not to be confounded in Judgment: We must not piece up want of legality with matter of convenience, nor the defailance of prudential fitness with a pretence of Legal Justice."[1]

This is one of the earliest clear statements as to the nature of that "positive completeness" which the "supreme" legislature has, but the "supreme" court has not, as to the difference between *jus dare* and *jus dicere*. It expressed the difference between judicial and legislative power in a way that has hardly even yet been entirely realized in England, in theory at least. From such a statement it is but a step to the declaration that "no Bill of Attainder or *ex post facto* Law shall be passed."[2]

But the old idea did not lose its effect at once. It was asserted by Twysden,[3] James Howell,[4] Hakewell,[5]

---

[1] Rushworth, *Strafford's Trial*, p. 53.
[2] *Constitution of the United States*, art i. sec. 9.
[3] *On the Government of England* (Camden Society), pp. 129, 131.
[4] *Somers Tracts*, vol. v. pp. 48, 51.
[5] *Modus Tenendi Parliamentum*, pp. 32, 33.

THE HIGH COURT OF PARLIAMENT

Judge Jenkins,[1] Nathaniel Bacon,[2] Petyt,[3] and others.

Prynne's *Soveraigne Power of Parliaments and Kingdomes* is particularly important. It was printed by order of the House of Commons in 1643, and probably sums up, better than any other writing we have, the constitutional views of the men who dominated the earlier sessions of the Long Parliament, and exhibits the theoretical basis of the revolution of the seventeenth century in England in its earlier stages.

If some of the leaders of the Parliament saw that the real question at issue was supremacy and not law, not so all. And even those who were keen enough to see so far could not miss the more obvious fact that in the England of 1641 the only justification for Parliament's actions which could win popular support was the justification of precedent. Prynne, then, voiced views that Pym and the other leaders wished to express, whether these were due to real conviction or only to motives of expediency.

In the book, Prynne cites the King's promise in Magna Charta not to deny nor defer justice and right, as an argument for frequent sessions of Parliament; and also tries to justify the act depriving the King of the power to adjourn or prorogue Parliament, on the precedent of previous statutory provisions—"that the King neither by his great nor privy seale, nor by Writ

---

[1] *Works*, pp. 48, 50.
[2] *Discourse on the Laws and Government of England*, part ii. p. 14.
[3] *Jus Parliamentarium*, pp. 29, 41-3, 55, 57, 74.

PARLIAMENT AS A COURT

or Letter could without just or lawfull cause assigned, prorogue or adjourne the Terme or sitting of any Courts of Justice, much lesse prorogue or dissolve his highest Court, and grand *Councell of the Realme*, the Parliament, or disable them to sit to redresse the kingdomes and Subjects severall grievances, or secure the Realm from danger; Which if he might lawfully doe at his pleasure, without the Houses joynt assents, there would necessarily follow, not onely a deferring and deniall, but likewise a fayler of Justice in the highest Court of Justice; which these Acts disable the King (who is so farre inferior to the Law, that he cannot so much as delay the smallest proceedings of it in any Court or Session, by his supreame power, by any meanes whatsoever) to effect in his meanest Courts, much lesse then in the greatest; from whence the subversion of Lawes, Liberty, Justice, and the whole Realme would ensue."[1]

In like manner, he argues, Parliament must have the power to annul any commission or proclamation of the King, because "the like power have all other Courts of Justice within the kingdome in some degree, when such Charters and Writs of the King are brought judicially before them, because they are Courts of the *Law, to which the King and all his Actions are and must be subject.* Now that which can thus question, cancell, disannull, revoke the Kings owne Royall Charters, Writs, Commissions, Patents, &c. though ratified

[1] *Soveraigne Power*, pt. i. p. 33.

with the Great seale and regall power, even against his will, must certainely be a Soveraigne power and Authority, which in point of Law and Justice is superiour to the King."[1] The apparent speciousness of this reasoning should not blind us to its importance. It exhibits the modern doctrine in process of development from the older theory. The old judicial interpretation is here made the precedent for the new parliamentary legislation. The flaw in this argument appears only when we see that the only ground on which a court could declare a grant or a patent invalid was a ground external to the court itself and beyond its discretion, namely, the law. This power is totally different from the right to reject such a grant for reasons known only to the Parliament. In short there is here the difference between the "negative completeness" of a court and the power of a sovereign lawmaking body which is "complete on its positive side" as well. But this was a distinction which undoubtedly most of Prynne's readers were not yet ready to make in 1643, and the argument must have been an effective one.

There were some who questioned the power of Parliament legally to do business in the absence of the King. This objection Prynne answers on the same general assumption by saying: "Though he be personally absent as a man, yet he is still Legally present in Parliament, (called the *kings* presence) as he is a King; as he is in all other his Courts of Justice, where all pro-

[1] *Soveraigne Power*, p. 34; see also p. 46.

PARLIAMENT AS A COURT

ceedings are entred, *Coram Rege*, though the King never yet sate personally in either of them."[1]

Prynne uses the same kind of an argument against those who deny the legality of a Parliament from which the bishops are excluded. "One puny Judge in the Courts of *Westminster* may and doth usually give judgement, and make binding Orders, though the Chiefe Justice and his Fellowes be negligently or wilfully absent: Much more then may the Lords and Commons now present, doe the like, in case of the Kings and other Members wilfull absence, of purpose to ruine both Parliament and Kingdome."[2] So he argues also that laws made in the reign of an usurper are nevertheless good laws, "because these Lawes, *and all other Judiciall Acts in Courts of Justice*, are the Acts of the Parliament and Courts themselves, which are lawfull: not of the usurping King, who is unlawfull."[3] "There is one cleare Demonstration yet remaining," he says, "to prove the supreme power of Parliaments above Kings themselves, which is this,"—that Parliament is the highest court of appeal. "Now this is an infallible Maxime, both in the Common, Civill, and Canon Law, that *The Court or person to whom the last appeale is to be made is the Supreamest power*."[4]

Again, the Resolutions against the King's Commis-

[1] *Soveraigne Power*, pt. i. p. 42.
[2] *Ibid.*, pt. i. p. 44.
[3] *Ibid.*, p. 49. The italics are mine.
[4] *Ibid.*, pp. 92, 93.

[157]

sions of Array, made by "the supremest Court" of Parliament, he declares to be lawful and binding on the King and every private subject; while the King's "*extrajudiciall* and illegal Declarations out of Parliament" in opposition are not to be obeyed, but are in "contempt" of Parliament's authority, and if not punished "will bring this *highest, greatest, and most honourable Court* . . . into greater contempt and lesse estimation with all men . . . then the basest Court of Pipouders is."[1]

In the same way he insists that if it is by statute treason to kill the Chancellor or any of the judges, "then much more must it be high Treason against the King and Kingdom, to warre against the highest Court of Parliament, or slay any Member of it, for doing their Offices and executing the Houses just Commands."[2]

The hazy views of the real character of parliamentary supremacy that still existed so late as 1653 are illustrated by the case of Captain John Streater, who had

---

[1] *Soveraigne Power*, pt. i. pp. 106, 107.
[2] *Ibid.*, pp. 108, 109. That the views expressed here were not entirely the result of the struggle with the King, but were an essential part of Prynne's political theory, appears in nearly all his works. For example, in his *Good old Fundamental Liberties*, he designates Parliament as *first* a council, *second* a court, and *third* a representative body to alter and repeal laws. The order is not accidental (*Introduction to the Christian Reader*). In his *Brief Register*, when stating the chief purpose of summoning Parliaments, the "promotion of publick Justice" comes before "the enacting of wholesome Laws" (pt. i. p. 434). See his *Plea for the Lords* (1658), p. 163, where he gives many valuable references, pp. 311, 312; also his *Abridgment of the Records* (1656), Preface, *passim*, where we find him using the judicial conception of Parliament to a different purpose — Parliaments which are the "best of all *Courts, Councils*, . . . when kept within their legal Bounds: so they become the greatest Mischiefs, Grievances to the Kingdom, when like the *Ocean* they overflow their banks."

PARLIAMENT AS A COURT

been committed to the Gate House by an order of the Parliament, and obtained a writ of Habeas Corpus returnable in the King's Bench. In the course of the hearing on the writ, there was much discussion of the character and efficacy of an "order of Parliament." It was insisted by the Commonwealth's counsel that "an Order hath force as well as an Act."[1] The case is the more interesting from the fact that there was no "Other House" in existence at this time. The result of the first hearing, held before the end of the short-lived Barebones Parliament, which had issued the order, was the remanding of Streater to the Gate House, the judges asserting the inability of any lower court to question what Parliament had done. "If the parliament should do one thing," said Chief Justice Rolle, "and we do the contrary here, things would run round."[2] To the objection of Streater's counsel that "the parliament hath not power to alter the laws," the Chief Justice answered: "Why, they have the legislative power, and may alter and order in such sort as they please; they may daily. If they find any thing that is fit to be reformed, they may alter and reform them, and make laws new. It is strange a counsellor should say this." To the objection that there was no cause of commitment in the Parliament's order, the Chief Justice answered: "It is true, here there is not. We are judges of the law, and may call inferior courts to an account.... In this case,

---
[1] 5 *St. Tr.*, 386.
[2] *Ibid.*

if the cause should come before us, we cannot examine it, whether it be true or unjust: they have the legislative power." As to the objection that this was but an order and not three times read in Parliament, he asks: "How can you tell but that it has been three times read?... But if it were but once read, we cannot call it into question, but must conceive it was on just grounds."[1] On the same point Judge Nichols also answered: "Why, their power is a law, and we cannot dispute any such thing. And whereas you affirm it was once pleaded here 'that the King was above the law, and might do what he pleased against the law,' that it was so here, I do not remember: but the parliament does not so."[2] Streater then demanded that notice should be taken of the condemnation of the King's arbitrary imprisonments in the debates in Parliament in 1628 over the Judges' decision in Darnel's case. The Chief Justice's answer is remarkable: "The King was plaintiff against them, and he was but a feoffee in trust: The Parliament is plaintiff against you, and they are a legislative power." The prisoner was accordingly remanded.[3] After the Parliament had come to an end, Streater's counsel moved for a new writ, and obtained it. The question now turned on whether a man could be detained on Parliament's order after the dissolution of the Parliament. The Attorney-General argued that "when kings die, it is true, that

[1] 5 *St. Tr.*, 386, 387.
[2] *Ibid.*, 387.
[3] *Ibid.*, 388.

Commissions do cease; but when Parliaments do dissolve, their acts do not cease. Besides, a parliament is the Supreme Court, and they do constitute other courts; and therefore it is not for other courts to question the proceedings of a parliament."[1] It was answered that "an Act or Order of parliament is not a Judgment of parliament. We are here *coram Protectore*."[2] The court took the latter view, and Streater was admitted to bail.

In 1642, when Charles had replied to Parliament's passage of the ordinance concerning the militia, and had commanded his subjects to pay no attention to the ordinance, the Lords had in turn protested "that when parliament, which is the supreme court of this kingdom, shall declare what the law of the land is, to have that not only questioned and controverted, but contradicted, and a command that it should not be obeyed, is a breach of the privilege of parliament."[3] In Hobbes's *Behemoth* this statement is commented on as follows: "I thought that he that makes the law, ought to declare what the law is. For what is it else to make a law, but to declare what it is. So that they have taken from the King not only the militia, but also the legislative power."[4] An even more interesting example of the transition from the old to the new is found in Filmer's *Freeholder's Grand Inquest:* "Every Su-

[1] 5 *St. Tr.*, 392.
[2] *Ibid.*, 393.
[3] *Parl. Hist.*, vol. ii. p. 1134.
[4] *English Works* (Molesworth), vol. vi. p. 290. See also 13 *St. Tr.*, 1428, for a similar statement.

preme Court must have the Supreme Power, and the Supreme Power is alwayes Arbitrary; for that is Arbitrary which hath no Superiour on Earth to controll it. The last Appeal in all Government, must still be to an Arbitrary Power, or else Appeals will be *in Infinitum*, never at an end. The *Legislative Power* is an *Arbitrary Power*, for they are *termini convertibiles*.

"The main Question in these our dayes is, *Where this Power Legislative remains?*"[1] Filmer's answer, of course, is that it remains in the King.

"The high court of parliament," wrote Sir Matthew Hale, "consisting of the king and both houses, is the supreme and only supreme court of this kingdom, from which there is no appeal. Wherever the dernier resort is, there must needs be the sovereignty; and so this word is constantly used and joined with it."[2] This might almost pass for sixteenth century doctrine, but he adds, a few lines later: "Again, if this should be, that the supreme jurisdiction without appeal, the dernier resort, were to the house of lords, then is the legislative power virtually and consequentially there also; or at least that power lodged in the king and both houses were insignificant. For what if the lords will give judgment against an act of parliament, or declare it null and void? If they have the dernier resort, this declaration or judgment must be observed and obeyed and submitted unto irremediably; for no appeal lies

[1] Page 40.
[2] *Jurisdiction of the Lords House*, p. 205.

PARLIAMENT AS A COURT

from their judgment, if they be the supreme court. And if it be said, this shall not be presumed they will do: I say, if this position were true, they may if they will."[1]

He argues that "the high court of parliament consisting of the king and both the houses of parliament are certainly the only supreme court of this kingdom, to whom the divolution of the last appeal or dernier resort doth belong," for, he says, "it is utterly inconsistent with the very frame of a government, that the supreme power of making laws should be in the king with the advice of both his houses of parliament, and judgment should be in one of the houses without the king and the other. A supreme power of making laws should be thus in the king, and monarchical; and the supreme decisive power or jurisdiction and dernier resort should be radically in the lords, and so aristocratical. Therefore it is not only *de facto* true in our government, but it is most necessary, that the supreme decisive power or jurisdiction and the dernier resort must be where the legislative power is."[2] This conjunction of the supreme court and the legislature Harrington also asserted: "Wherever the power of making Law is, there only is the power of interpreting the Law so made."[3]

Lord Hale has been charged with confounding the

---
[1] *Jurisdiction of the Lords House*, p. 206.
[2] *Ibid.*, p. 207.
[3] *A System of Politics: Works*, p. 509.

THE HIGH COURT OF PARLIAMENT

legislative with the judicial power in parliamentary proceedings.[1] In a sense it is true, but it is easy to forget that he was in the midst of a controversy. The exclusive jurisdiction of the Lords on appeal was not as undisputed as to-day, and certainly there were some precedents against it. After all, his reasoning was not so much at fault. He was correct in saying the Lords might declare an act of Parliament invalid if they would. At the time when he wrote it was not entirely unreasonable to imagine their willingness to do so.[2] The extent of the jurisdiction of the Lords was still a matter of controversy, and the distinction between *jus dare* and *jus dicere* was by no means yet clear to all. Only since this distinction has become perfectly clear and well understood has the danger that Hale dreaded disappeared, and it is difficult to say that there were no grounds whatever for his fears, when we consider that it was well along in the nineteenth century before the question was settled definitely when the judicial business of the House of Lords should be participated in by the whole house and when by the Law Lords alone. Moreover, the line between legislative and judicial power is a very fine one. Where the two powers are exercised by the same body, they cannot always be distinguished; where they are exercised by separate bodies, there are sometimes conflicts. Even in

---

[1] *Parl. Hist.*, vol. xxviii. p. 1095.
[2] This view is strengthened by reading the proceedings of both houses through the various phases of the long struggle between them in the reign of Charles II. See the Journals of both houses, *passim*.

PARLIAMENT AS A COURT

the United States, where the distinction between the two kinds of power is felt more keenly than almost anywhere else, it is not inconceivable that the Supreme Court might at some time disregard the distinction. Some of its recent decisions seem to indicate an unconscious tendency in that direction. It was probably a fear of this "arbitrary" action, and the influence of views derived from English legal and political writers like Harrington, that led to the varying views of the early American courts on the question of the power of a court to review the acts of a legislature.[1]

In England at the present day there seems little danger of encroachment by the courts upon the legislature, or *vice versa*. Their respective spheres have become pretty definitely marked. In a fairly recent decision it was said, "What is said or done within the walls of Parliament cannot be enquired into *in a court of law*."[2] The antithesis here is sharp. There is nothing of Parliament and "*other*" courts, or Parliament and "any inferior court." Except in the well-defined cases of the Lords' judicature in cases of appeal or in the trial

---

[1] On this point see Thayer, *Legal Essays*, p. 1 et seq., *The Origin and Scope of the American Doctrine of Constitutional Law;* Brinton Coxe, *An Essay on Judicial Power and Unconstitutional Legislation;* Bryce, *American Commonwealth*, ch. xxxiii.; W. M. Meigs, *The Relation of the Judiciary to the Constitution, American Law Review*, vol. xix.; E. S. Corwin, *The Supreme Court and Unconstitutional Acts of Congress, Michigan Law Review*, vol. iv., with references there cited; *The Conflict over Judicial Powers in the United States to 1870*, by Charles Grove Haines, Ph.D. (*Columbia University Studies in History, Economics, and Public Law*). On this question the debates over the Code Civil in France during the Consulate are most instructive.

[2] Lord Coleridge, C. J., in *Bradlaugh* v. *Gossett*.

of peers, Parliament is now thought of and spoken of purely as a legislature, and even questions of privilege so far as they properly belong to the houses are hardly considered any longer as judicial. In a country where so much depends upon precedent as in England, it is impossible to say that new circumstances may not arise leading to a furbishing of the old weapons, but it is safe to say that to-day the general idea of Parliament as a court is well-nigh forgotten.

"The separation of legislative and judicial functions is a refinement in the principles of political government and jurisprudence, which can only be the result of an advanced civilization."[1]

B. The Evidence of Words

"When states are departed from their original Constitution, and that original by tract of time worn out of Memory; the succeeding Ages viewing what is past by the present, conceive the former to have been like to that they live in; and framing thereupon erroneous Propositions, do likewise make thereon erroneous Inferences and Conclusions." Thus appropriately does Sir Henry Spelman begin his account "Of Parliaments."[2]

In no nation's history has this been more true than

---

[1] May, *Parliamentary Practice*, 9th ed., p. 754. For an excellent modern argument for the old view see Anstey, *On Blackstone's Theory of the Omnipotence of Parliament: Juridical Society Papers*, vol. iii. p. 305 et seq., especially p. 322 et seq. See also Hatschek, *Englisches Staatsrecht*, vol. i. p. 546, note 1.
[2] *Reliquiae Spelmannianae*, p. 57.

PARLIAMENT AS A COURT

in English history, and in no part of English history more than in the history of Parliament. The hardest thing for a historian of institutions to do, and the thing he oftenest fails to do, is "to think away distinctions which seem to us as clear as sunshine;" and yet, as Professor Maitland says, "this we must do, not in a haphazard fashion, but of set purpose, knowing what we are doing."[1] One thing above all others has made this "thinking away" so difficult for us, and that is the slow and almost unperceived changes that have occurred in the meanings of words. To no other single factor can be attributed so many misconceptions regarding the development of our institutions. As Selden says: "We have more words than notions, half a dozen words for the same thing. Sometimes we put a new signification to an old word, as when we call a *piece*, a *gun*. The word *gun* was in use in England for an engine to cast a thing from a man, long before there was any gunpowder found out."[2] This has again and again been noted as a special characteristic of English constitutional growth. Bagehot remarked it, and had to look behind the words to see that real working constitution which he described so brilliantly. "Language," he says, "is the tradition of nations; each generation describes what it sees, but it uses words transmitted from the past. When a great entity like the British Constitution has continued in connected outward sameness, but hidden inner changes, for many

[1] *Township and Borough*, p. 11.   [2] *Table Talk*, s. v. *Language*.

ages, every generation inherits a series of inapt words—of maxims once true, but of which the truth is ceasing or has ceased. As a man's family go on muttering in his maturity incorrect phrases derived from a just observation of his early youth, so, in the full activity of an historical constitution, its subjects repeat phrases true in the time of their fathers, and inculcated by those fathers, but now true no longer. Or, if I may say so, an ancient and ever-altering constitution is like an old man who still wears with attached fondness clothes in the fashion of his youth: what you see of him is the same; what you do not see is wholly altered."[1]

"In England," Seeley says, "it is our custom to alter things, but to leave their names unaltered."[2]

This change in the meaning of words, or, as often, the indiscriminate use of one word for more than one institution, frequently gives a valuable clue to the true nature of the institutions involved. For example, we often find a word used of one institution at one period, and later apparently transferred to another institution which may now be widely different from the first. In many cases this transfer is only apparent, for a closer inspection shows that the later institution is one of a number of branches into which the earlier institution has divided, the old name adhering to only one of the branches to the exclusion of all the others, and some-

---

[1] *The English Constitution* (American edition), pp. 69, 70.
[2] *Science of Politics*, p. 298. See Hobbes, *Leviathan*, part ii. ch. xxv.; also the judicious remarks of Professor Dicey, *Law of the Constitution*, p. 17.

times to the exclusion of the original parent institution itself. Whatever the character of the change, it is usually not unreasonable, in cases where the same word is used for several institutions now different, to conclude that they have not always been thus different.[1]

Instances of this process have already been noted, but there are many others, some of them comparatively modern, which throw light on the judicial side of Parliament's development. One or two of the most important of these it may be profitable to note. The early lack of separation of powers is shown in the various meanings of the word "assize;"[2] the fixity of early law by the word *établissement* (*stabilimentum*), which was long used in France; to say nothing of our own "statute." For more recent times a more important instance occurs in the different meanings formerly and to a certain extent still attaching to the word "jurisdiction." Prynne says that court which can question and banish or execute the King's greatest officers "must questionlesse be the highest *power and jurisdiction in the realme.*"[3] He speaks also of Parliament's "power and jurisdiction" in reforming the abuses of the King's menial servants and the expenses of his court,[4] and again of Parliament's "Sovereigne Power and Jurisdiction in making and

---

[1] On this point see Hearn, *Government of England*, 1st ed., pp. 260, 261.
[2] See Spelman, *Glossary*, and Du Cange, s. v. *Assisa; Oxford Dictionary*, s. v. *Assize;* Gneist, *Const. Hist.* (Ashworth's English translation), vol. i. p. 287, note; Stubbs, *Constitutional History*, vol. i. pp. 614-18, and p. 614, note 1.
[3] *Soveraigne Power of Parliaments and Kingdoms*, pt. i. p. 88.
[4] *Ibid.*, p. 89.

proclaiming Warre or Peace."[1] In like manner, he says the English Parliament has discussed and settled questions connected with "the Title and jurisdiction of the Crowne of Scotland."[2] In his *Fundamental Liberties* he speaks of "the Legislative Tax-imposing Power" as "the inseparable incommunicable Jurisdiction of our Parliaments alone."[3]

Clarendon speaks of "the temper of the people, the extent of the courts of law, and the jurisdiction of Parliaments, which at that time had never committed any excess of jurisdiction."[4]

It is clear that making general law, — so far as it was conceived that law was "made," — as well as the decision of particular cases, could then have been included under "jurisdiction," even when that word was used technically. Hale says so directly: "Jurisdiction," he says, "may be taken two ways. I. Less properly for acts of voluntary jurisdiction, which also takes in making constitutions and orders and ordinances. II. Properly for that judicial and coercive power *in foro contentioso*."[5]

Closely allied to "jurisdiction" is "judgement." There is abundant evidence that in Tudor times, and later, "judgement" was used of things we call legislative, as

[1] *Soveraigne Power*, pt. i. p. 90.
[2] *Ibid.*, pt. i. p. 98.
[3] Part i. p. 92.
[4] *History of the Rebellion*, book i.
[5] *Jurisdiction of the Lords House*, p. 30. See also 4 *Inst.*, Proemium. So a writer in 1684 speaks of Parliament as "the highest Judicature in this Kingdom," when he is evidently thinking of it in a "legislative" capacity. *Harleian Miscellany*, vol. v. p. 551 (ed. of 1745).

well as of things judicial. So John Knox says in 1558: "It is evident, that her [Deborah's] judgement or gouernement in Israel was no such usurped power."[1] Earlier, in Coverdale's version of the Psalms, we find, "I haue chosen the way of treuth thy judgments haue I layed before me."[2] In King James's version we find, "Now these are the *Judgements* which thou shalt set before them," where Coverdale, the Geneva and the Bishops' Bible have "lawes."[3] So also Lord Ellesmere in his speech in the Case of the *Postnati*, referred to above, speaks of the statute authorizing commissioners to treat with the Scots concerning the Union as "the judgement of the parliament."[4]

The words of Sir John Eliot are very explicit: "In this first & strickter signification [of *judicium*] it intends a power of Judicature; ye decision & determination of all home causes & controversies iudiciall, wch sence & acceptation is soe vulgar, as it needs noe authoritie to confirme it.... Yet there it does not terminat, as if merely it were design'd an Art of Judicature, & Justice, which haue proprietie wth in it. but it goes further, likewise to the larger sence & meaning which intends a power of gouerment, & soe it is the same wth *potestas* & *Imperium; summa potestas, summum imperium*, & *iudicium summum*, being paranomasia & Identities, hav-

---

[1] *First Blast of the Trumpet* (Arber's ed.), p. 41, quoted in the *Oxford Dictionary*, s. v. *Judgment*.
[2] Psalm cxix., quoted in *Oxford Dictionary* as above.
[3] Exodus xxi. 1, *Oxford Dictionary* as above.
[4] 2 *St. Tr.*, 662.

ing the selfe same sense and signification in the same latitude & extent."[1]

The oath imposed by Elizabeth's Act of Supremacy upon all holding office ecclesiastical or secular under the Crown brings out strongly the meaning of several important words. They had to swear that the Queen was "the only Supream Governor" of the realm and all her dominions in things both temporal and ecclesiastical, "and that no foreign Prince, Person, Prelate, State or Potentate, hath or ought to have any Jurisdiction, Power, Superiority, Preheminence, or Authority" in the realm, and to renounce and forsake "all foreign Jurisdictions, Powers, Superiorities and Authorities,"[2] etc. Commenting upon it Nathaniel Bacon says: "Now in regard *Offences and Enormities* are properly against Laws, the power to *visit* and *correct*, must also be regulated according to Laws, either of War, or Peace: Nor do these five words *Jurisdiction, Power, Superiority, Pre-eminence,* and *Authority,* contain any more *Supremacy,* or other sence; for two of them speak onely the Rank or Degree of the Queen in Government, *viz. Superiority* and *Pre-eminence* belongeth onely to her, and not to any other Foreign Power. And two other words do note her Right and Title thereto, by *Power* and *Authority* committed to her. And the other word denotes the thing wherein she hath *Superiority* and *Power, viz.* in *Jurisdiction:*

---

[1] *The Monarchie of Man* (ed. by Grosart), vol. ii. pp. 35, 37.
[2] 1 Eliz., cap. 1.

the nature of which word Ulpian (speaking of the nature of a mixt Government) explaineth thus: *Quando servata dictione juris judiciorum fit animadversio.* So as this *Supreme Authority in Jurisdiction,* is no other than *Supreme Power to visit correct, redress Offences,* or determine matters of doubt, by deputing fit persons to that end and purpose according to the Law; and this is all the *Supremacy* that appeareth to me, belongeth to the Crown in these times."[1]

C. THE EVIDENCE FURNISHED BY THE BEGINNINGS OF THE COMMONS AND THE EARLY ORGANIZATION OF PARLIAMENT

THE early English jury has always been to Englishmen and to others an object of admiration and investigation and a source of despair. Few things are more interesting or more important, and few more obscure. There is now no danger of confounding it, as was formerly done,[2] with the ancient suitors who pronounced the "judgement" under the old Germanic procedure. It is distinguished also from the *secta*, or suit witnesses, which a complainant might in early times be required to produce to strengthen his allegations, surviving to modern times in the conclusion of the declaration, " and therefore he brings his suit," etc. The ultimate acceptance of the inquisition, it is now believed,

---

[1] *Discourse of the Laws and Government of England,* part ii. p. 162. The second part of this book, from which this passage is taken, was first published in 1651. (*D. N. B., Nathaniel Bacon.*)

[2] Cf. the statements made by Erskine in his argument for a new trial in the great case of the Dean of St. Asaph's in 1784. 21 *St. Tr.*, 974 et seq., *Erskine's Speeches.*

THE HIGH COURT OF PARLIAMENT

was due more to royal than to popular pressure.[1] Unlike the *sectatores* or the compurgators, the members of the inquest were chosen by the King. Unlike the old suitors in the County Court, they pronounced no "judgement," but merely a statement of fact, a *vere dictum*, a verdict, while the King's judge now pronounced the judgement. It is clear that the *inquisitio* must be distinguished in origin and in character from these institutions that seem in some points so closely to resemble it. Unlike them, the recognition was "a body of impartial men, summoned by an officer of the law, to speak the truth"[2] concerning some matter. But, on the other hand, it is extremely improbable that these other forms of procedure were totally without influence upon the development of their new rival. "Things indicate," Professor Thayer says, "the breaking up and confusing of older forms; anomalies and mixed methods present themselves. The separate notions of the complaint *secta*, the fellow-swearers, the business witnesses, the community witnesses, and the jurors of the inquisition and the assize run together."[3]

Originally, in the King's courts, as in other courts, the King or his officer merely presided. He regulated the procedure; he did not pronounce the judgement. That was the work of the suitors. In the period immediately following the Conquest this appears to have

---

[1] There is probably less emphasis put upon the royal element than was the case a few years ago.
[2] Bigelow, *History of Procedure*, p. 334.
[3] *Preliminary Treatise on Evidence*, p. 18.

PARLIAMENT AS A COURT

been true of all the King's courts from the highest to the lowest. Nothing is more obscure, and hardly anything more important, than the process by which this procedure was changed into one where the King's officer is no longer a mere moderator, but a real judge; where he no longer asks for a "judgement" from the qualified suitors, but instead demands a *verdict* from a definite number of selected and impartial men. "The gradual intrusion of the sworn inquest, of the nascent trial by jury, soon begins to transfigure those courts in which the king presides by himself or his commissioners; justices and jurors begin to take the place of president and doomsmen, and this process is so rapid that we have nowadays some difficulty in describing the ancient courts without using foreign or archaic terms."[1]

Probably the most important consequence of this change was the growth of a distinction between law and fact. In all the older courts, where the suitors pronounced the judgement, in the *enquête par tourbe*, where the men of the fief declared what the custom was, no distinction was made, because it was unnecessary to make any, between law and fact. Traces of this remained in England in the rule that the existence of special customs should be declared not by the judges, but by twelve men.[2] But the juries that we find developed in England under Henry II, and apparently in Normandy

---

[1] *Pollock and Maitland*, 2d ed., vol. i. pp. 548, 549.
[2] Blackstone, *Comm.*, vol. i. p. 76; *Doctor and Student*, Dialogue I., ch. x.; Noy, *Maxims*, p. 18.

[175]

in the time of his father,[1] seem in practice to have confined themselves mainly to what we should call "matters of fact." This does not, however, imply the modern nice discrimination between law and fact. The line between the two may have been recognized,—some such distinction was prerequisite to the new powers and duties of the King's justices,—but as yet it was a very indefinite line.[2] The Grand Assize, for example, decided the *fact* of seisin, but there was law in that decision just as there is law in a jury's verdict in a case of criminal libel since Fox's Libel Act. The distinctive nature of the early inquest lay in the character of its members and in the method of choosing them, rather than in the subject-matter of their findings.

It is not strange, then, that the indefiniteness of law and fact in the older courts should leave its traces on the new *inquisitio* which grew up in those courts; and the mistake, so fundamental in English history, of con-

[1] Charles H. Haskins, *The Early Norman Jury: American Historical Review*, vol. viii. p. 616 et seq.
[2] The indefiniteness of the whole matter in the middle ages is not very surprising in the light of Lord Mansfield's great embarrassment in 1770, when Lord Camden propounded to him in the House of Lords his six questions on the duties of the jury in cases of criminal libel, the most searching of which was probably this: "Does the opinion [Lord Mansfield's recent opinion in granting a new trial in Woodfall's Case, although the jury had brought in a verdict of 'Guilty of printing and publishing *only*'] mean to declare, that in the case above mentioned, where the jury have delivered in their verdict guilty, that this verdict has found the fact only, and not the law?" 16 *Parl. Hist.*, 1321, 1322. See also *Annual Register* for 1771, pp. 34–6. "The dismay and confusion of Lord Mansfield was obvious to the whole audience" (Walpole, *Memoirs*, vol. ii. ch. xviii.), and he refused to make any answer or to agree upon any definite time to do so. Campbell's *Chief Justices*, ch. xxxvi.; May, *Constitutional History*, ch. ix.; Stephen, *History of the Criminal Law*, vol. ii. p. 324 et seq.

founding this *inquisitio* with feudal trial by peers was, after all, a very natural one.[1] For, in addition to what has been stated, there is an element—and a most important element—that is common to *enquête par tourbe* and jury, namely, their communal character. It is the essence of the decision given by the *enquête par tourbe* that it is at once a single and a collective decision. So also the continuity of the jury as an institution has depended on the fact that the verdict of the jurors was both single and collective. If the jurors had ever been questioned as single witnesses, their answers would have become mere separate bits of testimony instead of a verdict, and the jury would have disappeared in England as it did on the Continent. The jurors were, on the contrary, never mere witnesses. They were, from the very beginning, "representatives." The *vere dictum* to which they swore was not their individual opinion; it was the common belief of the countryside, and so this mode of trial was spoken of as *"per pais."*

This communal or representative element is no adventitious thing: it is an essential part of the institution itself, and was so from the beginning. Furthermore, the *inquisitio* was not a mere judicial instrument, in our modern technical meaning of judicial. We have been so influenced by the long subsequent history of the jury in matters now called judicial, that we are in danger of losing the fact that it was used originally for

[1] This mistake began very early. See Pollock and Maitland, *History of English Law*, 2d ed., vol. ii. p. 625, note 2, with references.

other purposes too. Henry II and his successors got their information from representatives. They were the representatives of the countryside, the *"pais,"* summoned before the King's councillors, the itinerant justices, in the full county court. The "presentment" made by these representatives was a statement of what was generally believed by the "country" concerning the matters on which the King desired information. These matters were whatever the King considered sufficiently important to him to instruct his itinerant justices to investigate. They might include such apparently particular facts as the case of a man appealed of murder, or a quarrel concerning property; or they might be general, such as a tax assessment or a presentment of all offences generally believed to have occurred since the last visitation. In the instructions to the itinerant justices in 1194 we find that the King or his ministers desire information on oath concerning such things as pleas of the crown, escheats, churches in the gift of the King, guardianship of minors where the King was interested, murderers of the Jews, and, what was more important to Richard, the pledges that had been in the possession of these Jewish money-lenders,[1] etc. If we wish to include activities so diverse as these under the one word "judicial," its meaning must be far wider and more comprehensive than the one we now give it.[2]

[1] *Form of Proceeding in the Judicial Visitation in 1194*, Stubbs, *S. C.*, p. 258.
[2] The promiscuous use of the inquest in the Angevin period shows that it was used indifferently to discover facts that we should label fiscal or judicial, and many that can hardly be properly put in either class. The men of that day made

PARLIAMENT AS A COURT

Historically, these different classes of cases may not all have come under the *inquisitio* at once. As we have seen, the jury may have been first applied to some with consent of parties, to others under pretence of a failure of justice in other courts, or even by a mere act of power. However that may have been, the *inquisitio* when once applied is applied to all, whether they be particular or general, "judicial," fiscal, or what not. Investigation shows that even our obvious distinction between the grand and the petty jury arose only when

no such distinctions. The subsequent history of the inquest in judicial matters in England, and the great place it occupied in the minds of men like Fortescue or Sir Thomas Smith as a national institution, are likely to obscure the undoubted fact that originally it was used for many purposes which we should call non-judicial. We no longer employ it, in the original form at least, in the assessment of taxes. We do use it in the presentment of crimes; but it is a mistake to think that originally the judicial use was any more characteristic than the fiscal. In fact, Brunner has shown that its origin is probably to be sought in the fiscal machinery of Charles the Great.

The attempt is sometimes made to push back into the earliest Angevin times a clear distinction such as existed later between the ordinary "judicial" business of the itinerant justices and that of the "General Eyre" which occurred at longer intervals and was concerned with "business of all sorts, not merely judicial." See, for example, A. T. Carter, *History of English Legal Institutions*, pp. 67, 68 (3d ed.). This distinction is one which arose only after Parliament had begun to take from the itinerant justices the "non-judicial" business which at an earlier date had constituted such a large part of their duties. See, generally, Holdsworth, *H. E. L.*, vol. i. pp. 115, 116; *Assize of Northampton*, chs. vi., viii., ix., xi. (Stubbs, *S. C.*, p. 152), Stubbs, *Historical Introductions to the Rolls Series*, p. 124 et seq.; *Select Charters*, p. 142; Madox, *Exchequer*, ch. iii. sec. x. (pp. 140-3 in ed. of 1769).

The provision in chapter eighteen of John's charter that the three possessory assizes should be held in the various counties before *justiciarii* sent out for that especial purpose does not imply the existence in 1215 of a general distinction between "judicial" and other administrative business. Cf. ch. viii. of the Articles of the Barons (Stubbs, *S. C.*, p. 291), and chs. xiii., xv., of Henry III's second reissue (Stubbs, *S. C.*, p. 345). See Mr. McKechnie's commentary on this provision, *Magna Carta*, p. 317 et seq.

men began to see that a presentment of common belief might be incorrect *in fact*. But even when the presentment had thus become traversable, it was not felt at once that the same jury which had sworn to common rumour should not also swear again to their opinion of the truth of the rumour. It was some time before a second jury was thought necessary.

The questions put by the judges to the people under oath must at times have been terribly searching. Rather than face them, we are told that the men of Cornwall in the year 1233 took to the woods.[1] The reason for this terror on the part of the subjects is also, in part at least, the explanation of the eagerness of the King to extend the operation of the *inquisitio* over so many different things. A few far-seeing men like Henry II might appreciate the value of the concentration of judicial administration which resulted from it, but all could see the financial advantage. Trial of causes meant profits. Justice and the profits of justice were synonymous to most feudal lords. Fees and fines were among the most important of their possessions.[2] The English court and the English realm were not different from their neighbours in this. Under the Norman kings "it was mainly for the sake of the profits that justice was administered at all."[3]

---

[1] *Ann. Dunst.* (*Annales Monastici*, Rolls Series, vol. iii. p. 135), quoted by Pollock and Maitland, vol. i. p. 202.

[2] Esmein, *Histoire de Droit Français*, p. 261.

[3] Stubbs, *C. H.*, vol. i. p. 418; Madox, *Exchequer*, chs. xii., xiv. The famous fortieth chapter of Magna Charta—*Nulli vendemus, nulli negabimus, aut differemus,*

PARLIAMENT AS A COURT

The significant points in the character of the early jury, therefore, are, first, that it was a royal means of ascertaining the general belief of a district on *any* subject desirable to know; and secondly, that it was a means involving the choosing of certain representative persons to "present" that general belief to the King's officers. But the difficulty was to find men who knew the things generally talked about, but who were at the same time "representative men." In questions concerning title this was simple enough. The substantial landed proprietors would be the best judges of questions of that kind; and so the Grand Assize, which was used in those cases, was composed exclusively of knights. But in many other matters, especially cases of alleged wrong-doing, there was greater difficulty. Those in the district who were most likely to know the kind of gossip which would form the basis of a presentment would in many cases not be the most trustworthy element of the population. It was necessary,

rectum aut justitiam—shows that the barons considered this one of their grievances. They were determined to stop the encroachments of the King's court on their own jurisdictions. The main aim was probably not, as was formerly assumed, to protect the poor from the oppression of exorbitant fees; it was rather to make it unprofitable for the King to draw cases into his courts. The chapter is closely related to chapter thirty-four, *Breve quod vocatur PRAECIPE de cetero non fiat alicui de aliquo tenemento unde liber homo amittere possit curiam suam.* They were both in the interest of the barons. Hence it is that Professor Jenks thinks this chapter thirty-four as really a hindrance to the advance of English liberty. *The Myth of Magna Carta: Independent Review*, 1904. There can be no doubt that it shut men out from the advantages of the King's courts and forced them back upon the inferior and often biased courts of the great nobles, from which they only escaped in time by a series of fictions invented by the King's judges themselves. See McKechnie, *Magna Carta*, p. 405 et seq.

however, that the justices' time be not wasted in investigating idle tales, or worse. The representatives must be credible as well as informed. We find, therefore, in the plea rolls instances where the jury is made up of two classes of persons,—those who furnish the facts, and those whose standing gives these facts sufficient credibility to furnish the basis of further proceedings. For example, in 1202, we find the plaintiff in a case conceding "that a jury may be made ... by lawful knights *and men who know the truth of the matter.*"[1] Notwithstanding this, the verdict is a single one. The facts may be directly known by only part of the jurors, but they are sworn to by all alike. This of course implies, within the jury itself, a process of examination and sifting of evidence by the knights before the final collective verdict is reached. There is thus in the very essence of the early jury, besides the mere duty of presenting facts, a representative function, and also a third function, which Maitland calls the "quasi-judicial element."[2]

These proceedings thus held before the justices

---

[1] *Select Civil Pleas* (Selden Society), No. 132. See also Bracton, lib. iii. cap. 22 (folio 143), where *juratores* and *villatae* are mentioned. The *juratores* and *villatae* are also referred to in chapter i. of the *Assize of Clarendon* (Stubbs, *S. C.*, p. 143). For discussions of the difference between *juratores* and *villatae*, see Starkie, *On Trial by Jury*, p. 25; Pollock and Maitland, *H. E. L.*, 2d ed., vol. ii. p. 644 et seq.; *Y. B. 12 and 13 Edward III* (Rolls Series), Mr. Pike's Preface, pp. lxxi, lxxii; Maitland, *Pleas of the Crown for the County of Gloucester*, Introduction, pp. xlii-xliv; and especially the remarks and citations of Professor Gross in his preface to the *Select Cases from the Coroners' Rolls* (Selden Society), pp. xxx-xxxiv.

[2] Pollock and Maitland, *History of English Law*, 2d ed., vol. ii. p. 624.

PARLIAMENT AS A COURT

itinerant were distinctly anti-feudal in character, and were strenuously objected to by the barons;[1] but the inquisitions of knights that reported periodically in this way to the King's officers have been generally recognized as an important stage in the history of English representative institutions. The character of the business dealt with on the circuits of these officers, or justices, is known mainly from the directions issued by the King to the justices mentioning the things to be investigated, and from the records of cases that have survived to our day. We have, so far as I know, no record of any petitions of a general nature presented by the knights to the King through these justices in eyre, but this is no evidence that the knights might not *complain* in their representative capacity of jurymen as well as swear to a presentment of criminals. Such things would not be so likely to be preserved as, for example, the records of concrete cases on which property rights depended.[2]

It is worthy of note, in passing, that after the Com-

---

[1] E. g. *Magna Charta*, cap. 34. Sir Robert Cotton believed that the Commons were first summoned to the Parliaments to weaken the power of the barons. It was a blow at their power, just as was the encroachment of the royal justice upon the manorial courts, which was accomplished largely through the agency of the jury. See Sir Robert Cotton's *Brief Discourse concerning the Power of the Peers and Commons of Parliament in Point of Judicature: Cottoni Posthuma*, p. 345 et seq., especially p. 349. Prynne combats this view in the preface of his *Abridgment of the Records*.

[2] Sir Erskine May says in reference to the period before Edward I, when the first parliamentary petitions appear: "It is conjectured that the parties aggrieved came personally before the council, or preferred their complaints in the country before the inquests composed of officers of the Crown." *Parl. Practice*, 9th ed., p. 606.

mons had become a regular part of Parliament, the petitions in the Rolls are directed to the King or the Council, just as would undoubtedly have been the case in the county court; for the itinerant justices were judges *coram rege*, and as such were, as we have seen, members of the King's Council.

It must surely be considered no great innovation if a King should at some time ask these "representative" knights to bring their information—and possibly their complaints—collectively before the assembled Council instead of before its members when scattered on circuit.[1]

[1] The first instance recorded is in 1213. "Before his [Edward I's] reign I have reason to believe that parties came up from the shires before the Council, and sometimes in great numbers, or their complaints were communicated to Parliament by inquests, which were brought down by various Officers of the Council; these inquests we may call examinations of witnesses." Testimony of Sir Francis Palgrave, in *Report on Public Petitions: Parl. Papers*, Session of 1833, vol. xii. p. 20. For a case of a jury ordered to appear before the Council in the reign of Edward I, see Note D (pp. 251, 252). An interesting case occurred in 1330. Sir Thomas Berkely was charged with the murder of King Edward II, who had been in his custody. The case was tried before the King in Parliament. Berkely placed himself on the country. A jury of knights was summoned, who appeared "*coram Domine Rege in Parliamento suo* apud Westmonasterium," and gave verdict of acquittal. *Rot. Parl.*, vol. ii. p. 57, No. 16. Sir Matthew Hale seems justified in saying that Sir Thomas Berkely was "unquestionably a peer of the realm." *Jurisdiction of the Lords House*, p. 91; *Lords' Report*, vol. i. p. 301; Dugdale, *Summonses; D. N. B., Berkeley, Family of*. But Hatsell thought he was a knight merely (*Precedents*, 2d ed., vol. iv. p. 73, note), and it is hard to explain why the man who is generally believed to have furnished the "singular and unfruitful precedent" (Harcourt, *His Grace the Steward and Trial of Peers*, pp. 337, 338) of the trial of a peer in Parliament by a jury of knights, should himself be designated in the record upon the Rolls of Parliament as "Thomas de Berkele, Mil'." "I marvel," says Selden, "the lords permitted the lord *Berkley* to wave his peerage, and put himself *super patriam*." *Judicature in Parliament: Works*, vol. iii. col. 1603. The author of *The Case Stated concerning the Judicature of the House of Peers in the Point of Appeals* (1675) [Lord Holles (?)], considered Sir Thomas Berkley a commoner (p. 20).

PARLIAMENT AS A COURT

This must have been a far more expeditious way for the Council to dispose of much of the fiscal and other business that would ordinarily have come to it eventually from the shires; and the very frequent occurrence of ordinary litigation in the earlier rolls, to say nothing of criminal cases brought before Parliament through the process of private appeals, shows that much of this business must have been "judicial" in nature.

There can be little question that the King's main motive in thus summoning knights to his Parliaments was a desire for revenue; but this we have found equally true of his use of the itinerant justices. The revenues from "justice" were a very important part of the King's income, but there is no reason to believe that the assessment of taxes was any less prominent among the duties of the justices when they were on circuit than when they were in Parliament. The blending of judicial, fiscal, and other business is characteristic of their work *in itinere*, as it is of their duties in "The King's Council in his Parliaments."

The summoning of representatives from the towns must at first also have been for fiscal reasons largely. But in the towns that had obtained exemption from the visits of the King's officials, there was doubtless the same fusion of functions that we find in those towns which were not differentiated from the country around them. In the favoured towns the point of contact with central institutions may have been to a greater extent than elsewhere the exchequer side of the Council, but this was a difference, for the early and formative years at least, in all probability relatively unimportant in practice, and in theory no difference at all.

Thus we have in time the King's Council in his Parliaments composed of persons from two estates of the realm, joined by representatives chosen from the knights of the shires and the citizens of the towns. Probably for a good while the relations of these new members of the Parliament toward the old were not very different from the relations existing when the Council went to meet the knights instead of their going to meet the Council. Now, as before, justice was administered in the King's name, and all other acts derived their legal validity from the will of the King, to which the petitions of the Commons, like the petitions of any other men or community of men in the kingdom, were an inducement, but nothing more. Only in certain specific matters, especially certain forms of taxation, had the King promised not to act without the assent of the estates vitally interested. These relations of Council and community subsisting before and after the summoning of the knights and burgesses left a lasting mark on English central institutions. To this day the King's judges continue to attend the House of Lords, summoned as of old by a different form of summons from that of the peers, but summoned still as a constituent part of "The King's Council in his Parliaments."

Through all their history, too, the Commons have

remained the "Grand Inquest of the Nation." Judges and inquest the two houses were before they were joined; Council and Grand Inquest they remained; and this conception of their origin, their character, their duties, and their privileges serves in large measure to explain throughout the history of Parliament, not only the claims of one house against the other, but also their common claims as the "High Court of Parliament."

An instance of the influence of these ideas in a very practical way is furnished by the uncertainty concerning the effect of a prorogation or a dissolution upon an impeachment, which gave rise to almost interminable debate so late as 1790, during the trial of Warren Hastings. The points which came up for discussion there show that even at that late day the judicial and legislative functions of Parliament were by no means clearly distinguished. It was argued on the one hand that a dissolution must put an end to an impeachment, as it would to any bill. On the other hand it was said the Court of Parliament is as permanent as any of the other courts. "It is a court perpetually existing. . . . Considering it as a court, which though, like all other courts, it has certain times of acting; yet, like all other courts, it has a constant existence, and cannot be annihilated."[1] But granting that Parliament's action in such cases was judicial, did not this put it within the power of the Lords alone, by their single resolution, to put an

[1] *Parl. Hist.*, vol. xxviii. p. 1112.

end to the case and thus defeat the wishes of the Commons? The idea was indignantly repudiated in the Commons: "If it gave up this, it gave up all, and, like salt that had lost its savour, was good for nothing."[1] This looks decidedly like the same old "confusion" of legislation and adjudication. To one of the members, "Gentlemen seemed to have law in their words and will in their meaning; to talk of parliamentary law, and reason about parliamentary power;"[2] and Pitt declared: "Parliament exercised two powers,—legislative, and judicial, which had their separate and distinct limits and duration. The confusion of these powers was the principal source of all the doubts upon the present question."[3]

It is true that with the extension of wealth and culture among the non-noble, and the birth of self-consciousness in the electorate, the Commons increased in power and importance until in time they deprived the King of his newly found legislative sovereignty. This at first they shared with the Lords, but in the end, through the control of the King's ministers maintained by the "Conventions of the Constitution," they have in modern times added to their former strength the

[1] *Parl. Hist.*, vol. xxviii. pp. 1033, 1034.
[2] *Ibid.*, p. 1143.
[3] *Ibid.*, p. 1093. See the whole debate in volume xxviii. of the *Parliamentary History*, p. 1018 et seq. An excellent summary of it is given by Sergeant Runnington in his edition of Hale's *History of the Common Law* (p. 55, edition of 1820). On the indefiniteness of the character of impeachment in earlier times, see Pike, *Const. Hist. of the House of Lords*, p. 228 et seq. The cases of impeachment from the earliest times are given in Hatsell, *Precedents* (2d ed., vol. iv.).

PARLIAMENT AS A COURT

King's legal prerogative, an addition which has made their power preponderant.

And yet, through all this long and wonderful process, the Commons, like Parliament as a whole, have retained much of their judicial character. For part of these judicial powers they entered into a long and bitter fight with the Lords, which resulted in some losses. Some other parts, however, as bills of attainder and impeachment, they retained until these fell into disuse or disfavour. Of all these powers, impeachment illustrates best that oldest characteristic of the Commons' House,—the function of presentment. They were there obviously the "Grand Inquest of the Nation." In the seventeenth century Filmer used this as an argument against their power. If the Commons were summoned only *ad faciendum et consentiendum*, they had no power to dissent.[1] In Fitzharris's Case it was said: "The Commons of England in Parliament are supposed to be a greater and a wiser body than a Grand-jury of any one county.... Will the law of England now suffer an examination, impeachment and prosecution for treason, to be taken out of the hands of the greatest and wisest inquest in England?"[2] So late as 1839 Lord Denman declared: "The Commons of England are not invested with more of power and dignity by their legislative character than by that which they bear as the grand inquest of the nation."[3]

[1] *The Freeholders' Grand Inquest*, p. 5. The title is significant.
[2] 8 *St. Tr.*, 286.   [3] 9 *Adolphus & Ellis*, 114.

THE HIGH COURT OF PARLIAMENT

Hardly anyone has doubted the judicial character of the Commons so far as this presentment of crimes is concerned. When, however, we come to the question of actual judgement, to the function originally exercised by the *Curia Regis*, the problem becomes more difficult. The Commons fought long and hard for a participation with the Lords in this important part of judicature. Precedents exist in the middle ages which could be cited for that participation; others exist that may be and have been cited against it. It is outside the purpose of this essay to enter the long controversy over this question, except to try to indicate how far the controversy arose out of the indefiniteness of the line between "legislation" and "litigation."

The best modern authorities seem to agree that the solution of the problem which has actually been made is on the whole the one most nearly in accord with ancient *practice*, namely, that jurisdiction in error should be in the Lords exclusively, but that neither house should have any original jurisdiction except in extraordinary cases when their privileges or their members are involved.[1]

[1] See especially on this subject: Pike, *Const. Hist. of the House of Lords*, pp. 281, 287-91, with references there cited; Holdsworth, *History of English Law*, vol. i. p. 175 and note, p. 176 and note, p. 180, and elsewhere; Hale, *Jurisdiction of the Lords House*, especially chs. xxi., xxii., and xxxiv., and Hargrave's valuable preface; Selden, *Judicature in Parliament;* Stubbs, *Const. Hist.*, vol. ii. (4th ed.), pp. 261, 636; Filmer, *Freeholders' Grand Inquest;* Coke, *Fourth Institute, Parliament;* Sir Robert Cotton, *A Brief Discourse concerning the Power of Peers and Commons of Parliament, in Point of Judicature: Cottoni Posthuma*, p. 343 et seq.; Prynne, *Plea for the Lords;* Prothero, *Documents*, Introduction, pp. lxxxiv, lxxxv; Gardiner, *History of England*, vol. iv. p. 122 et seq.; *The Works of Judge Jenkins*, pp. 107-13, 145-50; *The Case Stated concerning the Judicature of the House of Peers in the Point of Appeals* (1675).

PARLIAMENT AS A COURT

The arguments of the seventeenth century, when this great question was under debate, throw light upon the ideas then existing as to Parliament's judicial powers in general. But for the indefiniteness at that time still remaining in men's minds concerning the difference between law-making and law-declaring, the great controversy between the houses over judicature could hardly have occurred; but for the growth of a new idea of legislative sovereignty, the controversy could not have been settled so easily as it was. The complete victory of legislative sovereignty in England, and the entire disappearance of competition between the houses for judicature, were contemporaneous, but it was a long time before the one was complete or the other entire.

It is impossible here to do more than indicate briefly the lines of argument adopted by the two houses. They are best set forth in their historical and constitutional bearing, on the one side, by Prynne in his *Plea for the Lords*, and on the other, by Sir Matthew Hale in *The Jurisdiction of the Lords House*.

Thus Prynne argues: "It is a rule both of Law and justice, that no man can be an informer, prosecutor, and judge too of the persons prosecuted, & informed against it being contrary to all grounds of justice: therefore he ought to complain and petition to others for Justice. But the Commons in all ancient Parliaments, and in this present, have been informers and prosecutors (in nature of a Grand Inquest, to which some compare them, being summoned from all parts of the kingdom to present publike Grievances and Delinquents to the King and Peers for their redress) and thereupon have alwayes petitioned, complained to the King and Lords for Iustice against all other Delinquents and offenders in Parliament, not judged them themselves. . . . Therefore the House of Lords hath the proper right of judicatory vested in them, even in Cases of Commoners, not the Commons; who are rather Informers, Prosecutors, and Grand Jury men, to inform, impeach, than Judges to hear, censure, determine and give judgement."[1] Therefore, he concludes, the judicial power "resides wholly and solely in the King and House of Lords, not in the House of Commons; which hath no part nor share therein singly considered in it self, nor yet joyntly with the King and Lords, but only in some special cases and proceedings, as when and where the King and Lords voluntarily require their concurrence, or where the judgement and proceedings in Parliament are by way of Bill or Act of Parliament; or when a judgement passed or confirmed by Bill or Act to which the Commons consent was requisite, is to be altered or reversed, but in no other cases else, that I can find. To make this out beyond contradiction; it must be necessarily granted by all, and cannot be gainsaid or disproved by any, that this Supreme power of Judicature hath been vested in our Great Councils and Parliaments even from their beginning and original

---

[1] *Plea for the Lords*, pp. 309, 310. The italics of the original are not reproduced, as they have no significance.

institution, it being the *antientest,* as well as highest and honourablest of all other Courts: That it had this Soveraign Jurisdiction vested in it and exercised by it, both under our British, Saxon, Danish and Norman Kings, I have elsewhere evidenced, and shall anon make good by undeniable presidents."[1]

These must be taken to be Prynne's real views on this question. It is true, they contrast strangely with his argument, cited above (page 157), that Parliament can legally do business without the bishops, because the presence of the whole bench of judges is not necessary to the validity of legal decisions. But in 1643 Prynne had been trying to justify by precedent acts that were unprecedented, to cover under a veil of legality a contest that had passed into a struggle for supremacy.

In agreement with Prynne were such men as Lord Bacon,[2] Selden,[3] Filmer,[4] Judge Jenkins,[5] and Nathaniel Bacon.[6] On the other hand, Sir Matthew Hale insisted that "the supreme court of the kingdom is

---

[1] *Plea for the Lords,* p. 164. The same idea he expressed elsewhere: "The Commons have no more authority, right, reason, Jurisdiction to limit, or restrain this their [*i. e.* the King and Lords'] ancient right, Judicature, Priviledge (much lesse to abrogate) then the Grand or Petty Jury have to limit, regulate the Judges or Justices Commissions, Authority on the Bench; or the Tenants the Jurisdiction of their Lords Courts, or every Committee of the Commons House, the Excesses of the House it self." *Brief Register,* pt. i. p. 441.
[2] *Advice to Sir George Villiers.*
[3] *Judicature in Parliament: Works,* vol. iii. col. 1637.
[4] *Freeholders' Grand Inquest,* pp. 2-6.
[5] *Works,* pp. 107-13, 145-50.
[6] *Discourse on Government,* pt. ii. p. 14.

neither the house of lords alone, nor the house of commons alone; no, nor both houses without the king.— The high court of parliament, consisting of the king and both houses, is the supreme and only supreme court of this kingdom, from which there is no appeal."[1] With him Coke seems to agree,[2] and Sir Robert Cotton's statements anticipate Prynne's argument of 1643: "To infer, that because the Lords pronounced the sentence, the point of Judgment should be only theirs, were as absurd, as to conclude that no authority was left in any other Commissioner of *Oyer* and *Terminer*, than in the person of that man solely that speaketh the Sentence."[3]

All this is interesting here mainly from the fact that the arguments on both sides start from the ancient inquisitorial functions of the Commons.

The obvious explanation of the whole struggle lies in the fact that in the seventeenth century the Commons and the Lords were contending for a supremacy that was purely judicial, but the precedents on which both had to rely belonged to a time when the sharp distinction was not made between judicial and legislative. The number of lawyers in 1695 who would or could use the words "judgement" and "law" as practically synonymous terms was very limited indeed.

---

[1] *Jurisdiction of the Lords House*, p. 205. See also pp. 123-7, 205-8, *passim*.
[2] 4 *Inst.*, 23.
[3] *Cottoni Posthuma*, p. 352. See also some statements of Sir Robert Atkyns in *Sir W. Williams's Case*, 13 *St. Tr.*, 1413-15.

And yet that has to be done if we would understand the meaning of the older precedents.

It is amazing to note the comments that are made even in modern books upon the judicial activity of the early Commons. Such activity is usually dismissed with a statement that apparently there was a "confusion" of legislative and judicial power. This seems usually to dispose of the matter. Such explanations recur again and again, without so much as causing any anxiety or any desire to explain why these "confusions" are so frequent. Thus we still go on trying to decide the old question—impossible of solution only because it is not a proper question to ask—whether the judicial power in mediaeval times rested exclusively in the House of Commons or in the House of Lords. The only answer that can be given is that there was no separate "judicial" power in existence, if we mean judicial in the modern restricted sense. "Jurisdiction" was shared by the houses, but it was a jurisdiction that extended to the making of general rules as well as to the decision of particular cases. When the new, refined, and restricted meaning of the word had come to be the only one understood, it is evident at a glance what confusion must arise in trying to squeeze the old words into it; and also what contention must result if men of varying views were unconscious of the wrenching and twisting those old words had undergone in the process.

A very striking example of this unconscious desire to mould ancient institutions to fit modern conceptions occurs even in such a book as Pike's *Constitutional History of the House of Lords*, one of the most accurate and suggestive works on English parliamentary institutions. The case was one arising out of a petition to Parliament in 1414 by the son of the Earl of Salisbury, praying that his father's case might be reviewed and the errors redressed. The father had been put to death without a trial, but the temporal lords, with the assent of the King, had afterwards adjudged that his lands should be forfeited for treason. Of this case Mr. Pike speaks as follows:

"The petition and the subsequent assignments of error are hardly comprehensible according to any acknowledged legal principles. It was asked that errors alleged to have occurred, not in a Court below, but in Parliament itself, should be corrected in Parliament. Among the assignments of error were two which had relation to the Commons. In one the original 'declaration and judgement' were regarded as judicial acts; in the other they were regarded as legislative acts. In the one it was complained that they had been pronounced only by the Lords Temporal with the King's assent, whereas the judgement ought to have been given by the King, as sovereign judge, and by the Lords Spiritual and Temporal, with the assent of the Commons, or on their petition. In the other it was again maintained that the declaration and judgement were bad, as having been passed without petition or assent from the Commons, because the Commons 'are of right petitioners or assenters in respect of *that which is ordained for law* in Parliament.'

"A petition of error alternating between an attempt to redress in Parliament an error supposed to have been committed judicially in the High Court of Parliament itself, and an attempt to reverse an Act or Ordinance of Attainder, is a political curiosity, but seems very like a legal absurdity. It shows only the lengths to which men might be carried by political partisanship. In any case it has no bearing upon the authority to redress error arising in Courts below."[1]

I think even the small number of cases and statements that have been cited above from the great number in existence will show conclusively that in mediaeval England such proceedings would undoubtedly not have been looked upon either as "political curiosities" or "legal absurdities."

We all know that in France the "Parliament" actually remained a "court;" we are aware that Massachusetts had her legislative "General Court;"[2] and that in England itself, up to modern times, the Parliament was habitually *called* a court; but we have never taken this seriously. We have not accepted the fact that in the

---

[1] *Constitutional History of the House of Lords*, p. 291. I have mentioned this book in this way because it is one of the best books on the subject. No one whose work lies in English constitutional history can fail to acknowledge the help obtained from Mr. Pike's book. My footnotes show how much I have relied on it. Mr. Holdsworth's statement concerning such cases is guarded.— "But some of these cases *later* lawyers would perhaps deem rather legislative than judicial." *H. E. L.*, vol. i. p. 175.

[2] I owe the reference to the General Court of Massachusetts to the suggestion of Professor W. M. Daniels.

middle ages Parliament *really was* primarily a court, and only incidentally a "legislature." If all the consequences of this fact were understood, men would hardly ask whether in ancient times the "judicature" properly rested exclusively with the Lords or with the Commons. Possibly the present judicial arrangements in England may be as near to the ancient practice as changed conditions and modern ideas will permit, but the difference between the two is very great notwithstanding. It is indeed hard to see how it can be seriously contended that after all no important changes have occurred.

This is not equivalent to saying that the Commons after they became a part of Parliament became at once, or in fact ever became, the equals of the Lords in "judicature." However vague or large the meaning of that term may have been, one would be rash indeed to say, for example, that the Commons ever shared it with the Lords in the measure that they came to share the power, or rather the duty, of assenting to grants of taxes to the King. A study of the lists of *auditores*, or triers of petitions in Parliament, from the reign of Edward III on, fails to disclose the names of any commoners except the judges who were summoned to the House of Lords as a part of "The King's Council in his Parliaments;" and though these judges seem to have been regular members of these "committees," and may have voted on equal terms with the peers when present, their presence was not necessary to the validity of the

PARLIAMENT AS A COURT

committees' action, as was that of the peers. Fleta clearly indicates that in his day the *auditores* were a different court from "The King's Court in His Council in His Parliaments,"[1] but what the relation between the two was under the successors of Edward I it is impossible to say, though it is a point that must be cleared up before there can be any real understanding of the English central judicial system in the middle ages.[2] But the difficulty with the "Triers" does not end even there. Stubbs says: "By them was determined the court to which the particular petitions ought to be referred, and, if any required parliamentary hearing, the triers reported them to parliament."[3] In the Rolls, these triers are often officially delegated *oier, trier, et terminer*.[4] But what does *terminer* mean? Does it mean that such cases as were not allotted to the inferior courts, but reserved for hearing in Parliament, were actually determined by the *auditores*, unless these cases were of exceptional difficulty; or, on the other hand, were all the parliamentary cases passed along at once by the *auditores* for trial by the full Parliament? In the latter case, were the Commons ever to be included? Unfortunately, it is impossible to give categorical answers to these important questions. Practice

[1] Lib. 2, cap. 2. It cannot be said with certainty that the author had in mind the triers when he used the term *auditores speciales* in this passage: it seems to me probable.
[2] Maitland says the question is "still open." *Parl. Roll*, Introd., pp. xxxiii, xxxiv. See Note D at the end of this chapter (p. 251).
[3] *Const. Hist.*, vol. iii. p. 469.
[4] *E.g.* 5 Rich. II. (*Rot. Parl.*, vol. iii. p. 98); *post*, Note D to this chapter (p. 251).

may have varied, and our information is very limited. It seems fairly clear, however, that in all ordinary cases, the triers really "determined" the case before them. To deliver the petition was in most cases to answer it. To transmit it to a lower court implied a command to the lower court. This is what connects the parliamentary procedure so closely with the activity of the Chancery in issuing original writs. Without such a remission as this, or in the absence of an original writ, the inferior courts of the King could not entertain any case. "Nothing in the age that we are studying," Professor Maitland says, "is more remarkable than the narrowly limited powers of the courts of law, of the exchequer, of the chancery, more especially in all such matters as concern the king."[1] In all ordinary cases, then, the response of the triers was in the nature of a preliminary order, for, roughly speaking, it seems proper to say that the petition on which it was based need only make out what we should call a *prima facie* case. As most of the petitions were for redress of grievances which the petitioner believed could not be remedied in the ordinary courts, the frequent response by the triers that the existing law was sufficient, or a remission of the case to the ordinary courts, was in many cases a virtual refusal of the petition. Other cases, however, were apparently beyond the compe-

---

[1] *Parl. Roll*, Introduction, p. lxix. See also Madox, *Exchequer*, ch. iii. sec. vi. "Non potest quis sine brevi agere." *Fleta*, lib. ii. cap. 13, sec. 4. See also *ibid.*, lib. ii. cap. 34, sec. 1.

tence of the courts below, and such cases would be reserved by the triers. Numerous cases are to be found among the records endorsed by them *coram rege* or *coram consilio*. In most instances where the cases were not remitted to the ordinary courts, it is probable that the triers themselves, "if . . . on the face of the Petition they saw there was reason to entertain the prayer, . . . then gave . . . such remedy as the case required."[1]

For the more difficult cases probably the rest of the Council would be called in, as was done also in difficult cases before the judges of the Bench, as we have seen,[2] — those which had "the most of 'grace' in them" being reserved for the King's own ear.[3]

In trying to reconstruct these obscure institutions, one consideration must be kept steadily in mind, — that the triers for England, or for other parts of the King's dominions, were merely a part of the Council. It seems more correct to say this than to call them a committee of the Council, for their action seems to have been final in all cases which they did not transmit to the whole Council or to the King. We should be glad to know by what rules they were bound in determining or transmitting a case, — whether their discretion was large or small. If it was large, if they had powers nearly plenary, then they could hardly be a mere committee. If, on the

[1] Palgrave, *Parl. Papers*, Session of 1833, vol. xii. p. 19.
[2] *Ante*, p. 18 et seq.
[3] Maitland, *Parl. Roll*, Introd., p. lxx.

other hand, it was small, they might be more properly styled a committee of the Council. It would help us in deciding this question if we knew certainly the way they were appointed; but we do not. However far the discretion of the triers extended, when they called in their fellow councillors in difficult cases, the important thing to remember is that they were not invoking an external tribunal, a higher court of appeal. The procedure must have been analogous to the relations of the Councillors sitting as judges *coram rege* with the rest of the Council, where the distinction, as we have seen, between the larger and the smaller body was one more of convenience than of legal theory.

With reference to the relations of the triers to the courts below, the same caution is in point. The body of triers in all cases included the judges of those courts. The triers were thus no body entirely "external" to the ordinary courts, and the relations between them in cases of petitions were doubtless more free and informal, and their coöperation much closer and more sympathetic, than could have existed otherwise. The English judicial system has retained this general principle of coöperation in much greater measure than that of the United States, as appears in the *personnel* of their courts of appeal.

When the Commons' House becomes an indispensable part of Parliament, the question grows more intricate, and it is practically impossible to say how far the Commons participated in the settlement of petitions.

PARLIAMENT AS A COURT

After Henry IV's time we do find petitions addressed to the Commons,[1] but how far their powers extended in determining cases, it is hard to say. Most of the petitions received by them were undoubtedly transmitted at once to the Lords, and the well-known renunciation by the Commons of any share in judicial power in Henry IV's reign is often cited.[2] The renunciation in question came, however, at a time when the Commons looked upon parliamentary functions of all kinds as a duty rather than a privilege, and afterward, when opinions on such things had undergone a change, they may not have felt bound by this precedent in the way that Brady and Prynne try to make it appear.[3]

These questions are certainly obscure enough, and in view of these obscurities it would be unwarrantable to make definite assertions with assurance concerning the participation of the Commons in "judicature," or concerning the relations between the triers and the Council. It is not contended here that no line was drawn between business judicial and business non-judicial in

---

[1] "I can only trace one dubious and singular case before that period." Palgrave, in *Report on Public Petitions: Parl. Papers*, Session of 1833, vol. xii. p. 20.

[2] *Rot. Parl.*, vol. iii. p. 427 B (1399). See, for example, *The Case Stated concerning the Judicature of the House of Peers in the Point of Appeals* (1675), p. 29 et seq.

[3] Lest anyone should think that this desire on the part of the Commons to escape their duties was confined to matters *judicial* alone, reference may be made to the declaration of the Commons in the twenty-first year of Edward III, that they are not able to counsel the King *in matters of war*, and praying that they may therefore be excused. They also ask that these matters be decided on the advice of the Council, and promise that they will confirm any determination thus made. *Rot. Parl.*, vol. ii. p. 165 (1347).

Edward I's Parliament and afterward. Thus much, however, is contended, namely, that in the middle ages the line between judicial and non-judicial was far from distinct; that in the English Parliament of that age all business other than granting money to the King, and possibly also advising him on matters of national policy, was of a kind not susceptible of exact division into "judicial," or "legislative," or "administrative." Such lines of division eventually appeared, but to the end of the middle ages they were so vague that it is dangerous and misleading to accept them as the same lines that are drawn to-day with such exactness between the different activities of government.

The existence of some such lines of division may be indicated in the fact that the triers above mentioned consisted entirely of prelates, nobles, and judges; but even here it is to be noted that though "at least nine-tenths of the petitions have reference to the administration of law,"[1] as we might expect in the days before Parliament was a real lawmaking body, such petitions are in no way to be distinguished from others of a "non-judicial" character. They were, as Elsynge says, "for the most part petitions of private persons for re-

[1] Gneist, *Const. Hist.*, vol. ii. pp. 12, 13. "I should state that *ninety-nine out of every hundred* [petitions] presented by individuals related to individual grievances; that there are a few rare cases in which a complaint is made against a general law, but then it was a case where the general law was so mixed up with the particular case of the petitioner, that the Petition must not be considered as a Petition against the abstract principle of the law, but only against the particular application of it in his own case. Communities, such as the inhabitants of a forest or a shire, petitioned more frequently against general laws." Palgrave, in *Parl. Papers:* Session of 1833, vol. xii. pp. 20, 21.

PARLIAMENT AS A COURT

lief of any wrong done them, or for the king's grace."[1] If the triers considered the relief or favour a proper one, the petitioner might be sent to another court of law, or sometimes to Parliament, to obtain it; or he might be directed to the Council or the Chancellor.

The "relief" was as varied as were the petitions themselves. These were mainly "judicial," but not all. Sometimes, Maitland says, the petition is for something the King is bound to give in right; sometimes for a mere favour,—e. g. the petitioner asks to be allowed to pay in instalments money he owes the King.[2] "Generally the boon that is asked for is one which the king without transcending his legal powers might either grant or deny."[3] Nothing could better illustrate the essentially judicial character of Parliament, or the lack of definition of its powers, than this whole procedure by petition. For it appears that the initiation of the "acts" of Parliament is by petitions, which ordinarily "do not ask for legislation," and the resulting responses therefore "are not 'private acts of parliament'" of the modern kind,[4]—they are awards. The thing asked for in the petition may be the redress of a general grievance. Such petitions the triers would naturally send to the High Court of Parliament rather than to any inferior court, and Parliament's favourable action might result in the establishment of a general

---

[1] *The Manner of Holding Parliaments in England*, p. 273.
[2] *Parliament Roll*, Introd., p. lxviii.
[3] *Ibid.*, pp. lxvii, lxviii.
[4] *Ibid.*

rule—"legislation," we should say. But the triers themselves had no separate classification for cases of this kind. They also sent plenty of cases to the Court of Parliament, where the relief prayed was purely "judicial;" cases that in no way involved the necessity of laying down any general rule, that required no action of any kind not within the power of the ordinary courts. There is no assignable line of division between these two classes of cases. Both kinds are found in numbers on the rolls, promiscuously and indiscriminately. Most of the petitions that initiate the action on these cases come from individuals, and they ask for all manner of things, as restitution to lands and charters taken away by violence, reversal of outlawry, payment of a debt due by the King, a delivery of deeds, restoration to an office, etc. Often they are presented by a county or a city, as, for example, a request from the Cinque Ports for an explanation of their charter,—a strikingly "judicial" act. Or the petitioners may be a guild, as in the case of a petition from the London dyers, against false fulling of cloth.[1] Upon these may be based "acts" of Parliament which will satisfy the respective petitioners. These acts may be "judgements," or they may be "laws." Men of the day would probably have applied both words to them indiscriminately. When asked whether such petitions as these, when presented to the House of Lords, were not presented to them in their judicial rather than their legislative capacity, Sir Francis Pal-

[1] Elsynge, *op. cit.*, pp. 273-5.

grave replied: "The two capacities were so closely conjoined at that period, that it is almost a distinction without a difference. Every order which the Parliament made upon a Petition was a special law for that time and turn. They went on the broad and general principle, 'Parliament is to redress every grievance; we will redress it by a general law if we think it expedient so to do; we will cut the knot by a particular law, or an order applicable to your own case, if that be not sufficient.'"[1]

But in addition to these petitions of individuals, classes, or corporations, we have seen other petitions originating in the Commons themselves. Here, it might naturally be assumed, we must have matters of a different character. These petitions must be the ground of parliamentary action that we may call legislation. On examining the early rolls, however, we find no distinction made between these petitions from the Commons and the ones presented by individuals, and no difference between remedies given upon these different kinds of petitions. We find, as Maitland says, petitions of communities and even of the Commons, but they are mixed with individual ones, and seem not to have been treated differently,—the distinction came later.[2] Private petitions were of a decidedly "judicial" character. A petitioner might have to appear to make

---

[1] *Report on Public Petitions: Parl. Papers*, Session of 1833, vol. xii. pp. 20, 21.
[2] *Parliament Roll*, Introd., pp. lxxiv, lxxv. He is speaking of the Parliament of 1305.

THE HIGH COURT OF PARLIAMENT

good his petition if he did not wish to have it rejected.[1] This was no less true when the petition came from a community instead of an individual. "There is one class of Petitions," says Sir Francis Palgrave, "that are puzzling; those are Petitions presented by the community of a shire, and sometimes brought before a Parliament, and apparently not by the representative members. *There is one case of a county appointing an attorney to appear for them in Parliament for which they had regular Representatives!*"[2]

This "judicial" character of the parliamentary petitions is further illustrated by the manner in which they were received. Among the first acts of a Parliament was the appointment of "receivers of petitions." Elsynge points out that as the triers were always prelates, nobles, and judges, who had been summoned to Parliament, so the receivers were never men who had been summoned to Parliament. They were, in fact, at first clerks of the Chancery who were required to sit in

---

[1] *Parl. Roll*, No. 267, and Introduction, p. lxxiii.
[2] *Report on Public Petitions: Parl. Papers*, Session of 1833, vol. xii. p. 21. The instance referred to is in *Parl. Writs*, vol. i. p. 186, No. 11. The italics are mine. The communal organization of mediaeval England and the communal feeling accompanying must be premised if we are even faintly to understand the early representation in Parliament or the affairs of the shires that lie beyond and behind it. Without such a feeling the presenting jury could never have arisen and the iters of justices would have been utterly futile. The earlier examples of communal action and responsibility in Saxon or Norman times have often been commented on. Mr. Holdsworth gives some interesting examples from a later period. (*H. E. L.*, vol. ii. pp. 314, 315, and references cited.) The change from feudalism to nationalism was accompanied by a development from communities of the realm which might corporately appeal to the King for redress of grievances, to the solidarity of "The Commons in Parliament Assembled."

PARLIAMENT AS A COURT

some public and easily accessible place outside Parliament, to receive the complaints and requests of the petitioners.[1] It is unnecessary to point out at any greater length the "judicial" character of these proceedings from beginning to end. It is enough to note that they were the ordinary stages through which nearly all "legislation" passed, up to the time—about the end of the reign of Henry VI—when the Commons were able to impose upon the Parliament a "bill" instead of a petition. This, when it came, was undoubtedly a long step toward real "legislation;" but it is not difficult to show that the characteristics of this new procedure, as well as its name, are at first only slightly less "judicial" than the petitions out of which it grew.[2] Piers the Plowman could speak of "putting up a bill" in Parliament to institute an action for rape or seduction,[3]

---

[1] Elsynge, *op. cit.*, p. 271. But see Palgrave in *Parl. Papers*, Session of 1833, vol. xii. p. 21. See also Note D at the end of this chapter (p. 251).

[2] One of the best modern accounts of the procedure by petition is by Stubbs, *Const. Hist.*, vol. ii. (4th ed.), pp. 275-7, 604-10; vol. iii. (5th ed.), pp. 469, 478, 500, 501. Most of the above statements have been drawn from it and from the excellent account given by Elsynge, p. 262 et seq. See also May, *Parliamentary Practice* (p. 606 et seq. in 9th ed.); Hale, *Jurisdiction of the Lords House*, p. 25 et seq.; Holdsworth, *H. E. L.*, vol. i. pp. 173-5; Clifford, *History of Private Bill Legislation*, vol. i. p. 300 et seq.; Maitland, *Parliament Roll of 1305*, Rolls Series, Introduction, p. lvi et seq.; and the testimony of Sir F. Palgrave before the Select Committee on Public Petitions, *Parliamentary Papers*, Session of 1833, vol. xii. (MS. paging 153 et seq.) See also *post*, Note D at the end of this chapter (p. 251).

It may not be amiss here to call attention to the fact that it is to these petitions, so "judicial" in character, that we must trace back the "right of petition" which played so important a part in the Revolution of 1688, and passed in consequence into the Constitution of the United States, where it has had an important influence, especially upon legislative history.

[3] *Ante*, p. 117.

THE HIGH COURT OF PARLIAMENT

and the ordinances of 5 Edward II contain a requirement that Parliament shall be held at least once a year to decide cases "where the judges cannot agree." "And in like manner the Bills shall be finished which are delivered in Parliament, in such sort as Law and Reason demand."[1]

It is interesting to note that the receivers of the petitions who sent the petitioner to the proper court for his redress were probably the same clerks of chancery who also issued the original writs under which cases were instituted in the ordinary courts of the King, "clerici honesti et circumspecti, sworn to the King, learned in the laws and customs of England, whose duty it is to hear and examine petitions and complaints of complainants and to exhibit to these by the kings writ the remedy suited to the character of the injuries set forth."[2] It is here that we must look for

[1] *Statutes of the Realm*, vol. i. p. 165, art. xxix.
[2] *Fleta*, lib. ii. ch. 13. The following passage occurs in *A Treatise of the Maisters of the Chauncerie*, written between 1596 and 1603 : "Another part of ther service is in attendinge in the higher howse of parliament, whither they comme withowt writt as beinge a part of the same court. For both the parliament is somoned by writts owt of the chauncerie; the acts made are inrolled and kept in chauncerie; all commandements of that court are expedited, either by writs out of the chauncery, or by the chauncellors serjants at armes; the lord chauncellor is ever speaker of that howse, withowt further choice or appointment as is used about the speaker of the lower howse, and ought withowt any writt to attend there, (although the contrayrie have bene of late used by some of the pettie bag not well instructed of the auntient manner; for what neede hath the kinge to sende notice under his seale of the attendance to those whoe have the keping of the sayed seale?) and the clark of the parliament hath his fee owt of the hanaper as an officer of the chauncery. The reason of ther attendance there I take to bee, not onely for the receyving of petitions; but as the judges are there, that, by observinge the minds and reasons of the lords that make the lawes, they maie the more agreeable to ther

[210]

one of the most important links between the "judicial" activity of Parliament and that of the Chancellor and the judges of the King's other courts. The cases that would be sent for remedy to the Parliament would probably be those of greater importance or dignity, but there is nothing in the rolls of Parliament to indicate that these were less "judicial" in character than the ones sent to the Chancellor or the inferior courts. Furthermore, a comparison of the proceedings in both the Chancery and the Parliament shows that the initial procedure was practically the same in both. This was by a petition or bill. The words "petition" and "bill" are used interchangeably in the Chancery down to the Tudor times,[1] and the same is true in Parliament[2] as well as in the ordinary speech of the people.[3]

---

meaninge expound and interpreate the sayed lawes; soe the masters of the chauncery are there also, that they may likewise frame the writts that are to bee made upon those lawes in like correspondencie; and as the judges furthermore maye informe the lords, howe former lawes of this realme presentlie stand touching any matter there debated; soe may they bee alsoe informed by the masters of the chauncery (of which the greattest number have alwaies bene chosen men skillfull in the civill and canon lawes) in lawes that they shall make touchinge forraine matters, whowe the same shall accord with equitie, *jus gentium*, and the lawes of other nations. And therefore the auntient use hath bene, that not onelie the four appointed for resevours of petitions, but any of the masters of the chauncery, may take ther place amonge the rest in the higher howse, as I learn by the auntient masters of the court nowe livinge." *Hargrave's Tracts*, pp. 308, 309.

See also *Observations concerning the Office of the Lord Chancellor*, attributed to Lord Ellesmere, pp. 39-41.

[1] Kerly, *Historical Sketch of the Equitable Jurisdiction of the Court of Chancery*, p. 47, note 2.

[2] Clifford, *History of Private Bill Legislation*, vol. i. p. 300.

[3] "O verrey light of eyen that ben blinde,
O verrey lust of labour and distresse,

THE HIGH COURT OF PARLIAMENT

We find also, even as late as Henry VII, that parliamentary bills of a private character still end sometimes with a prayer, usually concluding with the familiar formula, "And your petitioner will ever pray," etc. The prayer has retained its place to the present time in bills in equity, and in Parliament to-day no petition will be treated as a true petition if the prayer is omitted.[1]

The growing power of the Commons, and the separation of the Council and the Chancery from Parliament, led in time to the growth of a jealousy between the Parliament and these two bodies.

The Council had become a body distinct from Parliament by the time of Richard II, or probably somewhat before; the Chancery also became definitely separate from the Council. Already the common law courts had a separate existence, while Parliament was an ad-

> O tresorere of bountee to mankinde,
> Thee whom God chees to moder for humblesse!
> From his ancille he made thee maistresse
> Of hevene and erthe, our bille up for to bede."
> Chaucer, *An A. B. C.*
>
> "A compleynt hadde I, writen, in myn hond,
> For to have put to Pite as a bille."
> *The Compleynte unto Pite.*

[1] Clifford, *History of Private Bill Legislation*, vol. i. p. 300; May, *Parl. Practice*, p. 609. A comparison of the petitions given in volumes one and two of the *Calendars of the Proceedings in Chancery* issued by the Record Commission, and also those in the Selden Society volumes on the Star Chamber and the Court of Chancery, with the ones in the *Rolls of Parliament*, discloses no essential difference between those addressed to Parliament and others. The most common ending of the prayer in the earliest extant petitions to the Chancellor was, "for God and in work of charity." Mr. Baildon says that the expression "Your petitioner will ever pray" appears about the middle of the fifteenth century. *Select Pleas in Chancery* (Selden Society), Introd., p. xxv.

PARLIAMENT AS A COURT

ditional competing tribunal; and besides, from about the time of Henry IV, we begin to find a considerable number of petitions of the usual kind directed to the House of Commons alone.[1] It is little wonder that we find under such circumstances somewhat of a scramble for business and for the fees coincident with it. This results in several contests, prohibitions, and evasions of the prohibitions by fictions such as "quominus" or "Bill of Middlesex."[2] There is evidence that the High Court of Parliament was not removed entirely above these jealousies.

It has been said that Parliament's jealousy of the Chancery, which appears in so many acts, was due to the fact that the Chancery was really exercising legislative powers. This is given as the reason for the celebrated provision of the Statute of Westminster II, providing that new cases shall in future be brought into Parliament and not tried under writs issuing out of Chancery except *in consimili casu* with an existing writ.[3] It may be true that this was due partly to the fact that these new writs were really "legislation," but a much more effective motive for the provision was the general jealousy between the conflicting "jurisdictions." From the reign of Richard II we find continual complaints in Parliament of the encroachments of the Chancellor, and "the fact that these complaints all

---

[1] May, *Parl. Practice*, pp. 607, 608.
[2] Kerly, *History of Chancery*, p. 12.
[3] Holdsworth, *H. E. L.*, vol. i. p. 196.

come from the Commons suggests that they may have been prompted rather by the professional jealousy of the Common Law lawyers, who, though often forbidden to sit, were found in the Lower House in large numbers, than by any real abuse of the Chancellor's powers."[1] It was natural that these lawyers should look askance at the power of the clerks of Chancery, now that it extended to the granting of new equitable remedies, as well as to the allotment of old cases in the granting of original writs or in their capacity as receivers of petitions.

The acts of Parliament against the Chancery, the multiplication of petitions to the House of Commons, and the great increase in the number of lawyers in that house, all tend to explain or to illustrate this jealousy. The evidence is very full for the increase in the number of lawyers, for their obnoxious activity, and for the attempts to exclude them. As early as 1330 objections were made to their presence in the Commons.[2] In 46 Edward III they were excluded by statute, along with the sheriffs, because "men of the law who follow divers businesses in the King's courts on behalf of private persons ... do procure and cause to be brought into Parliament many petitions in the name of the Commons which in no wise relate to them."[3] This pro-

---

[1] Kerly, *History of Equity*, p. 37 et seq., where are to be found references to the principal statutes passed to check the Chancellor's power. See also *Am. Hist. Rev.*, vol. xii. p. 1 et seq., for an account of these acts.
[2] Porritt, *Unreformed House of Commons*, vol. i. pp. 512, 513.
[3] *Ibid.*; *Statutes of the Realm*, vol. i. p. 394.

PARLIAMENT AS A COURT

vision greatly excited the wrath of Coke, who denied that this was a real statute.[1] Prynne, however, believed that it was, and considered it "most fit to be put in actual execution against such practising Lawyers, who make sute to be elected Parliament Members, only, or principally to get Clyents, Practice, and Pre-audience of others at the Barr, and to promote their Clients or Friends causes in the House, rather than diligently to discharge their publike Duties faithfully in Parliament, according to their trusts; as too many have done of later ages, as well as when this Ordinance was first enacted."[2] There is nothing new under the sun! Barrington says the opposition to the lawyers in Parliament was due to their being at this time "*auditors* to, and dependents upon men of property, receiving an annual stipend *pro consilio impenso & impendendo*, and were treated as *retainers*."[3] Professor Hearn comments on this statute with his usual insight: "Parliament was not then what it had become in the time of Lord Coke. A great part of its business was judicial, or at least semi-judicial. It was in contemplation of this business that maintainers were excluded."[4]

This jealousy of the common lawyers in Parliament was not directed at the Chancery alone; the jurisdiction of the Council was equally dangerous to their

[1] 4 *Inst.*, 48.
[2] *Abridgment of Records*, Preface. See also his *Observations on Coke's Fourth Institute*, p. 13.
[3] *Observations on the Statutes*, 2d ed., p. 302.
[4] *Government of England*, 1st ed., p. 489.

monopoly, and many acts of Parliament were levelled at it, which, as Professor Dicey says, "bear witness to the influence of the Common Law lawyers; since they are manifestly intended to do away with all legal proceedings except those in the Common Law Courts."[1] To make this statement perfectly accurate, we must remember that Parliament must be included among these "Common Law Courts."

D. "Acts" of Parliament

THE final outcome of the parliamentary business initiated by petition was the "act" or "award" (*agard*) of Parliament. Petyt defines an award of Parliament as "A final Resolution of particular original Cases, brought and given in full Parliament, upon publick Conference and solemn Debate; and not upon a Writ of Error before the Lords."[2] This definition may be accepted if it is borne in mind that in early times a "full" Parliament does not necessarily include the Commons,— a qualification that Petyt himself would have been the last to allow.[3] As the facts hitherto presented might lead us to expect, these awards, though generally "judicial," as we should say, and marked off from other activi-

---

[1] *Privy Council*, pp. 21, 22, where the principal statutes are mentioned; see also ibid., pp. 69, 70, 72, 73; Maitland, *English Constitutional History*, pp. 216-18; Palgrave, *King's Council*. For the general subject of lawyers in Parliament and its bearing on Parliament's character as a court, see in addition to the references noted above, Whitelocke, *Notes upon the King's Writt*, vol. ii. chs. 99, 100.

[2] *Jus Parliamentarium*, p. 32.

[3] See his *Antient Right of the Commons of England Asserted*.

ties of Parliament, were distinguished so imperfectly from other "acts" that the line is difficult to locate. An instance is afforded by a case in 6 Edward III. A writ of quo warranto was brought in the Court of Common Pleas against a franchise held by the Archbishop of York. For the Archbishop it was argued that the Common Pleas had no jurisdiction, because of the statute of Edward I directing that pleas of quo warranto should be held before justices in eyre, in the county. It chanced, however, that this particular franchise had been in litigation in Parliament a few years before this, but after the enactment of the Statute of Quo Warranto; and that the award there, which had been in the Archbishop's favour, had nevertheless contained a proviso allowing the King in future to have his writ against the franchise, *when and where he wished*. Therefore, when it was now contended that the proviso in the award was void against the statute, Schardelow replied: "When you sued by Petition to be restored to your possession, it was delivered to you in this Manner, *i.e.* that it was awarded in Parliament that the King might take his writ against you, when and where he pleased; and an award in Parliament is the highest Law that is: And since you make no Answer, we pray the Franchise may be seized into the King's Hands." And Herle, the Chief Justice, said: "You were restored to your Possession by an award of Parliament, and by the same Award it was adjudged, That you ought to answer the King when and where he pleased, and you would have the Benefit of this Award yourselves, and would oust the King of the Benefit of it, which cannot be done."[1] "From this case," says Petyt, "we may observe, that the Judges esteemed an Award in Parliament equal to an Act of Parliament, as to the inferior Courts, and able to exempt a particular Case awarded out of a general Act of Parliament."[2]

The "award" on which this case was based was an ordinary judgement,[3] but it is singularly like the mod-

---

[1] *Y. B.*, Hilary Term, 6 Edw. III., plea 15; Petyt, *Jus. Parl.*, p. 41.
[2] *Op. cit.*, p. 42.
[3] Petyt, *op. cit.*, p. 35. On the award generally, see also Gneist, *Const. Hist.*, vol. i. p. 418, note; Reeves, *H. E. L.* (Finlason's ed.), vol. ii. p. 654. This absence of distinction between acts and awards could be illustrated at considerable length from legal writings of the sixteenth and seventeenth centuries. I shall give three extracts, two of which are from writers opposed to the pretensions of the common lawyers. In the book entitled *The Privileges and Prerogatives of the High Court of Chancery*, sometimes, though perhaps wrongly, attributed to Lord Ellesmere, the following statements occur in criticism of the statute of 4 Henry IV., cap. 23, forbidding appeals from the King's courts: "One Court ought not to take upon them to Iudge and deside their own Iurisdiction, and the Iurisdiction of another of the King's Courts: But then *Bracton's* rule is to be holden: (that is) that the King's interpretation is to be expected, Who is to declare and expound all doubtfull or obscure words in *Chartis Regiis & factis regum:* For all Statutes are *facta regis*, made at the request and by the consent of the Lords Spirituall and Temporall and the Commons."

In the first edition in English of Finch's *Law*, published in 1627, at p. 233, we read: "The Parliament is a Court of the King, Nobility and Commons assembled, Hauing an absolute power in all causes. As to make Lawes, to adiudge matters in Law, to trie causes of life and death; to reuerse errors in the Kings Bench, especially where any common mischiefe is, that by the ordinarie course of Law there is no meanes to remedie: this is the proper Court for it. And all their Decrees are as Judgements. And if the Parliament it selfe doe erre (as it may) it can no where be reuersed but in Parliament."

Again in 1677, in a little anonymous book entitled *A Discourse of the Rise & Power of Parliaments*, it is said: "There was Law before Lawyers; there was a time when the *Common Customs* of the land were sufficient to secure *Meum* and *Tuum;* What has made it since so difficult? Nothing but the Comments

ern private bill, whose early development in Parliament Sir Erskine May describes as follows: "In the reign of Henry IV, petitions began to be addressed in considerable numbers, to the House of Commons. The courts of equity had, in the meantime, relieved Parliament of much of its remedial jurisdiction; and the petitions were now more in the nature of petitions for private bills, than for equitable remedies for private wrongs. Of this character were many of the earliest petitions; and the orders of Parliament upon them can only be regarded as special statutes, of private or local application. As the limits of judicature and legislation became defined, the petitions applied more distinctly for legislative remedies, and were preferred to Parliament through the Commons: but the functions of Parliament, in passing private bills, have always retained the mixed judicial and legislative character of ancient times."[1]

Through all their history, private bills have furnished one of the best examples of the fusion of legislation and adjudication, and through all that history down to

---

of Lawyers, confounding the Text, and writhing the Laws like a Nose of Wax, to what Figure best serves their purpose. Thus the great *Cook*, bribed perhaps by Interest, or Ambition, pronounced *that in the Interpretation of Laws, the Judges are to be believed before the Parliament:* But others, and with better Reason, affirm, That 'tis one of the great Ends of the Parliaments Assembling, To determine such causes, as ordinary Courts of Justice could not decide." The views of the last writer are the same as those expressed by William Petyt in his *Jus Parliamentarium*. Whatever other differences exist among these writers, it is clear that they have one thing in common, — the absence of a clear distinction between an "act" of Parliament and a judgement of Parliament.

[1] *Parliamentary Practice*, pp. 607, 608; see also Clifford, *History of Private Bill Legislation*, vol. i. p. 270; *Report on Public Petitions*, H. C. Papers, 1833, vol. xii.

THE HIGH COURT OF PARLIAMENT

the present, the line between these and public bills has been "very narrow, and has fluctuated from time to time."[1]

At first, of course, "special laws for the benefit of private parties, and judicial decrees for the redress of private wrongs, were not distinguished in principle or in form,"[2] *i. e.* there was no distinction between the "award" and the private bill. In like manner, "between public and private Acts no clear distinction was drawn."[3] In fact, this distinction has never become clear, and even to-day "It seems ... impossible to lay down a hard and fast rule as to the subjects which should and which should not be dealt with by private Bills."[4]

An interesting instance of the uncertainty as to the character of a statute is the well-known Statute of Waste of the twentieth year of Edward I. The first part is the record of an ordinary judgement or award. The second part has all the appearance of a regular "public" act.[5] There is another similar instance much later in the famous case of Richard Strode, a burgess of Parliament who had been convicted in the Stannary Courts of agreeing with the rest of the Commons upon a bill against certain abuses of the tinners. He was imprisoned and petitioned Parliament for a remedy,

---

[1] Ilbert, *Legislative Methods and Forms*, p. 30.
[2] May, *op. cit.*, p. 754.
[3] Clifford, *op. cit.*, vol. i. p. 343.
[4] Ilbert, *op. cit.*, p. 32.
[5] 20 Edw. I., stat. 2. The question whether it is a statute or not is discussed in *Y. B.* 7 *Edw. II.*, p. 231.

[220]

whereupon the following "act" was passed in the fourth year of Henry VIII: "All Suits, Condemnations, Executions, Charges, Impositions, put or hereafter to be put upon Richard Strode, and every of his Complices, that be of this Parliament, or any other hereafter, for any Bill, speaking, or reasoning of any Thing concerning the Parliament to be communed and treated of, shall be void."[1] As might be expected, opinions varied as to whether this was a private or a public act. In 1629 the judges resolved that the act "was a particular act of parliament and extended only to Richard Strode, and to those persons that had joined with him to prefer a Bill to the house of commons concerning Tinners," though they agreed that all other Parliament men "ought to have" immunity from prosecution for things said "in parliament by a parliamentary course."[2] In the same year Sir John Eliot's counsel asserted that Strode's case "hath always been conceived to be a general act, because the prayers, time, words, and persons are general, and the answer to it is general," also because it was on the statute roll.[3] Sir Robert Heath, for the King, denied that it was anything but "a particular act, although it be in print; for Rastal entitles it by the name of Strode: so the title, body, and proviso of this act are particular."[4] Sir Robert Atkyns, in his argument in the

[1] 4 Henry VIII., ch. viii. An account of this case is found in Prynne's *Plea for the Lords*, pp. 401, 402.
[2] 3 *St. Tr.*, 237.
[3] *Ibid.*, 297.
[4] *Ibid.*, 305.

case of Bernardiston v. Soame in 1674, declares that "tho' all in that act that concerns one Richard Strode is a private act, yet there is one clause which is a general act, and is declaratory of the ancient law and custom of parliament."[1] In his argument in Sir William Williams's Case he states the same view at greater length, and dismisses the resolution of the judges in 1629 as an extra-judicial opinion.[2]

This case has been given somewhat at length because it shows the importance of the distinction between private and public bills. So important a thing as freedom of speech in Parliament was involved in it. It is, however, unnecessary to give further examples from the past of the indefiniteness of the line between public and private bills, for even to-day the indefiniteness is almost as great as it ever was.[3]

The procedure on private bills likewise still retains many features that are judicial in character. For example, the private persons interested in the bill appear as suitors for or against it. If the parties interested do not take the necessary steps in advancing it, the bill is lost. Such parties must also pay the fees incidental to the procedure, as in other judicial cases, and the promoters of private bills in Parliament have even been restrained by injunction from proceeding with a bill, so far have they been identified with ordinary liti-

---
[1] 6 *St. Tr.*, 1083.
[2] 13 *St. Tr.*, 1429, 1430.
[3] Many recent illustrations are given by Ilbert, *Legislative Methods and Forms*, pp. 30-2.

PARLIAMENT AS A COURT

gants.[1] The bill is still formally styled a "humble petition," and ends with a prayer containing the formal words, "and your Petitioner will ever pray, &c.," and counsel are regularly heard by Parliament as in any other court, while every private bill is solicited by an agent whose duties are carefully prescribed.[2] But, as May says, while these private bills are "examined and contested before committees and officers of the house, like private suits, and are subject to notices, forms, and intervals, unusual in other bills; yet in every separate stage, when they come before either house, they are treated precisely as if they were public bills. They are read as many times, and similar questions are put, except when any proceeding is specially directed by the Standing Orders; and the same rules of debate and procedure are maintained throughout."[3] In short, private bills are still what they were in the middle ages, "a proceeding half legislative and half judicial."[4]

[1] May, *Parl. Practice*, pp. 756, 757, citing recent cases.
[2] *Ibid.*, p. 780.
[3] *Ibid.*, p. 758.
[4] Stubbs, *Const. Hist.*, vol. iii. (5th ed.), p. 478. On the general subject, in addition to the above references, see Maitland, *Constitutional History of England*, pp. 386, 387. On this subject Palgrave says: "Our Private Acts of Parliament have arisen out of the old course; all the Private Acts are only the ancient petitions for redress in a new shape. When a tenant for life petitions for a power of leasing, for instance, the Act is a special law made in form, but virtually a decree for the occasion, to redress a particular grievance arising perhaps from the acts of the parties. Still take it as you choose, it has the essence of a law.

"*Q.* Is that the 'Privilegium'?

"Yes, exactly so; and in consequence of the criminal jurisdiction having been entirely cut down by law, the practice of our modern Parliament in passing Private Bills, and granting powers of the before-mentioned description,

THE HIGH COURT OF PARLIAMENT

One important variety of these private bills is the Bill of Attainder. It is unnecessary to do more than mention these conspicuous examples of the union of legislative and judicial functions in Parliament. A few of the debates upon them may, however, profitably be noticed for the indications they give of the gradual growth of the idea of legislative sovereignty. From the beginning to the end of the history of these bills we find uncertainty in men's minds as to their character. This uncertainty took different forms at different times. Are they trials *per legem terrae* or *per legem parliamenti*? After the emergence of the idea of legislative sovereignty it is asked, Is the Parliament in a Bill of Attainder proceeding legislatively or judicially? Even after legislative sovereignty had become a generally accepted fact, the essential injustice of these acts caused men to revolt. They admitted, but admitted with a sigh, that "when supremacy and impunity go together, there is no remedy,"[1] and Atterbury remarked in his speech defending himself in 1723, "As to the justice of the legislature, in some respects it hath a greater power

---

are exactly the last remnants of the old Petitions for redress, where the ordinary court could not grant relief.

"*Q.* Are there many instances of Private Bills of that description?

"They grew up imperceptibly. From the time of Henry IV you find those applications gradually growing up into the regular shape of a Private Bill." *Testimony before the Select Committee of the House of Commons: Parl. Papers*, Session of 1833, vol. xii. p. 22. See also Hatschek, *Englisches Staatsrecht*, vol. i. pp. 121, 503.

[1] This very apt statement was made in the Commons in the course of the debate on the great case of *Shirley* v. *Fagg* in 1675. *Grey's Debates*, vol. iii. p. 195.

than the sovereign legislature of the universe: for he can do nothing unjust."[1]

Henry VIII, when he revived this oppressive procedure, was in doubt as to the legality of condemning a man unheard, and called upon the judges for an opinion; who answered, "that it was a dangerous question, and that the High Court of Parliament ought to give examples to inferiour Courts for proceeding according to Justice, and no inferiour Court could do the like; and they thought that the High Court of Parliament would never do it." But when "pressed to give a direct answer," they reluctantly admitted "that if he be attainted by Parliament, it could not come in question afterwards, whether he were called or not called to answer," and the Act of Parliament which was passed accordingly, Coke admits, "did bind, as they resolved." "Yet," he says, "might they have made a better answer," for "no man ought to be condemned without answer," as Magna Charta and other statutes provide.[2]

When Bills of Attainder were again revived in the time of the Stuarts, the same uncertainty remained, and was even accentuated by the growth of the idea of Parliament's legislative sovercignty. The remarkable speech of Lord Digby against them has been noted above,[3] a statement that caused his former friends to attack him "with an implacable rage and uncharitable-

---

[1] 8 *Parl. Hist.*, 287.
[2] 4 *Inst.*, 37, 38. See also the account of Henry's use of attainder in Reeves, *H. E. L.*, vol. iii. pp. 423-5, 506, 507.
[3] *Ante*, p. 153.

ness upon all occasions," Clarendon says.[1] But even St. John, who believed, if Clarendon reports him correctly, that Parliament could kill Strafford as easily and as legally as they could "knock foxes and wolves on the head,"[2] felt the necessity of explaining to the Lords at great length the reasons, legal and practical, for substituting the bill of attainder for impeachment,[3] and "the bill had not that warm reception in the house of peers, that was expected."[4] Much was made of the fact that the bill was supplemental in character. Facts enough had been submitted to prove everything but a technical breach of the law. The substitution was merely "to husband time;"[5] "to obviate those Scruples and Delays, which through disuse of proceedings of this nature, might have risen in the manner and way of proceedings."[6]

In 1667, when the Lords had sent the bill against Clarendon down to the Commons, complaint was made in the latter house that "The lords will neither secure

---

[1] *Rebellion*, book iii.

[2] "He averred, 'That, in that way of bill, private satisfaction to each man's conscience was sufficient, although no evidence had been given in at all:' and as to the pressing the law, he said, 'It was true, we give law to hares and deer, because they be beasts of the chase; but it was never accounted either cruelty, or foul play, to knock foxes and wolves on the head as they can be found, because they be beasts of prey.' In a word, the law and the humanity were alike; the one being more fallacious, and the other more barbarous, than in any age had been vented in such an auditory." Clarendon, *Rebellion*, book iii.

[3] See the whole remarkable speech, Rushworth, *Strafford's Trial*, p. 675 et seq.; some extracts are given *ante*, pp. 151, 152.

[4] Clarendon, *Rebellion*, book iii.

[5] Rushworth, *op. cit.*, p. 677.

[6] *Ibid.*, p. 676.

nor summon him, but will condemn him unheard; and this they put you upon, which is against honour and justice;" but it was admitted at the same time, "That the power of parliaments is indeed great; it hath no bounds but the integrity and justice of parliaments."[1] In the House of Peers Lord Strafford protested that "The commitment upon a general Impeachment hath been heretofore, and may be again, of most evil and dangerous consequence,"[2] as he of all men living had best reason to know.

Fenwick's attainder in 1696 brought out the strongest expressions against the procedure by bill in such cases, even though the guilt of the accused could hardly be doubted, and notwithstanding the fact that one of the two witnesses requisite by statute had been induced by Fenwick's wife to leave the kingdom. Practically the whole of that long case bears upon the question under discussion; only a few statements are here given. For one thing, it was alleged on Fenwick's side that the bill must set forth the acts committed, in the nature of an indictment, "For in all courts of judicature this is a certain rule, You must proceed *secundum allegata et probata;* and you shall not go about to prove a thing unless it be alledged."[3] In answer to these statements it was said, "If they were in Westminster-Hall they would be in the right: but this house is not bound to those

[1] 4 *Parl. Hist.*, 399.
[2] *Ibid.*, 403.
[3] 5 *Parl. Hist.*, 1008.

forms: for I believe the enacting clause would do the business of Sir J. F. well enough, if all the rest were laid aside."[1]

The argument was made in Fenwick's favour that it was "an untrodden path" to bring such a bill before proof was offered, and it was insisted that "what is justice in Westminster-Hall is so here, and every where."[2] One speaker declared: "It is said, we are not tied up to the rules of Westminster-hall; and that parliaments may denominate crimes after they are committed; but I never did hear that the parliament did take upon them to determine that to be evidence which is not evidence in any court in the world.... Why, by parity of reason may not two affidavits do by help of the legislative power?"[3] Another said: "The birth-right that we have is in our laws; and I did ever think till now, that the laws were not only made for Westminster-hall, but for the subjects of England;... Here have been great mistakes between the power of parliament and the jurisdiction of it; the power of parliament is to make any law, but the jurisdiction of parliament is to govern itself by the law.... It hath passed here for current, That the parliament hath a power to declare what they will treason, though so by no other law; It is the greatest mistake in the world."[4]

On the other hand, it was said, "There is lodged in

[1] 5 *Parl. Hist.*, 1015.
[2] *Ibid.*, 1019; see also 1016, 1017, 1020, 1030, 1047, 1087.
[3] *Ibid.*, 1037.
[4] *Ibid.*, 1093, 1094.

the legislative a power to judge those crimes that are sheltered behind the law."[1] "The inferior courts are to go by the letter of the law; and whoever can avoid that, is to escape punishment there; but the legislative is not to be dallied with;"[2] and the legislative power was defined as "a power that can make laws, and abolish them; a power that is superiour to all other powers whatsoever."[3] It is little wonder that one member of the Commons wearily declared, "I can't tell under what character to consider ourselves, whether we are judges or jurymen,"[4] and another, "We sit in so many capacities, it is hard to distinguish in what capacity we are here."[5] The bill passed and Fenwick was executed, but the majorities were small in both houses.[6]

In later cases of pains and penalties we find the same doubts recurring,[7] but enough has been said to show the uncertainty and indefiniteness that have always marked these proceedings.[8]

E. Parliamentary Privilege

If the whole length of parliamentary history be had in view, it will appear how late in that history parliamentary privilege became an important question. The

---

[1] 5 *Parl. Hist.*, 1039. [2] *Ibid.*, 1106. [3] *Ibid.*, 1070. [4] *Ibid.*, 1068. [5] *Ibid.*, 1108.
[6] *Ibid.*, 1154-56. For other interesting statements occurring in the course of the debate, see *ibid.*, 1031, 1032, 1038, 1085, 1096, 1098, 1113.
[7] For example, in the case of Bishop Atterbury, *Parl. Hist.*, vol. viii. pp. 210, 211, 237, 238, 295, 298, 349, 350.
[8] See also on the general subject of bill of attainder, Hatschek, *Englisches Staatsrecht*, vol. i. pp. 121, 240. A convenient résumé of Bills of Attainder since 1329 is to be found in Hatsell, *Precedents*, 2d ed., vol. iv.

THE HIGH COURT OF PARLIAMENT

earliest recorded case of great importance is Thorpe's, in 31 Henry VI. The High Court of Parliament, the "supreamest," the "most honourable," the "most authenticall" court, was of such dignity that its privileges in the early time were not questioned. Prohibitions and other process might issue against other courts, but the dignity of Parliament saved it generally from interference. It will be noted how few important cases of privilege arose before 1640, and how many are found in the later years of the Stuarts. This is by no means an accident. The exercise of legislative powers on an unheard of scale, the uncertainty regarding the respective jurisdictions of the two houses, the struggle between the King and the Parliament, all tended to bring out bold assertions of privilege, and on the other hand determined attempts to limit it. Thus, much of the strife over privilege, though by no means all, arose from the legislative activity of Parliament. The privilege that was asserted in all these cases of whatever kind was, however, in its origin the result of Parliament's "judicial" character, if that word may be used at all in speaking of those times; and the marks of this origin have remained upon it to the present day. Privilege, in fact, furnishes the most striking; though one of the latest to appear, certainly one of the most lasting; and on the whole, one of the most convincing of all the instances of the eminently judicial character of Parliament that can be pointed to.[1]

---

[1] Professor Redlich will not admit that there is any other. He says: "The conception of the House of Commons as a court of law is rather to be looked upon

PARLIAMENT AS A COURT

When, in the thirty-fourth year of Henry VIII, the Commons set up their privilege against the Court of as a claim which arose under the pressure of political needs; as such it had an extraordinarily strong and productive influence on the development of one branch of the *lex et consuetudo parliamenti*, namely, *Privilege*. Consequently, as will be more exactly explained below, the notion had a certain influence upon internal parliamentary law. But in their essential features the procedure and order of business have from the first grown out of the political exigencies of a supreme representative assembly with legislative and administrative functions." *The Procedure of the House of Commons*, by Josef Redlich, English translation by A. Ernest Steinthal, vol. i. p. 25. In a note to this passage Professor Redlich mentions Coke as the representative of the view that Parliament was a court, and comments as follows: "But anyone who closely follows the party strife of the sixteenth and seventeenth centuries under the leadership of the learned jurists of those times will have little difficulty in seeing that their constitutional arguments, at times bordering on the fantastic, were mere cloaks for the political claims to power made by the majority of the House of Commons, and by sections of the nation which it represented." To anyone who has read this essay up to this point, I hardly need say that this view seems to me to be based upon a misreading of the sources from which our knowledge of the history of England before, during, and after the sixteenth and seventeenth centuries is derived. In so saying, I do not wish to underrate the importance of the *actual* legislative work of Parliament in the sixteenth and seventeenth centuries or in centuries before. For the sixteenth and seventeenth centuries at least, I have been investigating what men thought about the work of Parliament rather than that work itself. And men's theories and explanations usually lag far behind the changes in their actual practice. Parliament was a nationally representative body in the sixteenth and seventeenth centuries. No other court was. It was also a large body, composed of two houses. These are facts which go far toward accounting for its unique procedure, so unlike that of all other courts in most ways. It also possessed at that time, and had long possessed, powers that we rightly call legislative.

To say, however, that the procedure and order of business in Parliament in all their "essential features" have "*from the first* grown out of the political exigencies of a supreme representative assembly," seems to me to convey an idea that is contrary to the weight of evidence and utterly foreign to the habit of mind prevailing among Englishmen of the period under discussion. And even if we could believe that the great leaders on both sides in the constitutional struggle of the seventeenth century did not sincerely hold a constitutional theory that colours all their utterances, must we assume that they were not only insincere but stupid as well, in thinking it necessary to use such "mere cloaks" for their real opinions and designs? The words of Professor Goldwin Smith, though used in another connection, are applicable here: "If some of the pro-

King's Bench in the case of Ferrers, the King declared: "We be informed by our Judges, that we at no time stand so highly in our estate Royal as in the time of Parliament; wherein we as Head, and you as Members, are conjoyned and knit together into one body politick, so as whatsoever offense or injury (during that time) is offered to the meanest Member of the House, is to be judged, as done against our person, and the whole Court of Parliament: which prerogative of the Court is so great (as our learned counsel informeth us) as all Acts and Processes comming out of any other inferiour Courts, must for the time cease, and give place to the highest."[1]

As was said in the Commons in 1593, "This Court for its Dignity and highness hath priviledge, as all other Courts have; And as it is above all other Courts, so it hath priviledge above all other Courts; and as it hath priviledge and Jurisdiction too, so hath it also Coercion and Compulsion; otherwise the Jurisdiction is nothing in a Court, if it hath no Coercion."[2]

This is no doubt the proper explanation of the origin of Parliamentary privilege; and the speaker was correct also when he said that privilege must carry with it "coercion and compulsion." But when the Parlia-

---

fessions were hollow, that only proves the strength of the general feeling which demanded the tribute." All this can be said without taking sides on the question of the relative merits of the historical claims of the Commons and the Lords in their great struggle with each other for jurisdiction in the seventeenth century.

[1] *Parl. Hist.*, vol. i. p. 555; Prynne, *Brief Register*, part iv. pp. 855, 856, 862 et seq.
[2] D'Ewes, *Journals*, p. 145.

ment, and more especially the Commons, had assumed the control of the machinery of government, it is easy to see what an extension must almost of necessity be made to this doctrine.

Coke, in an oft-quoted passage, sets forth, but with no thought of legislative sovereignty, the doctrine of a *lex parliamenti*. "And," he says, "as every Court of Justice hath Laws and Customs for its direction, some by the Common Law, some by the Civil and Cannon Law, some by peculiar Laws and Customs, &c. So the High Court of Parliament *Suis propriis legibus & consuetudinibus subsistit*. It is *Lex & Consuetudo Parliamenti*, that all weighty matters in any Parliament moved concerning the Peers of the Realm, or Commons in Parliament assembled, ought to be determined, adjudged and discussed by the course of the Parliament, and not by the Civil Law, nor yet by the Common Laws of this Realm used in more inferiour Courts; which was so declared to be *secundum legem & consuetudinem Parliamenti*, concerning the Peers of the Realm, by the King and all the Lords Spiritual and Temporal; and the like *pari ratione* is for the Commons for anything moved or done in the House of Commons: and the rather, for that by another Law and Custom of Parliament, the King cannot take notice of any thing said or done in the House of Commons, but by the report of the House of Commons: and every Member of the Parliament hath a judicial place, and can be no witness. And this is the reason that Judges ought not to give any opinion of a matter of Parliament, because it is not to be decided by the Common Laws, but *secundum legem & consuetudinem Parliamenti:* and so the Judges in divers Parliaments have confessed. And some hold, that every offence committed in any Court punishable by that Court, must be punished (proceeding criminally) in the same Court, or in some higher, and not in any inferiour Court, and the Court of Parliament hath no higher."[1]

When we try to define this *lex et consuetudo Parliamenti* our trouble begins, and many questions arise in the attempt. Is the House of Lords a court of record or not? It has been said to be so in its judicial capacity, but not in its legislative.[2] It certainly has exercised the power of imprisonment for a term extending beyond its own session, but there has been much hesitation on this point.[3]

Even more argument has been expended on whether the Commons are a court of record or not, a question which, even to-day, as Sir Erskine May says, "would be difficult to determine; for this claim, once firmly maintained, has latterly been virtually abandoned although never distinctly renounced."[4] There is little doubt that under the Tudors the Commons did occasionally exercise powers usually belonging to none but courts of record. In 1531 King Henry VIII wrote to Lady

---

[1] 4 *Inst.*, 15.
[2] May, *Parl. Practice*, 9th ed., p. 110, citing Lord Kenyon.
[3] *Ibid.*, p. 111.
[4] *Ibid.*

PARLIAMENT AS A COURT

Worsley commanding her to desist from troubling Sir Thomas Bradshaw concerning a matter long at variance between them, as the House of Commons had decided that he was not culpable.[1] In Fitzherbert's Case in 1592, the House of Commons declared itself to be a court of record.[2] Coke also insisted that the Journal of the Commons was a record, and attempted to justify it by an act of Henry VIII's reign.[3] Sir Erskine May has collected from the Journals of the House numerous instances where the Commons during Elizabeth's reign fined offenders and committed them to the Tower for definite periods.[4] The House itself plainly felt that it had gone too far in Floyde's Case in 1621, when it imposed a fine and other punishment upon a man for words that in no way concerned the dignity or privilege of Parliament; but though the Commons receded from the case, they disavowed any intention of giving up any of their claims, and in the course of the case Sir Edward Coke reasserted their claim to be a court of record. So late as 1666 the House of Commons imposed a fine of £1000.[5]

This contention of the Commons was denied as strenuously as it was asserted. For example, by Prynne in his *Plea for the Lords,* and by Filmer, who went so

---

[1] *Letters and Papers of Henry VIII.*, vol. v. No. 117; A. F. Pollard, *Henry VIII.*, p. 259, note.
[2] D'Ewes, *Journals*, p. 502.
[3] 4 *Inst.*, 23; 6 Henry VIII., cap. 16. This statute merely mentions a license which must be "entered of Record in the Book of the Clerk of Parliament."
[4] May, *Parl. Practice*, p. 113.
[5] May, *op. cit.*, pp. 111-14 and references there cited.

THE HIGH COURT OF PARLIAMENT

far as to say that "The House of Commons, which doth not minister an Oath, nor fine, nor imprison any, but their own Members (and that but of late in some Cases) cannot properly be said to be a Court at all; much less to be a part of the Supream Court, or highest Judicature of the Kingdom."[1]

This confusion—"one of the most difficult questions of constitutional law that has ever arisen"[2]—arose out of the mixed and uncertain functions of Parliament. Members of Parliament, on account of the dignity of the High Court in which they "had judicial place," were protected from insult or from process of inferior courts by the ordinary judicial methods of punishing contempt. From the fact that other courts could not question these acts of the "most authenticall court," its methods of procedure within its own walls, and even the extension of that procedure beyond its walls, as in cases of contempt, were looked upon as coming under a special law different from the law of the land. This was a natural conclusion in the days when the memory of a separate ecclesiastical jurisdiction was still fresh in England, and when even the law merchant was not yet reduced by the advancing dogma of legislative sovereignty to a place too low to be comparable with the common law.

As was said in the Queen's Bench by one of the judges so late as 1704, in the case of Ashby v. White,

---

[1] *Freeholder's Grand Inquest*, p. 5.
[2] May, *op. cit.*, p. 169.

PARLIAMENT AS A COURT

concerning a commitment by the Commons, "to be committed by one law, and to judge of the commitment here by another law, would be a strange thing: for the House do not commit by the authority of the common law, but by another law, 'Legem et Consuetudinem Parliamenti;' for there are in England several other laws, besides the common law, viz. the ecclesiastical law, the admiralty law, &c. and there is the law and customs of parliament, where they have particular laws and customs for their directions."[1]

So long as Parliament kept out of conflict with other organs of the commonwealth the indefiniteness that exists in the *lex parliamenti* might cause little disturbance. But Parliament had long been a lawmaking body as well as a court, and by the sixteenth and seventeenth centuries was beginning to find it out. The problem was serious enough before. It had often been impossible to decide when Parliament or one house of Parliament was bound by the *lex terrae* and when only by the *lex parliamenti;* to distinguish between what it *must* do as a court administering the common law of the land, and what it *might* do by virtue of its own peculiar laws of procedure.

But now, when Parliament men were coming gradually to see more clearly the distinction between the judicial and the legislative part of their work, the problem of the *lex parliamenti* began to be more complicated than ever. If before it had been hard to distinguish

[1] 14 *St. Tr.*, 854.

privilege from ordinary adjudication, it now became doubly hard to distinguish adjudication from legislation; and this at a time when the great accession of parliamentary business in the seventeenth century made a solution more necessary. In legislation was Parliament (or either house alone) bound by the *lex terrae*, by the *lex parliamenti*, or by no law at all? Under the influence of the modern view of Parliament's discretion incident to its omnipotence, we easily answer these questions; but the great influence of the idea of fundamental law still obtaining over the minds of men of the seventeenth century is shown by the fact that though they were accustomed to the *actual* discretion of Parliament, and hence were unable to say that in legislation it was bound by the *lex terrae*, we do find them saying that even in legislative matters, Parliament is bound by the *lex parliamenti*. Thus the Attorney-General said in Fitzharris's Case: "I would observe there are three things to be considered of the parliament; the legislative part, the matters of privilege, and the judicial part proper to this case. *For the legislative part*, and matters of privilege, both Houses do proceed only 'secundum legem et consuetudinem parliamenti.'"[1] And in Streater's Case in 1653, where the objection, as we have seen, was to commitment by a mere *order* of Parliament, the court answered: "We must submit to the legislative power."[2]

[1] 8 *St. Tr.*, 315.
[2] *Ante*, p. 159; 5 *St. Tr.*, 386.

PARLIAMENT AS A COURT

This double indefiniteness in the meaning of *lex parliamenti* comes directly from the haziness of the line between legislation and adjudication; and from that indefiniteness, in turn, arose the almost hopeless contradiction in the decisions of English courts on these matters, which remained for a hundred years and more to make the subject of privilege one of the most difficult in the whole range of English constitutional law.

The apparent dilemma that resulted arose from reasoning somewhat as follows: The Commons (for it was usually in that house that these questions arose) are a court, and a court higher and more honourable than the King's other courts of law: it is not fitting that any inferior court call in question the higher: the inferior courts must therefore accept without question as *lex parliamenti* and inviolable every decision of the Commons upon their own privileges. Besides, the whole doctrine of the binding character of judicial precedents requires that a decision of a higher court must be accepted without question by a lower. Even though the House of Commons may have no power to legislate by itself, its decisions must in regular judicial course bind any inferior court.

The Commons themselves clung to this view with the greatest tenacity, because to relinquish it would subject the decision of their privileges in the last instance to their rivals, the House of Lords.

But, on the other hand, privilege is an exception to the ordinary law; an enlargement of existing privileges would be an encroachment on the law of the land; if the Commons should do that, it would really be legislation, which can be legally enacted only by King, Lords, and Commons together.

If the former contention should prevail, it is clear that in questions of privilege the duties of the inferior courts would be restricted to the mere ministerial enforcement of the judgement pronounced by the house whose privileges were involved. This dilemma needed only an actual extension of privilege on the part of the Commons to become the basis of a great constitutional struggle. Clarendon at the beginning of the struggle laid down the principle generally accepted to-day as the proper solution. "We are," he represents the Commons as saying, "and have been always confessed, the only judges of our own privileges; and therefore whatsoever we declare to be our privilege, is such: otherwise whosoever determines that it is not so, makes himself judge of that, whereof the cognizance only belongs to us." "And this sophistical riddle hath perplexed many, who, notwithstanding the desperate consequence they saw must result from such logic, taking the first proposition for true, which, being rightly understood, is so, have not been able to wind themselves out of the labyrinth of the conclusion: I say the proposition rightly understood: they are the only judges of their own privileges, that is, upon the breach of those privileges, which the law hath declared to be their own, and what punishment is to be inflicted upon

PARLIAMENT AS A COURT

such breach. But there can be no privilege, of which the law doth not take notice, and which is not pleadable by, and at law."[1]

In striking contrast to this statement, the House of Commons declared so late as 1837, "That for any court or tribunal to assume to decide upon matters of privilege inconsistent with the determination of either house of Parliament thereon, is contrary to the law of Parliament, and is a breach and contempt of the privileges of Parliament."[2] The present view of the law was well stated in the case of Stockdale v. Hansard when it was said: "The proposition contended for goes no further than to say that each house is a court of exclusive jurisdiction, as the ecclesiastical courts, the admiralty court, and the court of exchequer, are with respect to particular branches of the law. They have not power to make the law, but only an exclusive authority to declare it on particular subjects. It does not follow that they can extend their jurisdiction."[3]

Between the statement of this view by Lord Clarendon in the seventeenth century and its iteration in the nineteenth, there is a period of struggle, confusion, and hesitation, relieved, however, by the luminous opinions of Lord Holt in the case of the Aylesbury men, when he decided against an extension of the privileges of the Commons,[4] and in Rex & Regina v.

[1] *History of the Rebellion*, book iv.
[2] 92 *Commons Journals*, 418, quoted in May, *Parl. Practice*, p. 183.
[3] 9 *Adolphus & Ellis*, 32, 33.
[4] 2 Ld. *Raymond*, 1105.

[241]

Knollys, where he decided on like grounds against the Lords.[1]

In this long period one case deserves especial mention here. The great case of Sir William Williams has hardly received the notice it deserves in our histories of the English Constitution. Along with the cases of the Seven Bishops and Godden *v.* Hales, it must be considered one of the immediate causes of the Revolution. It was the occasion of one of the most important clauses in the Bill of Rights, and probably therefore of the like provision in the Constitution of the United States. Sir William Williams, Speaker of the Commons, for signing *ex officio* the order of the house authorizing the publication of Dangerfield's narrative, was found guilty in the King's Bench and fined ten thousand pounds,—circumstances of considerable constitutional importance, surely. The case is important on account of its nature and its influence upon the Revolution, but its chief interest for this discussion is the fact that it turned so largely on the judicial conception of Parliament. This appears all through the argument of Sir Robert Atkyns in Williams's defence, which was published in 1689. His whole contention is based upon the idea that Parliament is a court. Thus he argues that no indictment lies for what is done in a course of justice or in a way of legal proceeding: "But what has been done by the defendant, and by the House of Commons in this case, hath been done in a

[1] 1 *Ld. Raymond*, 10.

PARLIAMENT AS A COURT

course of justice, and in a way of legal proceedings, and that in the highest court of the nation."[1]

One of the most striking things about Atkyns's argument is his use of the *Lex et Consuetudo Parliamenti*. This had always been of indefinite extent, but in general it applied to procedure and privilege mainly. Atkyns now apparently makes it so general that if a case comes before Parliament on appeal, it is decided by the *lex parliamenti* instead of the *lex terrae;* which looks very much like a fusion of legislative and judicial functions that merits the term confusion when used so late as 1688.[2] He apparently also includes within the *lex parliamenti* the discretion of Parliament in the passage of laws,[3] and this had been done before.[4] He cannot be rid of the old idea that in all its actions Parliament is bound by some law: if not the *lex terrae*, then the *lex parliamenti*. Even in the exercise of its discretion (acting *ex arbitrio*, as Spelman would say)[5] it is bound by a law, the *lex parliamenti*. In other words, he has made the transition to the idea of legislative sovereignty, but he has done it under the old forms and with the old terms. Parliament is still a court and its functions are in the main judicial, but under its *lex parliamenti* it may do any act it pleases and shall never be questioned for it beyond its walls.

He is resting his contention ultimately on the old ju-

---
[1] 13 *St. Tr.*, 1384.   [2] *Ibid.*, 1425.   [3] *Ibid.*, 1427, 1428.
[4] *Fitzharris's Case* (1681). See *ante*, p. 238.
[5] Spelman mentions certain (judicial) functions of Parliament as "meerly *Legal* and not *Parliamentary* or *ex arbitrio*." *Reliquiae*, p. 82.

dicial idea of Parliament. This, however, involved one great difficulty. He is trying to extend judicial privileges and immunities to all forms of parliamentary action.

But did not "Parliament" in the judicial sense mean the Lords alone? Appeals from the courts of law had been heard there exclusively for a long time, and though the Lords had abandoned their claim to try original cases where peers were not involved, they had lately vindicated their doubtful right in the case of appeals from the Court of Chancery. This difficulty Atkyns avoids in characteristic style: It must be remembered, he says, "that the parliament ... is one entire body, and that their power in the right of it is entire, though as to the exercise of it, it is distributed into parts, and is divided: nor can the House of Lords exercise any power as an House of Parliament, or as a court for errors, without the House of Commons be in being at the same time. Both Houses must be prorogued together, and dissolved together; like the twins of Hippocrates, they live and die together, and the one cannot be in being, without the other also, at the same time be in being too."[1]

Statements of the judicial character of Parliament keep on recurring up to the nineteenth century, in cases of privilege.[2]

---

[1] 13 *St. Tr.*, 1424. For other parts of this interesting argument bearing on this point, see columns 1410, 1411, 1422, 1423, 1429, 1433, 1437, and the valuable references there cited.
[2] For example, in *Ashby* v. *White* (14 *St. Tr.*, 728, 853, 855); in the *Case of Brass Crosby* in 1771, 19 *St. Tr.*, 1147; *Burdett* v. *Abbott*, 14 *East*, 159, 160.

PARLIAMENT AS A COURT

In fact, the whole question of the privileges of the House of Commons remained uncertain just so long as the judicial character of the house remained undefined, and that in turn remained undefined so long as there was uncertainty concerning the boundary between legislation and adjudication. The particular phase of the question concerning privilege was settled with a prospect of finality by the case of Stockdale v. Hansard. In that case Lord Chief Justice Denman said: "It can hardly be necessary to guard myself against being supposed to discuss the expediency of keeping the law in its present state, or introducing any and what alterations. It is no doubt susceptible of improvement; but the improvement must be a legislative act. If we held that any improvement, however desirable, could be effected under the name of privilege, we should be confounding truth, and departing from our duty; and if, on such considerations, either house should claim, as matter of privilege, what was neither necessary for the discharge of their proper functions, nor ever had been treated as a privilege before, this would be an enactment, not a declaration, or, if the latter name were more appropriate, it would be a declaration of a general law, to be disregarded by the courts, though never, I hope, treated with contempt. It would also be a declaration of a new law; and the word 'adjudge' can make no difference in the nature of the thing."[1]

[1] *Adolphus & Ellis*, 151–3. See also *Howard* v. *Gossett*, 10 Q. B., 359; *Bradlaugh* v. *Gossett*, 12 Q. B. D., 271.

THE HIGH COURT OF PARLIAMENT

For this period of some two hundred years there is a masterly summary of the cases on parliamentary privilege in Chapter VI of Sir Erskine May's *Parliamentary Practice*, and another equally good in Part III of Broom's *Constitutional Law*. To these the reader is referred for further proof of the point which it has been the object of this chapter to illustrate; namely, that the great doubt and uncertainty that so long clouded the decisions upon the important question of parliamentary privilege arose almost entirely from Parliament's character as a court; from the inability to see clearly the lines between its varied powers in that "judicial" capacity; and from the confusion of those judicial powers with the discretionary power which the theory of parliamentary legislative sovereignty necessarily implies.[1]

---

[1] On the general subject of Privilege in this connection, see the parts of Broom's *Constitutional Law* (2d ed.) and May's *Parliamentary Practice*, referred to above; also Hale, *Jurisdiction of the Lords House*, Hargrave's Preface, pp. ciii-cxxvi (for the case of *Skinner* v. *The East India Co.*); *ibid.*, pp. cxxxiv-clxi (*Shirley* v. *Fagg*); *ibid.*, pp. clxxxii-iv (*Case of Charles Knollys*); *Dyer's Reports*, 60 A; 13 *Cobbett's State Trials*, 1369-1442, *passim* (*Sir William Williams's Case*); 14 *St. Tr.*, 695 et seq., *passim* (*Ashby* v. *White*); 8 *St. Tr.*, 223 et seq., *passim* (*Fitzharris's Case*). Exhaustive references to other cases will be found in May and Broom, and in the great case of *Stockdale* v. *Hansard*, 9 *Adolphus & Ellis*, 1 et seq., especially in Lord Denman's opinion, p. 106 et seq. The most important source of all, of course, is to be found in the Journals of the houses themselves. See in index volumes under "Privilege," and especially the cases of *Shirley* v. *Fagg*, *C. J.*, vol. ix. p. 329 et seq., *passim*; *Fitzharris's Case*, *C. J.*, vol. ix. p. 711 et seq.; *Fenwick's Case*, *C. J.*, vol. xi. p. 577 et seq., *passim*. See also Hatsell, *Precedents* (2d ed., vol. i.); 4 *Inst.*, 1 et seq.; and the minute exhaustive chapter in Prynne's *Brief Register* (vol. iv. pp. 622-869); *Lex Parliamentaria*, by G—— P——, Esq. (1698); *Miscellania Parliamentaria*, by William Petyt (1680).

PARLIAMENT AS A COURT

Note A
Judicial Interpretation of Edward III's Statute of Treason
(*Page* 117)

In the third year of Richard II, John Imperial, ambassador from Genoa, was murdered by two citizens of London. The case was debated in both houses and declared to be treason. "This declaration," Hale says, "being by the king and both houses of parliament was a good declaration pursuant to the act of 25 E. 3." *History of the Pleas of the Crown* (1736), vol. i. p. 263. "Note it well," says Coke, "this case was not referred to the Judges, but declared in and by Parliament." (12 *Reports*, 16.) Hale clearly implies that this declaration in Imperial's case was an "act" which would not be valid unless made by both houses. This elastic clause in the Statute of Edward III came up for discussion in Strafford's Trial. (*State Trials*, vol. iii. p. 1475; Rushworth, *Strafford's Trial*, pp. 676, 677, 699, 700.) Again, in the Earl of Clarendon's Case, it was asked: "Hath the Parliament declaratory Power now? Yes, but it must be by King and Parliament, so it was in the case of the *Genoua* Ambassador. The Judges would not conclude the Articles Treason, nor would the Lords alone; and if you come to an equal declarative Power with them, you must examine witnesses, or go by a Bill." (2 *St. Tr.*, 565, Hargrave's ed.)

Hale, and Clarendon's judges, Mr. Holdsworth thinks, here mean to assert that a judgement of Parliament in pursuance of this clause of the statute of 25 Edward III is a legislative act. (*H. E. L.*, vol. i. p. 188, note 3.) I can hardly think so, at least in Hale's case, for Hale goes on to say that the declaration is not in force in his own day. "Because it was but a particular case, and extended not to any other case, as a binding law but only as a great authority." (*Pleas of the Crown*, vol. i. p. 263.) It is true, Hale does, as Mr. Justice Stephen points out (*History of the Criminal Law of England*, vol. ii. p. 252), declare that the case of Tresilian and others in 11 Richard II was not within this statute of 25 E. III, "because the king and commons did not consent *per modum legis declarativae*, for the judgment was only the lords." (*P. C.*, vol. i. p. 264.) But this is by no means to declare that a proper declaration under the statute must be a "legislative" act. Hale only asserted that certain declarations were warranted by the statute because made by both houses, and that other declarations and judgements were unwarranted by it because made by the Lords alone. He says nothing about "legislative" acts, and his argument in his *Jurisdiction of the Lords House* would indicate that he did not mean "legislative" acts. For him a valid judgement as well as a valid statute required the action of both houses. In the passage in question he is thinking of the judicial functions of Parliament rather than the legislative, though in fact it is apparent that he makes no clear distinction between them, as will be noted later. Mr. Justice Stephen himself believes the clause of the statute in question referred to judicial acts (*H. C. L.*, vol. ii. p. 252), and Mr. Holdsworth seems to agree with him (*H. E. L.*, vol. i. p. 188, n. 3). For the Case of John Imperial, see also *Rot. Parl.*, vol. iii. p. 75 B., and *3 Inst.*, 8. These varying interpretations, if they serve no other purpose, show how hazy and indefinite the line of division between acts judicial and acts legislative remained even to the time of Lord Hale.

Note B. Early Cases Determined in Parliament
(Page 117)

BRACTON says : " Si autem aliqua nova et inconsueta emerserint, et quae prius usitata non fuerint in regno, si tamen similia evenerint, per simile judicentur, cum bona sit occasio a similibus procedere ad similia. Si autem talia nunquam prius evenerint, et obscurum et difficile sit eorum judicium, tunc ponantur judicia in respectum usq; ad magnam curiam, ut ibi per consilium curiae terminentur: licet sint nonnulli qui de propria scientia praesumentes, quasi nihil juris ignorent, nolunt alicuius consilium expetere: in quo casu honestius et consultius eis foret consilium habere quam aliquid temere definire, cum de singulis dubitare non sit inutile. Sedem quidem judicandi, quae est quasi thronus dei, non praesumat quis ascendere insipiens et indoctus, ne lucem ponat in tenebras, et tenebras in lucem, et ne in manu indocta, modo furientis, gladio feriat innocentem, et liberet nocentem, et ex alto corruat quasi a throno dei, qui volare inceperit antequam pennas assumat." Lib. i. cap. ii. secs. 7, 8.

There are many cases in the Year Books and Rolls of Parliament that show the practice. See, for example, *Rot. Parl.*, 18 Edward I. (vol. i. p. 44); also vol. i. pp. 301, 307.

PARLIAMENT AS A COURT

In the time of Edward III such cases are especially numerous: e. g. Hil. 1 E. III., fol. 7 B; Mich. 39 E. III., fol. 21 A. In the second of these cases, which arose from the omission of a proper name from a writ, Judge Thorp declared that in a previous similar case, the writ had been taken into Parliament, where "the Lords who made the writ stated what their intention was," namely, that in all such cases the process should be amended. Here we find the Parliament interpreting a statute,—in litigation,—a proceeding that we think of as strictly judicial.

In the next year Thorp is apparently referring to the same case. He says he and a fellow judge went to the Council and demanded of those who made the statute, to know if the record could be amended. They were told that it could. Trin. 40 E. III., fol. 34 B. See also Mich. 13 Henry IV., fol. 4.

In another case, involving the title to land, occurring in the thirty-ninth year of Edward III, Judge Thorp speaks of a previous case similar to the one then before him, which had been tried in Parliament ("in autiel cas de Giles Blaket il fuit parle in Parliament"), in which the judges had been commanded that when any such case came before them, they were not to proceed to judgement without good advice. "Wherefore," he says, "sue to the Council, and as they wish us to do, we will do, and otherwise not in this case." Mich. 39 E. III., fol. 35 A. In the eighteenth year of Edward III we find another case where the judgement of the court is *par avise de Counsel le Roy.* Lib. Ass., fol. 60 B. See also Lib. Ass., fol. 256 B.

In a case in 9 Henry V (1421) (*Rot. Parl.*, vol. iv. p. 153), we find the following statement: "Et pur tant, que sur grantes altercations et disputations, queux par long temps feurent en la dite Chancellerie, par entre les Conseils des ditz parties, sur les materes suisdites euz et moevez, et des queux mon dit Seigneur le Chanceller, et les Clercs du Roi de sa Chancellerie, pur difficulte ne purrient brievement et droitement estre avisez a faire ceo que la Leie y vorroit cell partie, mon dit Seigneur le Chanceller adjurna la matere a ceo mesme Parlement, et attermina et referra les ditz parties illoeqes d'oier ceo, que purroit estre terminez par advis de mesme le Parlement, selonc l'effect de l'auncien Estatuit de Westm' secounde." On the general subject, see also 2 *Inst.*, 408; Petyt, *Jus Parliamentarium*, p. 15 et seq.; Reeves, *H. E. L.*, vol. ii. p. 290 et seq.; Prynne's *Abridgment of the Records*, Preface.

NOTE C. THE RELATIONS OF CHANCERY AND PARLIAMENT
(*Page* 133)

"Nor are there found any Bills, and Decrees in *Chancery*, before the 20th. of H. 6. Such causes as since that time were heard in that Court, having formerly been determined in the Lords House of Parliament, as may seem from the number of *Petitions* in *Parliament*, of that nature, which are yet extant." Dugdale, *Origines Juridiciales* (1680), p. 37. "Note that in ancient time, where the matter was against reason, and the party had no remedy by the Common Law, it was used, to sue for remedy in Parliament, and the Parliaments were holden of course, twice every year, but now most of those sutes are in the Chancery, and the Parliaments are not so often holden." *Certaine Observations concerning the Office of the Lord Chancellor*, "Composed by the Right Honorable, and most Learned, *Thomas* Lord *Ellesmere*, late Lord Chancellor of England" (1651), p. 47.

In this "ancient time" there is observable the same concurrent activity of the Parliament and the Chancellor, in his granting of new writs. There has been some difference of opinion upon the question whether the Chancellor's jurisdiction in early times was mainly *supplendi gratia* or *corrigendi gratia*. The granting of *new* remedies would naturally be connected more closely with the Chancellor's oversight of his subordinates in their capacity of receivers of petitions and his own functions as a member of the Council; his part in the administration of the common law would be mainly due to his power of issuing original writs. Both of these great powers, however, were originally exercised by the Chancellor, not as an individual official, but as a member of the Council; it may almost be said by virtue of the power delegated by the Council. The main fact to be noticed in this early and formative period, in the relations between the Chancellor and the Council, is the same one we have already noticed in the relations of the Council and the King's other courts,—an absence of legal distinction. Important stages in this early development are marked by the *Provisions of Oxford* of 1258, where the barons compelled the Chancellor to promise "That he will seal no writ, except-

PARLIAMENT AS A COURT

ing writs of course, without the commandment of the king and of his council who shall be present" (Stubbs, *S. C.*, p. 389); and by the twenty-fourth chapter of the Statute of Westminster II, which required new cases to be brought into Parliament, but also allowed the Chancellor in future to issue new writs "in consimili casu cadente sub eodem jure" with the old. In the *Provisions of Oxford* we see not so much a fear of the Chancellor's power as a determination on the part of the barons to prevent his being answerable to the King alone for its exercise. The nature of the provisions of the Statute of Westminster II is discussed in the text (pp. 115, 116). See also *ante*, p. 116, note. On this subject generally, see Holdsworth, *H. E. L.*, vol. i. pp. 196, 197; Jenks, *Law and Politics*, pp. 143, 144, 145; Stat. 27 Eliz., ch. viii., quoted above (p. 132); Kerly, *History of Equity*, ch. i.; Hardy, *Introduction to the Close Rolls;* Spence, *Equitable Jurisdiction of the Chancellor*, vol. i. p. 322 et seq.

Note D. The Auditores or Triers of Petitions in Parliament
(*Page* 209)

The name *auditor* seems originally to have been applied to one whose duties were judicial rather than fiscal (Du Cange, s. v. *Auditor, Auditores*), and for a long time in England it was used of judicial officers as well as fiscal. The author of *Fleta,* in his chapter on the Courts in England, speaks of Auditors specially appointed who can hear but not finally determine cases ("Habet etiam curiam suam coram Auditoribus specialiter a latere Reg[is] destinatis, quorum officium non extenditur nisi ad Justiciar[em] et ministros Regis, et quibus non conceditur potestas audita terminare, sed Regi deferre, ut per ipsum adhibeantur poenae secundum meritorum qualitates." Lib. ii. cap. ii. sec. 4). There is an interesting case on the Rolls of Parliament of 1290 bearing out this statement, in part at least. (*Rot. Parl.*, vol. i. pp. 20, 21.) It arose from the interference by the King's bailiffs with rights exempt by charter. As a result, the abbot whose rights had been invaded sued the bailiffs "coram Episcopo Wynton & Sociis suis Auditoribus" at Westminster. The parties placed themselves on the country, and a jury of twenty-four from Southampton, where the alleged wrong was committed, was brought before the *auditores*. However, on the appearance of the parties and the jury, the auditors decided that they had no power to proceed further in the case, because it really concerned the King, the bailiffs having no interest in it save in their capacity of tax collectors. They therefore set a day for the parties "*and the jury likewise*," to appear before the King and his Council.

In the same year, on account of complaints of undue influence upon ministers and clerics in London, "Preceptum est per Consilium Auditorum querelarum in Civitate Lond." that the said ministers be removed until the cases in which they were interested were disposed of. (*Rot. Parl.*, vol. i. p. 48.) We find on the Rolls another case in the same year, where the men of Appleby " petunt auditores" for relief for injuries sustained. (*Rot. Parl.*, vol. i. p. 51.) And still another, again from the year 1290, where Richard, a clerk of Southwark, "petit Auditores quod inde audiatur," because the King had treated as escheated a house he had bought of Isaac, a Jew of Southwark, which house the King had allowed the Jew *per cartam* to sell. (*Rot. Parl.*, vol. i. p. 58.)

Section 40 of the Ordinances of the Barons in 1312 provided that a bishop, two counts, and two barons should be appointed in each Parliament, " de oier & terminer " all the complaints against the King's ministers for breach of the ordinances. (*Rot Parl.*, vol. i. p. 286.)

In the Parliament Roll for 1314-1315 we find the heading, "Responsiones Petitionum Angl' per Auditores earundem facte in Parliamento Regis apud Westm' post octab' S'c'i' Hillarii, anno regni sui octavo." (*Rot. Parl.*, vol. i. p. 314.)

In 1330 complaint was made because the Chancellor had altered the endorsement of a petition after it had been received, which was illegal and against his oath—"desicome Peticion endosse en Parlement, et livre par l'Auditour d'ycelle a la place des Roules en la Chauncellerie, doit de reson estre de Record, et nient estre change en avantage ou prejudice de nully." (*Rot. Parl.*, vol. ii. p. 45.)

In 1332 directions were given for the receiving and trying of petitions by the "Triours et Terminours," who are also spoken of as "Auditours." (*Rot. Parl.*, vol. ii. p. 68.) Soon after this it becomes usual to find at the opening of Parliament, as, for example, in 1381, that "certeins Clercs de la Chancellerie sont assignez de les resceivre,

PARLIAMENT AS A COURT

et certeins Prelatz, Seigneurs, et Justices de les veer, oier, trier et terminer." (*Rot. Parl.*, vol. iii. p. 98.)

In 1390 the record of the appointment of receivers and triers restricts the petitions to things "which cannot be redressed by the Common Law of the Land." (*Rot. Parl.*, vol. iii. p. 277.) But the present-day use of the term " common law " is probably much more exclusive and definite than the meaning of the term in 1390,—"the term ' Common Law ' not being used in the confined sense that we give to it in the present day, but as indicating the ordinary mode of proceeding in the ordinary courts of justice." (Testimony of Sir F. Palgrave, *Parl. Papers*, Session of 1833, vol. xii. p. 19.)

In 1340 the Barons' ordinance of 1312 was made permanent by statute and applied to cases of all sorts, where delays or other grievances in the ordinary courts are complained of.

Unlike the *auditores* of Edward I's day, the "committee" under this ordinance might determine as well as hear, unless in their judgement the case should be too difficult to be determined without further assistance, when they might resort to Parliament for a decision. If they wished, they might consult the great officers, members of the Council or the judges, but if this was done, it would seem probable from the wording and general tenor of the act, that those so consulted were to have no power beyond that of advising. (14 Edward III., Stat. 1, cap. v.) Lord Hale, however, thought they had "a co-ordinate voice as well as the lords" (*Jurisdiction of the Lords House*, p. 156); and it is probably true, as he contends, though the actual words of this statute seem hardly to support it, that the judges who were regularly appointed along with the lay and spiritual peers among the triers, both before this statute of Edward III and after it, had a "voice of suffrage" equal with the rest, instead of a mere " voice of advice," "as . . . appears by the composure and power of the *auditores querelarum* appointed by the King in parliament; which consisted as well of the chancellor treasurer and justices, as of lords, and their power not only preparative to the house of lords but decisive." He continues: "But yet further it is most evident beyond all dispute, that though the record either by writ or petition were removed into the lords house, and virtually and interpretatively the judgment of affirmation or reversal was theirs; yet the actual decision and determination (in antient times even after the decay of the power of the *consilium regis*) was given by a select number of lords and judges, nominated by the king in parliament, or at least by the king with the advice of the lords." (*Jurisdiction of the Lords House*, p. 156.)

So far as I know, there is nothing in the later rolls to show that any distinction was made between the peers and the judges who were always appointed to serve with them as triers. Lord Hale's contention is supported by the studies of Professor Baldwin upon the oath taken by the Councillors, as noted above in the text, pp. 34, 35.

The above instances indicate the close relation between the courts and Parliament.

With clerks of chancery acting as receivers, and judges of the law courts serving among the *auditores*, along with the Chancellor, it could hardly be otherwise.

There are several questions of great importance on which we know very little, some of which have been referred to in the text. For example: Did the receivers of petitions ever have any such discretion in parliamentary petitions as that which at one time they seem to have exercised in their capacity of clerks of chancery when they issued original writs?

What was the criterion by which the triers adjudged some petitions fit for hearing in Parliament and others suitable for the inferior courts? How far is the body of triers or auditors, including both peers and judges, to be identified with "The King's Council in his Parliaments," and was there any distinction between the powers and duties of the peers and those of the judges?

These questions in our present state of knowledge cannot be certainly answered, but it seems clear, as we study these institutions more closely, that the "judicial" functions of Parliament grow very close to, and are indifferently distinguished from, the activity of the other courts of the King. The ancient writ of *audita querela* granted by the chancery clerks bears a name singularly suggestive of the *auditores querelarum* in Parliament. Was there any great or essential difference between *querelae* which the clerks directed to the judges and other *auditores querelarum* in Parliament, and the ones they sent to the same judges in the inferior courts? In the book published in 1641 as

PARLIAMENT AS A COURT

Lord Ellesmere's, with the title *The Privilege and Prerogatives of the High Court of Chancery*, reasons are given for the passage of the Statute 4 Henry IV., cap. 23, concerning appeals upon cases decided in the King's courts. The author says, "But before the making of this Statute; there bee many precedents and records to prove, that the King and his Councell, and the King's Commissioners appointed to be auditors *querelarum* & Court of Rome, & some pretending to have power" assumed to examine and reverse judgements, wherefore the statute.

Accounts of the receivers and triers are given in Coke, 4 *Inst.*, 10, 11; Prynne, *Observations on Coke's Fourth Institute*, p. 14; Elsynge, ch. viii.; Clifford, *History of Private Bill Legislation*, vol. i. p. 271 et seq. Prynne believed that the Masters of Requests had their origin in the Receivers of Petitions (*Obs. on the 4th Inst.*, pp. 14, 52). According to the view now seemingly held by the best authorities, this can hardly be true except in the most general sense.

The duties of the Receivers and those of the Masters of Requests were similar in general character, and in that sense a general continuity of function might probably be shown between the Receivers in the days of their activity and the later Masters of Requests. That the one office is a direct offshoot of the other, however, would seem to be impossible, if the Court of Requests as a definite organization had an origin as late as the date now generally accepted for it. See Mr. Leadam's introduction to *Select Cases in the Court of Requests* (Selden Society); Holdsworth, *H. E. L.*, vol. i. p. 207 et seq. But see Spence, *The Equitable Jurisdiction of the Court of Chancery*, vol. i. p. 351.

Though Prynne's supposition may be unfounded, I cannot help thinking that there is a very close connection between the general development of equity jurisdiction and the double functions of these clerks of chancery who acted as receivers of parliamentary petitions as well as drafters of original writs; between the activity of the judges in the King's ordinary courts and their duties as *auditores querelarum* in the High Court of Parliament. And it can hardly be accidental that the ancient writ of *audita querela*—when we consider its character—should bear a name so like the name of the auditors. Still less can it be an accident that the regular choosing of receivers in Parliament begins to be noted on the Rolls in the earlier years of Edward III (see *ante*, pp. 208, 209; Elsynge, p. 263 et seq.), while there is good evidence that the first use of the writ of *audita querela* corresponds almost exactly in time. In 1343 Stonore, Chief Justice, said of the writ, "Quite recently there was no such suit." *Y. B. 17 E. III.*, Rolls Series, pp. 370, 371. See also Mr. Pike's introduction to that volume, pp. xl, xli. In the next year it was said in the course of a case, "*Audita Querela* was given quite recently, that is to say in the tenth year of the reign, *in Parliament*, on account of the mischief, and it was never given before." *Y. B. 18 E. III.*, Rolls Series, p. 308. The italics are mine. See Holdsworth, *H. E. L.*, vol. ii. p. 503, and note 3. On the writ of *audita querela* generally, see Jacob's *Law Dictionary;* Fitzherbert's *New Natura Brevium*, p. 102 et seq. The writ itself is to be found in the *Register of Writs*, vol. i. pp. 149, 150 (1687).

CHAPTER IV

The Relations of "Judiciary" and "Legislature"

NOT least important among the results of the growth in modern times of the doctrine of legislative sovereignty is the change it has wrought in the relations between the judges and Parliament. The most striking characteristic of the growth of law in recent times is the prominence of legislation. Legislation derives its authority from an " external body or person." " Its obligatory force is independent of its principles." The motives of the makers of a law are absolutely immaterial if they have clearly and unequivocally expressed their intention. After that intention has been expressed, only two things remain : in the first place, to explain that expression of intention and adapt it to cases not specifically foreseen; in the second place, to enforce it. The former of these may be done by the legislature itself by supplementary or "expository " acts, or it may be left by the legislature to the courts. In the performance of this function the courts in England have, in modern times, to use Sir Frederick Pollock's expression, " treated Acts of Parliament as proceeding from a wholly external and unjudicial authority."[1] The clear *ipse dixit* of Parliament, covering a particular case, is all they want, all they dare seek for. Neither the mo-

---

[1] *First Book of Jurisprudence*, p. 331.

tives nor the righteousness of Parliament's action is open to question or investigation. The only argument in a court of law, upon a case clearly covered by parliamentary legislation, is the argument from authority. Parliament is looked upon in a purely objective way. "They have the legislative power."[1] Such is the theory and such is the consciously attempted practice.

But in the past it was far otherwise, and the traces of the past are still to be found. This is more notably true in the United States, where the doctrine of legislative sovereignty has had less influence than in England, in the great powers exercised by our courts, by virtue of their inherent character, or under the interpretation of the constitutional phrase "due process of law." We have seen that formerly the legislature in England was in reality a court, that legislation was not sharply differentiated from adjudication. Conversely, this is but to say, as Mr. Justice Holmes does, that "in substance the growth of the law is legislative"—and he is here referring to judge-made law. "And this in a deeper sense than that what the courts declare to have always been the law is in fact new. It is legislative in its grounds. The very considerations which judges most rarely mention, and always with an apology, are the secret root from which the law draws all the juices of life. I mean, of course, considerations of what is expedient for the community concerned. Every important principle which is developed by litigation is in fact and

[1] *Ante*, p. 159.

at bottom the result of more or less definitely understood views of public policy; most generally, to be sure, under our practice and traditions, the unconscious result of instinctive preferences and inarticulate convictions, but none the less traceable to views of public policy in the last analysis."[1]

At a time when this tendency was far more marked than it is now even in the United States, when the courts shared largely in this "legislative" growth, because legislation was not a separate function, nor the work of one body exclusively, the relation of the "other courts" to Parliament was far different from what it is to-day. Parliament to them was not foreign, not external, not exclusively legislative or nearly so; it was another body more like themselves than unlike, more honourable, and of greater dignity, but still a court. A like difference from present-day conditions is observable in the treatment of Parliament's acts by the other courts. These acts were not the solemn inviolable declarations of a foreign "legislative" body, the sovereign power in the state, to whom absolute and unquestioning obedience is due. On the other hand, the treatment of statutes by the courts was free and

[1] *The Common Law*, pp. 35, 36. Cf. the resolution of the judges of the Court of King's Bench, below, p. 292. Cf. Austin: "I cannot understand how any person who has considered the subject can suppose that society could possibly have gone on if the judges had not legislated, or that there is any danger whatever in allowing them that power which they have in fact exercised, to make up for the negligence or the incapacity of the avowed legislator. That part of the law of every country which was made by judges has been far better made than that part which consists of statutes enacted by the legislature." Note to Lecture V.

familiar. They were to be scrutinized, were often condemned, and the motives of their makers freely commented on. They, like the High Court in which they originated, were not "external" nor "unjudicial."

"There has been a natural tendency on the part of the judges," says Sir Courtenay Ilbert, "to place a narrow construction on enactments which appeared to them to conflict with what they have regarded as fundamental principles of common law, to round off their angles, to adapt them to their environment by means of ingenious and sometimes far-fetched glosses; and the process has occasionally been carried to such an unwarrantable extent as to justify the expression of driving a coach and four through Acts of Parliament." "But," he adds, "the action of the courts is to be judged in the light, not of a few petulant or captious criticisms by individual judges, but of their general course of conduct; and they have as a rule loyally adhered to their functions of being, not critics of the legislature, but interpreters of the law."[1] As a description of present-day conditions in judicial England the last of these sentences is entirely accurate. When the attempt is made to make this applicable to the sixteenth century it becomes misleading, and, in fact, is contradicted by abundant evidence. "If you ask me, then," said Sir Henry Hobart, in the case of Sheffield v. Ratcliffe, "by what rule the judges guided themselves in this diverse exposition of the self same word and

[1] *Legislative Methods and Forms*, pp. 6, 7.

sentence? I answer, it was by that liberty and authority that judges have over laws, especially over Statute laws, according to reason and best convenience, to mould them to the truest and best use."[1] So, also, Lord Ellesmere quoted with approval from Justice Croke : " Vpon this reason it is, that some lawes, as well statute lawe as common law, are obsolete and worne out of use: for, all humane lawes are but *leges temporis:* and the wisedome of the judges found them to bee vnmeete for the time they liued in, although very good and necessarie for the time wherein they were made. And therefore it is saide 'leges humanae nascuntur vigent, et moriuntur, et habent ortum, statum, et occasum.'"

"By this rule also," he says, " and vpon this reason it is, that oftentimes aunicent lawes are changed by interpretation of the judges, as well in cases criminal as ciuile." Then follow numerous instances. " By this rule it is also," he continues, " that words are taken and construed, sometimes by extension; sometimes by restriction; sometimes by implication ; sometimes a disjunctiue for a copulatiue; a copulatiue for a disjunctiue; the present tense for the future; the future for the present; sometimes by equity out of the reach of the wordes; sometime words taken in a contrary sence; sometime figuratiuely, as *continens pro contento,* and many other like: and all of these, examples be infinite, as well in the ciuile lawe as common lawe."[2]

[1] *Hobart's Reports,* p. 346.
[2] 2 *St. Tr.*, 674, 675. This is an extract from the argument published in 1609 as the Speech of the Lord Chancellor in the Exchequer Chamber in the *Case of the*

THE HIGH COURT OF PARLIAMENT

A few only of these "infinite" examples of this "liberty and authority" will be given here. In one case it was said naïvely that the judges would "strain hard" rather than declare a statute void.[1] Their straining was at times almost equally hard the other way.[2] The expressed doctrine was, that if the words were obscure, they were to "be expounded most strongly for the public Good. For Words, which are no other than the Verberation of the Air, do not constitute the Statute, but are only the Image of it, and the Life of the Statute rests in the Minds of the Expositors of the Words, that is, the Makers of the Statutes. And if they are dispersed, so that their Minds cannot be known, then those who may approach nearest to their Minds shall construe the Words, and these are the Sages of the Law, whose Talents are exercised in the Study of such Matters."[3]

But in determining what was in the minds of the makers of the statutes great latitude was exercised. For example, the Statute of Gloucester[4] provided that the disseisee should recover damages in a writ of entry upon *Novel Disseisin* against him that was found tenant after the disseisor, but Littleton declared that if the disseisor had made a deed of feoffment to B, C,

---

Postnati. The words here quoted were quoted in part by Hakewel in his *Modus Tenendi Parliamentum*, written probably shortly before the outbreak of the Civil War and published in 1671, pages 93-95.

[1] 10 *Mod.*, 115.
[2] 2 *Brooke's Abridgment,* folio 120 B (*Parlement & Statutes*); *Comyn's Digest,* s. v. *Parliament* (R. 10).
[3] *Plowden,* p. 82.
[4] 6 E. I., ch. i.

[262]

and D, but livery of seisin had been made to B and C only; after the death of B and C, the disseisee could not recover damages from D, if D had not been at the livery, and had not consented to it, nor taken the profits of the land.[1]

This "interpretation," then, simply dispensed with the statute in a particular case, an "Exposition" which was declared in a case in the second year of Elizabeth to be "founded upon the Intent of the Makers of the Act, and upon good Reason. And yet it seems contrary to the Text, which says generally that *the Disseizee shall recover Damages against him that is found Tenant after the Disseizor*. And *Littleton* says that in the said Case he is found Tenant after the Disseizor, and yet the Disseizee shall not recover Damages against him, but it was the Intent of the Legislature that made him say so. And that their Intent was so, he gathered from Reason, for Reason would never suffer him to pay damages to the Disseizee, where he never assented to the Wrong done to the Disseizee, and never received nor intended to receive any Profits of his Land."[2]

After a review of other similar judgements, the case continues: "From which Cases it appears that the Sages of the Law heretofore have construed Statutes quite contrary to the Letter in some Appearance, and those Statutes which comprehend all things in the Letter they have expounded to extend but to some Things,

[1] *Tenures*, sec. 685.
[2] *Plowden*, pp. 204, 205.

and those which generally prohibit all People from doing such an Act they have interpreted to permit some People to do it, and those which include every Person in the Letter they have adjudged to reach to some Persons only, which Expositions have always been founded upon the Intent of the Legislature, which they have collected sometimes by considering the Cause and Necessity of making the Act, sometimes by comparing one Part of the Act with another, and sometimes by foreign Circumstances. So that they have ever been guided by the Intent of the Legislature, which they have always taken according to the Necessity of the Matter, and according to that which is consonant to Reason and good Discretion."[1] In another similar case the Chief Justice said, "that, which Law and Reason allows, shall be taken to be in Force against the Words of the Statutes."[2]

Cases such as these are numerous. It is unnecessary to cite more, but it must be clearly evident from these that judicial "interpretation" in the sixteenth century was widely different from that of the twentieth century. Enactments based on a misconception of fact were also in some cases denied binding effect in the courts.[3]

---

[1] *Plowden*, p. 205.

[2] *Ibid.*, p. 88 (6 and 7 Edward VI). See also, for example, *ibid.*, pp. 109, 110, 304, 364; Wingate, *Maxims*, Maxim 35, No. 23; Maxim 70, No. 70; 2 *Brooke's Abr.*, fol. 122 A; 1 *Rep.*, 24; *A Treatise concerning Statutes or Acts of Parliament*, "written by Sir Christopher Hatton, Late Lord Chancellor of England," published in 1677; Holdsworth, *H. E. L.*, vol. ii. pp. 366-70.

[3] *The Earl of Leicester's Case*, *Plowden*, pp. 398-400, and cases there cited; Wingate, *Maxims*, Maxim 28, No. 31, and references.

RELATIONS OF JUDICIARY AND LEGISLATURE

An interesting example of interpreting statutes is to be found in the history of the Statutes of Jeofail. One of these statutes (18 Elizabeth, cap. 14) enacted "that all defaults in form in any writ original or judicial, count, declaration, plaint, bill, or demand, are remedied, and judgment for them shall not be stayed." On an action for trespass, where the defendant had caught fish in waters belonging to the plaintiff, it was contended for the defendant that the omission in the declaration "of what nature the fish were, pikes, tenches, breams, carps, roaches, &c.," and the absence of any statement of the number of the fish taken, were fatal; and to this objection "it was agreed by the whole court, that the omitting of the nature and number of the fish, was a matter of substance, and not of form to be remedied by the said Statute of 18 Eliz."[1]

The clearest proof of Mr. Justice Holmes's belief, quoted above, that the work of courts is really legislative, is furnished by the persistence of fictions. One example will be enough. Coke says: "An obligation made beyond the seas may be sued here in England, in what place the plaintife will. What then if it beare date at *Bourdeaux* in *France*, where shall it be sued? And answer is made, that it may be alleaged to be made *in quodam loco vocat' Burdeaux* in *France*, in *Islington* in the county of *Middlesex*, and there it shall be tried, for whether there be such a place in *Islington*

[1] *Playter's Case*, 5 Rep., 35. See also *Bishop's Case*, 5 Rep., 37; Reeves, *H. E. L.*, vol. ii. p. 676, note *a* (by Finlason); *Jacob's Law Dictionary*, s. v. *Jeofail*. A list of the statutes is given in Blackstone, *Com.*, vol. iii. p. 408, note *a*.

or no, is not traversable in that case"![1] Comment is hardly necessary.

The main objection always brought against fictions is that they encroach upon the powers of the legislature. This is the burden of Bentham's complaints, for in the transparent fiction, instanced above, there could, of course, be no question of deception. " Can it be conceited for a moment," asks Austin, " by any reasonable person, that fines and recoveries (for example) ever deceived anybody, or were intended to deceive? that the authors of these absurdities hoped to impose upon the nobility whose great estates they were trying to break down? or that heirs in tail, or remaindermen and reversioners, were *trepanned* out of their interests by that

---

[1] *Co. Litt.*, p. 261 B. "The object sought to be attained by such fictions," says Professor Salmond, "is of course the indirect alteration of the law, and their efficiency for this end is obvious. For the practical effect of any rule of law depends on two things — the nature of the rule itself, and the nature of the facts to which it is applied. To alter the practical effect, therefore, it is necessary to alter either the law or the facts. And the only method of altering the facts is the establishment of conclusive presumptions contrary to them. Thus the rule of law that an English court could take no cognisance of a bond executed beyond the seas, would, if applied to the fact that Bordeaux is beyond the seas, have prevented any action being brought on a bond executed at Bordeaux. The rule of law being unchangeable, the only way to avoid this result was to alter the fact of Bordeaux being beyond the seas, and this was effected by a nontraversable allegation that the bond was executed at a certain place called Bordeaux in France in Islington in the County of Middlesex. ... This is the famous fiction whereby English courts obtained jurisdiction in transitory actions in which the cause of action arose abroad. We find it in use as early as the reign of Edward III." *Essays in Jurisprudence and Legal History*, pp. 9, 10. See also Lord Mansfield's opinion in *Mostyn* v. *Fabrigas*, in 1775, *Cowper's Reports*, p. 170 et seq., especially his reference to the allegation in a declaration that a vessel was seized "*on the high seas, videlicet in Cheapside.*"

ridiculous juggling? Such a conceit is really more absurd than the foolery to which it relates."[1]

The very transparency of these fictions underlying fines and common recoveries brings out in stronger relief the great power, and what would seem in our day the amazing audacity, of the judges. By a mere ruling that the truth of certain statements universally known to be untrue might not be questioned, they effectually and permanently defeated the designs of the nobility and rendered absolutely ineffectual the clearly expressed will of Parliament. Speaking of the celebrated Taltarum's Case, John Hill Burton says: " It may ... without much exaggeration be affirmed, that, in the reign of Edward the Fourth, the principal enactment of the Statute *De Donis* was *repealed by a judicial sentence.*"[2] Judges who could as a matter of course do

[1] *Lectures on Jurisprudence*, 4th ed., vol. ii. p. 629.
[2] *Compendium of the Law of Real Property*, p. 231, quoted by W. D. Lewis, Esq., in *Juridical Society Papers*, vol. i. p. 374. Nothing in the history of English Law better illustrates the actual legislation by the courts than their treatment of the Statute *De Donis*. They rather than the Parliament represented the will of the nation, — and the nation as such was beginning to have a will, — and their action was sanctioned by King and people. Nothing in English law is better known than these facts, but it is amazing that their true significance should be so little recognized. Mr. Scrutton is not going too far when he says, "The class legislation of Parliament was defeated by the national legislation of the judges." *Land in Fetters*, p. 76. For the opposition of the judges here is direct, conscious, successful, and generally approved. It is directed against an odious piece of " class legislation " which the Parliament has formally enacted in words too clear to be misunderstood, and has refused again and again to repeal. And there can be no question of the intention of the makers of the act. The judges are trying to defeat that intention, not to give effect to it. They are guided by "considerations of what is expedient for the community." All this is clearly brought out in Coke's account of the matter. Speaking of the evil state of affairs caused by the statute, he says: " And the same was

such things as these had a conception of their office, and of their relation to the law and the lawmaking body, far different from that existing to-day; and their actual doing with impunity year after year these things so vitally important to many is the best proof that that conception was not materially repugnant to the feelings and beliefs of that part of the English nation which held the balance of power.

Another illustration of this freedom of interpretation is found in the case of statutes declaratory of the common law.

Coke says in his *Fourth Institute*, "Of acts of Parliament some be introductory of a new Law, and some be declaratory of the Ancient Law, and some be of both kinds by addition of greater penalties or the like."[1]

Again he says: "To know what the Common Law

---

attempted and endeavoured to be remedied at divers Parliaments and divers bills were exhibited accordingly (which I have seen) but they were always on one pretence or other rejected. But the truth was, that the Lords and Commons knowing that their estates-tail were not to be forfeited for felony or treason; as their estates of inheritance were before the said act, (and chiefly in the time of H. 3. in the Barons war) and finding that they were not answerable for the debts or incumbrances of their ancestors, nor did the sales, alienations, or leases of their ancestors bind them for the lands which were entailed to their ancestors, they always rejected such bills: and the same continued in the residue of the reign of E. 1. and of the reigns of E. 2. E. 3. R. 2. H. 4. H. 5. H. 6. and till about the 12th year of E. 4. When the Judges on consultation had amongst themselves, resolved, that an estate tail might be docked and barred by a common recovery; and that by reason of the intended recompence, the common recovery was not within the restraint of the said perpetuity made by the said act of 13 E. 1." *Sir Anthony Mildmay's Case*, 6 *Rep.*, 40, 41. Note the perplexity into which these fines and recoveries threw the Student and the Doctor in Saint Germain's Dialogue. *Doct. and Stud.*, Dialogue I., ch. xxvi.

[1] Page 25.

was before the making of any Statute, (whereby it may be known whether the Act be introductory of a new Law, or affirmatory of the old) is the very lock and key to set open the windows of the Statute."[1]

The application by the judges of a different rule of interpretation to such acts or such parts of acts as *they* considered declaratory—for that is just what was done—indicates at once the commanding position of the Common Law and the power of the judges. For it is to be noted that the declaratory nature of an enactment was determined by the judges nine times out of ten, not from any expression of intention on the part of the lawmakers, but by the mere fact that the subject matter of the act in question, in the opinion of the judges, came within some rule of the existing law, that mystery to which they alone were initiated. Important results might follow from the exercise of this great power. The commonest was the rule "that a Statute made in the affirmative, without any negative expressed or implyed, doth not take away the Common Law."[2] So it was seriously urged in the trial of the Earl of Strafford that the act of Edward III defining treason was merely in affirmance, and therefore any words or actions that could be proved to be treasonable according to the law existing previous to that act, might properly constitute treason in 1640, though they were not within the terms of the statute.[3]

[1] 2 *Inst.*, 308.   [2] *Ibid.*, 200.
[3] Rushworth, *Strafford's Trial*, p. 699 et seq.

The language used by Coke, in reference to the Act of 3 Henry VII which organized the Court of Star Chamber, seems strange to our ears, but was not so when uttered: "The second conclusion is, that the Act of 3 H. 7. being in the affirmative is not in some things pursued. For where the Act directeth that the Bill or Information should be put to the Lord Chancellor, &c., all Bills and Informations in that Court are constantly and continually directed to the King's Majesty, as they were before the said Act; and it is a good rule, that where the Act of 3 H. 7. is not pursued, there (if there be many judicial presidents in another sort) they must have warrant from the ancient Court; and yet it is good (as much as may be) to pursue this Act, there being no greater assurance of jurisdiction than an Act of Parliament. And where there be no such presidents, then the Statute as to the Judges must be pursued. . . .

"Fifthly, where it is said in this Act, 'And to punish them after their demerits after the form and effect of Statutes made,' &c. The Plaintiff may choose whether he will inform upon such Statutes as this Act directeth, or for the offence at the Common Law, as he might have done before this Act: which proveth that this Act taketh not away the former jurisdiction."[1]

In addition to these cases where the judges openly

---

[1] *4 Inst.*, 62, 63. See also *ibid.*, p. 40, marginal note; *Co. Litt.*, lib. 2, cap. 10, with Hargrave and Butler's notes (Nos. 153-9); *Plowden*, 111, 112; Hawkins, *History of the Pleas of the Crown*, vol. ii. p. 56. For a more modern instance, see the arguments against Dowdeswell's proposed libel Act in 1771, *Parl. Hist.*, vol. xvii. pp. 54, 58.

deprived a law or a statute of practical effect by a false assumption of fact, or altered its application on the ground of its declaratory nature, there are assertions—some of them mere dicta, it is true, but not all; and too numerous to be entirely accidental—that statutes are void entirely, because against reason or the fundamental law. Some of these have been noticed already under the head of "The Fundamental Law." "We find," says Sir Frederick Pollock, "a series of dicta, extending to the early part of the eighteenth century, to the effect that statutes contrary to 'natural justice' or 'common right' may be treated as void. This opinion is most strongly expressed by Coke, but, like many of his confident opinions, is extra-judicial. Although Coke was no canonist, we may be pretty sure that it was ultimately derived from the canonist doctrine prevailing on the Continent of Europe. In England it was never a practical doctrine."[1]

One who holds the prevailing view that a developed legislative sovereignty was in existence in Coke's time must consider these frequent statements as "confident," "petulant," or "captious," but their frequency, and the reputation of those who made them, render this easy explanation rather hard to accept.

Instead of being occasional, captious, or inexplicable, these cases represent the continuance of ideas prevalent and common in mediaeval times, not only in England, but in all Christendom. Gierke says: "The

[1] *The Expansion of the Common Law*, pp. 121, 122.

properly Medieval and never completely obsolete theory declared that every act of the Sovereign which broke the bounds drawn by Natural Law was formally null and void. As null and void therefore every judge and every other magistrate who had to apply the law was to treat, not only every unlawful executive act, but every unlawful statute, even though it were published by Pope or Emperor."[1]

It may be admitted that one great source of such opinions was the canonists; not the sole source, however, for such canonist doctrines could have had but little effect where such a theory existed as the present-day one of the omnipotence of Parliament. It cannot be denied, probably it might easily be shown, that the division of allegiance between Pope and King had been one great source of the attempts in mediaeval England to set limits to the powers of the organs of the state. It does seem somewhat superficial, however, to explain those resulting attempts as mere accidents, nothing more than chance explosions of ill-temper or arrogance.

This influence of the Church upon the attitude even of the common lawyers is shown by the nature and occasion of the earliest appearance of statements denying the validity of unrepealed statutes.

The Church was no more willing to allow the law of the state to override its canons in England than elsewhere. If the two came into conflict, the secular law

[1] *Political Theories of the Middle Age*, translated by F. W. Maitland, p. 84. See also the references given by Gierke in support of this statement.

must yield. This principle was undoubtedly accepted by the churchmen in England. It was set forth in the provincial canons.[1] In defence of it Becket lost his life, and his death gave it new vitality.

The first known recognition of the principle that an unrepealed statute might be void, occurring in a secular court, seems to have been in the twenty-seventh year of Henry VI, and it is connected more or less directly with the old quarrel of Church and State. The Statute *De Asportatis Religiosorum*, of 35 Edward I, provided that abbeys should have a common seal, which was to remain in the custody of the Prior and four others of the House and be left for safe keeping under the private seal of the Abbot, "so that the Abbot or Prior, which doth govern the House, shall be able of himself to establish nothing." If any writings or contracts were entered into or "sealed with any other Seal than such a common Seal, kept as aforesaid," they were to be adjudged "void and of no force in law." In the year 27 Henry VI one brought suit against an abbot upon a grant of an annuity made by the abbot's predecessor, and sealed with the convent seal. It was alleged that the seal had not been in the keeping of the prior and the four as the statute required, and that therefore the grant was void. The decision, however, was that the grant was good notwithstanding the stat-

---

[1] Lyndwood, *Provinciale* (1679), p. 263. "I have looked in vain for any suggestion that an English judge or advocate ever called in question the statutory power of a text that was contained in any of the three papal law-books." Maitland, *Canon Law in the Church of England*, p. 9.

ute, "et loppinion del court que cest statut est voide, quar est inpartinent destre observe,"[1] the reason being that if the seal were in the keeping of the four, the abbot could seal nothing with it; for if it were in his hands, then it must be out of their keeping, and therefore every sealed document would be necessarily void.

This seems reasonably clear. Apparently a grave injustice would have been done here if the grantee of the annuity in question, or his successor, had been deprived of the benefit of the grant. It seems equally apparent that the statute made the grant void. To prevent the injustice, the common law judges here simply say the statute—meaning the portion of it concerning seals—is void and of no effect, the reason being a piece of verbal jugglery, which surely could deceive no one. There was here no "impossibility of performance," other than a dialectical impossibility such as might be created to avoid almost any statutory requirement, no matter how plain. Coke, however, gravely repeats the reasoning in Fitzherbert: "This branch (as it hath been resolved) is impossible, and inconvenient to be observed: impossible, because it is hereby enacted, [then follows a summary of the provision of the statute] for, if it be kept in custody under the seal of the Abbot, then no writing can be sealed by the Abbot, and if the Abbot taketh it out, and seal, &c. then is it not kept in custody under his private seal; and therefore it was resolved by the whole Court of the Common Pleas,

[1] *Fitzherbert's Abridgment*, Annuitie No. 41.

that this branch being impossible to be observed, is void; the Court also resolved, that it was inconvenient: for they said, that if the statute should be observed, every deed that passed under the common seal might be undone by a simple surmise, &c."[1]

Out of this Blackstone, in his turn, evolves the mild doctrine that "acts of parliament that are impossible to be performed are of no validity,"[2] which is not unlike a truism; and this rather lame conclusion seems to be the construction put by most modern commentators upon the words of Henry VI's judges.

But can the words "cest statut est voide, quar est inpartinent destre observe" be dismissed so easily? The statute in this case was not declared to be void because it was physically impossible to carry it out. The impossibility was one of the judges' own making, and it was made because there were other reasons—reasons of "public policy," it may be—why the statute should not be obeyed. The judges were here openly refusing to give force to the obvious intention of the makers of the statute. It is true they veiled this refusal under the thinnest of pretences, but who in that day could have been deceived by it? Can Sir Frederick Pollock to-day be wholly right when he says the judges declared the act inoperative, "not because it was contrary to natural justice, but because they could make no sense of it at all"?[3]

---

[1] 2 *Inst.*, 587. See also *Dr. Bonham's Case*, 8 *Rep.*, 118.
[2] *Commentaries*, vol. i. p. 91.   [3] *Expansion of the Common Law*, p. 122.

THE HIGH COURT OF PARLIAMENT

Furthermore, it is to be observed that the declaration that the statute is void is here probably no *obiter dictum*. It seems likely from the existing summary of the case in Fitzherbert that the decision in favour of the validity of the grant turned directly upon the invalidity of the statute. If this be a correct analysis of this case, it must seem a little hazardous to say that "No case is known ... in which an English court of justice has openly taken on itself to overrule or disregard the plain meaning of an Act of Parliament."[1] The case may be an exceptional one, but it must be reckoned with. No doubt one great reason for the misconception as to this case is Coke's unfortunate rendering of "inpartinent" as "impossible," as noted above. On a review of the case it becomes evident that the real reason for the declaration concerning the statute is to be found in the statement noted by Coke as above, that "the Court also resolved, that if the statute should be observed, every deed that passes under the Common Seal might be undone by a simple surmise," no doubt a great hardship and injustice in most cases. Nevertheless, no court of to-day would dream of avoiding such inconveniences, however great, by a remedy so heroic as an open or even a covert disavowal of the authority and validity of the act itself.[2]

[1] Pollock, *First Book of Jurisprudence*, p. 252.
[2] The fullest treatment of this remarkable case is to be found in the late Brinton Coxe's *Judicial Power and Unconstitutional Legislation*, p. 153 et seq., to which I am indebted for many of the above references. For the relation of this decision to the provisions of the canon law on the subject, see especially Coxe, pp. 157-60.

Another case, somewhat later, which brought out strong expressions from the judges against the validity of an act, was one reported in the Year Book of 21 Henry VII. This case arose directly out of a collision of the rules of the canon and the common law. The only point of the case which in any way touched the question here at issue was the question whether the King could be made a Parson by Act of Parliament. It was argued: "It seems that the King cannot be called parson by act of Parliament, for no temporal act can cause a temporal act to make a temporal man have spiritual jurisdiction."[1] "For," the serjeant continues, "if it was ordained by act, etc., that such a one should not tender tithes to his curate, the act would be void, for concerning such a thing as touches merely the spiritualty, such temporal act cannot make any ordinance: the same law, if it was enacted that one parson should have the tithes of another. Thus by this act which is merely one of a temporal court, the king cannot be made to have any spiritual jurisdiction." This point was argued back and forth, and was concluded by Frowike, the Chief Justice, in these words: "As to the other matter, whether the King can be parson by act of parliament; as I understand, it is not a great matter to argue: for I have never seen that any temporal man could be parson without the agreement of the Supreme Head. And in all the cases which have been put,

---

[1] *Y. B. 21 H. VII.*, pl. 1 (p. 2). The clumsy repetition may be due to the careless copyist, but the meaning is clear enough.

namely of the benefices in Wales, and the benefices which laymen have in their own use, I have seen the matter: the king had them by assent and agreement of the Supreme Head. Thus a temporal act, without the assent of the Supreme Head, cannot make the King a Parson."[1]

The above case, turning as it does directly upon the validity of temporal legislation in a field admitted to be ecclesiastical, is not so instructive as the case that preceded, but the language used is significant enough when coming from a common law judge.

The same view of the limitation of Parliament's power over spiritual matters was partly the cause of the death of Sir Thomas More, once Chancellor of England. Roper tells us that Sir Richard Rich, the Solicitor General, who was trying to draw some incriminating admission from Sir Thomas More, put this question to him: "'Admitt there were, Sir,' quoth he, 'an Acte of Parliament, that all the Realme should take me for the King, would not you (Mr. Moore) take me for the King?' 'Yes, Sir,' quoth Sir Thomas Moore, 'that would I.' 'I put the case further' (quoth Mr Rich) 'that there weare an Acte of Parliament that all the Realme should take me for the Pope; would then not you, Mr. Moore, take me for the Pope?' 'For answeare,' quoth Sir Thomas Moore, 'to your first case, the Parliament may well (Mr Rich) meddle with the

---

[1] *Y. B. 21 H. VII.*, p. 4; Brinton Coxe, *op. cit.*, 147-53; *Brooke's Abridgment, Parlement & Statutes*, No. 28 (vol. ii. fol. 120 B, ed. of 1573).

stat of temporall Princes; but to make aunsweare to your [second] case, I will put you this case, Suppose the Parliament would make a Law, that God should not be God, would you then, Mr Rich, saye God weare not God?' 'Noe, Sir,' quoth he, 'that would I not, sithe noe Parliament may make any such Law.' 'Noe more' (sayd Sir Thomas Moore, as Mr Rich reported of him) 'could the Parliament make the Kinge suppreame head of the Church.'"[1] When asked on his trial why judgement should not be given against him, he replied, as Roper reports, "'Forasmuch as, my Lord,' (quoth he) 'this Indictment is grounded upon an Act of Parliament, directly oppugnaunt to the Lawes of God and his holye Church, the supreame goverment of which, or of any part thereof, maye no temporall Prince presume by any lawe to take uppon him as rightfully belonginge to the See of Rome.'"[2] After this the Chancellor demanded the opinion of the Chief Justice of the King's Bench on the sufficiency of the indictment, who gave this significantly evasive answer: "I must needes confesse, that if the Acte of Parliament be not unlawfull, then is not the Indictment in my conscience insufficient."[3]

The author of the dialogue of the *Doctor and Student*, though an opponent of ecclesiastical power, evidently had in mind the same limitation of Parliament's

[1] Roper's *Life of Sir Thomas More* (edited by J. R. Lumby), p. xlvi.
[2] *Ibid.*, p. l.
[3] *Ibid.*, p. li.

authority, for in discussing the validity of a statute which should forbid the use of torches, tapers, etc., at burials, he concludes: "It were a good statute, and ought to be observed, as well by spiritual men as by temporal; and this I take to be the reason why, for all goods, though they be in the hands of spiritual men, be temporal concerning the body, and nourishing the body, as they do to temporal men. . . . And all temporal things the King and his progenitors, as in the right of the crown, have in this realm alway ordered and judged by his laws: and therefore I suppose that the parliament may enact, that there shall not be laid upon a deceased person but such a cloth, or thus many tapers or candles set up about him."[1]

Further on he says: "Verily there is a writ in the Register (which is a book of the law of England) that no sheriff shall impanel any priest upon any inquest, and that writ may every priest have, that will sue for it. And I think right well, that that writ is grounded upon the law of the realm: taking in that point his effect upon the law of God. And therefore I think, that the parliament may not enact, that priests should go universally upon inquests; but to enact, that in this special case [*i. e.*, as to whether a man were sufficiently learned to be a priest], which is not mere temporal, but to enquire of the sufficiency of learning, and that to a good and necessary purpose, I suppose the parliament

[1] Additions to Dialogue II., ch. i.

may assign them to it without breaking the liberty of the church."[1]

It is not hard to imagine why such statements become rarer after 1534, but the persistence of this old idea in England, notwithstanding the modern doctrine of the omnipotence of Parliament, is shown when a bishop of the Church of England, in the middle of the nineteenth century, could renounce communion with the Archbishop of Canterbury because he thought the archbishop had endangered the rights and liberties of the Church, in obeying the Queen's monition based upon the provisions of an act of Parliament.[2]

If anyone doubts whether this view still survives or not, let him read the communications sent to the Royal Commission on Ecclesiastical Discipline in 1904 by priests of the Church of England whose conduct of the service of the Church had been under criticism. Many of these close with a statement which had evidently been adopted by agreement: "Possibly I may be acting contrary to some decisions of the Judicial Committee of the Privy Council; but I deny the competence of that tribunal as a final Court of Appeal in matters relating to the doctrine, discipline, and ceremonial of the Church."[3]

---

[1] Additions to Dialogue II., ch. xi. See, on this subject, Roscoe Pound, in *Harvard Law Review*, vol. xxi. p. 393 et seq.
[2] This arose out of the celebrated Gorham Case in 1850. On it see, for example, Hore's *History of the Church in England*, vol. ii. p. 351.
[3] *House of Commons Sessional Papers*, 1906, vol. xxxiii. (Minutes of Evidence, vol. i. pp. 8, 15, 16, 18, 27, 36, 44, 46, 48, 53, 100, 103, etc.).

THE HIGH COURT OF PARLIAMENT

Among the appendices to the Report of the Commission is a Memorial addressed to the Archbishop of Canterbury, signed by 2519 clergymen, in which they declare, "that loyalty to the Church of England compels them to repudiate the competence of any such tribunal as the Judicial Committee of the Privy Council to over-rule the plain meaning of the Rubrics of the Book of Common Prayer or to interpret and determine the doctrine and discipline of the Church of England."[1]

[1] Appendix B (vol. xxxiv.). An interesting parallel to these modern views, as to the competency of a lay court to review the judgements of a spiritual one, is found in the Articles exhibited by the Clergy to the Privy Council in the reign of James I, with the answer of the common-law judges. Among other things, the clergy pray (sec. 16, 2 *Coke's Inst.*, 611) that where the statutes concerning tithes are in dispute, "then the said three Statutes may be thoroughly debated before your Lordships, lest under pretence of a right, which they challenge, to expound these kind of Statutes, the truth may be over-born, and poor Ministers still left unto Country trials, there to justifie the right of their tithes before unconscionable Jurors in these cases." In reply, the judges declared: "We never heard it excepted unto heretofore, that any Statute should be expounded by any other then the Judges of the land; neither was there ever any so much over-seen, as to oppose himself against the practice of all ages to make that question, or to lay any such unjust imputation upon the Judges of the Realm."

Again (in sec. 20, 2 *Inst.*, 614), the clergy challenge the claim of the temporal judges to determine "causes of Faith and Religion," and to prevent by Prohibitions their trial in ecclesiastical courts — "which conceit, how absurd it is, needeth no proof, and teacheth us, that when matters meerly Ecclesiastical are comprised in any Statute, it doth not therefore follow, that the interpretation of the said matters doth belong to the Temporal Judges, who by their profession, and as they are Judges, are not acquainted with that kind of learning." To which the judges answered, "And for the Judges expounding of Statutes that concern the Ecclesiastical government or proceedings, it belongeth unto the Temporal Judges; and we think they have been expounded as much to their advantage, as either the letter or intention of Laws would or could allow of. And when they have been expounded to their liking, then they could approve of it; but if the exposition be not for their purpose,

RELATIONS OF JUDICIARY AND LEGISLATURE

The jurisdiction of the Judicial Committee of the Privy Council as a court of final appeal in ecclesiastical cases, it need hardly be said, is based on parliamentary enactment.[1]

All the above cases deal more or less with ecclesiastical matters, and in most of them, therefore, the declarations against the validity of statutes are based on a want of jurisdiction in the secular courts (including the court of Parliament[2]) over matters belonging to the courts of the Church, rather than on the character of the enactments themselves.

Turning now to the cases of a more distinctly secular nature, we find there also many free criticisms of statutes on the part of the judges, extending at times to a declaration that statutes may be void.

For a long time, practically the only kind of "enactment" found in mediaeval England was the Assizes. The term "assize" may have been used, as Stubbs suggests, because of the special sanctity of the term "law," as used in Scripture and in the Roman jurisprudence.

---

then they will say, as now they do, that it appertaineth not unto us to determine of them." The judges close their answer to the whole petition by saying, "For the Judges doing but what they ought, and by their oaths are bound to do; it is not to be called in question: and if it fall out, that they err in judgment, it cannot otherwise be reformed, but judicially in a superiour Court; or by Parliament." (2 *Inst.*, 618.)

[1] 3 and 4 Wm. IV., ch. xli. See especially Finlason, *The Judicial Committee of the Privy Council.*

[2] Note that in the argument quoted above (on page 277) the statute in dispute is spoken of as "this act *which is merely one of a temporal court,*" and cf. what is said above, at page 119, concerning the meaning of "jurisdiction" in earlier times.

Another reason for the use of some other term than "law" is the fact that in theory "law" then practically meant ancient and unchangeable custom, while these assizes dealt largely, or could be made to seem to deal almost entirely, with administrative machinery in which changes might occur. Surely some changes of great importance were thus brought about, as the Assizes of Clarendon and Northampton, for instance, will show. If, then, these assizes were "tentative" and "temporary," as Stubbs says, they were, nevertheless, the most authoritative form of *enactment* that existed at that time. But we find, notwithstanding its importance, that such an assize "is liable to be set aside by the judges where they find it impossible to administer it fairly;"[1] which is not surprising when it is remembered that the assizes had been made with the advice of the Curia, where sat the same judges who were now to enforce them. At a time, for example, such as the reign of the absentee Richard I, when the men of the Council were practically the rulers of England, it is not at all strange that these men should by their own authority discontinue an assize they found inconvenient or unsuitable.[2] When enactments began to

---

[1] Stubbs, *Const. Hist.*, vol. i. pp. 615, 616.

[2] An interesting case in the next reign is reported by Hoveden under the year 1201, with the heading, "De relaxatione Statuti regis Ricardi" (referring to his Assize of Measures) as follows: "Eodem anno Hugo Bardulfi, et alii quidam justitiarii regis, venerunt ad nundinas Sancti Botulfi, volentes capere in manu regis pannos laneos qui non habebant duas ulnas de latitudine infra lisuras, secundum assisam Ricardi regis. Quo audito, mercatores effecerunt adversus praedictos justitiarios, quod panni eorum non capiebantur, et quod diutius

be placed upon the Statute Roll, these conditions were not sharply changed.

Henry III's reissue of Magna Charta in 1225 is one of the first and, without doubt, the best known of the enactments among the early statutes.[1] The first instance I shall give of the judges declaring a statute void concerns Magna Charta itself, and arises out of the determination of the judges that no man must be a judge in his own case, one of the principles of justice which the common law judges strove hardest to uphold in all ages.

In chapter twelve of the reissue it is ordained that the assizes of *novel disseisin* and *mort d'ancestor* should not be taken unless in the proper counties. It was nevertheless decided in 18 Edward II that an assize of *novel disseisin* to regain a lordship in the Marches of Wales was rightly held in the English county of Gloucester, though this was a violation of a negative command of Magna Charta itself, "and the reason is notable, for the Lord *Marcher* though he had *jura Regalia*, yet could he not do Justice in his own case,"

non teneret assissa illa Ricardi regis, neque de latitudine pannorum, neque de mensuris bladi; et ut liceat eis de caetero facere pannos suos latos vel strictos sicut eis placuerit. Unde praedicti justitiarii magnam adepti sunt pecuniam ad opus regis, in damnum multorum. Vitanda est turpis lucri causa." Vol. iv. p. 172 (Rolls Series).

[1] The Statute Roll begins in the latter part of the thirteenth century. Parliamentary enactments made before that time are found on rolls that are made up in the main of records which to-day would be considered more judicial than legislative. The Record Commissioners denied that Henry's reissue was a statute (S. R., vol. i. p. xxxiv, note). The section concerning the assizes, however, was repeated in Edward I's reissue, which is on the Statute Roll.

"and therefore," says Coke, "this case of necessity is by construction *excepted out of the Statute.*"[1]

In the famous case of Dr. Bonham, in the sixth and seventh years of James I, Lord Coke cited a number of cases in support of his theory that "in many cases the common law will controul acts of Parliament, and sometimes adjudge them to be utterly void."[2] One of the most important of these has been noticed already.[3] Of the others, the earliest and probably the one most questioned from Lord Ellesmere's days onward, is Thomas Tregor's Case, of the eighth year of Edward III.[4] In that case, Herle, Chief Justice, used these words: *Ils sont ascun statutes faitz que celuy mesme qui les fist ne les voleit pas mettre en fait.* This seems to mean: "There are some Statutes made which he himself who made them does not will to put into effect." Coke, in quoting this, made an important addition. The whole passage should be given: "And it appears in our books, that in many cases, the common law will con-

---

[1] 2 *Inst.*, 25. The italics are mine. This case is reported in *Fitzherbert's Abridgment*, Assise, No. 382. See also a case in 21 Henry III (*Fitzherbert*, Briefe, No. 881), where, notwithstanding the well-known provision that the common pleas should be held in some fixed place, it was said, "Et quamvis prohibeatur quod communia placita non sequantur Curiam &c. non sequitur propter hoc quin aliqua placita sigularia sequantur dominum regem." See also Coke, as above. Mr. Holdsworth (*H. E. L.*, vol. ii. p. 366, and note 4) cites a case from *Rot. Parl.*, vol. ii. p. 41 (4 Edward III., No. 52), in which certain petitioners declare to be contrary to law the statute by which the lands of the Templars were transferred to the Hospitallers: "Et disoient que ce sunt contrarie a Ley, issi que cel Estatut se fist contre Ley et contre reson." See also Holdsworth, *op. cit.*, vol. ii. p. 369, and note 1.

[2] 8 *Rep.*, 118.

[3] *Ante*, p. 273 et seq.

[4] *Y. B. 8 E. III.*, Pasch. pl. 26.

troul acts of Parliament, and sometimes adjudge them to be utterly void: for when an act of Parliament is against common right and reason, or repugnant, or impossible to be performed, the common law will controul it, and adjudge such acts to be void; and therefore in 8 E. 3. 30. a. b. Thomas Tregor's case on the Statute of W. 2. c. 38. & *artic. super chartas*, c. 9. Herle saith, some statutes are made against law and right, which those who made them perceiving, would not put them into execution." [Then follow some other precedents.] Now here, apparently, Coke is assuming that at least one reason for not enforcing the statute was its being against reason or law. Sir Frederick Pollock, on the other hand, in commenting on it remarks that " Plenty of modern statutes have been inoperative in practice, not because the common law controlled them, but because they were in fact unworkable;"[1] thus evidently implying that we have here nothing more than a law which has been allowed to become a dead letter through inadvertence or absence of any wish to enforce it *on the part of the legislator;* or, at most, a law physically impossible of enforcement.

There is here a radical difference of interpretation between Coke and Sir Frederick Pollock. Herle may have meant the one thing, or he may have meant the other. Certainly, his bare statement, as reported in the Year Book, is not sufficient alone to bear Coke's inference. Coke was in this instance probably quoting from

[1] *First Book of Jurisprudence*, p. 251, note.

memory, as he seems to have done frequently, and sometimes with serious results; but the quotation as he made it, we must consider, was not a chance utterance carelessly made. It undoubtedly represents Coke's settled conviction. An explanation of this very passage was later demanded of him, and in an answer directed to the King himself he repeated the statement word for word, prefacing it with the declaration, "The words of my report do not import any new opinion, but only a relation of such authorities of law, as had been adjudged and resolved in ancient and former times."[1] It is hardly possible that his attention had not been called to the addition he had made to Herle's words, and yet he considered that he himself had brought forward no new opinion. He clearly considered that Herle's words could mean only one thing, and that the addition of the words "against law and right" in no way changed their original sense.

It is, then, quite true to say that Herle's bare words are not sufficient, taken by themselves, to bear out Coke's conclusions, but it is a different matter entirely to say positively that those conclusions were wrong. He cited other cases which certainly do go far to show that his interpretation may have been the right one. One or two of these have been noted, and others remain to be discussed.

At all events, Coke's interpretation, whether deduced rightly or wrongly from earlier precedents, must be

[1] *Bacon's Works* (edited by Montagu), vol. ii. p. 506 (American ed.).

looked upon by a student of English constitutional law and history as most important evidence of what the common lawyers of the early seventeenth century accepted as the only legally and historically sound position to be taken upon this important question. This, after all, is for our discussion a more important matter, perhaps, than the determination of the real meaning of Herle's words. And yet, it seems to me, those words are so significant that some explanation should be sought. That they refer merely to the disuse of the statute, or to the physical impossibility of enforcing it, I cannot believe.

One very striking thing about the whole case is the fact that Coke is apparently citing these words of Herle — "There are some Statutes made which *he himself who made them* does not will to put into effect"—as proof of the power of the *judges* to disregard the statute concerning the college of physicians which was under discussion in Bonham's Case. What possible relation can there be between the opinions of the *judges* and the opinions and desires that *the makers of the law* begin to entertain subsequent to the passage of the act? Under modern conditions, no relation whatever; for to-day, the will of the legislature is assumed to be expressed in the act itself. Even if the lawmaking body wholly changes its mind subsequent to the passing of an act, this in no way alters the attitude of the courts to the act. They must be guided according to the clear intent expressed in the act itself, and would not think of regarding any change in the minds of the legislators, unless that change had been put in the official form of an amending or repealing statute. In other words, we to-day keep our legislation and adjudication in entirely separate compartments.

In Herle's time this was not so. We have seen that judges were continually appealing to Parliament for help and advice in difficult cases, and we shall presently find them asking the meaning of statutes. Sometimes these appeals were made to a different Parliament from the one which had made the enactment. Moreover, we shall see that the judges who decided the cases in the courts were also entrusted with a large part of the business of the Court of Parliament, both "judicial" and "legislative." We shall also find that the wording, and, in fact, all but the bare main principles of the acts, were for long the exclusive work of the same judges. Therefore, when Herle says that the *makers* of the statutes often will not to enforce them, is it certain, as is usually assumed, that he means the *"legislature"* exclusively? Is it not possible that Coke was as nearly right when he cited the statement to prove the right of the *courts* to review "legislation"? But would it not be still nearer to the truth to say, in view of the close relations of judges and Parliament, of the fusion of functions judicial and legislative which we have found in both the High Court of Parliament and the inferior courts, and above all in view of the manifest absence of any clear distinction between a judgement and a law, between judicature and legislation, in the time of Edward III, —in view of all this, would it not be better to say that Herle would probably have considered an alteration of a statute by a subsequent statute, and a modification of it, or even a refusal to enforce it, by the *courts;* as actions not essentially different in character?[1]

It is absolutely necessary to rid ourselves of the modern idea of the law-making and law-interpreting bodies as mutually exclusive, and external to each other, if we wish to understand the meaning of Herle's words. So understood, they would seem to bear Coke's interpretation as readily, or possibly more readily, than the interpretation suggested by the more modern doctrine of legislative sovereignty.

But we must not forget that Coke himself lived under influences different from those of the middle ages. For over a century Parliament had, to a great extent, ceased the judicial activity that so marked it in the time of Edward III. It was natural, then, that Coke should argue that this power of review should in his time be in the ordinary courts, since the Parliament, though entitled to exercise it, was not doing so to any great extent.

If the High Court of Parliament was not actually exercising to the full all the indefinite powers properly belonging to it, what more natural than that the other courts of the common law should be the proper place

---

[1] But see the article by Professor Roscoe Pound, in *Harvard Law Rev.*, vol. xxi., at p. 391.

for the exercise of them? It is to be expected under these circumstances, when the lines between adjudication, legislation, and administration were not keenly felt, that Coke should insist that most of these indefinite powers should remain in the end with those of his own craft. The resolution of the judges in Bagg's Case would seem to show that this feeling was shared by his fellows of the common law: "And in this case, first, it was resolved, that to this court of King's Bench belongs authority, not only to correct errors in judicial proceedings, *but other errors and misdemeanors extrajudicial,* tending to the breach of peace, or oppression of the subjects, or to the raising of faction, controversy, debate, or any manner of misgovernment; so that no wrong or injury, either public or private can be done, but that it shall be (here) reformed or punished by due course of law."[1]

It is not strange that Coke was called upon to explain this case to the King.[2] It claimed "jurisdiction" for the common law courts over the very matters which, as the King and Bacon and Ellesmere contended, belonged to the King or to his Council, many of them matters that we do not ordinarily think of as belonging to the courts at all.[3]

[1] 11 *Rep.*, 98. The italics are mine.
[2] The letter of explanation entitled *The Humble and Direct Answer to the Last Question arising upon Bagg's Case* is printed in Montagu's edition of *Bacon's Works*, vol. ii. p. 507 (American ed.).
[3] But cf. the non-judicial powers often exercised by our courts in the United States; for example, the power of granting licenses for the sale of intoxicating

RELATIONS OF JUDICIARY AND LEGISLATURE

But the King and Bacon and Ellesmere in opposing the exercise of these great powers by the common lawyers were very far from denying the legitimacy of the powers themselves. They never object to judicial criticism of statutes unless that criticism comes from the common law judges. On the contrary, while repudiating the exclusive claim of the common lawyers to exercise such extensive and indefinite powers, they themselves were striving with all their might to have those same powers exercised by the Council and the Court of Star Chamber,—bodies that we think of as judicial rather than legislative,—or even by the Court of Chancery. Notwithstanding some utterances provoked by the claims of the common lawyers, these men were really basing their legal and political theories on the prevailing idea of a fusion of powers: they were no advocates of legislative sovereignty, and they would hardly have understood the explanation now usually accepted of the relations which existed in the middle ages between the courts and "those who made the law." This is put beyond doubt by the words of Lord Ellesmere himself. It was probably Bagg's Case that he had in mind in his speech to Sir Henry Montagu when the latter was sworn Chief Justice of the King's Bench in place of Coke. In that speech the Chancellor reminded Sir Henry of his grandfather, Edward Montagu, formerly Chief Justice of the Common Pleas,

---

liquors in the State of Pennsylvania. Of course no one looks upon these as judicial.

how "He challenged not power for the Judges of this Court to correct all misdemeanors as well extrajudicial as judicial, nor to have power to judge Statutes and acts of Parliament to be void, if they conceived them to be against common right and reason; but left the King and the Parliament to judge what was common right and reason. I speak not of impossibilities or direct repugnances."[1] Such language in the eighteenth or twentieth century would clearly be an assertion of legislative sovereignty over judicial power: in the early seventeenth, it was merely a denial of the competency of the common law judges in this respect. It was far from implying that such matters were wholly beyond "judicial" cognizance.

It is probably true that in all England the common law had no opponent so bitter as Lord Ellesmere. There is no doubt that he was thus regarded by the common lawyers.[2] But notwithstanding this opposition to the pretensions of the common lawyers, Ellesmere himself could declare, after citing Coke's own words in Bonham's Case: "And the Judges themselves *do play the Chancellors' parts upon statutes*, making construction of them according to equity, varying from the rules and grounds of law, and enlarging them, pro bono publico, *against the letter and intent of the makers*, whereof our

---

[1] *Moore's Reports*, p. 828.
[2] He was, Sir James Whitelocke says, "the greatest enemye to the common law that ever did bear office of state in this kingdome; he was therupon termed viscount Breaklaw for viscount Brackley." *Liber Famelicus* (Camden Society), p. 53.

books have many hundreds of cases."[1] Such statements cannot be reconciled on any theory of parliamentary sovereignty.

A struggle was inevitable. When it came, it arose from the determination of the "prerogative courts" to exercise unchecked those large and indefinite powers which they claimed as the heirs of the old Council. The Court of Parliament and the courts of the common law had equal right to claim descent from the ancient Curia. It would be a cause of surprise if dissension and even war should not result from a situation so serious. For the claims of both parties in the great contest had an historical foundation. These different bodies, all tracing their legitimate descent from the ancient Curia, had formerly worked in greater harmony, but now changed conditions had set them in opposition to each other, and a new line of kings was on the throne, that knew not the full importance of preventing a rupture, who were short-sighted enough to identify themselves and their prerogatives with one party exclusively. By this, new elements were brought into the quarrel, and it eventually required the sacrifice of the King and thousands of his subjects before a solution of the great question was reached. When reached, it was not the solution sought by either of the original parties. Bacon and Strafford, who embody the highest and best aims of the prerogative party, were seek-

[1] *The Earl of Oxford's Case*, 13 Jac. I., *White and Tudor's Leading Cases in Equity*, 6th ed., vol. ii. pp. 648, 649. The italics are mine.

ing a balance of powers in the state, but with an administrative system removed to a large extent from the ordinary course of the law, as is found in a measure over much of the Continent to-day. Parliament took up the quarrel of the common lawyers, as we have already seen. The victory of the Parliament led to a system in which both the King's ministers and the courts of law had to take a subordinate place; the modern theory of legislative sovereignty will brook no equal for the sovereign lawmaking body.

If, then, the above was really Coke's view of this important matter, it was in full accord with his general theory and with that of his contemporaries: Coke's statement, however, can hardly be truly said to be an accurate description of the practice on this important matter prevailing in the time of Edward III, though it would seem to be as near to that practice as the more modern view, which is, that Herle had in mind merely the subsequent attitude of the "legislature." If the latter was Herle's meaning; if they "who made the act" exercised afterwards no power beyond that of a modern legislature; no power of a judicial character, no control and supervision over the actual operation of the act, then Herle's famous remark was of no practical significance whatever, and no importance must be attached to it at all. In view of all the circumstances, I cannot think that this was his real meaning.

The next case cited by Coke in Bonham's Case was another occurring in the reign of Edward III and reported by Fitzherbert. Briefly stated, the case was as follows: The Statute of Westminster Second, chapter 21, enacts that in case a tenant fail for a period of two years to perform the services due from his land, then the lord may have a writ of *cessavit* to recover the tenement. This writ the statute expressly extends to the heirs of the lord. Nevertheless, in 33 Edward III, Willoughby, Justice, denied this remedy to the heirs of a deceased lord, notwithstanding the statute.[1] The reason was, Coke says, "because in a *Cessavit* the tenant before judgment may render the arrearages and damages, &c. and retain the land, and that he cannot do when the heir brings a *Cessavit* for the cesser in the time of his ancestor, for the arrearages incurred in the life of the ancestor do not belong to the heir: and because it would be against common right and reason, the common law adjudges the said act of Parliament as to that point void."[2]

Coke in Bonham's Case cites in support of his theory several other cases, which may be seen in the report, including the case of the abbey seals mentioned above.[3]

[1] *Fitzherbert's Abr.*, *Cessavit*, 42; *F. N. B.*, p. 209 F.
[2] 8 *Rep.*, 118. These reasons are not given in Fitzherbert's report of the case, which is very brief, but they may be correct ones, nevertheless. See also 2 *Inst.*, 460.
[3] In addition to the ones already given may be mentioned one or two cases of Elizabeth's reign in which, if the judges did not always say that statutes were void, they acted as though they could be. One such is *Lord Cromwell's Case* in the King's Bench in 20 Elizabeth. Henry Lord Cromwell brought an action *de scandalis magnatum* against Ed. Denny, Vicar of Northlinham in Norfolk, for certain words uttered against him contrary to the Statute of 2 Richard II., cap. 5. But the plaintiff in his declaration misrecited the act

THE HIGH COURT OF PARLIAMENT

That statutes were not held in great reverence in mediaeval times is shown not merely by the decisions

in question. The act says, "whosoever shall" do so and so "shall incur," etc. This was changed so as to read, who "shall *not*" do it "shall incur," etc. It was moved by the defendant's counsel that the declaration was therefore insufficient, but in return it was urged that the act in question was a private act; that the courts could therefore take no notice of it *ex officio*, but must take the act as the party had alleged it, which, of course, would, if true, dispose of the charge of insufficiency in the declaration.

It was decided by the whole court that the act was a public and not a private act. But "it was likewise resolved, that if the act was private, and that the court ought to take it to be such as is alledged; then the said act was against law, and reason, and therefore void: for as it is alledged, those who do not offend shall be punished, and that was *condemnare insontem & demittere reum;* wherefore judgment was given against the plaintiff *quod nihil capiat per billam.*" 4 *Reports*, 12, 13.

A case where the Court's action was very significant occurred in the Exchequer in 31 Elizabeth. Sir Thomas Gresham had levied a fine of some manors in Norfolk to the use of himself, his wife, and their heirs, but with the power of revocation on payment of a certain sum. Later, Sir Thomas revoked the uses, complying, as he thought, with the necessary conditions, and afterwards raised several new uses and estates of some of the manors, which he held *in capite*. After Sir Thomas's death, in the twenty-third year of Elizabeth, it was decided by the justices that the revocation was void, and that therefore all the manors accrued to his widow as survivor. Following this decision, the revocation was declared by private act of Parliament to be good and binding in law, and soon after Lady Gresham was summoned into the Exchequer to answer a fine to the Queen, because the new uses which Sir Thomas had raised before his death constituted an alienation of lands held *in capite*, and the alienation had been accomplished without royal license. The contention of the Crown, of course, was valid only if the new uses were good, and these, in turn, could stand only if the revocation were upheld. But the revocation had been by act of Parliament declared to be valid and binding. Nevertheless, it was held by the Court, that as Sir Thomas had died before the passage of the act validating the revocation, Lady Gresham was discharged by survivorship; and as every alienation without license implies a wrong and a trespass, Lady Gresham must be discharged of the fines for the alienations, because "an act of Parliament, to which the Queen, and all her subjects are parties, and give consent, cannot do a wrong." 9 *Reports*, 106, 107. The reason the act could not do a wrong was, of course, merely because the judges, when *they* decided it was wrong, refused to enforce it. See also cases in *Brooke's Abr.*, *Parlement & Statutes* (vol. ii. fol. 120 B, ed. of 1573).

and dicta of the judges, but by the words of the statutes themselves. Thus, a statute of Edward III speaks of a previous statute as "certain Articles expressly contrary to the Laws and Customs of our Realm of England and to our Prerogatives and Rights Royal . . . pretended to be granted by Us by the Manner of a Statute."[1] Coke's definition of *mala in se* as breaches of the common law and *mala prohibita* as breaches of statute, referred to above, shows how far he ranks the perfection of the customary law above the statutory law.[2] In fact, it is clear that he and his contemporaries retained the old distinction between law and enactment. Statutes were not ordinarily to be disregarded, "there being no greater assurance of jurisdiction than an Act of Parliament, where there be no . . . presidents" to the contrary; but statutes, made by the High Court of Parliament, and orders of other courts correcting errors in judicial proceedings and "other errors and misdemeanors extra-judicial," which might make changes in the working or the administration of the law, could never affect the sacred principles of the common law created by immemorial tradition and founded upon the unalterable principles of reason and revelation. As for the judges of Henry II, the assizes were not " law," neither was a statute "law" to Coke. The idea

---

[1] 15 Edw. III. (1341), 1 *S. R.*, 297. Similarly, in 15 E. II. (1 *S. R.*, 185), a statute was declared to be "sinfully and wrongly made and granted, against Reason and common Right, and against the Oath of our Lord the King which he made at his Coronation."

[2] 4 *Inst.*, 63.

that law can be "made" is very modern. The opinion of one of Coke's contemporaries and enemies has already been quoted. In whatever points Lord Ellesmere differed from Coke, and there were many, he agreed — and his testimony as Chancellor is of great value — that "the wisdom of the judges" had in times past found some of the laws "unmeete for the times they liued in."[1]

If we turn now from cases and statutes to the works of systematic writers on law, we find some evidence that they believed statutes might be void in some cases. So the author of the *Doctor and Student* says, "Of the Law of Reason, the which by doctors is called the law of nature of reasonable creatures,"—"Against this law, prescription, statute nor custom may not prevail: and if any be brought in against it, they be not prescriptions, statutes nor customs, but things void and against justice."[2] Again, he says, "If any general custom were against the law of God, or if any statute were made directly against it: as if it were ordained that no *alms* should be given for no necessity, the custom and statute were void."[3]

Coke's writings, of course, are the place where we find most frequent expression of this attitude of the

---

[1] See also *ante*, p. 294, where Lord Ellesmere, in commending Chief Justice Montagu for not declaring statutes void, makes this significant exception: *I speak not of impossibilities or direct repugnances.*

[2] Dialogue I., ch. ii.

[3] *Ibid.*, ch. vi.; see also *ibid.*, chs. **iv.**, xix., xxvi.; Dialogue II., ch. xv.; Noy, *Maxims*, p. 1.

[300]

judges toward statutes. We have noted some instances above. Another is his comment on the statute of 11 Henry VII, empowering justices of assize and justices of the peace to hear and determine cases on mere information. This statute was the especial object of Coke's wrath,—a statute "which had a fair flattering preamble," but "tended in the execution ... to the high displeasure of Almighty God, the great let, nay the utter subversion of the Common Law, and the great let of the Wealth of this Land."[1] Likewise in his account of the conference concerning Proclamations in 8 James I, Coke says, "But 9 H. 4 an Act of Parliament was made, that all the Irish people should depart the realm, and go into Ireland before the feast of the Nativity of the Blessed Lady, upon pain of death, which was absolutely *in terrorem*, and was utterly against the law."[2]

When we come to that great series of constitutional questions which came up for settlement before the King's judges in the years preceding the civil wars, there is one important problem in the solution of which we get great assistance from a knowledge of this traditional attitude of the judges toward the statute law. In assessing the relative legal merits of the claims of the Crown lawyers and of those on the side of Parliament, this point, it seems to me, has been somewhat neglected. We too readily assume the sacred and inviolable character of the enactments of Parliament. When the King's

[1] 4 *Inst.*, 39-41. See also *ante*, p. 64, n.
[2] 12 *Rep.*, 76.

judges, therefore, "excepted certain cases out of the Statute" where the King was concerned; where they declared to be legal some royal act which he had done without statutory warrant, or sometimes in the face of a statute; we accept without qualification the outcries of the parliamentarians. We assume that as the judges are the King's creatures, they are always simply doing his bidding, regardless of the law; or, at least, are less considerate of it than of royal favour. But, I submit that this is unfair to the judges in some cases. Judges were accustomed to "except cases out of the Statute" in cases of necessity, when injustice would result, or when the public good demanded it.[1] They also declared acts void if contrary to "law." There was, therefore, nothing unusual, nothing unprecedented, when the King's judges made exceptions out of the law where the King's prerogatives were concerned. This does not necessarily imply in all cases that they put the King "above the law." They were acting as judges had done for centuries. This must be said in explanation, not in entire justification, of the views and actions of men who in many cases honestly took a narrow legal view of the situation. To men who could see, the law offered but an incomplete solution. The King must be checked in the performance of acts that could reasonably be interpreted as *strictly legal*, or the substance of Englishmen's liberties would soon be gone. The bare law was not sufficient protection against the King, when the

[1] *Ante*, p. 263; *Plowden*, pp. 204, 205; 2 *Inst.*, 25.

King was arrayed against the people. That law had grown up, its precedents had been formed, in times when the King and the other organs of the commonwealth were still working in harmony, before the King had come to look upon himself as *above* and separate from his people, before the people themselves were enough conscious of their political existence apart from the Crown to realize an antagonism between Sovereign and subject. Now, under the new and altered conditions, the old law was breaking down. It offered no sufficient protection to the subject, when the King without a breach of it could oppress him and discover legal means of taking, without his consent and even against his will, so much of his property that the government was thus rendered independent of him entirely, deaf to his complaints, and able to ignore them with impunity.

These things a statesman should have seen; many of them did see. And hence we find even many loyal supporters of prerogative joining with the more radical to keep the King within bounds. The business of the judges, however, was in the main different, and properly different. They were to give effect to the existing law. Their training led them to look backward, not forward. It is a mistake, then, to be surprised at their action; it is unjust to cover them with indiscriminate censure. In arguing for the legality of ship-money, Weston was probably not so far beyond the law when he so pertinently replied to his opponents, "If you say, the acts of parliament should give way to necessity, then you have answered all you have objected:—This is not the only case of necessity. . . . And shall not the acts of parliament give way to necessity for defence of the kingdom? What though there have been petitions in parliament to have it decreed, that this kind of charge should not be laid upon the subject? Admit it had been so decreed in parliament, yet by the law of equity they ought to be charged; and in all reason they ought to be charged towards the defence of the kingdom."[1]

Even more explicit in his statement of the old doctrine was Sir Edward Crawley, one of the justices of the Common Pleas: "Admit, I say, there were an express act, That the king, were the realm in never so much danger, should not have aid from his subjects, but in parliament, it is a void act; will any man say such an act shall bind? This power is inseparable from the crown, as the pronouncing of war and peace is: such an act is manifestly unreasonable, and not to be suffered; . . . You cannot have a king without these royal rights, no, not by act of parliament."[2]

[1] 3 *St. Tr.*, 1075. Weston was one of the Barons of the Court of Exchequer.
[2] *Ibid.*, 1085. See his statement more at length; also Justice Croke's similar opinion, *ibid.*, 1160.
    So Sir William Jones, a justice of the King's Bench, declared: "I will tell what I have heard adjudged in this case. In the parliament held 1 Jac. there were two things expressly moved: One, That there might be no wardship or tenure of the King: The other, that the king might not allow surveyors. To these questions, after long disputes, it was answered by the whole parliament, that such an act of parliament to top the prerogative of tenures would be void, because it is inherent in the crown, for every man holds immediately or mediately of the king." *Ibid.*, 1190. St. John in replying to these arguments clearly

RELATIONS OF JUDICIARY AND LEGISLATURE

Under the Commonwealth we have noted the gradual change from the old view of the supremacy of law to the new one of the supremacy of Parliament. This comes out in the treatment of the statutes. For example, in Streater's Case, in 1653, we find this interesting dialogue:

Freeman (counsel for Streater), arguing against the form of the return in a habeas corpus, "My lord, every Return ought to have these two things in it; the Cause and how long he shall be a prisoner: and so you have it in Magna Charta, p. 54. My lord, all acts of parliaments against the laws of the land, are in themselves void. The law is above the parliament.

"*Judge.* Good Sir, do not stand to repeat these things before us.

"*Freeman.* My lord, I do know it; they may pass their acts according to law, but not against law. The lord Dyer hath it so in his Reports.

"*Judge.* When we are in examination of a prisoner, will you come and overthrow the acts of parliament?

had in mind the difference between a law and an enactment, though he naturally magnified the importance of the latter to the utmost. Speaking of the decision of the judges in the ship-money case and comparing it with the decision of Richard II's judges upon a statute, he said: "In that of Rich. 2, it was for overthrowing but one act of parliament, *which was likewise introductive of a new law;* for the commission had no rise from the common law; for in truth it was derogatory to the crown: *It had only the strength of the parliament to support it,* which was sufficient; it was for the common good. But here the endeavour was at once, not to blow up one act of parliament, but all; *and these not introductive, but declaratory of the common law.* . . . That of Rich. 2, was but the blowing up of the upper deck; this of the common law, and the statutes too, and the old foundations, and all the structures built upon them, all together." 3 *St. Tr.,* 1280.

"*Freeman.* My lord, I refer it to your lordship's judgment, whether this gentleman ought to be kept in prison without cause shown."[1]

So it was said further on in argument for Streater, "Parliaments ever made laws, but the judges of the law judged by those laws. Who will question but that the warrant of a justice of Peace, shewing lawful cause of imprisonment, is of greater force in law, than an Order of Parliament shewing no cause of imprisonment?"[2]

The case of Day v. Savadge is one of the best known cases in which this principle is set forth. There it was stated *obiter* that "even an act of parliament, made against natural equity, as to make a man judge in his own case, is void in itself; for *jura naturae sunt immutabilia*, and they are *leges legum.*"[3]

During the parliamentary proceedings against Clarendon in 1667, Sir Heneage Finch, afterwards famous as Lord Chancellor, said: "And tho' I know not what the *Legislative* Power of a Parliament cannot do, yet it is not in the Power of the Parliament, King, Lords nor Commons, to declare anything to be Treason, which is not in the Common-Law Felony before."[4] His great uncle had expressed views very similar.[5]

The new temper of the judges is seen in the quotation above from Streater's Case. The judge must

---

[1] 5 *St. Tr.*, 372, 373.
[2] *Ibid.*, 381.
[3] *Hobart's Rep.*, p. 87.
[4] 2 *St. Tr.* (Hargrave's edition), 560.
[5] *Finch's Law* (1627), book i. ch. vi.

uphold the power of Parliament. In that case Chief Justice Rolle certainly did not do it in a very impressive manner against the precedents cited by counsel. With the Restoration, we find some indications of a return to the old theory, especially when the prerogative was in question; but this very matter formed so important a part of the ground of struggle in 1688, and was so prominent in the Revolution settlement, that few echoes of the older doctrine are to be heard after the Revolution. Lawyers and judges, of course, for a while, remembered the old theory. Some twelve years after the Revolution the great Chief Justice Holt made his well-known comment on Dr. Bonham's Case: "What my Lord *Coke* says in Dr. *Bonham's Case,* in his 8 *Co.,* is far from any extravagancy, for it is a very reasonable and true saying, That if an act of parliament should ordain that the same person should be party and judge, or, which is the same thing, judge in his own cause, it would be a void act of parliament; for it is impossible that one should be judge and party, for the judge is to determine between party and party, or between the government and the party; and an act of parliament can do no wrong, though it may do several things that look pretty odd; for it may discharge one from his allegiance to the government he lives under, and restore him to the state of nature; but it cannot make one that lives under a government judge and party."[1]

[1] 12 *Mod. Rep.*, 687. See, generally, Roscoe Pound in *Harvard Law Rev.*, vol. xxi. p. 390 et seq.

THE HIGH COURT OF PARLIAMENT

Since then, we meet now and then with a vague statement of the older view, especially in relation to international law,[1] but it is safe to say that the whole attitude of the courts had changed. What had before been customary and accepted—as we believe has been sufficiently shown at length above—now becomes unusual and no longer representative of the generally accepted theory. Blackstone was no doubt expressing current belief when he said: "Where some collateral matter arises out of the general words, and happens to be unreasonable; there the judges are in decency to conclude that this consequence was not foreseen by the parliament, and therefore they are at liberty to expound the statute by equity, and only *quoad hoc* disregard it. Thus if an act of parliament gives a man power to try all causes, that arise within his manor of Dale; yet, if a cause should arise in which he himself is a party, the act is construed not to extend to that, because it would be unreasonable that any man should determine his own quarrel. But, if we could conceive it possible for the parliament to enact, that he should try as well his own causes as those of other persons, there is no court that has power to defeat the intent of the legislature, when couched in such evident and express words, as leave no doubt whether it was the intent of the legislature or no."[2]

I shall simply ask the reader to look back at the

[1] See Note A at the end of this chapter (p. 329).
[2] *Commentaries*, vol. i. p. 91.

cases that have been given, in proof of the statement that the courts in the sixteenth and seventeenth centuries did not agree in theory and did not carry out in practice the doctrine contained in the last of these sentences of Blackstone. His studies had made him familiar with the cases denying Parliament's omnipotence and the reasoning therein contained. He repeats these in what Sir Frederick Pollock aptly calls the "ornamental part" of his introduction, but he repeats them as a lesson he has learned. It was no part of his scheme, and his later statements concerning Parliament contradicted it utterly. The fact is, he misunderstood the meaning of these older statements. He interpreted them in the light of a theory which would have been repudiated if it had been known to the men who originally gave these decisions and made these statements, and thus he gave them a different meaning.

It is true, about Blackstone's time there was one last whisper of the old theory brought out by the stress of colonial government, but it soon died away,[1] and the doctrine of the legislative supremacy of Parliament has since been practically unquestioned in English courts of law. In America James Otis had used the old argument against writs of assistance — "No Acts of Parliament can establish such a writ; . . . An act against the constitution is void."[2] And there it was destined

[1] Lord Camden and Pitt on the repeal of the Stamp Act, *Parl. Hist.*, vol. xvi. pp. 168, 169, 171, 179, 195. Compare the "Declaratory Act" of the same year and the statements of Lord Chancellor Northington and others.
[2] *John Adams's Works*, vol. ii., appendix, p. 525.

THE HIGH COURT OF PARLIAMENT

to continue and influence the course of government and the decisions of courts for generations; but in England, the life had gone out of the theory, and parliamentary omnipotence occupied the whole field.[1]

It may be important to point out in a little more detail one phase of the decline of the doctrine that courts may declare an act of Parliament void. I mean the upholding by the courts in the time of James II of the King's dispensing power. It is unnecessary here to go generally into the history of the dispensing power or cases illustrating it.[2] It will be enough to try to show its relation to the general attitude of the judges toward the statutes. It is pretty well established that a dispensing power of somewhat indefinite boundaries was acknowledged up to the Revolution to belong to the King. It arose partly from the sacredness of the King's prerogatives and partly from the prevailing view of the authority of statutes. The distinction we have noticed

---

[1] See, generally, Dicey, *Law of the Constitution;* Lowell, *The Government of England,* vol. ii. chs. lxi., lxii.; Hatschek, *Englisches Staatsrecht,* vol. i. pp. 137, 138; *Juridical Society Papers,* vol. iii. p. 305 et seq.; Dwarris, *On the Statutes* (1848), part ii. ch. xi. p. 694 et seq.

[2] See on that subject, Broom, *Const. Law,* 2d ed., p. 492 et seq.; Anson, *Law and Custom of the Constitution,* vol. i. (4th ed.), p. 326 et seq.; Maitland, *Constitutional History of England,* pp. 302-6; Hearn, *Government of England,* 1st ed., pp. 46-9; Brinton Coxe, *Legislative Power,* pp. 165-71; Hallam, *Const. Hist.,* ch. xiv.; *Thomas* v. *Sorrell, Vaughan's Rep.,* p. 330; *Godden* v. *Hales,* 11 *St. Tr.,* 1165; and several important pamphlets discussing the dispensing power appended by the editor to the report of Hales's Case in 11 *St. Tr.,* 1200 et seq. Several of these are by Sir Robert Atkyns, and were also published in a volume entitled, *Parliamentary and Political Tracts,* written by Sir Robert Atkins (2d ed., 1741). See also W. Petyt, *Jus Parliamentarium;* Finch's *Law* (1627), pp. 234, 235; *The Birth and Parentage, Rise and Fall of Non Obstante, Luders' Tracts* (1810), Tract V.

the judges making between "law" and statute is here important. This is seen in the distinction between *mala in se* and *mala prohibita*. This distinction Coke considers the same as that between "law" and statute.[1] So the King might dispense with a statute forbidding *mala prohibita*. Such things were illegal merely because made so by the statute, and having nothing better to support them, the King might except individual cases out of the statute; but his power did not extend to the common law, nor to acts declaratory of the common law.

This dispensing by the King is very similar to the practice of the judges already noticed, when, on account of some injustice or hardship, they "excepted out of the Statute" some particular case.[2] In the case of a "law," generally speaking, the judges could not declare it void, nor could the King dispense with it; but in the case of a statute, cases of hardship or injustice might be "excepted out of it" by the judges, and individuals might, in like manner, be excepted from its operation by the King, as their offence was merely *malum prohibitum*. Clearly, these exceptions were in both cases due, in great part, to the lower estimation in which statutes were held as compared with the principles of the common law. They were also partly due to the fact, noted above, that in the absence of a clear

[1] On this point see 4 *Inst.*, 63; 12 *Rep.*, 76, and 11 *St. Tr.*, 1253, 1285, 1286, where Coke's explanation of these terms is disputed. For Blackstone's view see *Commentaries*, vol. i. pp. 54, 57. Vaughan refused to accept Coke's definition; see *Thomas* v. *Sorrell*.

[2] *Ante*, pp. 263, 302; 2 *Inst.*, 23, 25; *Plowden*, pp. 204, 205; Dwarris, *On the Statutes*, vol. ii. p. 622 et seq. (1848).

definition of legislation, that power was by no means the exclusive possession of the Parliament. The dispensing power, like the issuing of proclamations, was a part of those undefined rights which the King exercised by himself or through his Council. In the case of the dispensing power, this was apparently recognized by the judges as legitimate, provided it did not extend to the principles of the "law," which, according to the orthodox theory, neither the King, nor the Parliament, nor themselves, could alter in any material matter.

It is interesting to note how the power of the judiciary, which, in the beginning of the long constitutional struggle under the Stuarts, had been pitted against prerogative and had at first been looked upon by the parliamentarians as an aid, is now invoked by prerogative as a protection against legislative aggression. Here, as usual, we see the conservatism of the law. Through the changes of the civil war it had remained practically unaltered, while the nation had moved rapidly. It was invoked by Coke against James I because James's pretensions were an *innovation;* it was employed by James II against the novel doctrine of legislative supremacy.[1]

[1] It is no less interesting to find in 1688 many of the arguments *against* the dispensing power still based on Parliament's old "judicial" supremacy. Sir Robert Atkyns said, "The King and both Houses were of opinion, that they could make a Non Obstante in such case void. The judges are of a contrary opinion, that a Non Obstante shall make void the statute. Here is an inferior court over-ruling and controuling the judgment of a superior court." 11 *St. Tr.*, 1232. This is also the basis of Petyt's whole argument in his *Jus Parliamentarium,* a book which was written in opposition to the theory that judges could uphold the King's power of dispensing with a statute.

RELATIONS OF JUDICIARY AND LEGISLATURE

The great subject of Prerogative is not within the scope of this essay, which is taken up with the nature of Parliament's supremacy rather than with its extent. Incidentally, however, this has entailed a brief consideration of such a branch of prerogative as the dispensing power. One other branch is connected with our subject almost as closely as the dispensing power; namely, the question of ordinances and royal proclamations, their nature and enforcement.

It is clear that by Edward III's time some distinction existed between statutes and ordinances. The former were more permanent than the latter, and more difficult to change. Attempts have frequently been made to distinguish them with much greater definiteness than this. It has been said that an act of the King and Council without the Commons was an ordinance, while all three must agree on a "statute;" that enactments of new law were statutes, declarations of the old law only ordinances; that all enactments placed on the Statute Roll were statutes, all others mere ordinances, etc. The effort has also been made to push the distinction between the two kinds of enactment back beyond the reign of Edward I. Apparently, these attempts have been unsuccessful, signally so for the earlier period. For example, the great assizes of Henry II antedate the Statute Roll; they appear in many cases to be nothing more than directions to the King's judges. We have seen how they might be set aside by the judges, and this is not surprising in a time when laws were not made but declared. Nevertheless, if these were not "statutes," no statutes then existed. Filmer long ago pointed out that even Magna Charta and the Charter of Forests had only the form of letters patent, and also many enactments hardly less important.[1] Maitland shows that if the consent of the Commons were requisite, it is doubtful whether "those two pillars of real property law," *Quia Emptores* and *De Donis Conditionalibus*, may be included among the statutes.[2]

Prynne in almost all his constitutional works denies the difference between ordinance and statute, though Coke as strenuously asserts it. The modern view is much in favour of Prynne rather than Coke. Gneist, for example, says, "Under the system of personal government, single decisions, temporary administrative measures, and permanent ordinances were all confused together. Frequently petitions that had been granted lay inoperative for years before the enactments affecting the same were carried out or published. As a rule, at the close of the parliamentary sittings, the council sorted the confused mass of resolutions, and provided for their being duly carried out. It was specially the business of the justices to select such enactments as, being of a permanent nature, should be entered upon the 'roll of the statutes' for the cognizance of the courts."[3]

---

[1] *Patriarcha*, ch. iii. sec. 16.
[2] *Const. Hist. of England*, p. 187.
[3] *Const. Hist.* (Eng. trans.), vol. ii. p. 23; see also *ibid.*, pp. 24, 25; Stubbs, *C. H.*, vol. ii. p. 426 et seq.; Maitland, *C. H.*, pp. 186-8. On the general subject, see, in addition, Gneist, *C. H.*, vol. ii. p. 149, note; Pike, *Const. Hist. of*

RELATIONS OF JUDICIARY AND LEGISLATURE

"Legislation," such as we could say existed in those times, did not belong exclusively to Parliament, even after the Council had separated from it. The King had formerly considered himself the real source of all "legislative" power, and a certain, or, as Maitland says, an uncertain, part of this power was still recognized as his. So late as 1390 the Commons petitioned that the Chancellor and Council would not, after Parliament ended, make an ordinance contrary to the common law, or to statutes already in existence or to be enacted by that Parliament. They could get no better answer than that what had been done before should continue, saving the King's prerogative.[1]

The conciseness and generality of the statutes that we meet with on the earlier rolls we shall find to be due to the fact that they were to be interpreted by judges able at need to amplify and correct them; and even in circumstances of hardship, or injustice, to except cases out of them. But the common law judges were not the only ones able to do this. The King and his Council were also sharers in these powers. By the dispensing power they could "except cases out of the

the House of Lords, pp. 321, 322; Amos's edition of Fortescue's *De Laudibus*, pp. 59-61; Clifford, *History of Private Bill Legislation*, vol. i. p. 332; Hargrave and Butler's Notes to *Coke on Littleton*, p. 159 B, note 292; 2 *Inst.*, 643, 644; 4 *Inst.*, 25; Ruffhead's preface to his edition of the statutes, vol. i. p. xiii; Maitland, *C. H.*, pp. 256-8, 302; Barrington, *Observations on the Statutes*, 2d ed., p. 36; Anson, *Law and Custom of the Constitution*, vol. i. (4th ed.) pp. 243-9; Hale, *Jurisdiction of the Lords House*, p. 32; Parry, *Parliaments and Councils of England*, p. 124 and note; Hatschek, *Englisches Staatsrecht*, vol. i. p. 114; Prynne, *Observations on Coke's Fourth Institute*, p. 13.

[1] *Rot. Parl.*, vol. iii. p. 266; Stubbs, *Const. Hist.*, vol. ii. p. 618.

statute" as well as the judges. So, by the power of making ordinances, the King could supplement the law. This latter power we naturally think of as "legislative" or as "administrative," and far from "judicial." But it is necessary to remember that the common law judges claimed a share in it in Bagg's Case, noted above, and it is not without significance that even Locke does not separate *judicial* administration from the rest. Thus it is that the older statutes leave so much to be done by interpretation—which really includes dispensation, be it the dispensation of judge or Council—and by ordinance.

For the Tudor period at least, then, there is justification for saying that "legislation" was still vaguely considered as the act of the King. It is true, many things could be done only with consent of Parliament. This had been true for centuries of most forms of taxation. But, after all, the residuum of legislative power was still felt in a general way to be in the King. Even in questions of taxation this was the case, and where the King's right of taxing without Parliament could not be shown by precedent or enactment to have been taken away from him, the judges of the seventeenth century usually decided that the right was still in the King. Loud as were the complaints of the parliamentary lawyers, it is not so clear that James I was acting beyond his rights in Bate's Case, or that his son was violating the fundamental law in collecting tonnage and poundage without a parliamentary grant. It is assuming too much to say that the judges who upheld such actions were in all cases the mere tools of the King.[1] The sharp distinction now made between the King in Council and the King in Parliament was then not so sharp. Parliament was not exclusively legislative, nor was its legislation exclusive. It did much business that was judicial, and many of its "acts" which we style "legislative" were still conceived of as done under the precept *ad consentiendum* rather than *ad faciendum*.[2] On the other hand, much "legislative" business never got into Parliament at all. The extensive use of these royal proclamations is an indication of it, as well as the great executive and legislative powers exercised by the Privy Council under Henry and Elizabeth.[3]

These facts and the indefiniteness of "jurisdiction" out of which they arise suggest a comparison between the "secondary legislation" up to the seventeenth century and that of the period subsequent. There is no modern constitutional state but must have a power

---

[1] On *Bate's Case* see Gardiner, *History of England*, vol ii. pp. 1-11; Hall, *Custom-Revenue in England*, vol. i. p. 145 et seq. For the question of tonnage and poundage, see especially, Gardiner, *op. cit.*, vol. vi. p. 322 et seq.
[2] See Note B at the end of this chapter (p. 330).
[3] Speaking of the Tudor proclamations, and the legal characterizations of them as *quoad terrorem populi* only, Dicey says the Tudors themselves looked upon them otherwise: "Their constant aim was to give proclamations the force of laws, and thus to render the King's Council a legislative body. Had that endeavour succeeded, the Council would have occupied the position of a French Parliament; a body to which, both in origin and history, it bore a close resemblance." *Privy Council*, p. 92. He gives instances of the proclamations on p. 93. See also on this subject, Hallam, *Const. Hist.*, ch. v.

THE HIGH COURT OF PARLIAMENT

lodged somewhere, which can meet emergencies not foreseen or covered by the existing law, and one that is not hindered by the delay of the courts or by the necessity of waiting for the assembling of the legislature. As Bishop Stubbs says, "The executive power in the state must have certain powers to act in cases for which legislation has not provided, and modern legislation has not got beyond the expedient of investing the executive with authority to meet such critical occasions. The crown is able on several matters to legislate by orders in council at the present day, but by a deputed not a prerogative power; but there are conceivable occasions on which, during an interval of parliament, the ministers of the crown might be called upon to act provisionally with such authority as would require an act of indemnity to justify it."[1]

The Continental countries have met this need by a vesting of legislative power in the hands of administrative officials. In England this has hitherto not been adopted except in a very small way. The outcry over the "forty days' tyranny" in 1766, when Chatham by an Order in Council laid an embargo on grain, showed the feeling of Parliament on such matters.[2] The present agitation in the United States over "Government by Commission" is due in part to a similar feeling.[3]

And yet in the England of the sixteenth, and part

---

[1] *Const. Hist.*, vol. ii. p. 619.
[2] *Parl. Hist.*, vol. xvi. p. 245 et seq.; *Annual Register* for 1767, pp. 45-8.
[3] See Note C at the end of this chapter (p. 331).

of the seventeenth century, powers were exercised without statutory warrant, which extended even further than those exercised to-day on the Continent under the protection of the *droit administratif*. The proclamations of Henry VIII, of Elizabeth, of James I, and Charles; the enforcement of these by the Council and the Court of Star Chamber, to say nothing of the activity of those "courts" in matters non-"judicial,"—all these point to a "legislative" activity outside the "legislature," which we, the heirs of the Long and the Revolution Parliaments, can hardly understand. Though in England there is no *séparation des pouvoirs*, as on the Continent, the judicial power has been separated from the rest of administration. On the Continent, curiously enough, the very theory of separation has prevented this, to a certain extent. For example, in France the *Conseil d'État* has had to take on judicial functions in addition to administrative, because as an executive body its acts must not, according to the theory of the separation of powers, be reviewable by the judiciary. So in a roundabout way they have returned to conditions somewhat resembling those in England when the proclamations of the Council were enforced by the Council itself or by the Star Chamber. In Tudor England, however, these conditions were due to no *separation* of Powers, but to a *fusion* of powers. To-day, "Government by Commission" is resisted because it is an encroachment upon the judiciary, as well as upon the legislature, for we divide judicial administration from the rest of administration, and all administration from legislation. The contest between Council and common law courts in the time of Coke, we are too ready to think, must, therefore, have been a struggle of the "judiciary" against the "executive," an attempt to prevent "executive aggression." The contest should be looked at rather as a *competition* for "jurisdiction."

But, notwithstanding this great difference, due to the indefiniteness of governmental powers in the earlier time, the Council of the Tudors and a French *Conseil d'État* have many common characteristics, and the Council has usually attracted the attention of Continental observers.[1]

It is necessary now to look back over these instances where the King's judges excepted cases out of statutes as against reason, law, or the prerogative; or where others of the King's officials did the like under the dispensing power, or made and enforced proclamations without statutory warrant. Some explanation of this free and familiar treatment thus accorded to statutes is necessary if we are to have any clear understanding of these great constitutional questions. Such an explanation, to be in any sense adequate, can, I believe, be reached only through a consideration of the relations formerly subsisting between the ordinary courts and the High Court of Parliament; of the activity of the judges

[1] See, generally, Gneist, *Englische Verwaltungsrecht*, vol. i. secs. 11, 12, 44; Jellinek, *Gesetz und Verordnung*, p. 20 et seq.; Hatschek, *Englisches Staatsrecht*, vol. ii. p. 102. See also Note D at the end of this chapter (p. 334).

of the ordinary courts in parliamentary business; of the uncertainty of the line that divided what we call the "judicial" part of the business from "legislation;" and, finally, of the character of the "acts" in which that "legislation" was embodied.

The peculiarly commanding position of the courts in countries whose institutions are English must not be considered an accident. On the Continent, where representative legislative assemblies are, to a greater extent than in England, a modern and a conscious creation, the courts of law have a lower place. It has been the peculiar fortune of England that her mediaeval High Court of Parliament survived the disintegration of feudal ranks, to have infused into it the new vigour of nationality. Thus it retained in unbroken continuity its ancient powers and functions, which were large and indefinite. Without losing them it became also in time the mouthpiece of the nation, and the supreme lawmaking body. On the Continent, for the most part, the feudal assemblies went down with the wreck of feudalism, or became so feeble or occasional, for one reason or another, that their feudal traditions were well-nigh lost. There the connexion between the traditions of the feudal council and the modern legislature was broken. The latter did not acquire strength till the former had disappeared. In England, on the contrary, the feudal Curia broadened out into the modern Parliament, without break of continuity, by a process so imperceptible and natural that we can point specifically to but few of the changes that transformed it.

It inherited from feudal times the general and undefined powers which we have seen to be a leading characteristic of feudal assemblies. But the very indefiniteness of those powers made it impossible for the High Court completely to monopolize them; they were shared by the Council and the other law courts, which, in fact, had a common ancestry with the High Court itself. Thus, these separate bodies, each having an unbroken history from the time when it separated from the Curia, the common parent of all, had "jurisdictions" that were by no means mutually exclusive, but were in many things concurrent. It was not until this sharing of "jurisdiction" had turned into competition, and competition into an antagonism which resulted in the ultimate supremacy of the High Court and the subjection of its competitors, that foreigners began to be actively interested in English institutions. Therefore, when the shock of the French Revolution had cleared the way for a conscious reconstruction on the Continent, it was to the English constitution that men turned, but it was to the English constitution as seen by a Montesquieu, the post-revolutionary constitution.[1] So Montesquieu had written, "There is no liberty, if the judiciary power be not separated from the legislative and executive. Were it joined with the leg-

---

[1] Esmein, *Éléments de Droit Constitutionnel* (5th ed., 1909), p. 399. See, on the separation of powers generally, *ibid.*, pp. 392-475.

islative, the life and liberty of the subject would be exposed to arbitrary control; for the judge would be then the legislator. Were it joined to the executive power, the judge might behave with violence and oppression." Again he says, "The national judges are no more than the mouth that pronounces the words of the law, mere passive beings, incapable of moderating either its force or rigour."[1] Thus we find the "séparation des pouvoirs" which occupies so important a place in Continental constitutions. There, the legislature is non-judicial and its acts are external to the courts, which tend to be, even more than in modern England, "mere passive beings." Even where a written constitution has been adopted, in many cases the power has not been given to the courts to decide whether legislative acts conform to its provisions or not.

In the United States, on the other hand, where, notwithstanding a thoroughgoing separation of powers, the earlier spirit of English judicial institutions has been least influenced by the doctrine of legislative sovereignty, we find a much larger measure of that old indefinite "jurisdiction" still remaining in the courts of law. In England before the civil wars, it has been shown that this indefiniteness was greater still. To it we must ascribe in greatest measure that activity of the courts which to-day would be considered an unwarranted interference with the "law-making body."

That activity was evidenced in many ways. We have

[1] *Spirit of Laws*, bk. xi. ch. vi.

noticed to what an extent the judges of the King's ordinary courts shared in the work of Parliament that may be classed as judicial; how they were always among the triers of petitions, and how they were summoned to the King's Council in his Parliaments. We have also noticed how difficult cases were referred to this court; and how indefinite was the line between an "award" in which the judges must often have had practically the deciding power, and an "act."

In the case of a "legislative act" itself, from almost the first, their influence was very great. For even of such "acts" as we may imagine being made without their participation, we know that for a long period the wording, and, in fact, everything but the main principle, was the work of the judges exclusively. The barons, it may be, decided upon the main lines, but the whole reduction of these bare principles to the form and nature of a "statute" was the work of the judges, often after the barons had dispersed. This meant not merely the penning of the statutes: it extended to the form, and probably, to some extent, to the subject matter itself.[1] The brevity of the statutes when completed shows how much these judges who framed them were intentionally leaving to be interpreted by themselves or their colleagues in the light of the individual circumstances through which the statutes would be brought before them in the courts. This brevity is in strong contrast with the minute provisions by which the average

[1] May, *Parl. Practice*, 9th ed., p. 519.

modern *legislature* seeks to render impossible any freedom of interpretation by the judicial branch of the government.

There is nothing strange, then, in the fact that these same judges who drew the statutes practised and handed on to their successors a free-and-easy way of interpreting their own work.[1] Why should a judge have any great awe of a statute which perhaps he himself, or, at most, his predecessors in office, had helped to make; of which possibly the whole form and expression had been the work of himself and his colleagues of the Bench? So, when counsel in a case in 1305 argued for a certain construction of the Statute of Westminster Second of 1285, he was cut short by the Chief Justice with the remark: "*Do not gloss the Statute; we understand it better than you do, for we made it!*"[2]

The relations of ordinary court and High Court of Parliament were undeniably very close. We cannot, we should not, think that judges kept their "judicial" and their "legislative" and their "administrative" business totally separate and distinct from one another. On the contrary, we find a judge in 1338 in a case argued

[1] "In the last place we may consider how much hath been attributed to the opinions of the king's judges by parliaments, and so find that the king's council hath guided and ruled the judges, and the judges guided the parliament." Filmer, *Patriarcha*, ch. iii. sec. xviii.

[2] *Y. B. 33-35 E. I.* (Rolls Series), pp. 82, 83; Pollock, *First Book of Jurisprudence*, pp. 330, 331. In 1341, in a case where the interpretation of the Statute *De Donis* was in dispute, Sharshulle mentioned a previous case—probably the one above—where Herle said that the strongest argument for one side of the case was the construction given by Hengham, "who drew the Statute." *Y. B. 15 E. III.* (Rolls Series), pp. 392, 393.

before him judicially insisting that certain words of a franchise under litigation had been inserted by the Council, and must, therefore, have one particular meaning.[1] We have numerous cases of the judges consulting Parliament when they were uncertain of the meaning of an act, not formally in the way of appeal, but merely for advice on the construction of the statute; and this was sometimes the same Parliament that actually made the statute: sometimes it was one totally different.[2] The persons in Parliament who, in these cases, gave the desired advice, there can be little doubt, were for a long time the ones who had actually drawn the statute, namely, the judges. There seems, in short, to have been an informal give and take between the judges in and out of Parliament. Parliament was not "external" to the courts below it. The case of the Stauntons, referred to above from the Year Book of Edward III, is inexplicable under any other supposition.[3]

We cannot, under such conditions, imagine the judges treating statutes with the deference due to the solemn formal act of an external and sovereign legislative assembly. We should be surprised to find anything but the free, informal handling of statutes which we do find, and this is still easier to understand when we keep in mind the vagueness of the line between acts and awards. Sir Frederick Pollock says: "In the Middle

[1] *Y. B. 12 and 13 E. III.* (Rolls Series), pp. 14-17.
[2] See Petyt, *Jus. Parl.*, ch. ii.; 2 *St. Tr.*, 675, 676; *ante*, p. 115 et seq.
[3] *Ante*, p. 113, note.

Ages legislation was not the primary business of Parliament, and the rule that the king cannot legislate without Parliament was established only by degrees. Early statutes, therefore, are of a mixed character, containing both legislative and administrative provisions. We can hardly separate the declaration of new law from the enforcement of old, the establishment of novel remedies for novel mischiefs or newly detected shortcomings from the king's executive instructions to his officers. The King in his Council is alike ready to make fresh rules, to provide fresh machinery for the better working of existing rules, and to dispense justice in extraordinary cases. Law-making is not yet regarded as a distinct branch of sovereign power, external to the judicial authority, requiring strict and literal obedience, but entitled to nothing more. . . . In later times the judges have treated Acts of Parliament as proceeding from a wholly external and unjudicial authority."[1]

It is in this, then, that we are to look for the explanation of those decisions which have caused such embarrassment to modern constitutional lawyers. It is not enough to dismiss them as "captious" or "petulant;" they are too numerous and important for that. We want an explanation of them rather than a criticism. The explanation here offered is to be found in these characteristics of the mediaeval Parliaments and courts below which we have been describing; and the

[1] *First Book of Jurisprudence*, pp. 329-31.

continued existence of these traditions among lawyers and judges long after the change had set in which was to transform the ancient Court of Parliament into the sovereign legislative body we know to-day.[1]

---

[1] See T. C. Anstey, *On Blackstone's Theory of the Omnipotence of Parliament, Juridical Society Papers*, vol. iii. p. 305 et seq., especially p. 323.

RELATIONS OF JUDICIARY AND LEGISLATURE

Note A. Parliamentary Omnipotence and International Law
(*Page* 308)

The most interesting case on this subject is probably *Regina* v. *Keyn*, L. R. 2 Ex. Div., p. 63 et seq. The principle really at issue in that case does not directly affect parliamentary sovereignty, but some of the comments upon it do. The validity of the three-mile rule in international law and the discussion as to its acceptance as a part of the law of England have in reality little to do with the question of Parliament's omnipotence. The issue in *Regina* v. *Keyn* was merely whether this three-mile rule had been incorporated in the law of England or not. It is difficult to see how this involved Parliament much more directly than a similar discussion regarding any part of the customary law not mentioned in any act. In 1876, when the case was decided, no court would have recognized the validity of a rule of international law in flat violation of an act of Parliament. It seems rather unnecessary to say, as Sir J. F. Stephen does in commenting on this case, "The English courts no doubt administer in such cases what they conceive to be the principles accepted by all nations, but they do so because they are part of the law of England, and if Parliament were to pass an act expressly and avowedly opposed to the law of nations, the English courts would administer it in preference to the law of nations, whatever that may be." (*History of the Criminal Law*, vol. ii. p. 36.) No one will question the truth of this, but it is not to the point. The question whether international law is a part of the law of England is a very interesting one, but it affects the theory of parliamentary omnipotence only in the same general way that the whole question of the basis of "judge-made" law affects it. It has little more to do with the omnipotence of Parliament than the question whether the Law Merchant or even the rule of primogeniture is a part of the law of England. They are all illustrations of the indefinite powers still exercised by the courts of England,—powers which, according to the Austinian theory, may be reconciled with the supremacy of the "definite superior" through the dictum that what the sovereign permits, he prescribes. (*Austin*, Lecture xxxviii.)

The words of Lord Mansfield in *Heathfield* v. *Chilton* (4 Burrow, 2016), — "the act of parliament of 7 *Ann. c.* 12. did not *intend* to alter, nor *can* alter the law of nations," — if taken with the context and with the statute itself, are not directly or indirectly a denial of the validity of the statute, and cannot be compared with the utterances of the sixteenth and seventeenth century judges. See also his opinion in the case of *Triquet* v. *Bath*, 3 *Burrow*, 1480, 1481. In general, also, see Stephen, *History of the Criminal Law of England*, vol. ii. p. 29 et seq.; Roscoe Pound in *Harvard Law Rev.*, vol. xxi. p. 394 et seq.

NOTE B. PARLIAMENT AS AN ADVISORY COUNCIL
(*Page* 317)

THIS feature of Parliament's activity is well brought out in Raleigh's dialogue on the Prerogative of Parliaments in England. The Justice and the Councillor are discussing impositions, and the Justice asks, "Now, my lord, What prejudice hath his Majesty, his Revenue being kept up, if the Impositions, that were laid by the Advice of a few, be in Parliament laid by the general Council of the Kingdom, which takes off all Grudging and Complaint? — *Couns.* Yea, Sir; but that, which is done by the King, with the Advice of his private or Privy-council. is done by the King's absolute Power. — *Just.* And by whose Power is it done in Parliament, but by the King's absolute Power? Mistake it not, my Lord; The three Estates do but advise, as the prime Council doth; which Advice, if the King embrace it, becomes the King's own Act in the one, and the King's Law in the other; for without the King's Acceptation, both the publick and private Advices are but as empty Egg-shells." (*Harleian Miscellany* (edition of 1745), vol. v. p. 206.)

Somewhat the same idea was expressed later by Hobbes: "Neither a Counsellor (nor a Councell of State, if we consider it with no Authority of Judicature or Command, but only of giving Advice to the Soveraign when it is required, or of offering it when it is not required, [)] is a Publique Person. For the Advice is addressed to the Soveraign only, whose person cannot in his own presence, be represented to him by, another. But a Body of Counsellors, are never without some other Authority, either of Judicature, or of immediate Administration: As in a Monarchy, they represent the Monarch, in delivering his Commands to the Publique Ministers: In a Democracy, the Councell, or Senate propounds the Result of their deliberations to the people, as a Councell; but when they appoint Judges, or heare

Causes, or give Audience to Ambassadors, it is in the quality of a Minister of the People: And in an Aristocracy the Councell of State is the Soveraign Assembly it self; and gives counsell to none but themselves." *Leviathan,* part ii. ch. xxiii. See also *ibid.,* ch. xxv.

As we go back from the Tudor times this can be seen in the *Pronunciationes Parliamenti,* made at the opening of new Parliaments, usually by the Chancellor. It was then as now the custom to open Parliament by an address or sermon in which the purposes of the calling of the Parliament were impressed on the members. As may be seen from the examples below, much stress was put on business that we call judicial; and what is not judicial is consultative, advisory rather than legislative. It is business natural to the King's old advisory council: only by looking toward the future can we properly call it legislative. For example, at the opening of the Parliament in 15 Henry VI, the Chancellor, the Bishop of Bath and Wells, declared the three objects of the Parliament to be: (1) The Justice and Peace of the King's subjects, (2) a ready sale for English commodities, (3) Protection of the realm and seas against enemies and rebels. (*Rot. Parl.,* vol. iv. p. 495.) In 2 Henry IV Sir William Thyrning, chief justice of the King's Bench, by the King's command opened Parliament with the declaration that they were called in order that the Church and other persons and corporations should enjoy their liberties, that all good laws should be executed and justice truly administered, and that nothing should be done in derogation of the common law. (*Rot. Parl.,* vol. iii. p. 454.) Such examples might be added almost indefinitely. See Elsynge, ch. vi.

Note C. The Delegation of Power by Parliament
(*Page* 318)

The feeling in the United States against "Government by Commission" extends not merely to commissioners appointed without statutory warrant, but also to those based upon an act of Congress. This involves the constitutional question as to the ability of Congress to delegate its legislative power, a subject recently much discussed. In the Parliaments of the Norman period this question could hardly arise. Even so late as the reign of Edward I, we have found the Council making laws after the rest of the Parliament had gone home. This, however, was no delegation of power, for theoretically the Council seems to have *been* the Parliament. In 1337, however, it was enacted by statute that wool was not to be exported until the King and Council provided otherwise. (*S. R.*, vol. i. p. 280; Stubbs, *C. H.*, vol. ii. p. 619, note 2.) In 1385 Parliament ordained that a staple should be held in England, but the place, time, and manner, it was said, "ordinabitur postmodum, per Consilium Domini Regis, auctoritate Parliamenti. Et quod id quod per dictum Consilium in hac parte fuerit ordinatum, virtutem Parliamenti habeat pariter et vigorem."(*Rot. Parl.*, vol. iii. p. 204, quoted by Stubbs, *C. H.*, vol. ii. p. 619, note 2.) In these cases, it ought to be borne in mind that we are not able to say *with absolute certainty* that the *consilium* was considered a different body from Parliament; and if it was not, of course there was no delegation. But it is generally admitted that by 1385, at least, the Council was separate from Parliament.

In the twenty-first year of Richard II, a statute was passed naming commissioners who were empowered to hear and determine petitions "come leur meulx semblera par lour bone advys et discrecion." (21 Rich. II., cap. xvi.)

The wrongful acts of the commission so created were the ground for the repeal of all the acts of Parliament of 21 Richard II, after the deposition of the King (1 Henry IV., cap. 3); and in the Articles drawn up against Richard, one of the charges against him is that he "subtlely procured and caused to be granted" the provision for the appointment of the commission—"et hoc de voluntate Regis: in derogationem Status Parliamenti, et in magnum incomodum totius Regni, et perniciosum exemplum. And that they might seem to have some colour and authority for such their doings, the King caused the Parliament Rolls to be altered and blotted at his pleasure, against the effect of the said grant." *Rot. Parl.*, 1 Henry IV. (1399), No. 25 (vol. iii. p. 418); *Parliamentary History*, vol. i. p. 257. See also *Rot. Parl.*, vol. iii. p. 426, No. 70. In his will Richard bequeathed the royal treasure to his successor only on the condition that the statutes of the twenty-first year of his reign were observed and also the ordinances of the commission. This is complained of in the charges against him, as a defence of "statutes and ordinances which are erroneous and unjust, and repugnant to all law and reason." (*Parl. Hist.*, vol. i. p. 263.)

RELATIONS OF JUDICIARY AND LEGISLATURE

In the heat of the struggle with Rome, the Parliament, in 1533, in the long preamble of the act concerning Peter's Pence and Dispensations, declared that all laws of religion observed in England up to that time had existed only by sufferance of the King and people, —the truth or falsity of which is of no importance here. Then they continue: "It standeth therefore with natural Equity and good Reason, that in all and every such Laws human made within this Realm, or induced into this Realm by the said Sufferance, Consents and Custom, your Royal Majesty, and your Lords Spiritual and Temporal, and Commons, representing the whole State of your Realm, in this your most high Court of Parliament, have full Power and Authority, not only to dispense, *but also to authorize some elect Person or Persons* to dispense with those, and all other human Laws of this your Realm, and with every one of them, as the Quality of the Persons and Matter shall require." (25 Henry VIII., cap. 21.)

Six years later Parliament passed the celebrated Statute of Proclamations (31 Henry VIII., cap. 8, 1539), which Maitland calls "the most extraordinary act in the Statute Book." (*C. H.*, p. 253.) This statute enabled the King with advice of his Council to issue Proclamations "under such Penalties and Pains as to him and them shall seem necessary, which shall be observed as though they were made by Act of Parliament." It is declared that this is not to prejudice any Person's "Inheritance, Offices, Liberties, Goods, Chattels, or Life;" but anyone willingly disobeying "shall pay such Forfeitures, or be so long imprisoned, as shall be expressed in the said Proclamations," and anyone leaving the realm to escape such punishment is to be adjudged a traitor. In the Parliament of 1542-3 it was enacted that nine of the King's Council might give judgement against violators of these proclamations (34-35 Henry VIII., cap. 23). The Statute of Proclamations, Stubbs says, "is one of the most curious phenomena of our constitutional life: for it employs the legislative machinery which by centuries of careful and cautious policy the parliament had perfected in its own hands, to authorize a proceeding which was a virtual resignation of the essential character of parliament as a legislative body; the legislative power won for the parliament from the king was used to authorize the king to legislate without a parliament." (*Const. Hist.*, vol. ii. pp. 619, 620.)

THE HIGH COURT OF PARLIAMENT

The act, with its supplement, was repealed in the first year of Edward VI. (1 Edward VI., cap. 12, sec. v.) The view of the matter held by the lawyers is contained in the well-known resolution of the judges as given in *Coke's Reports*, vol. xii. pp. 74-6.

Sir William Anson sums up these resolutions in convenient form. (*Law and Custom of the Constitution*, vol. i. p. 323.) In briefest wise these resolutions declare that the King may not by proclamation create an offence where none existed by the law before, and that he has no prerogative but what the law of the land allows him. "But the King for the prevention of offences may by proclamation admonish his subjects that they keep the laws, and do not offend them; upon punishment to be inflicted by law." It will be noticed that these resolutions say nothing directly upon the question of the delegation of legislative power, neither do they pronounce upon the validity or extent of the jurisdiction of the Court of Star Chamber beyond saying that an offence not punishable there could not be made so by the King's proclamation.

Notwithstanding these resolutions, the King's proclamations went on without interruption and were given force by the Star Chamber. This continued until that tribunal was abolished by the Long Parliament, and it was no doubt a main cause of the abolition.

After the establishment of parliamentary sovereignty in England, it is needless to say, this question of *delegated* authority practically disappears. The legality of proclamations does not cease to be a burning question, but its importance is henceforth confined to Proclamations based on prerogative alone. In the United States, however, this is a living constitutional issue. For some remarks of Prynne on this subject, provoked by the ordinances under the Commonwealth, see his *Good Old Fundamental Liberties*, vol. i. pp. 92, 93; *Brief Register*, vol. iv. pp. 602-5. For a modern account of the whole subject generally, see Anson, *Law and Custom of the Constitution*, vol. i. pp. 321-5.

NOTE D. SECONDARY LEGISLATION IN ENGLAND
(*Page* 320)

THE similarity of conditions in Tudor England and on the Continent to-day under the *Droit Administratif* has never been more clearly stated than by Professor Dicey in the following extract from the seventh edition of his *Law of the Constitution:* "From the accession of the Tudors till the final expulsion of the Stuarts the Crown and its servants maintained and put into practice, with more or less success and with varying degrees of popular approval, views of government essentially similar to the theories which under different forms have been accepted by the French people. The personal failings of the Stuarts and the confusion caused by the combination of a religious with a political movement have tended to mask the true character of the legal and constitutional issues raised by the political contests of the seventeenth century. A lawyer, who regards the matter from an exclusively legal point of view, is tempted to assert that the real subject in dispute between statesmen such as Bacon and Wentworth on the one hand, and Coke or Eliot on the other, was whether a strong administration of the continental type should, or should not, be permanently established in England. Bacon and men like him no doubt underrated the risk that an increase in the power of the Crown should lead to the establishment of despotism. But advocates of the prerogative did not (it may be supposed) intend to sacrifice the liberties or invade the ordinary private rights of citizens; they were struck with the evils flowing from the conservative legalism of Coke, and with the necessity for enabling the Crown as head of the nation to cope with the selfishness of powerful individuals and classes. They wished, in short, to give the government the sort of rights conferred on a foreign executive by the principles of administrative law. . . .

"The doctrine, propounded under various metaphors by Bacon, that the prerogative was something beyond and above the ordinary law is like the foreign doctrine that in matters of high policy (*acte de gouvernement*) the administration has a discretionary authority which cannot be controlled by any Court. The celebrated dictum that the judges, though they be 'lions,' yet should be 'lions under the throne, being circumspect that they do not check or oppose any points of sovereignty,' is a curious anticipation of the maxim formulated by French revolutionary statesmanship that the judges are under no circumstances to disturb the action of the administration, and would, if logically worked out, have led to the exemption of every administrative act, or, to use English terms, of every act alleged to be done in virtue of the prerogative, from judicial cognizance." (*Law of the Constitution*, pp. 365, 366 (7th ed., 1908); see also *Privy Council*, pp. 92, 93.)

CHAPTER V

The Political History of Parliamentary Supremacy

THE England of the Tudors was an "organic state" to a degree unknown before Tudor times, and forgotten almost immediately afterward. Professor Seeley says: "In our system 'republic' or 'commonwealth' are terms very suitable to describe what we have called the organic state. An organic state . . . springs up by the effort of the social organism to resist a hateful pressure, that is, by a striving towards the common good or commonweal. Opposed to this are all states which we have called inorganic, because they rest upon the violent effort of some group or section to coerce the community for its own advantage."[1]

In this sense Tudor England was an "organic state," taking "organic" here to indicate that the various parts of the state are in such relation the one to the other that no "group or section" or individual is raised above and beyond the state, imposing laws upon it from without, but not subject to those laws. It could not be better stated than in the phrase of Henry VIII himself quoted below,—a "body politic, knit together," in which all members, both ruler and ruled, are working in harmony for the interests of the commonwealth. It is unnecessary to our purpose to go further into the question of

[1] *Introduction to Political Science*, p. 183.

PARLIAMENTARY SUPREMACY

what "organic" really implies, or to discuss the validity of Seeley's general theory on that point.

That the theory briefly described above was the view concerning the nature of the State in general acceptance in Tudor England by both King and people, would not be difficult to show. Feudalism had given way to nationality, and of the "commonwealth" that resulted the King was a real component part. Account for it as we may: by the decay of feudalism, by the disappearance of so many of the old nobility in the previous civil wars, by the influence of the Reformation or of the New Learning, by the increase and wider diffusion of wealth; the fact remains that the King was recognized by the people as the proper centre of the state, but that they also regarded King and people as dependent on each other, both parts of the one whole—the "commonwealth."

This feeling was expressed by a writer of the time of Henry VIII, when he said, "A kyng is annoynted, to be a defence vnto the people, that thei be not oppressyd nor oueryocked; but by all godly and polytick meanys to seke the comon welth of hys people."[1]

Staunford defined Prerogative as "a priuiledge or preheminence that any person hath before an other, which as it is tollerable in some, so is it most to be permitted & allowed in a prince or soueraigne gouernor of a realme. For besides that, that he is the most excellent & worthiest part or member of the body of the commonwealth,

[1] *Complaynt of Roderyk Mors* (Early English Text Society), p. 10.

so is he also (through his good gouernance) the preseruer, nourisher, and defender of al the people being the rest of the same body. And by his great trauels, study and labors, they inioy not only their liues, lands & goodes but al that euer they haue besids, in rest, peace, and quietnes."[1]

And Hooker said: "In Kingdoms therefore of this quality the highest governor hath indeed universal dominion, but with dependency upon that whole entire body, over the several parts whereof he hath dominion; so that it standeth for an axiom in this case, The king is *major singulis, universis minor*."[2]

This view was not confined to the people, for Henry VIII himself declared to Parliament in Ferrer's Case, "We at no time stand so high in our estate royal as in the time of parliament; when we as head and you as members, are conjoined and knit together into one body politic."[3]

In the body politic thus "knit together," the nobility occupied a relatively unimportant place. Things were changed since the time when the barons could compel a king to dismiss a hated minister and be ruled by a committee of themselves. This decline in the fortunes of the nobility Sir Walter Raleigh graphically presents in the words of the Justice in his dialogue on the Prerogative of Parliaments: "Your Lordship may remem-

[1] *An Exposition of the Kinges Praerogatiue*, fol. 5 (1st edition, 1567).
[2] Book viii, *What the power of dominion is*.
[3] *Parl. Hist.*, vol. i. p. 555.

ber," he says to the Counsellor of State, "in your Reading, that there were many Earls could bring into the Field a thousand barbed Horses, and many a Baron five or six hundred barbed Horses; whereas, now, very few of them can furnish twenty fit to serve the King. ... The Force, therefore, by which our Kings in former Times were troubled, is vanished away: But the Necessities remain. The People, therefore, in these latter Ages, are no less to be pleased than the Peers; for, as the latter are become less, so, by reason of the Training through *England*, the Commons have all the Weapons in their Hands. ...

"My good Lord, the Wisdom of our own Age is the Foolishness of another: the Time present ought not to be preferred to the Policy that was, but the Policy that was, to the Time present. So that, the Power of the nobility being now withered, and the Power of the People in the Flower, the Care to content them should not be neglected, the Way to win them often practised, or, at least, to defend them from Oppression."[1]

This was shrewd advice, and it well describes the general course adopted by the Tudor sovereigns. Of the reign of Elizabeth, Harrington, in his *Art of Law Giving*, wrote: "The growth of the people of *England* since the ruines mentioned of the Nobility and the Clergy, came in the Reign of Queen *Elizabeth* to more then stood with the interest, or indeed the nature or possibility of well-founded or durable Monarchy; as was

[1] *Harleian Misc.*, vol. v. pp. 192, 193 (edition of 1745).

prudently perceived, but withall temporized, by her Council, who (if the truth of her Government be rightly weighed) seem rather to have put her upon the exercise of Principality in a Commonwealth, then of soveraign power in a Monarchy. Certain it is, that she courted not her Nobility, nor gave her mind, as Monarchs seated upon the like order, to Balance her great men, or reflect upon their power now inconsiderable; but ruled wholly (with an art she had unto high perfection) by humoring and blessing the people."[1] "The Tudor monarchy was essentially a national monarchy."[2]

This did not escape the keen and practical eye of Raleigh. He makes his Justice in the Dialogue say, "If it be a Maxim in Policy to please the People in all Things indifferent, and never suffer them to be beaten, but for the King's Benefit (for there are no Blows forgotten with the Smart, but those) then I say, to make them Vassals to Vassals, is but to batter down those

---

[1] Pages 17, 18. Also in *Harrington's Works* (1737), p. 390.
[2] Prothero, *Documents*, Introduction, p. xviii. Professor Burgess sums this up as follows: "By the middle of the fifteenth century the actual power of the state had passed from the aristocracy to the people. It remained now for the people to organize themselves and seize the sovereignty. . . . The people were not yet far enough advanced in the development of their political consciousness to create an entirely independent organization. An *existing* institution must furnish them the nucleus. They were deeply conscious of their hostility to the aristocracy. There remained, then, only the King. He, too, was hostile to the aristocracy. Through their common enemy, the King and the people were referred to each other. In the organization which followed, called in political history the absolute monarchy of the Tudors, the people were, in reality, the sovereign, the state, but, apparently, the King was the state. England under the Tudors was a democratic political society under monarchic government." *Political Science and Comparative Constitutional Law*, vol. i. p. 93.

mastering Buildings, erected by King *Henry the Seventh*, and fortified by his Son, by which the People and Gentry of *England* were brought to depend upon the King alone. Yea, my good Lord, our late dear Sovereign kept them up, and to their Advantage, as well repaired as ever Prince did. *Defend me, and spend me,* saith the *Irish* Churl."[1] Such a system as this is based on mutual concession. At first, when the people were less conscious of their power, the King could go further in the appearance of absolutism. Later, when "the nation had outgrown the tutelary stage,"[2] greater caution was necessary.

If ever there should appear a king devoid of such caution,—and the Stuarts were such kings,—or if a spirit of opposition should arise in the people or in the body now representing them, this "body politic" must be split. People and King, or better, possibly, the people through the King, were exercising vast and indefinite powers. There was no questioning of the legality of this so long as neither party was dissatisfied. Let either, however, press too far his rights against the other, and there must follow a struggle for supremacy. The Tudor system could not be permanent. It was based on the common antagonism of King and people toward the nobility; upon the incompleteness of the development of political self-consciousness among the people and the consequent retarded development of their repre-

[1] *Harleian Misc.*, vol. v. pp. 207, 208.
[2] Prothero, *Documents*, Introduction, p. xxix.

sentative organ; and, lastly, upon the wisdom, adroitness, and consequent popularity of the Prince himself. These were temporary causes. The first two were gradually losing their force. The loss was made up under Elizabeth by greater adroitness and greater concessions. The catastrophe was brought on by the absence of these in the time of her successors. The final result was probably inevitable; it might, however, have been postponed and made more gradual, and the deplorable accompaniments might have been avoided, by a continuance of the caution so characteristic of the Tudors. In justice to the Stuart kings it must be said, however, that people and King had been exercising jointly powers which could never be suddenly assumed in severalty by either without a struggle to the death. In so far, the constitutional struggle of the seventeenth century was inevitable. The English constitution under the Tudors was not unlike an unstable chemical compound. Any violent concussion was likely to break it up into its elements.[1]

Raleigh, in the dialogue above mentioned, clearly sees these conditions and is prophetic of their probable results: "If," says the Justice, "the House press the King to grant unto them all that is theirs by the Law, they cannot, in Justice, refuse the King all that is his by the Law. And where will be the Issue of such a

[1] "The distribution of the functions of government is made necessary by the growth of the community in magnitude and complexity. It is not an effect of the advance of popular principles, and it would take place none the less if there were no advance of popular principles." Seeley, *Political Science*, p. 300.

Contention? I dare not divine, but sure I am, that it will tend to the Prejudice both of the King and Subject."[1] He clearly saw how dangerous Tudor precedents would be in a divided state. Where law and precedent can be properly and honestly cited by two powerful and uncompromising antagonists, the struggle between them cannot by any possibility be kept within constitutional bounds—a revolution is inevitable. The men of the Tudor period had had in mind a commonwealth of which the King was a member. "King in Council" had not yet been arrayed against "King in Parliament." They had not anticipated "the case of a divergence between the elements of which Parliament was composed."[2] But that divergence at length came, and the very closeness of the tie between King and people under the Tudors served to make the rent between them the wider under the Stuarts. Under the latter kings, as Sir William Anson says, "Both parties appealed to the letter of old statutes, and neither seemed to see that with the change of times, and after the long lapse of political interest under the Tudors, the mediaeval constitution needed to be restated, or even recast."[3]

It is necessary to look briefly at the causes of this great divergence and of the revolution of the seventeenth century which substituted for the "organic"

---

[1] *Harleian Misc.*, vol. v. p. 208 (edition of 1745).
[2] Prothero, *op. cit.*, Introduction, p. cxxiv.
[3] *Law and Custom of the Constitution*, vol. i. (4th ed.), p. 35.

state of the Tudors new conditions and a new theory of government.

One of the most potent of those causes was, doubtless, the breach with Rome. We have already noticed the meaning of the words "supreme" and "supremacy" before the Reformation. The idea was dimly felt when the claims of the Emperor had to be met, but the Emperor's claims were never a very practical danger in England. With the breach with Rome, however, and the rival claims that followed, "supremacy" gained a more vivid meaning. A consideration of the oaths required of Englishmen from the Act of Supremacy of Elizabeth's first year until the eighteenth century will reveal the great influence of the idea of the King's independence of any foreign ruler upon the whole question of the King's position in the state.[1] A strengthening of the King's supremacy over foreign potentates, however, could not but carry with it the heightening of his dignity and power at home, and a widening of the distance between him and his subjects. And so it actually happened.

Opposition to the papal power had, up to the sixteenth century, centred mainly in the head of the state. First it was the claims of the Emperor, as set forth, for example, by Ockham and Lewis of Bavaria. As national monarchies developed, new claims were asserted against papal supremacy. But, as in the case

---

[1] See Prynne, *The Soveraigne Power of Parliaments and Kingdoms*, vol. i. pp. 104, 105; *Bacon on Government*, pt. ii. p. 162.

of the Empire, they were always asserted in favour of the personal head of the state,—the monarch. It was natural, under such circumstances, that a school of writers should eventually spring up to defend the papal supremacy by a denial of the monarchical theory, and we find that this was the case, both on the Continent and in England.[1] The memory of Elizabeth's excommunication, of the Armada, and of the Gunpowder Plot; the fear excited by the wonderful recuperation of the Catholic Church with its attendant dangers for England, joined with this attack on the theory of monarchy in the interest of the Papacy,—all these things contributed to heighten the pretensions of the King, not only in his own mind, but in the minds of his subjects as well. A Divine Right of Kings arose against the Divine Right of the Pope. We may not go so far in agreement with Mr. Figgis as to say: "That complete sovereignty is to be found in some person or body of persons in the State is a necessity of effective anti-papal argument,"[2] or: "A doctrine of sovereignty vested by Divine Right in the King was the indispensable handmaid of a national Reformation;"[3] but it is hard to escape his conclusions when he says: "It is to the conception of a single supreme authority in the State, that men are inevitably driven in seeking to formulate an anti-papal theory."[4] "If phrases slip in which grant to

---

[1] Figgis, *From Gerson to Grotius*, Lecture V.
[2] *Divine Right of Kings*, p. 91.
[3] *Ibid.*, p. 92.
[4] *Ibid.*, p. 90.

kings an unconditioned omnipotence, which few of them ever dreamed of exercising, that is rather because no one as yet is concerned to deny them, than because they are construed strictly or regarded as of much importance."[1] "Thus it is obedience, rather than a theory of government, that writers in the sixteenth century insist upon."[2] "Obedience must be absolute and immutable, or the Pope will find it possible to make good some part of his claim. This can only be if the power of the Crown be regarded as God's appointment and non-resistance as a Divine ordinance."[3] "English controversialists, in answering the theory of the Papal supremacy, were driven to propound a doctrine of the Divine Right of secular governments, which is in its essential meaning no other than the Imperialist theory of two centuries and a half before."[4]

Inevitable as this process may have been, it had, and could not fail to have, the result of breaking up that "body politic" in which the King and his subjects were "knit together." It was impossible to raise the King's pretensions against the Pope without also raising them against the people. Here is where it becomes harder to follow the lead of Mr. Figgis. With the contract theory in mind, he says: "The believers in Divine Right teach that the State is a living organism and has a characteristic habit of growth, which must be

[1] *Divine Right of Kings*, p. 92.
[2] *Ibid.*, p. 93.
[3] *Ibid.*, p. 95.
[4] *Ibid.*, p. 105.

investigated and observed. Their opponents believe the State to be a mechanical contrivance, which may be taken to pieces and manufactured afresh by every Abbé Siéyès who arises."[1]

It may be that most anti-royalists seized on Locke's contract theory as a weapon against the King, but royalists also used that weapon, of whom Hobbes is the best known. This did undoubtedly augment and strengthen a tendency toward a mechanical, artificial conception of the state. But that tendency was already in existence, and with all its defects it may, nevertheless, be traced in great part back to a source no other than Divine Right itself. It may have been inevitable, it certainly is easily explicable, that competition with Rome should raise the King to a height never claimed before; how can it be denied that it also raised him farther above and away from his subjects than he had ever been before? By it the King was erected above his subjects and beyond his laws. The "organic" commonwealth of Sir Thomas Smith or Harrison becomes a thing forever past. The King is no longer an integral part of his state; James I could never say, as Henry VIII had done, that he and his subjects were knit together in one body politic. Instead, he says: "Kings are justly called Gods, for they exercise a manner of resemblance of Diuine power upon earth: For if you wil consider the Attributes to God, you shall see how they agree in the person of a King. God hath power

[1] *Divine Right of Kings*, p. 259. See also pp. 249-51.

to create, or destroy, make, or vnmake at his pleasure, to giue life, or send death, to judge all, and to bee judged nor accomptable to none: to raise low things, and to make high things low at his pleasure, and to God are both soule and body due. And the like power haue Kings: they make and vnmake their subjects: they haue power of raising, and casting downe: of life, and of death: Judges ouer all their subjects, and in all causes, and yet accomptable to none but God onely. They haue power to exalt low things, and abase high things, and make of their subjects like men at the Chesse: A pawne to take a Bishop or a Knight, and to cry vp, or downe any of their subjects, as they do their money. And to the King is due both the affection of the soule, and the seruice of the body of his subjects:... For to Emperors, or Kings that are Monarches, their Subjects bodies & goods are due for their defence and maintenance."[1] This does not impress one as a very "natural" or a very admirable theory of government. Even when stripped of the absurdities of James's foolish and bombastic rhetoric, the theory here laid down is plain absolutism. And James was not alone in holding it; witness Filmer and the devotees of passive resistance. Fortunately, there were steadying hands. Bacon, though tainted with obsequiousness, was a statesman. Devotion to prerogative with him meant no preposterous claim such as these, and the same may

---

[1] *A Speach to the Lords and Commons of the Parliament at White-Hall*, March 21, 1609, *Works of James* I., p. 529; see also *Works*, pp. 537, 557, for similar sentiments.

be said of Strafford and Clarendon after him. It is hard to be enthusiastic over such a theory as that of James when compared with the solidarity of a "body politic" such as Tudor England. Henry VIII, with all his oppression and cruelty, never went so far as to violate that feeling that he and his people were joined as members in one commonwealth, and even his most atrocious acts he was careful to clothe in the form of law. James, on the contrary, notwithstanding the great unifying force of a common national fear of foreign attack, and the rallying of the nation to protect its religion from destruction, and though by nature far more humane than Henry VIII, placed himself almost at the outset of his reign directly against those conservative feelings of Englishmen which were held in their most extreme form by the common lawyers. Thus it was that the great contest started. As Divine Right had arisen in protest against papal theories and claims, now the supremacy of the law was invoked, in turn, against Divine Right. The state which fundamental law presented was one with balanced powers, or rather of undefined, but never unlimited, powers. Thus the opponents of Divine Right fell back upon conservatism, as was natural. We have already noticed the reliance put by them upon the fundamental law. That law, however, had been affected by the influences of the Tudor régime. Powers had then been conceded to the King as a member of the "body politic" which could not safely be left in the hands of a king who believed he could "cry up or

THE HIGH COURT OF PARLIAMENT

downe" his subjects "like men at the Chesse." The opponents of the prerogative were therefore in time forced by the exigencies of the struggle to go far beyond the conservatism of the lawyers. The conservatives on both sides, to use the contemptuous but penetrating words of Hobbes, "dreamt of a mixed power. . . . That it was a divided power, in which there could be no peace, was above their understanding,"[1] whereas, as he himself pointed out truly enough, this implied "two powers, which, when they chance to differ, cannot both be obeyed."[2] The whole trouble was that at the time when the powers had been conceded, when the precedents had been created, no such division or difference existed or was anticipated. Thus it was that parliamentarians, in opposing the Divine Right of Kings, found but blunted weapons in the precedents of the law, and perforce had to oppose to that novelty another theory, more novel still, the theory of the Divine Right of Legislatures, Parliamentary Omnipotence. Different as these two theories are, they are alike in finding no precedent in the common law. Legislative sovereignty, by either King or Assembly, is not warranted by the earlier precedents. The changes by which the principle was finally grafted upon the English constitution are rightly called "The Revolution."

And yet both parties were alike under the necessity

[1] *Behemoth: English Works* (edited by Molesworth), vol. vi. p. 319.
[2] *Ibid.*, p. 246.

of justifying their position by an appeal to precedent, and the precedents to which both appealed were often identical, the result of the growth of two divergent interpretations of the same facts and institutions. These varying interpretations, arising out of the more or less unconscious and usually ingenuous acceptance by both parties of the new principle of legislative sovereignty, led one party to ascribe a limitless power to the King, the other, to Parliament; while both relied for precedents upon a King and a Parliament neither of whose powers had ever been, nor had ever before been thought to be, without limit. They were now setting up in opposition to each other the claims of a Parliament and of a King, which before had been left indefinite, because their powers had been exercised in common and without collision. It is little wonder that when thus wrenched out of their environment and thrust into the turmoil of 1641, these peaceful precedents should furnish apparently legitimate grounds for constitutional views as diverse as those of Pym and of Strafford. On these precedents, interpreted in the new light of legislative sovereignty, at least a plausible constitutional argument can be made for both an omnipotent Parliament and a King of unlimited power.

In thus describing the Tudor period and comparing its political theory with that of later times to the disparagement of the latter, it will be understood that I am referring to theory only. The England of

THE HIGH COURT OF PARLIAMENT

Henry VIII or Elizabeth was no Elysium, nor was that of the Stuarts so bad as it is often represented. Furthermore, when the beauties of the Tudor commonwealth are here mentioned, it must not be assumed that these conditions could necessarily be reproduced to-day, or that they would be an improvement if they were. As a theory of government, the Tudor "body politic" was a finer and truer ideal of government than the divided state of the Stuarts and their successors. This is all that is meant.

It is a problem of some interest and importance to try to discover as nearly as possible the exact time when the new theory of parliamentary sovereignty was first acted on *practically*. That time may be designated with as much particularity as is usually possible in such matters. Probably no better date could be given than May 27, 1642, when the Lords and Commons drew up their declaration in answer to the King's proclamation forbidding his subjects to obey the Parliament's order for mustering the militia. This remarkable declaration, an extract from which is given at the end of this chapter,[1] well illustrates many of the points I have been trying to make. In it we see an illustration of the fusion of powers in the only precedents Parliament could cite. Because, they argued, the King's *judges* could not be coerced or restrained in their duties, therefore the Lords and Commoners in Parliament, the King's Highest Court, had power not only to adjudge and determine

[1] See Note A (p. 389).

PARLIAMENTARY SUPREMACY

individual cases against the King's grants, but to do anything necessary for the peace and safety of the kingdom, though the King in person should oppose. Here is parliamentary sovereignty in the making. The uncontrolled exercise of such new powers as we see displayed in this great declaration, when once assumed, could never again be wholly lost. And so, after the anarchy of the Interregnum was over, we find Parliament on a firmer basis than ever before. It is true, that as the Revolution draws near, there is a temporary disturbance, but if we survey the period following 1660 and compare the regularity of the Parliaments with the long and uncertain intervals that occurred in the sessions up to 1640, the force of Seeley's dictum becomes manifest, when he says, "At the Restoration, as I understand the matter, and not at the Revolution, the English monarchy and the system of government took the form which they retained throughout the eighteenth century."[1] From the Restoration, "the permanent Parliament takes its place . . . among English institutions, and with a certain interval in the closing years of Charles II and in the reign of James II, an exceptional, revolutionary period, we have had it ever since."[2] "The great idea of that generation,"—the generation of the Civil Wars and the Commonwealth,—"which is to be clearly distinguished from the dreams, idle or premature, in which it occasionally indulged, was to give Par-

[1] *Political Science*, p. 253.
[2] *Ibid.*, p. 258.

liament permanence and solidity."[1] This permanence also had its effect upon the ordinary administration of the law in the courts. It should not be forgotten that it was the Long Parliament of the Restoration that gave the death-blow to the *Oath Ex Officio,* and it was its successor that passed the *Habeas Corpus Act.* There were periods of startling exception, but it may be said generally that the courts were fast acquiring that exclusively *judicial* cast which marks them to-day to such an extent that we can with difficulty imagine anything different. The temptation to use the courts for social or political objects was, as Professor Lowell points out, greatly lessened by the frequency and regularity of the sessions of Parliament. "If a grievance was felt, if a change was wanted, if an obstacle blocked the way, the result desired could easily be brought about by a statute which was immediately enforced by the courts as a part of the law of the land."[2] "Parliament is henceforth really an organ" of the state.[3] The Revolution secured and established guarantees for the permanance of this new order. From that time and up to the present the practice as well as the theory of parliamentary sovereignty may be said to have been definitely settled.

Such being the process by which practical parliamentary sovereignty arose, let us turn to a brief consideration of the modern theory. Political theory has

---

[1] Seeley, *op. cit.*, pp. 258, 259. See the whole interesting passage, pp. 253-9.
[2] *Government of England,* vol. ii. p. 476.
[3] Seeley, *op. cit.*, p. 257.

usually grown from actual conditions. The modern German theories of sovereignty, for example, are deeply coloured by the peculiarities of German federalism. The modern doctrine of parliamentary sovereignty is no exception. As held in England, it is a reflection of actual conditions, and the conditions antedate the theory. As a theoretical explanation of those conditions, it is of the utmost importance. When, however, it is set up as a principle of universal validity and application, or when the assumption is made that its permanence is absolutely assured in the British Empire at least, it is well to recall its recent origin, the circumstances attending its gradual growth, and the present geographical limitations upon its claims to universality. Sir Frederick Pollock truly says, the English doctrine of absolute sovereignty is not capable of being usefully applied to constitutions of the type of the Constitution of the United States. "In fact it is a generalization from the 'omnipotence' of the British Parliament, an attribute which has been the offspring of our peculiar history, and may quite possibly suffer some considerable change within times not far distant."[1]

Parliamentary sovereignty *is* comparatively recent in origin; nothing, for example, can be plainer than that the idea is contrary to all mediaeval notions. "It is very necessary for us to remember," says Professor Maitland, "that the men of the thirteenth century ... had not clearly marked off legal as distinct from moral

[1] *First Book of Jurisprudence*, p. 261.

THE HIGH COURT OF PARLIAMENT

and religious duties, had not therefore conceived that in every state there must be some man or some body of men above all law.... No, we have to remember that when in the middle of the seventeenth century Hobbes put forward a theory of sovereignty which was substantially that of Bentham and of Austin, this was a new thing, and it shocked mankind. Law had been conceived as existing independently of the will of any ruler, independently even of the will of God; God himself was obedient to law: the most glorious feat of his Omnipotence was to obey law."[1]

Legislative sovereignty, then, can hardly be safely pushed back much beyond the Reformation. In fact, many of the causes which produced the Reformation underlay the doctrine of legislative sovereignty as well. But even after the forces were actively at work which produced the new conditions, it required considerable time for a theory to arise from them. As is usual in such cases, the beginnings of the new order were not perceived by contemporaries. Sir Thomas Smith has been hailed as their discoverer. We have given the reasons why we prefer the conclusions of Sir Thomas Smith's editor on this point.[2] During and after the civil wars, the new theory made rapid progress,[3] and its general acceptance to-day can hardly be denied by anyone. It must also be admitted that the doctrine as held

---

[1] *Const. Hist.*, p. 101. See also Gierke, *Political Theories of the Middle Age* (tr. by Maitland), p. 93.
[2] *Ante*, p. 128 et seq.
[3] *Ante*, p. 150 et seq.

PARLIAMENTARY SUPREMACY

in England furnishes a fairly satisfactory explanation of the working and also of the accepted theory of the English constitution following the Revolution.[1] It could hardly be otherwise, for it was in reality a deduction from that constitution itself. But herein is its very weakness. "Theories of sovereignty," Mr. Brown says, "have been more often apologies for a cause than the expression of a disinterested love for truth."[2] This theory, indeed, became in time much more than a mere "apology for a cause;" it was based upon actual conditions. But in erecting it into a universal principle of politics, are we not making the mistake to which Mr. Figgis objects in the upholders of contract, the mistake of trying "to transform a temporary instrument in a particular struggle into an eternal truth"?[3] May we go so far as rightly to say that the doctrine is a permanent one even in England? The theory is a proper generali-

---

[1] From the strictly legal point of view it is open to the same criticism which may be made of the new distinction between legal and practical sovereignty. See *post*, p. 379 et seq.

Professor Dicey has shown, in what is probably the most brilliant part of his *Law of the Constitution*, how the great and extensive powers which remained a part of the King's legal prerogative, even after 1688, have since been gradually transferred, by means of the "Conventions of the Constitution," from the King to his ministers, and have thus, owing to the fact that the House of Commons really controls the ministers, become the legal basis for the preponderance of the Commons over the Lords, a fundamental characteristic of the latter-day English constitution. "The prerogatives of the Crown have become the privileges of the people. . . . If government by Parliament is ever transformed into government by the House of Commons, the transformation will, it may be conjectured, be effected by use of the prerogatives of the Crown." See *The Law of the Constitution*, 7th ed., p. 461 et seq.

[2] *The Austinian Theory of Law*, p. 272.

[3] *Divine Right of Kings*, p. 265.

zation of the governmental conditions in post-revolutionary England. It bears the marks of the time and place of its growth, for it is English, not universal, not even British. Growing up at a time when the problem of imperial control of "self-governing colonies" was unknown, it contained within it no solution for that problem.

If any doubt exists on that score, the history of the events leading up to the American Revolution should be enough to answer them. On its theoretical side, that conflict was the result of the failure of the constitution to meet new conditions. Nothing strikes us more forcibly than the poverty of new political ideas displayed in history. On the whole, probably it is better so, but there have been bad results as well as good. In America a few separate trading factories, with charters suitable for the corporate government of mere trading factories,—charters made, in fact, in imitation of the charters to the great trading companies, of which the East India Company had been the latest,—had grown in reality to be separate commonwealths of Englishmen three thousand miles beyond the sea. Here was a problem of government absolutely new.

The wonderful growth of the English constitution has largely been silent, steady, and without sudden breaks. This has given it a continuity and a solidity unknown in the rest of Europe. Paroxysms are generally no better for the body politic than for the natural body. But it should not be forgotten that the success of this

PARLIAMENTARY SUPREMACY

process of "broadening down from precedent to precedent" has been due to the other fact that in England political *conditions*, as well as the constitution which accompanied them, were changing slowly and very gradually.

When, however, the natural and inevitable instincts of nationalism in the Englishmen of North America began to be importunate in the eighteenth century, it came as a rude shock. These commonwealths beyond the sea, it is true, had not grown up overnight. Their development also had "broadened down" only a little less slowly than England's. But to the English statesmen of the eighteenth century, with few exceptions, this process had been unnoticed or meaningless.

The well-known stories of ministerial ignorance of American geographical conditions have created a notion of that ignorance probably exaggerated;[1] nevertheless, the failure of the ministers to grasp the meaning or understand the spirit of colonial institutions is only too well proved. It is not surprising that the true conception of the British Empire should be hidden from them. There is no gift more rare than the power to interpret contemporary events,—except, possibly, the ability to understand past ones. Parliamentary sovereignty and ministerial responsibility, for example, were both on the ground a long time before they were discovered. When even present-day statesmen and historians make the mistake of "confounding the his-

[1] See the valuable study of Mr. G. L. Beer, *British Colonial Policy, 1754-1765*.

tory of England with the history of Parliament,"[1] it should hardly occasion surprise that the English borough-mongers of the eighteenth century, the actors in the "petty struggles" of an oligarchic Parliament, should have been oblivious to those "other and vaster enterprises" which were moulding the history of the British Empire for all future time. On a comprehensive consideration of the career of Chatham, even, it seems probable that the key of it is to be found in his determination to check the power of France in the world rather than to create a great colonial empire.

The significance of these facts for us is this: Colonial development had proceeded in another environment and, therefore, along different lines from that of the mother country. The forces that were shaping that peculiar development in America had little or no influence upon the institutions of old England, and for long were almost unperceived there. When, therefore, in the course of their development, these colonial institutions approached maturity and demanded recognition, that demand came as a surprise. It was unexpected and unprovided for. Englishmen suddenly awoke to find on their hands a commonwealth, or, rather, a series of commonwealths, to be governed, instead of a trans-oceanic "plantation" to be farmed. They were unprepared. The conditions were strange to them and there was no machinery ready.

Tried statesmen are suspicious of untried machinery,

[1] Seeley, *Expansion of England*, p. 122 (American ed.).

and generally rightly so; but it is no more short-sighted to adopt expedients hitherto untried than to assume that methods which have been in successful operation in one country must, therefore, be equally successful under all conditions and under any sky. That is just what English statesmen of the eighteenth century did in the emergency. Criticism of such methods does not necessarily imply the adoption of utility as the sole principle of political action. The mistake of these English statesmen was not so much in failing to devise new remedies, as in totally ignoring colonial precedents in their choice of old ones.

Instances of this may easily be found. The charters mentioned above are one. To the end, English statesmen insisted on interpreting them by the same narrow legal rules as would have been applied to three acres of ground in the Manor of Dale. Some of the colonial charters had been granted to trading corporations. Under them the company had such power over the adventurers who became virtually its employés as such companies usually had by charter. These charters to trading companies again are probably connected with the early charters to municipalities, through the activity of guild life. Thus, old institutions were progressively adapted to new and strange uses.

It may be cause for surprise that the Virginia Charter of 1609 should give to the governing body of a trading corporation—a body organized primarily for gain, be it remembered—"full and absolute Power and Authority to correct, punish, pardon, govern and rule" all English subjects who should "from Time to Time adventure themselves in any Voyage thither" or ever afterward inhabit there. For this purpose the Company had authority in defect of any instructions from the Privy Council to make ordinances or constitutions "according to the good Discretion of the said Governor and Officers respectively, as well in Cases capital and criminal, as civil."[1] These were, however, to be "as near as conveniently may be" agreeable to the Laws and Statutes of England. It certainly seems to us a strange proceeding to grant to the directors of a commercial company such powers as these, which amount to the power of life and death over its employés. To men of that day it was not strange; it had been done in India and elsewhere. Furthermore, there were in existence at the time in England municipal corporations with powers fully as extensive. As late as 1650 we find felons beheaded in Halifax by virtue of no royal warrant whatever, but merely "by the ancient custom and liberty of Halifax, whereof the memory of man is not to the contrary."[2] And it is said that powers equally great are to be found in some municipal charters still in existence.[3]

[1] Poore, *Charters and Constitutions*, vol. ii. p. 1901.
[2] Stephen, *History of the Criminal Law of England*, vol. i. p. 269. For earlier instances, see Miss Bateson's *Borough Customs* (Selden Society), vol. i., especially pp. 74, 76, 77.
[3] "Several small villages in Kent have charters by which they might, apparently, still try people for their lives, but as the county justices and the

PARLIAMENTARY SUPREMACY

Fortunately, the last of the Virginia charters was annulled in 1624, but before that there must have been a good deal of irritation in a colony which has been described as little better than "a profitable slave-gang administered for the benefit of the Company in England."[1]

It is easy to blame the statesmen of the time for conditions like these. The fault, however, was with the machinery more than with the men. The institutions which had grown up and around the feudal conditions of mediaeval England had been wrenched away from their surroundings and applied to colonies planted three thousand miles away in a practically uninhabited land. It is little wonder that these primitive charters broke down under the strain when thus made to do duty as constitutions for rapidly growing commonwealths of Englishmen at the ends of the earth. Nothing better illustrates the paucity of political ideas. It was a fundamental, a fatal confusion of corporation charter and instrument of government.

In like manner, the proprietary charters were in form and substance modelled upon English feudal grants of an earlier age. And lest anyone should think this a matter of form merely, let it be remembered, for example, that in the case of the "three lower counties" consti-

---

assizes had always concurrent jurisdiction, the power has been forgotten and has become, practically, obsolete." Stephen, *History of the Criminal Law*, vol. i. p. 119.

[1] Doyle, *English Colonies in America* (Virginia, Maryland, and the Carolinas), p. 140.

tuting the modern state of Delaware, the government of William Penn rested upon no better legal basis than the bare deeds for the soil by which it passed from the Duke of York to Penn. This is a recrudescence of feudalism, to be sure; and a more striking example of the confusion of ownership and jurisdiction, of a deed with an instrument of government, it would be hard to find. As has been said, the charters under which this "trans-Atlantic Empire" was governed were interpreted in complete disregard of the fact that they were really the "constitutions" of extensive commonwealths. Like any other corporation charter they could be dissolved in the regular way, and a constitution regulating the political affairs of thousands abolished for some act *ultra vires* committed by the grantees. Even Lord Holt advised that the Charter of Maryland might be practically withdrawn without any legal process and without cause shown, provided the revenues of *the proprietor* were secured to him.[1]

I am not citing these as examples of oppression peculiarly colonial. They were not. Exactly the same treatment was accorded, for example, to the great city of London, and it was probably strictly legal. But legal or illegal, it was impossible that such things should continue. The English Revolution would not have occurred if these things had been illegal: and the same is true of the American Revolution. The worst feature of things like these was their strict legality. Had they been ille-

[1] Chalmers's *Colonial Opinions* (1858), pp. 65, 66.

gal, they might have been thrown off without a revolution. Though not contrary to law, they are examples of the dire results that may follow from the employment of worn-out and obsolete institutions to meet new and unusual conditions. When brought to this new test they had collapsed. All this furnishes a remarkable parallel to the break-down of the Roman constitution under the Republic, caused by the fiction that the local laws of a city could be spread thin enough to do duty as a constitution for the greater part of the civilized world.

In this case great and growing commonwealths inhabited by Englishmen—and Englishmen, it will be shown, who inherited the traditions of the Tudor "body politic"—were regarded, and in strict law rightly regarded, in the same light as any English municipal corporation. It certainly is a prime cause of the American Revolution that the colonial assemblies in America could never rise to a higher legal status than that of the select body of some little piddling incorporated village in mediaeval England. For it must not be forgotten that that revolution was no revolution if the colonists were merely seeking redress for illegal wrongs. No such claim can safely be made for them. Their contention may have been justified in political theory, or in abstract right, or even upon a proper interpretation of the English constitution under the Tudors and earlier; but under the post-revolutionary constitution their claims must be ruled out of court. Lord Chancellor

Northington's answer in 1766 is based on a sound interpretation of the existing law: "My lords, I seek for the liberty and constitution of this kingdom no farther back than the Revolution: there I make my stand. And in the reign of King William an act passed avowing the power of this legislature over the colonies."[1]

As in 1688 England itself destroyed what might, with show of truth, be argued to be the legitimate powers of the King, so in 1776 the Americans, by another Revolution, threw off an authority which was unquestionable on its merely legal side.

It is reasonably clear, then, that, *on its theoretical side*, the American Revolution was primarily a struggle to repudiate the legal claims of an imperial Parliament. Those claims, as the Lord Chancellor so clearly brought out, arose from the legally accepted theory of parliamentary sovereignty. Strict adhesion to that theory in its first really great test had led to the division of the British Empire; it had "rent asunder the English race."

No large changes in the law followed the loss of the American colonies, but a great difference in the administration of it. Thus have grown up the great self-

---

[1] *Parl. Hist.*, vol. xvi. p. 171. "The provisions in the Bill of Rights, also," says Professor Lowell, "and the famous clause in Magna Charta [concerning "taxation"], were not intended to restrain in any way the legislative power of Parliament. These great bulwarks of English liberty as they were quite properly called, were very effective in shielding the people against attacks on the part of the king. . . . But they have put no check upon legislation. To so great an extent is this true, that private property in England is, on the whole, less secure from attack on the part of the government to-day than it was at the time of the Stuarts." *Essays on Government*, pp. 81, 82.

governing colonies. But what an anomalous condition has resulted! Great empires of Britons in all quarters of the globe theoretically subject to the commands of an English assembly which dares not coerce them. Who believes that Parliament would dare exercise the power that is legally hers? Only by her forbearance is the tenuous bond retained between her and her great and powerful self-governing colonies. These relations must be altered or they will be severed. From the point of view of mere law, the relation of Great Britain and her own colonists beyond the seas is almost as far from settlement to-day as it was in 1775. For, in fact, notwithstanding many changes in detail, the fundamental relations of Imperial Parliament and subordinate colonial legislature are the same to-day as they were in the eighteenth century. Forbearance to exercise legally existing powers is now the only cement that holds the empire together.[1] Such forbearance, it is true, can now be exercised as was impossible in the eighteenth century, under the vicious economic doctrines then universally held; but a federal empire composed of powerful states cannot long be held together by mere forbearance. It is unreasonable to expect fair weather all the time, and such a federation is likely to be shattered by the first severe storm.

Maitland significantly says: " Some friendly critics

[1] "The legislative supremacy of Parliament over the whole of the British dominions is complete and undoubted in law, though for constitutional or practical reasons, Parliament abstains from exercising that supreme legislative power." Sir H. Jenkyns, *British Rule and Jurisdiction beyond the Seas*, p. 10.

would say that in the past we could afford to accept speciously logical but brittle theories because we knew that they would never be subjected to serious strains. Some would warn us that in the future the less we say about a supralegal, suprajural plenitude of power concentrated in a single point at Westminster—concentrated in one single organ of an increasingly complex commonwealth—the better for that commonwealth may be the days that are coming."[1] Again, in another place, he says: "Standing at the beginning of a century and in the first year of Edward VII, thinking of the wide lands which call him king, thinking of our complex and loosely-knit British Commonwealth, we cannot look into the future without serious misgivings. If unity of law—such unity as there has been—disappears, much else that we treasure will disappear also, and (to speak frankly) unity of law is precarious. The power of the parliament of the United Kingdom to legislate for the colonies is fast receding into the ghostly company of legal fictions."[2]

[1] Maitland, Introduction to Gierke's *Political Theories of the Middle Age*, p. xliii.
[2] *English Law and the Renaissance*, p. 33. In another place he says: "The modern and multicellular British State—often and perhaps harmlessly called an Empire—may prosper without a theory, but does not suggest and, were we serious in our talk of sovereignty, would hardly tolerate, a theory that is simple enough and insular enough, and yet withal imperially Roman enough, to deny an essentially state-like character to those 'self-governing colonies,' communities, commonwealths, which are knit and welded into a larger sovereign whole." Introduction to Gierke, p. x. Again, still speaking of the colonies: "Even the right or power to impose taxes has never been abandoned, though it is not exercised. Students of Austin's Jurisprudence may find some interest in noticing this case: the sovereign body habitually refrains from making

PARLIAMENTARY SUPREMACY

When we read in the preamble of the federal constitution of Australia, "Whereas the people of New South Wales, Victoria, South Australia, Queensland, and Tasmania, humbly relying on the blessing of Almighty God, have agreed to unite in one indissoluble Federal Commonwealth under the Crown of the United Kingdom of Great Britain and Ireland, and under the Constitution hereby established," the question naturally arises: What would the Australians actually do, if the Imperial Parliament, in the due exercise of its legal prerogatives, were to give the "Commonwealth" serious cause for dissatisfaction?

Apparently, the existing theory of parliamentary sovereignty, which has undoubtedly served a valuable purpose in England, is not comprehensive enough for the British Empire. With new conditions, changes in machinery must be made to meet them and the theory must follow.[1]

Objections have also frequently been made to the English theory of parliamentary omnipotence from a less practical point of view. German theorists, for example, have had few kind words for it.

I shall not willingly plunge into the abyss at the bottom of which, it may be hoped, some solution of the problem of sovereignty lies. I shall merely indicate briefly one or two objections that have been urged, or,

---

laws of a certain class and must suspect that if it made such laws they would not be obeyed." *Constitutional History*, p. 339.

[1] See Note B at the end of this chapter (p. 390).

as it seems to me, may be urged, against the theory of legislative sovereignty as held in England, and these objections will be of an historical rather than a purely logical kind. They may, in fact, be compressed into one. The theory now embodied in the doctrine of parliamentary sovereignty is mechanical, artificial, inconsistent with natural growth, in a word, unhistorical. This is the charge brought—and rightly brought—against the contract theory. But its opponent, the theory of Divine Right, and the theory of parliamentary sovereignty, which in a sense that is historically true is the legitimate successor of Divine Right, are little less artificial. Alike, they break up the body politic into fragments. They create an unnatural separation between governor and governed. Bacon warned James I against bargaining with his people at the time of the "Great Contract." That transaction, however, was the natural corollary of a theory which set the people and the King off against each other. A recent writer says: "One may say, then, that a strongly characteristic feature of the development of the theory of sovereignty during this period was the individualistic-contractualistic tendency. The emphasis on the individual came from the Reformation, the form of contract from the Roman law."[1]

As Gierke expresses it, . . . "In so far as the Community was a 'Subject' of rights, and stood apart from and either above or below the Ruler, this 'Subject' could not be identified with the Whole organized and

[1] Merriam, *History of the Theory of Sovereignty since Rousseau*, pp. 36, 37.

unified Body, since the Head was being left out of account. Rather a separate 'Subject' was made of 'the People:' a 'Subject' that could be contrasted with 'the Government.'"[1]

The process which resulted in this division had started with the King. The underlying individualism may have been the creature of the Reformation, or more properly of the Renaissance, but the fact remains that the people were "knit together" with the King into one body politic until the claims of Divine Right placed the King practically outside the commonwealth. By that act the body politic was split up; its members became mere "subjects," mere individuals,—*disjecta membra*. "Our *Trimmer*," says Halifax, "thinks that the King and Kingdom ought to be one Creature, not to be separated in their Political Capacity; and when either of them undertake to act apart, it is like the crawling of Worms after they are cut in pieces, which cannot be a lasting motion, the whole Creature not stirring at a time."[2] But now the King and his people have ceased to be "one creature." Instead, we have the inspiring picture of James I haggling with his people over the terms of the "Great Contract;" of his son, in the interval of civil war, weighing the relative advantages of the *Propositions of New Castle* and the *Heads of the Proposals;* of Charles II coolly balancing the amount the people will grant him in Parliament for carrying out

---

[1] *Political Theories of the Middle Age*, translated by Maitland, p. 71.
[2] *The Character of a Trimmer* (1699), pp. 12, 13.

the will of the majority of the nation, against the sum he can get from England's greatest enemy in return for thwarting the desires of his people and betraying their interests and their religion. We see the Parliament choosing treasurers and auditors to prevent royal misuse of supplies; we become familiar with transactions like that of Tonnage and Poundage in 1629; we are not surprised when the Minister of George II and the Opposition are found bidding against each other in Parliament with the people's money for the distinction of pandering to the luxurious or lascivious tastes of the heir apparent; nor when the real leader of the Opposition buys his way back from a traitor's exile by gifts of money to the King's mistress, and the King carries out his part of the sordid bargain by forcing the Minister's reluctant assent to the introduction of the bill effecting it, even by threats of dismissal from office.

In some of these examples we begin to see the growth of the modern idea of "checks and balances," of setting off against each other rival organs of the state, each one with a defined sphere of action, and therefore each determined to prevent by jealous watchfulness the encroachment of the others upon that sphere. The success of this system in the United States, where it has had a consistent development, is hardly yet so conspicuous as to warrant us in setting it up as the "last word" in political theory. In all the examples, it is evident that the sovereign's interest and the subjects' interest have really become antagonistic.

PARLIAMENTARY SUPREMACY

In the beginning, Parliament represents the claims of the "subjects," and therefore denies the validity of the King's pretensions, including the claim of sovereignty. In the death struggle which ensues "Parliament is forced to make new claims and by degrees to grasp at supremacy, lest it should lose old rights or even forfeit equality."[1] With the successful issue of the struggle, Parliament assumes as of right those very powers it formerly denounced. Practically all the English political theories of the later seventeenth century, whether contractual or patriarchal, presuppose a sovereign and subjects in antithesis if not in antagonism. Divine Right truly "has stamped upon the English mind the conception of sovereignty," and, Mr. Figgis continues, "thereby rendered a service which can hardly be overestimated by all who value clearness of political vision."[2] This seems undeniably true. Historically, all modern political philosophy is based on the discovery of sovereignty made in the sixteenth and seventeenth centuries. This would probably be admitted even by those who in recent years have held that the very idea of sovereignty is incompatible with conditions existing in a modern composite state. For most theorists who take a position less extreme than this, the conception of sovereignty set forth in substance by Bodin and Hobbes underlies the whole theory of the state and is postulated by it. Whatever

[1] Figgis, *Divine Right*, p. 231.
[2] *Ibid.*, p. 144.

our view may be, it is hard to overrate the debt we owe to Bodin and to Hobbes.

But, if we look at England alone, our sense of gratitude is vastly lessened when we remember that the bearer of this sovereignty is out of all organic connection with the state or with his subjects. Mr. Figgis himself sees the unreality and artificiality of this product. He says, "What is needed now-a-days is that as against an abstract and unreal theory of State omnipotence on the one hand, and an atomistic and artificial view of individual independence on the other, the facts of the world with its innumerable bonds of association and the naturalness of social authority should be generally recognized and become the basis of our laws, as it is of our life."[1]

This want will never be supplied by Austin's "definite political superior." His theory is based on the dismembered state of the seventeenth century. It is as unhistorical as the despised original compact. "It is a mistake," says T. H. Green, "to think of the state as an aggregation of individuals under a sovereign."[2]

The English doctrine of parliamentary sovereignty grew up in the seventeenth century. It bears the marks of that period. It is the result of strife, not of growth.[3]

[1] *From Gerson to Grotius*, p. 206 (1907).
[2] *Political Obligation*, p. 139.
[3] It will be understood that by "parliamentary sovereignty" I mean the theory as it is actually held in England. In criticising this theory I do not wish to be understood as objecting to the general theory of political sovereignty. The objection here insisted on is directed entirely at the location of the bearer of the sovereignty, not at the theory in general. I have used the term

PARLIAMENTARY SUPREMACY

No creation of that period of stress could be anything but artificial. The theory of sovereignty is artificial because the whole theory of the state had become so.[1]

In saying this, however, due credit must not be denied to the English theory of parliamentary omnipotence. Whatever defects may be seen in it, it accomplished its purpose. It disposed forever of the King *legibus solutus*, even if it did bring into being a Parliament *legibus solutum*. The protection of the rights of individuals in the seventeenth century demanded a power able to cope on equal terms with the King.

"legislative sovereignty" to describe the English theory, because I could not find any substitute, but I wish to disclaim any intention of criticizing a general theory of legislative sovereignty. Whether that be a *sine qua non* of correct political speculation or not, the sovereignty certainly need not be located in a "definite political superior" which is out of all natural relation to the state itself.

[1] This is admirably stated by Mr. Merriam: "Again, it is to be observed that an adequate conception of the unity and personality of the State was wanting throughout the period under consideration. As already seen, the movement in the earlier phases of the development was toward the organization of two public persons in the same State, the people on the one hand, and the Government on the other, with reciprocal rights and duties. Neither the people nor the Government constituted the whole State. Later, the State was absorbed either in people or in Government. With Hobbes, the Government swallowed up the State, and became the sole representative of its personality, so that the Government could truly say 'L'État c'est moi.' Or, with Rousseau, the people became the Government, and the Government was lost in the State. Hobbes saw a particular organ, the special bearer of power, but not the organism. Rousseau saw the organism as a whole, the general bearer, without organs capable of exercising sovereign power. And lastly the idea of personality, whether of the people or a part of the people, was at best of a wholly unreal and artificial character. Except where an individual was sovereign, the ruling body was a person only by the grace of fiction, persona representata, persona ficta — one in the place of many. Person was an abbreviation for a sum of individuals, and the bearer of the sovereignty not a real entity. The only real persons were individuals, all others were fictions." *History of the Theory of Sovereignty*, pp. 37, 38.

The result was the omnipotent Parliament. It is not unnatural, then, that men looked back to 1689 as the "glorious" Revolution. We must admit the probable necessity of a doctrine of parliamentary sovereignty in the seventeenth century. To say, however, that it was inevitable, even to say that in its age it was a necessity and a benefit, is not to justify the conditions which made it necessary, or the circumstances from which it arose. Above all, a recognition of the services it performed in its day should not lead us to think that this theory is fit to become a political formula of universal validity.

Abuses usually get themselves tolerated because they are sheltered under institutions whose past services render them immune from attack.

The body of irresponsible nominees, who in the eighteenth century called themselves the House of Commons, were trading on the credit of the Revolution Parliament. When parliamentary omnipotence has become a means of punishing "subjects" for breach of privilege in fishing in Mr. Joliffe's pond,[1] or killing Lord Galway's rabbits;[2] when election petitions are made mere tests of party strength, settled by a strict party vote in the House of Commons itself, with absolute indifference to the expressed will of the electors, and in supreme disregard of their legal rights, but "All the arts,

---

[1] *Commons Journals*, vol. xxvi. p. 698.
[2] *Ibid.*, vol. xxiii. p. 505. A list of such "breaches," containing many other instances equally trivial, is given in the report of the case of *Stockdale* v. *Hansard*, 9 *Adolphus & Ellis*, 10-13.

PARLIAMENTARY SUPREMACY

money, promises and threats ... are applied, and self-interest operates;"[1] when even Edmund Burke can plume himself on his consistency in "uniformly and steadily" opposing "for many years together" "the reforms in representation and the bills for shortening the duration of parliaments;"[2] and when the Chancellor of England refuses to look beyond the Revolution for the "liberty and constitution" of England, even to save an empire;[3] we may begin to suspect that the doctrine of parliamentary omnipotence has about outlived its usefulness. The first of the great evils resulting from it, the corruption and irresponsible character of Parliament, has since been obviated by a series of most important rules, the majority of which, however, the disciples of parliamentary omnipotence would not permit us to designate as laws, but only as "conventions," though a breach of them would inevitably result in revolution: the other evil, the colonial problem, remains.

It becomes evident, then, that in the eighteenth century, men on both sides of the sea were looking in vain to Parliament for the protection of individual rights. The American Revolution was the logical sequel to the Revolution of 1689. It applied to Parliament as well as to the King Locke's doctrine of the responsibility of the governor to the governed. Thus it was not wholly without excuse that the Opposition could speak

---

[1] Horace Walpole, quoted by Sir W. Anson, *Law and Custom of the Constitution*, 4th ed., vol. i. p. 170.
[2] *Appeal from the New to the Old Whigs.*
[3] *Ante*, pp. 365, 366.

of the American forces as "our army,"[1] or Charles James Fox refer to the report of an American defeat as "the terrible news from Long Island."[2]

The fault, if fault there was, on the part of the English statesmen, lay not in the adoption of the doctrine of parliamentary sovereignty, but rather in retaining it, to the detriment of the subject and of the Empire, after its day of usefulness was over.

The rooted conservatism of the English mind has many things to its credit. It is hardly possible to overestimate its beneficent results, but our just praise should be tempered with discrimination: it has occasionally done some harm as well as good.

Divine Right may have been inevitable. Once in existence the struggle between it and Parliament certainly was so. To the theory and the struggle we owe the doctrine of the omnipotence of Parliament. In exchange, however, was given the grand conception of the English Commonwealth. This conception men are now painfully trying to regain. "Even where legal absolutism can be attributed to some definite legislative in-

[1] Quoted from Lady Minto's *Life of Sir Gilbert Elliot*, in Lecky's *History of England*, vol. iv. p. 76 (American edition).
[2] Letter of Fox to the Marquis of Rockingham, dated October 13, 1776, Russell's *Memorials of Fox*, vol. i. p. 130 (American edition). . . . "Above all, my dear Lord, I hope that it will be a point of honor among us all to support the American pretensions in adversity as much as we did in their prosperity, and that we shall never desert those who have acted *unsuccessfully* upon Whig principles, while we continue to profess our admiration of those who succeeded in the same principles in the year 1688." *Ibid.* Our opinion of the truth of the historical facts implied in this advice is not affected by any doubts we may have of the entire propriety of attributing them exclusively to "Whig principles."

stitution, sooner or later the question is certain to arise whether, after all, formal supremacy can be attributed to that institution save as an organ of the State. . . .

"Although the location of the sovereign varies in the different legal theories of different nationalities, it seems probable that the Jurisprudence of a near future will recognize that the State itself is the true sovereign, and that such a body as the Parliament of Great Britain should be described, not as the sovereign, but as the sovereign-organ."[1]

Upon our attitude toward the English theory of parliamentary omnipotence will also depend our view of the distinction made by Mr. Bryce and Professor Dicey between legal and political sovereignty. The legal sovereign, according to Mr. Bryce, is "the person (or body) to whose directions the law attributes legal force, the person in whom resides as of right the ultimate power either of laying down general rules or of issuing isolated rules or commands, whose authority is that of the law itself."[2] The practical sovereign is "simply the strongest force in the State, whether that force has or has not any recognized legal supremacy."[3]

It is hard to see what advantage this new distinction

---

[1] Brown, *The Austinian Theory of Law*, pp. 284-7. See also T. H. Green, *Lectures on Political Obligation*, pp. 96, 98, 104, 113. For probably the best general account of the various theories, see Jellinek, *Allgemeine Staatslehre* (2d ed.), pp. 123 et seq., 421 et seq., 526 et seq. See also, in addition to the references already noted, Gierke, *Johannes Althusius* (2d ed., 1902).

[2] *Studies in History and Jurisprudence*, p. 505.

[3] *Ibid.*, p. 511. See also Dicey, *Law of the Const.*, 7th ed., pp. 68 et seq., 424, 425.

has to offer to political science. After all, it does little but postpone the difficulty, for the distinction is strictly subsidiary to the doctrine of parliamentary sovereignty. It stands or falls with that.

There is, however, another difficulty incident to it somewhat more definite. In distinguishing between sovereignty legal and sovereignty practical, Mr. Bryce uses the following illustration:

"The fact that the House of Commons, a part of the Legal Sovereign of England, is chosen by the people, and that many members of the House of Lords, another part of the Legal Sovereign, have been appointed by the Crown, does not affect the Sovereignty of Parliament, because neither the people nor the Crown have the right of issuing directions, legally binding, to the persons they have selected."[1] Presumably Mr. Bryce here has reference exclusively to legal matters, and not mere custom, for he speaks of "directions, *legally* binding." He is not speaking of the "conventions of the Constitution," he means the "law of the Constitution." But when he says that the Crown cannot issue *legally* binding directions to Parliament, does he mean to say that the Crown cannot *legally* issue a "direction" to the Parliament ordering its dissolution? If non-legal convention is put aside,—and it must be if we are considering a strictly *legal* sovereign,—what is to prevent the Crown from proroguing or dissolving an existing Parliament whenever so inclined? And what direct *legal*

[1] *Studies*, p. 510.

PARLIAMENTARY SUPREMACY

pressure can be brought to bear on the Crown to summon another one until ready to do so? If we adhere to the strictness of this legality, we find a rather peculiar sovereign resulting. One, in fact, whose very precarious existence is dependent upon the whim of a power outside itself. It is no answer to this to say that it is the "King in Parliament" who does these things. Where is the "King in Parliament" during the interval between the dissolution of one Parliament and his issuing writs for a new one? If parliamentary supremacy is thus to be defended by arguments from mere law, it seems that the question asked by Judge Jenkins in 1647 is still pertinent, — "The King assembles the Parliament by his Writ, adjournes, prorogues, and dissolves the Parliament by the Law at his pleasure, as is evident by constant practise, the House of Commons never sate after an adjournment of the Parliament by the King's Command: where is the supreame power?"[1]

---

[1] *The Works of Judge Jenkins*, p. 57. Compare the words of Hobbes: "Seeing then all Lawes, written and unwritten, have their Authority, and force, from the Will of the Common-wealth; that is to say, from the Will of the Representative; which in a Monarchy is the Monarch, and in other Common-wealths the Soveraign Assembly; a man may wonder from whence proceed such opinions, as are found in the Books of Lawyers of eminence in severall Commonwealths, directly, or by consequence making the Legislative Power depend on private men, *or subordinate Judges* [these italics are mine]. As, for example, *That the Common Law, hath no Controuler but the Parliament;* which is true onely where a Parliament has the Soveraign Power, and cannot be assembled, nor dissolved, but by their own discretion. For if there be a right in any else to dissolve them, there is a right also to controule them, and consequently to controule their controulings." (*Leviathan*, pt. ii. ch. xxvi.)

It is interesting in this connexion to note Mr. Bagehot's enumeration of powers which the Crown could still exercise in the year 1872, by virtue of the prerogative alone. He says, in the introduction to the second edition of his *Eng-*

THE HIGH COURT OF PARLIAMENT

For all practical purposes, Parliament has been the unquestioned lawmaking organ since the Revolution, but such legalistic distinctions as these are somewhat embarrassing.

The more general objection to this distinction between legal and practical sovereignty tells against the whole theory of parliamentary sovereignty as held in England: it is unhistorical. Mr. Bryce himself says of it: "It has nothing to do with the actual forces that exist in a state, nor with the question to whom obedience is in fact rendered by the citizens in the last resort. It represents merely the theory of the law, which may or may not coincide with the actual facts of the case, just as the validity of the demonstration of the fifth

---

lish Constitution: " I said in this book that it would very much surprise people if they were only told how many things the Queen could do without consulting Parliament, and it certainly has so proved, for when the Queen abolished Purchase in the Army by an act of prerogative (after the Lords had rejected the bill for doing so), there was a great and general astonishment.

"But this is nothing to what the Queen can by law do without consulting Parliament. Not to mention other things, she could disband the army (by law she cannot engage more than a certain number of men, but she is not obliged to engage any men); she could dismiss all the officers, from the General Commanding-in-Chief downwards, she could dismiss all the sailors too; she could sell off all our ships of war and all our naval stores; she could make a peace by the sacrifice of Cornwall, and begin a war for the conquest of Brittany. She could make every citizen in the United Kingdom, male or female, a peer; she could make every parish in the United Kingdom a 'university;' she could dismiss most of the civil servants; she could pardon all offenders. In a word, the Queen could by prerogative upset all the action of civil government within the government, could disgrace the nation by a bad war or peace, and could, by disbanding our forces, whether land or sea, leave us defenceless against foreign nations." (American edition, pp. 31, 32.) Cf. Dicey, *Law of the Constitution*, 7th ed., pp. 22-4 and elsewhere; the comments of Professor Lowell, *Government of England*, vol. ii. pp. 473, 474, and note; and Dr. Hatschek, *Englisches Staatsrecht*, vol. i. p. 546, note.

proposition in the first book of Euclid has nothing to do with the accuracy with which the lines of any actual figure of that proposition are drawn."[1]

The analytical school has always prided itself on keeping close to the ground, on avoiding the metaphysical speculations of which others have been guilty. "Not what law ought to be, but what law is" has been its cry. What could be more divorced from actual fact than a theory such as this, which avowedly "has nothing to do" with actual conditions? "The conception of legal sovereignty as inhering in a portion of the community needs then to be revised by reference to the fact that such portion is but an organ of the community as a whole. When we have escaped from the tyranny of mere forms, and have overcome the superstition that we must not regard things in their totality, when we have learnt that, on the contrary, it is only when we so regard them we can hope to comprehend them, we shall find some place in legal theory for ideas which have already profoundly affected less conservative branches of learning. We shall not fear to think of the State as a unity, a personality, a sovereign—a sovereign in whose presence the visible ruler can aspire to no higher title than that of sovereign-organ."[2]

The analogy suggested between political science and geometry is, on the whole, unfortunate. In geometry, we knowingly agree upon premises which in some cases

[1] *Studies*, p. 509.
[2] Jethro Brown, *The Austinian Theory of Law*, pp. 286, 287.

we are aware will not square exactly with actual fact. To do this in political science is a very questionable proceeding. We may not play fast and loose with our facts. The methods of the Schoolmen are no more in place in political science than in geology. Modern natural science has made all its advances by rejecting the exclusive use of the mediaeval deductive method. It has been the one great contribution of the analytical school in England to emphasize the practical advantage of separating jurisprudence from ethics, of restricting the science to the data furnished by law actually existing now or in the past. Consciously to desert this point of view and ignore utterly "the actual forces that exist in a state," to adopt the deductive methods of geometry, is to return to the unreality and *a priori* dogmatism that to-day rightly condemns the political philosophy of Rousseau. We cannot be satisfied in the twentieth century with a theory which confesses that it "has nothing to do with actual conditions." "While we talk logic, we are unanswerable; but then, on the other hand, this universal living scene of things is after all as little a logical world as it is a poetical; and, as it cannot without violence be exalted into poetical perfection, neither can it be attenuated into a logical formula. Abstract can only conduct to abstract; but we have need to attain by our reasonings to what is concrete."[1] Happily, England has long ago broken free from the conditions which created the doctrine of parliamentary

[1] Newman, *Grammar of Assent*, p. 268.

omnipotence. Some day the tardy theory may catch up with the facts.

Whatever may be its defects in nature and form, parliamentary sovereignty is the substitute which in England has taken the place of the organic theory of the sixteenth century. In America the problem was met in another way. In the Tudor state, as we have seen, the departments of government were not clearly separated. Its main characteristic was a fusion of powers. While this has by no means entirely disappeared in England, the legislative supremacy of Parliament has utterly changed it. In America the old fusion of powers was replaced not by the elevation of one of the organs of government above the rest, as in England, but by a series of elaborate checks to prevent that very thing. A "separation of powers" certainly took place in both England and North America; it was, however, by no means so far reaching, in England at least, as Montesquieu imagined he saw it to be, and far less complete than the modern Continental theory.

For, notwithstanding the great changes made, the old foundations remained. In England, as we have seen, the old indefiniteness in the powers of courts long influenced their action, notwithstanding the newer doctrine of parliamentary sovereignty, and has never wholly disappeared; while in America the doctrine of checks and balances has been far less effective than the English doctrine of parliamentary supremacy, in narrowing the scope of judicial action. American courts still retain much of their Tudor indefiniteness, notwithstanding our separation of departments. They are guided to an extent unknown now in England by questions of policy and expediency. The Supreme Court has acted again and again on the principle that it may reverse its decisions, a principle which the House of Lords has definitely accepted as inadmissible.[1] In short, in America many of those traditional powers and functions have remained in the courts which in England have to a greater extent been excluded by the rigour of the doctrine of parliamentary sovereignty. These differences are now very marked, but they are also to be seen in the English colonies in North America long before independence. The colonists retained to a marked and unusual degree the traditions of Tudor England. In all our study of American institutions, colonial and contemporary, institutions both of public law and private law, this fact must be reckoned with. The breach between colonies and mother country was largely a mutual misunderstanding based, in great part, on the fact of this retention of older ideas in the colonies after parliamentary sovereignty had driven them out in the mother country. These facts have often been noticed. Thus Professor Dicey says, "American institutions are the direct outgrowth of English ideas, and in the main of the English ideas which prevailed in England during the democratic movement of the seventeenth century."[2]

[1] *London Tramways Co.* v. *London County Council. App. C.*, 375 (1898).
[2] *Law of the Constitution*, p. 527. "Curiously enough," says Professor Lowell, "the political evolution of America branched off from that of England early

PARLIAMENTARY SUPREMACY

Speaking of the practice of courts in declaring statutes void, Professor Lowell says: "With the growth, however, of the doctrine of the omnipotence of Parliament, it vanished from the courts early in the eighteenth century; but this was the point where the stream of political thought in the American colonies separated from that of the mother country, and the doctrine not only contributed indirectly to the evolution of constitutional law in the United States, but has been occasionally repeated in express terms by American judges."[1]

It is not within the scope of this essay to compare

in the eighteenth century, nearly a couple of generations before the revolt of the colonies, and while the legal tone of thought was at its height. American institutions are still in some respects singularly like those of England at the death of Queen Anne, and not least in the power of legal tradition, which was rather intensified than weakened by its transfer to the new world. Thereafter the changes in the British Constitution found no echo on the other side of the Atlantic, largely no doubt because taking the form of custom, not of statute, they were not readily observed." *Government of England*, vol. ii. p. 472.

[1] *Government of England*, vol. ii. pp. 480, 481. See also Coxe, *Legislative Power*, pp. 214, 215. On this subject Hatschek says: "Von der siegreichen Revolutionspartei wird aber 1688 in dem Rechtsfalle L. Mayor and Commonalty of London v. Wood, und zwar durch den Mund des Richters Holt behauptet, dass ein Gesetz, das z. B. jemanden gerade zum Richter in eigener Sache bestellte, gegen das Common law und gegen die Vernunft, daher ungültig wäre. *So wurde selbst nach der glorreichen Revolution den Richtern ein materielles Prüfungsrecht der Gesetze zugestanden, eine Doktrin, die damals nach Nord-Amerika kam und hier, fruchtbaren Boden fassend, sich bis auf den heutigen Tag erhalten hat.* In England aber nahm nach der glorreichen Revolution die Doktrin einen anderen Weg. Die zur Herrschaft kommende liberale *Whigdoktrin* lässt sich die Steigerung der parlamentarischen Allmacht deshalb gefallen, weil sie in ihr das Mittel zur Einschränkung der Königlichen Prärogative sieht. Die Allmacht des Parlaments habe die englische Freiheit gerettet. Daher die Willensäusserungen dieses allmächtigen Parlaments keiner Macht auf Erden untergeordnet seien. *Die Suprematie des Parlaments bedinge die Koordination des Gesetzesrechts (Statute law) und des Common law.*" *Englisches Staatsrecht*, vol. i. p. 138. See also a letter of Thomas Jefferson to Judge Tyler dated 1812, *Jefferson's Works* (Washington, 1854), vol. vi. pp. 65, 66.

THE HIGH COURT OF PARLIAMENT

the present English and American systems, or to trace the effect of the older English ideas upon the growth of our constitutional system. That system, however, can be properly understood, in its origin, development, workings, and spirit, only in the light of precedents and traditions which run back to the England of the civil wars and the period before the civil wars.[1]

---

[1] The further development of these principles in the American constitution is to be treated in a forthcoming volume, by Professor Edward S. Corwin, to be entitled, *The Growth of Judicial Review*.

PARLIAMENTARY SUPREMACY

NOTE A. PARLIAMENT'S FORMAL ASSERTION OF SOVEREIGNTY—
THE DECLARATION OF MAY 27, 1642

(*Page* 352)

THE following is an extract from the act: "The Question is not whether it belong to King or no, to restrain such Force, but if the King shall refuse to discharge that Duty and Trust, whether there is not a Power in the two Houses, to provide for the Safety of the Parliament and Peace of the Kingdom, which is the end for which the Ordinance concerning the Militia was made, and being agreeable to the Scope and Purpose of the Law, cannot in reason be adjudged to be contrary to it, for although it do affirm it to be in the King, yet it doth not exclude those in whom the Law hath placed a Power for that purpose, as in the Courts of Justice, that Sheriffs and other Officers and Ministers of those Courts, and as their Power is derived from the King by his Patents, yet cannot it be restrained by his Majesty's command, by his great Seal or otherwise, much less can the Power of Parliament be concluded by his Majesty's command, because the Authority thereof is of a higher and more eminent nature then any of those Courts.

"It is acknowledged that the King is the Fountain of Justice and Protection, but the Acts of Justice and Protection are not exercised in his own Person, nor depend upon his pleasure but by his Courts, and by his Ministers who must do their duty therein, though the King in his own Person should forbid them: and therefore if Judgments should be given by them against the King's Will and Personal command, yet are they the King's Judgments.

"The High Court of Parliament is not only a Court of Judicature, enabled by the Laws to adjudge and determine the Rights and Liberties of the Kingdom, against such Patents and Grants of His Majesty as are prejudicial thereunto, although strengthned by his Personal Commands, and by his Proclamation under the Great Seal, but it is likewise a Council to provide for the necessity, to prevent the imminent Dangers, and preserve the publick Peace and Safety of the Kingdom, and to declare the King's pleasure in those things that are requisite thereunto, *and what they do herein hath the stamp of Royal Authority, although His Majesty seduced by evil Council, do in his own Person oppose or interrupt the same,* for the King's Supream and Royal

THE HIGH COURT OF PARLIAMENT

pleasure is exercised and declared in this High Court of Law and Council after a more eminent and obligatory manner, then it can be by any personal Act or Resolution of his own." (Rushworth, *Collections*, vol. iv. pp. 551, 552.)

"By this memorable declaration," says John Allen, "which was the groundwork of all the subsequent proceedings of the parliament in the civil wars that ensued, it is obvious that the two houses not only separated the politic from the natural capacity of the King, but transferred to themselves the sovereign authority attributed to him by lawyers in his ideal character. They assumed to themselves the supreme power of the state, retaining nothing of monarchy but the name." (*Royal Prerogative*, 1849, pp. 83, 84.)

Note B. Parliamentary Sovereignty and the British Empire
(*Page* 369)

Since the above was written my friend, Mr. F. R. Carpenter, has called to my attention the similar conclusions which Mr. Frederick Scott Oliver has reached from a comparative study of the conditions of the American colonies after independence and those existing to-day in the British Empire, in his recent book on Alexander Hamilton, from which the following is an extract:

"When, however, we come to inquire closely into this matter of sovereignty, we are amazed to find how strong a likeness there is between the States of America before the Union and the British Empire at the present day. The difference lies in the dispositions of the two people, not in their political circumstances. In spite of our aspiration towards sovereignty (so strong and universal as almost to amount to a belief that somewhere in the empire a clear sovereignty does actually exist), in spite also of the fact that we are haunted by no fixed idea which confounds strong government with tyranny, we are victims of the same disease. There is no sovereignty. Everything hangs on sentiment, influence, and management. In the Three Kingdoms sovereignty so far has not been impaired; but outside these islands it is a very different matter. The theory of the empire seems hardly to have moved a step forward since the War of Independence. . . .

"The theory, indeed, of sovereignty is complete and without a

PARLIAMENTARY SUPREMACY

flaw, but it is also startling if we view it from a democratic standpoint. The imperial sovereignty which is exercised in the name of the King actually resides in the British Prime Minister, a gentleman who holds his office at the pleasure of the majority of the British House of Commons. Therefore, in the ultimate appeal, a majority of British voters is the supreme power in the empire. One democracy — for the time being the most numerous — holds a sovereignty, not merely over those portions of the King's dominions where, as in the case of India, the form of government is frankly autocratic, but over other democracies whom we think of, and who think of themselves, as self-governing. . . . But what has never been questioned since the War of Independence is that a democracy pretending to a sovereignty over other democracies is either a phantom or the most intolerable of all oppressions.

"In regard to the foreign affairs of the empire, sovereignty appears to best advantage. But even here, when carefully examined, its tenure is precarious, its warrant, in reason if not in law, is dubious. The true meaning of the situation is no less painful than it is plain. The most powerful member of a loose confederacy is content to defend her fellow-members from foreign attack for so long as they are willing to acquiesce in her policy. . . . But what is clear equally to the optimist and the cynic is that the other states will cease to acquiesce at the moment when our foreign policy has the appearance of being in serious conflict with their interests or their honour. The equilibrium is so unstable that no argument upon tradition can persuade us it has any of the elements of safety. Even with fine weather it is only a miracle that maintains it, and under rain or storm there must be a shifting of the balance that can have no issue but disintegration.

"Leaving foreign affairs upon one side, we are equally dismayed by the lack of any efficient check, not merely upon colonial legislation, but also upon purely British legislation. This want may imperil the very existence of the union if there is no power equal to the task of restraint or co-ordination, no courage equal to the exercise of such power, no judgment capable of directing the courage. And such is unfortunately the case. On British legislation there is not even a formal veto, while the veto upon colonial legislation is scrupulously preserved only because it is hardly ever exercised. Even if a colony desired to institute polygamy or slavery, or to practise repudiation, it would be a matter of the utmost delicacy to defeat its intention. For the exercise of the only veto which exists is, in plain words, the tyranny of one parliament over another—of one democracy over another.

"The theory of the British constitution is, as it stands, clearly intolerable, except in disuse. The powers which are imagined to exist in it would never stand the strain of being put in force. . . . The consequences being so obvious, we have declined upon a timid make-believe, and for the sake of peace and goodwill have laid sovereignty upon the shelf, regardless of the fact that sovereignty is the very essence of union.

"If the government of Great Britain and Ireland, which we term somewhat grandiosely the Imperial Parliament, desires anything to be done which requires colonial co-operation, it must go like the old Continental Congress, hat in hand, arguing, persuading, cajoling, and entreating. By a fine tradition it has the full dignity of sovereignty; but in reality it is as impotent as the Continental Congress, and only less ridiculous because it has learned from experience the timid wisdom not to court rebuffs.

"Our real reliance is upon the sentimental quality of each great emergency to produce a dramatic co-operation. But it is wise to remember that in a dramatic impulse, though there is *élan*, there is not, and cannot be, much staying power. The tie of affection or kinship is the raw material of union, not union itself. '*Influence*,' said Washington, '*is not government*.' A power which we refuse to influence we can hardly grant to sentiment. The union we complacently acknowledge is a mere shadow—not a political fact, but a poetical fancy. It has the health of an invalid who is free from pain so long as he will lie still in one position. Such is its present frailty, that in a protracted struggle of varying fortune it must almost inevitably fall asunder.

"The hope and strength of our great empire are in popular government, but the hope will be disappointed and the strength will fail if the need of a true sovereignty be overlooked. Sovereignty can never be secure while it rests upon a confusion of legal formulas and brittle sympathies; but only when it has been founded boldly upon the free and deliberate choice of the citizens of the empire" (pp. 475-9).

A more accurate, penetrating, or vigorous statement could hardly be desired.

Index

Absolute, meaning of the word, 129 sqq., and notes, 142.
Act of settlement, 77.
Aid, 59.
Analytical school of English *jurisprudentes*, 383, 384.
Army, their view of the fundamental law, 91.
Articles exhibited by the Clergy to the Privy Council temp. James I, 282 n.
Arundel, Archbishop, 69, 70.
Ashby v. *White*, 236 sq.
Assemblies, on the Continent, lost their feudal traditions, 321; colonial, had no higher legal status than an incorporated village, 365.
Assize, 44, 131; possessory assizes, 178 n. 2; of *Darrein Presentment*, 44; of *Novel Disseisin*, 44, 262 sq.; the word, 169, 283 sq.; distinguished from "laws," 284; its temporary character, 284; may be set aside by the judges, 284 and note; of Measures, 284 n.; of *Mort d'Ancestor*, 285.
Atkyns, Sir Robert, his argument in defence of Sir William Williams, 242 sqq.; on the dispensing power, 312 n.
Attainder, Bill of, 224 sqq.; St. John on, in the Earl of Strafford's Case, 151 sqq.; opinion of Henry VIII's judges on, 225.
Atterbury, Bishop, 224, 229 n.
Audita Querela, Writ of, 254, 255 sq.
Auditor. See Petitions, Triers of.
Aula, 30 n.
Austin, John, 259 n., 329; his conception of law, 144; on fictions, 266; his theory based on the dismembered state of the seventeenth century, 374.

Australia, federal constitution of, 369.
Award of Parliament, 114, 205, 216 sqq.
Aylesbury Men, Case of (*Regina* v. *Paty et al.*), 241 sq.

Bacon, Francis, Lord Chancellor, 193, 335; on Magna Charta, 64 sq.; on new laws, 73; on the jurisdiction of the courts of common law, 292 sqq.; on prerogative, 295 sq., 348 sq.; warns James I against the "Great Contract," 370.   [193.
Bacon, Nathaniel, 154, 172, 173 n.,
Bagehot, Walter, 128, 167; on prerogative, 381 n.
Bagg's Case, 292 sq., 316.
Barons, relations of the King with, in England, 9 sq., 15; loyalty to their order rather than to their country their main motive, 15 sq.
Barrington, Daines, on the obnoxious activity of lawyers in Parliament, 215.
Bate's Case, 316.
Battle, wager of, 131.
Becket, Thomas, Archbishop of Canterbury, 13; and the Constitutions of Clarendon, 45 n.
Bentham, Jeremy, 105, 266.
Berkely, Sir Thomas, Case of, 184 n.
Berkley, Sir Robert, his opinion in the Case of Ship-Money, 149.
Bernardiston v. *Soame*, 222.
Bible, occurrence in the various English versions of the word "judgement," 171.
Bigamy, statute of, 115.
Bill of Middlesex, 213.
Bills, substituted for petition, 209; their "judicial" character, 209 sq.; conclude with a prayer, 212.

[395]

INDEX

Bills, private, 142, 218 sqq.; procedure on, 222 sq.

Blackstone, Sir William, 311 n.; and the Cabinet, 127; on legislative sovereignty, 141; on statutes impossible of performance, 275; on void statutes, 308 sq.

Bodin, Jean, 373 sq.

Bonham's Case, 147, 286.

Bracton, his enumeration of the courts, 19, 20 n.; on fundamental law, 66, 101 sqq.; on the jurisdiction of Parliament, 248.

Brady, Robert, on the Norman monarchy in England, 7, 11; on the composition of the early Parliaments, 28.

Brenchley, William, 39.

British Empire, legal theory of, contrasted with actual conditions, 367 sqq.; too extensive for the existing theory of parliamentary sovereignty, 369; sovereignty in, 390 sqq.

Bryce, James, his distinction between legal and political or practical sovereignty, 379 sqq.

Burgesses, summoned to Parliament, 21; their relations with the King's Council in his Parliament, 25; their part in Parliament's "judicial" business, 25 sq.

Burials, the use of torches, tapers, etc., at, 280.

Burke, Edmund, on parliamentary reform, 377.

Camden, Charles Pratt, Lord, 176 n., 309 n.   [a court, 122.

Camden, William, on Parliament as

Canon Law, and common law, 272, 277; Sir T. More on, 278 sq.

Canterbury, Archbishop of, 281.

Cartwright, Thomas, on Parliament as a court, 121.

Castile, King of, his suit against the King of Navarre in the Court of the King of England, 111 and note.

Cessavit, Writ of, 297.

Chancellor, 252. *See* Chancery.

Chancery, Court of, 38, 200, 250 sq., 293; its relation to the Council in early times, 18 n.; its relation to Parliament, 115 sq., 132 sqq., 250 sq.; jealousy of, in Parliament, 213 sq.; clerks of, 210 n., 252, 254; Masters in, 210 n. *See* Chancellor.

Charlemagne, 10.

Charles I, 371.

Charles II, his secret dealings with Louis XIV, 371 sq.

Charters, 46; of Henry I, 46 n.; of Stephen, 46 n.

Of the Forests, 65; not on the Statute Roll, 314.

Colonial (royal), made to do duty as constitutions, 358 sqq.; rigid interpretation of, 361; (proprietary) 363 sq.; made an instrument of government, 364.

Municipal, 362 and note.

See Magna Charta.

Chatham, William Pitt, Earl of, 318.

Checks and balances, 372; in America, 385.

Church, the, 272; law of, to prevail over statutes in ecclesiastical matters, Sir T. More's view, 278 sq.; view of some churchmen of the present day, 281 sq.

Church of England, 73; not separate in organization in the middle ages, 13 and note.

Clarendon, Assize of, 284.

Clarendon, Constitutions of, 45 and note, 48, 111 and note.

Clarendon, Edward Hyde, Earl of, on the meaning of "jurisdiction," 170; on Strafford's trial, 225 (and

[396]

INDEX

note)sq., 306; his trial, 226 sq., 247; on parliamentary privilege, 240 sq.; on prerogative, 349.

Clopton, Walter, Chief Justice of the King's Bench, 40.

Coke, Sir Edward, 147 sqq., 194, 247, 265 sq., 271, 274 sq., 286 sqq., 300, 312, 335; on Statute of Gloucester, 48; as the "discoverer" of Magna Charta, 58 n.; on Magna Charta, 64 and note; on statutes and the old law, 73 sq., 74 n.; his quarrel with James I, 75 sq.; on the common law, 80; on the fundamental law, 82, 83 sq.; on Parliament as a court, 139 sqq.; on the Commons as a court of record, 235; on the exclusion of lawyers from Parliament, 214 sq.; on *lex parliamenti*, 233 sq.; his account of the evasion of the Statute *De Donis* by the judges, 267 n.; on declaratory statutes, 268, 270; on the statute of 3 H. VII organizing the Court of Star Chamber, 270 sq.; on declaring statutes void, 276, 286 sqq.; on Sir T. Tregor's Case, 286 sqq., 296; on *Cessavit*, 297; on statute 11 H. VII for determining cases on mere information, 301; on ordinance and statute, 314.

Colloquium, 28, 112.

Colonies, American, their growth to maturity in the eighteenth century, 359; ministerial ignorance of, 359 sq.; their growth divergent from England's, 360; their demand for recognition, 360; their retention of the ideas prevalent under the Tudors, 386 sq., 386 n.

Self-governing, their relations with Parliament, 366 sqq., 390 sqq.

Comminaltie de la terre, 104. *See* Communities of the Land.

Commissioners, Lords', on the Dignity of a Peer, 48 sqq.

Common recoveries, 267 (and note) sq.

Commons, House of, 21 sqq., 38.

Its functions as a part of Parliament, 26, 190 sqq.; Prynne on, 191 sqq.

As a court of record, 139, 234 sq.; as the Grand Inquest of the Nation, 187 sqq.; its judicial character in impeachment, 187 sqq.; its dealings with petitions, 202 sqq., 219; its renunciation of judicial power, 203; not necessary for a "full" Parliament, 216; privileges of, 230 sqq.; fines and imprisonment for a definite term imposed by, 235; its share in Parliament's jurisdiction, 244; its corruption and irresponsible character in the eighteenth century, 376.

Commonwealth, the Tudor, 336 sqq., 340 n., 378.

Communities of the Land, their relation to Parliament, 208 n.

Concilium, 17 and note.

Confirmatio Cartarum of 1297, 49.

Conseil d'État, 319, 320 and note.

Conservatism, of the English people, its merits and defects, 378.

Consimili Casu, Writs *in*. *See* Writs in Consimili Casu.

Constitution, English, unbroken history of, 8; its framework complete by the fourteenth century, 38; effect of precedent in the development of, 146; its character under the Tudors, 342; its silent steady growth, 358 sq.

Roman, its break-down under the Republic, 365.

Written, effect of, on power of judicial review, 5 sq., 323; reasons for absence of, in England, 61 sqq.; in

INDEX

England during the Interregnum, 92 and note.
Contract theory of government, 347.
Convention, 140.
Conventions of the Constitution, 188.
Cosin, Richard, on Parliament as a court, 121.
Cotton, Sir Robert, 194; his view of the reasons for first summoning the Commons to Parliament, 183 n.
Council, 15, 27 n. 2, 32, 35, 38 and note, 48 and note, 201, 293; its varied functions, 16, 30, 134 sq.; its relation to Parliament and the other courts of the King, 17 sqq., 23 sqq., 28, 132 sqq., 320, 332; its composition in early times, 22 sqq.; its part in the "judicial" business of the Parliament, 25 sq.

Judges in, 31 sqq., 39 sqq.; Prynne's views, 33; their oath, 34 sq.; their importance, 35 sqq.

Its jurisdiction and that of the House of Lords, 32 sq., 33 n.; estimate of, by Queen Elizabeth, 37; its importance in the Tudor and Stuart period, 37 and note; laws declared in, 45; its activity in the Tudor period, 136, 319; its relation to trial by jury, 183 sqq., 251 sq.; its relation to the Triers of Petitions, 201 sqq., 254; jealousy of it in Parliament, 212 sq., 216 sq.

Courts, their commanding position in England, as compared with the Continent, 321.

In the United States, have retained much of their ancient indefinite power, 323, 385 sqq.

In England, before the civil wars of the seventeenth century the courts still had much of their mediaeval "jurisdiction," 323, 385 sq.

The King's Courts, encroachment of, on the manorial and communal courts, 43 sq.; relations to Parliament, 113 n., 119 sq.; jury trial in, 174 sqq.; their limited power of initiative, 200; relation to the Triers of Petitions in Parliament, 202.

Courts of common law, their "legislative" functions, in Tudor and early Stuart times, 134 sq., 258 sqq., 267 n., 292 (Bagg's Case); descended from the ancient *Curia*, 295, 322; their jealousy of the Council, 320.

"Prerogative Courts," their struggle with Parliament in the seventeenth century, 295.

Court of Common Pleas, 286 n.; its relation to the Council in early times, 18 (and note) sq.

Court of King's Bench, its relation to the Council in early times, 18 (and note) sqq., 23 sqq.

Court of Exchequer Chamber, act of 1585 concerning, 132.

The word, 119, 126. *See Curia.*

See Chancery, Court of; Star Chamber, Court of; Council; Parliament.

Crawley, Sir Edward, his opinion in the Ship-Money Case, 304.
Croke, Sir James, 261.
Cromwell, Oliver, on the fundamental law, 86 sq., 91; on Lilburne's Trial in 1649, 89.
Cromwell's Case, 297 n.
Curia (the word), 29 sq., 30 n., 111 and note.
Curia Regis, 26; under the Norman kings in England, 7, 8 sq.; the parent of all the courts in England, including Parliament and the Privy Council, 295, 321.
Customs, 96 sqq., 131; declared in feudal courts, 44; declared in the

[398]

INDEX

King's Council, 45; the basis of mediaeval law, 46 sqq., 51 sq.; Filmer on, 96; in relation to the law of reason, 106 sq.; special, method of proving, 175.

Customs revenue, 316.

Darrein Presentment, Assize of, 44.
Day v. Savadge, 306. [273.
De Asportatis Religiosorum, Statute,
De Donis Conditionalibus, Statute, 74 n., 267 and note; doubt as to its being a statute, 314.
De la Pole, Michael, Chancellor, impeachment of, 39; Selden's opinion concerning, 40.
De Tocqueville, on the Supreme Court of the United States, 3 sq.
Declaration of May 27, 1642, by Parliament, assuming sovereignty, 389 sq.
Delaware, basis of William Penn's government in, 364.
Delegation of power by Parliament, 331 sqq.
Denman, Chief Justice, on the nature of parliamentary privilege, 245.
Dicey, Professor, on federalism and litigation, 3 sqq.; on the relations between kings and their assemblies in feudal times, 9 sq.; on "secondary" legislation in England and on the Continent, 334 sq.
Digby, George, Lord Digby, Earl of Bristol, his speech on Strafford's Attainder, 153, 225 sq.
Dispensing power, 310 sqq.
Divine Right of Kings, 75 sq., 370; origin and growth of the theory in England, 345; necessity for the theory, 345 sq.; results of the theory, 346 sqq.; statement of, by James I, 347 sq.; placed the King outside the commonwealth and split up the body politic, 371; its contribution to political theory, 373; the forerunner of parliamentary sovereignty, 378.
Doctor and Student, 105 sqq.; on the relation of statutes to the customary law, 72; on common recoveries, 268 n.; on void statutes, 279 sqq., 300.
Doddridge, Sir John, on Parliament as a court, 122.
Droit Administratif, 317 sqq., 334 sq.
Dugdale, Sir William, 250.

Ecclesiastical Discipline, Royal Commission on, communications addressed to, on the authority of the Judicial Committee of the Privy Council, 281 sq.
Edward the Confessor, Laws of, 45 n., 46 n., 53.
Edward I, 16, 49 sq., 51, 116 n.; summons knights and burgesses to Parliament, 21; legislative activity of his reign, 48.
Edward II, his deposition announced by one of the judges in the Council, 36.
Election petitions, settled by a party vote in the House of Commons, 376 sq.
Eliot, Sir John, 335; on the meaning of "judgement," 171 sq.; Case of, 221.
Elizabeth, Queen, her opinion of privy councillors, 37; indulged the common people, not the nobility, 339 sq., 342.
Ellesmere, Thomas, Lord, 171, 218 n., 250, 254 sq., 261, 300; his views of the judges' functions in Parliament, 137 sq.; on the jurisdiction of the courts of common law, 292 sqq.; an opponent of the common lawyers, 294; on the construction of statutes, 261, 294 sq.

[399]

INDEX

Elsynge, Henry, on petitions, 204 sq., 206; on receivers of petitions, 208 sq.; on the *Pronunciationes Parliamenti*, 331.

Emperor, his claim of authority over England, 344; his claims against the Papacy, 344.

Enquête par Tourbe, 43, 175, 177.

Entails, Statute of, 74 n.

Equity, its growth proportionate to the decline of Parliament's judicial activity, 133.

Établissement, 169.

Ethelbert, King, his dooms, 97.

Exchequer, its relation to the Council in early times, 18 n.

FEDERALISM, substitutes litigation for legislation, 3 sqq.

Fenwick, Sir John, Attainder of, 227 sqq.

Ferrers' Case, 232, 338.

Feudal immunities, the basis of national liberties, 16, 52 sq., 54 sqq.

Feudalism, its importance in mediaeval English history, 6 sq., 9; involves a fusion of public and private rights, wrongs, and remedies, 114.

Fiction, 47, 63, 213, 265 sqq.

Filmer, Sir Robert, 189, 193, 348; on the Norman monarchy in England, 7, 11; on the powers of the judges in the early Council, 34 n.; on legislative sovereignty, 96, 161 sq.; on the Commons as a court of record, 235 sq.

Finch, Sir Heneage, on Parliament's inability to declare treason, 306.

Finch, Sir Henry, on an award of Parliament, 218 n.

Fitzharris, Edward, Case of, 189, 238.

Fitzherbert's Case, 235.

Flambard, Ranulf, 8, 12.

Fleta, its author's remarks on the relation of Council and Parliament, 20 and note; fundamental law in, 68 and note; on prerogative, 101; on triers of petitions, 251.

Floyde's Case, 235.

Foreigners, opposition to, by English barons, 15.

Fortescue, Sir John, 53; his distinction between *Dominium Regale* and *Dominium Politicum et Regale*, 72.

"Forty days' tyranny," 318.

Fox, Charles James, his attitude toward the revolutionists in America, 378.

Fox's Libel Act, 176.

Franchises, 53 and note.

Freeman, 11, 12; on the continuity of the English central assembly, 8 sq.

Frowik, or Frowick, Chief Justice, 277.

Fundamental Law, 42 sqq., 46, 51 sq., 53, 55 sq., 57, 61 sqq., 84 n.; Prynne on, 65 sq., 84 sq., 85 n.; in Bracton, 66; in the reign of Henry III, 66 and note; in Fleta, 68 and note; in the reign of Richard II, 68 sqq.; Mr. Figgis on, 70 sq.; Manwood on, 72 sq.; James I's idea of, 79 (and note) sq., 82 and note; origin of the expression, 81 sqq.; Pym on, 83; Wentworth on, 83; Coke on, 82, 83 sq.; Selden on, 85; Judge Jenkins on, 85 sq.; Cromwell on, 86 sq.; different interpretations of, by royalists and parliamentarians, 88; as used by the republicans, 88 sqq., 90 sqq.; as viewed by the army, 91; *vs.* Divine Right, 349 sq.

Fusion of powers, the, explains relations of Parliament to other courts, 119, 126 sq., 150, 164 sqq., 188, 204, 219 sq., 245, 246, 293, 319.

INDEX

Gᴇᴏʀɢᴇ II, 372.
Gloucester, Statute of, 48, 262 sq.
Godden v. *Hales*, 242, 310 n.
"Government by Commission" in the United States, 318, 319, 331, 334.
Grand Assize, 43, 44, 176.
Grand Inquest, the Commons as, 187 sqq., 191 sq.
"Great Contract," between James I and his subjects, 370, 371.
Gresham's Case, 298 n.

Hᴀʙᴇᴀs *Corpus Act*, 354.
Hakewell, William, 153.
Hale, Sir Matthew, his views concerning the powers of the judges in the Council, 33 and note, 36, 37; on the supremacy of Parliament, 162 sq.; on the meaning of "jurisdiction," 170; on the jurisdiction of the Commons, 193 sqq.; on the declaration of treason pursuant to the act of 25 E. III, 247 sq.; on triers of petitions in Parliament, 253 sq.
Halifax, George Savile, Marquis of, his "Trimmer" on the relation of King and State, 371.
Halifax Gibbet Law, 362.
Halla, 31 n.
Hankeford, Sir William, 39.
Harrington, James, 87 and notes, 165; on Elizabeth's government, 339 sq.
Harrison, William, 347; his description of Parliament, 131.
Hastings, Warren, Case of, 187 sq.
Heads of the Proposals, 371.
Heathfield v. *Chilton*, 329 sq.
Henry I, his charter, 46 n., 53.
Henry II, 23; and the Constitutions of Clarendon, 45 and note.
Henry III, 16; his reissue of Magna Charta in 1225, 285.

Henry VIII, 347; on the privileges of Parliament, 232; his letter to Lady Worsley, 234 sq.; his characterization of the "organic" state, 336, 338; his relations with his subjects, 349.
Herle, William, Chief Justice of the Common Pleas, his statement in Tregor's Case, 286 sqq., 296.
Hobart, Sir Henry, 260 sq.
Hobbes, Thomas, 130, 347, 350, 373; on legislative sovereignty, 95 and note, 161; on Parliament as a body merely advisory to the King, 330 sq.; on the Crown's power to dissolve Parliament, 381 n.
Holmes, Justice, his views of the legislative activity of the courts, 258 sq.
Holt, Sir John, 241 sq.; his comment on Bonham's Case, 307; his advice concerning the Maryland Charter, 364.
Hooker, Richard, on Parliament's power to alter the law by statute, 73; his Erastianism, 73 n.; on the King in the commonwealth, 338.
Howell, James, 153.

Iʟʙᴇʀᴛ, Sir Courtenay, his view of the proper attitude of judges toward acts of Parliament, 260.
Impeachment, 187 sq.
Imperial, John, Case of, 247 sq.
Inquest, a statute requiring priests to go generally upon, would be void, 280 sq. See Jury, Trial by.
Institutions, the nature of their development, 167, 168 sq.
Instrument of Government, 86.
Interpretation, judicial, 257 sqq.
Irish people, statute of 9 H. IV requiring them to depart the realm, 301.

INDEX

James I, on old and new laws, 74; his struggle with Coke, 75 sq.; his theory of the kingship, 78 sqq., 347 sqq.; his idea of fundamental law, 79 sq.; his idea of his relation to his subjects and theirs to him, 347 sq.

Jenkins, David, Judge, 154, 193; on fundamental law, 85 sq.; on the power of the Crown to dissolve Parliament, 381.

Jeofail, Statutes of, 265.

Jones, Sir William, his opinion in the Ship-Money Case, 149.

Judgement (the word), 170 sqq.

Judges: their powers and functions in the Council, 31 sqq., 39 sqq., 323 sq.; Prynne's views, 33.

Their importance in the Council, 35 sqq.; form of summons to Parliament, 33 (and note) sq.; their part in the drafting of statutes, 36, 324, 325 and note; independence of, 76 sq.

In Parliament, Lord Ellesmere on, 137 sq., 186, 198 sq., 352 sq.; their relation to the King, 149, 317; their attitude toward acts of Parliament, 257 sqq., 289 sqq. (Tregor's Case), 294, 325 sqq.

Their attitude toward the royal prerogative in the seventeenth century, 301 sqq.; Bacon on, 335.

Judicature and legislation, relation between, 257 sqq.

Judicial Committee of the Privy Council, its authority in ecclesiastical causes, 281 sq.

Juratores, 182 n.

Jurisdiction (the word), 169 sq.

Jury, trial by, 57, 63, 173 sqq.; law and fact in, 175 sq.; the verdict in, 177; not narrowly judicial in character, 177 sqq., 178 n. 2; the presentment, 178; grand and petty jury, 179 sq.; importance of, in fiscal matters, 180; case of a jury ordered to appear before the Council, 184 n., 251 sq.; a jury of knights in Parliament, 184 n. *See* Inquest.

Justices Itinerant, 178 n. 2, 183 sq., 185, 186.

Justiciarius, 31 n.

King, his powers and duties in feudal times, 9 sq.

King of England: his power in the Norman period, 9 sq.; his relations with his barons, 9 sq., 15 sq.; his right to refuse assent to bills, 65 sq.

The King and the law, in Bracton, 66; in Fleta, 68 and note; in Fortescue, 72; in Manwood, 72 sq.; in the theory of James I, 78 sqq.

The King and the commonwealth, 75 sqq.

His relations with Parliament and the other courts, 149; Prynne's view, 154 sqq.; the proper judge of the necessity for levying ship-money, 304; his supremacy, 344.

Relations with the Church, 272; cannot be made a parson, 277 sq.

As Supreme Head of the Church, Sir T. More's view, 279; his relation to the commonwealth, 336 sqq.; his legal demands and Parliament's, 342 sq.; his changed relation to his subjects after the Reformation, 344 sqq. *See* Monarchy.

Knights, summoned to Parliament, 21; their relations with the King's Council in his Parliament, 25; their part in Parliament's "judicial" business, 25 sq.

Knox, John, 171.

Lambard, William, on Parliament as a court, 123 sq.

[402]

INDEX

Law, to be distinguished from enactment, 284, 299, 311 sq.; conservatism of the, 312.
    Feudal, 42 sq.
    Common, 43 sq., 131, 253; Mr. Figgis on, 70 sq.; and the kingship, 75 sqq.; and statute, St. John on, 84; Milton on, 94; and Canon Law, 272, 277.
    International, its relation to parliamentary sovereignty, 308, 329 sq.
    Judge-made, 258, 329.
    Of nature, 97 sqq., 105 sqq., 272.
    Of reason, 264; in the *Doctor and Student*, 98 sq., 105 sqq., 300.
    Of God, 278 sq., 300.
    Constituent, its relation to ordinary legislation, in the United States, 4; in the German Empire, 5; in Switzerland, 5; reasons for absence of, in England, 61 sqq.
Law and fact in the early jury, 175 sq.
Law Merchant, 329.
Laws, in feudal times "not enactments but records," 42 sq.; of Edward the Confessor, 45, 46 n., 53; Anglo-Saxon, 42; of William the Conqueror, 46 n.
Lawyers, 81, 217 n., 219 n., 293; feeling of James I toward, 76, 80, 81; excluded from Parliament, 214 sqq.; their attitude toward Divine Right, 349.
Leges Barbarorum, lack of distinction between crime and tort in, 114.
Legislation, 42, 46 sqq., 257; paucity of, in mediaeval England, 42 sqq., 51, 327; in Parliament of 1305, 48; in reign of Edward I, 48; the assizes the only form of, in early England, 284; not exclusively Parliament's, 315, 317, 319; the act of the King, 316; "secondary," in England and on the Continent, 317 sqq.
Legislative sovereignty, 94, 103 sqq., 137, 140 sqq., 148, 156, 161, 162, 224 sqq., 243, 293, 294, 296, 306, 350, 373, 375 n.; in Smith's *Commonwealth*, 128 sqq.; in Strafford's Trial, 151 sqq.; in Streater's Case (1653), 159 sq., 305 sq.; leads to the attributing of unlimited power to both King and Parliament in the seventeenth century, 351; first definitely assumed by Parliament, 352; a new thing in the seventeenth century, 355 sq.; the theory as held in England, mechanical and unhistorical, 370; makes a sharp distinction between sovereign and subject, 370 sq.; the service of the theory to political science, 373 sq.
    Defects of the theory in England, 374; the result of strife, not of growth, 374 sq.
    Service of the theory to England, 375.
Levellers, on fundamental law, 87.
Lewes, the Song of, 66 n.
Lex parliamenti, 139, 224, 233 sqq., 243 sq.
Liberties, of classes become those of the nation, 52 sq.
Lilburne, John, his trial in 1649, 89; on fundamental law and Parliament's power, 89 sq.; on Magna Charta, 91.
Locke, John, 377; did not separate judicial from other administration, 316, 347.
Logic, insufficiency of, 384.
Long Parliament, 85, 104, 154.
"Lords Appellant," 39.
Lords, House of, 38, 139, 163 sq.; beginning of a separate jurisdiction of, 32 sq., 33 n.; as a court of record,

[403]

INDEX

234; exclusiveness of its jurisdiction, 244; will not reverse its decisions, 386.

Magna Charta, 46, 49 and note, 54 sqq., 83, 95, 154, 178 n. 2, 183 n.; punishment for contemptuous remarks concerning, 13; a feudal not a national document, 14, 54 sqq.; its importance due to its embodying the idea of a fundamental law, 55 sq.; the later interpretation of, 57 sq.; not on the Statute Roll, 314; its reissues, 58 sq., 285; omissions in the reissues, 58 sq.; an unalterable law, 59 sqq.; Francis Bacon on, 64 sq.; Coke on, 64 and note; Prynne on, 65 sq.; Lilburne on, 91.

Magnum Concilium, 17.

Malum prohibitum, 108, 299, 311 n.

Mansfield, William Murray, Lord, 176 n.

Manwood, John, on the fundamental law, 72 sq.

Maryland, Lord Holt advises that its charter may be taken away, 364.

Massachusetts Convention of 1780, 87 n.

Masters of Requests, 255 sq.

Maxims, as a ground of the law of England, 106 sqq.

Measures, Richard I's Assize of, 284 note.

Merton, statute of, 48 n., 74 n., 112.

Mildmay's Case, 267 n.

Milton, John, 130; on the common law, 94; on parliamentary sovereignty, 94.

Monarchomachs, the, 345.

Monarchy, the English: under the Norman kings, theories concerning, 7 sq., 11 sq., 14; feudal theory of, 9 sqq.

Under the Tudors, 336 sqq., 340 n.; theories in its support against the Papacy, 345 sqq.

See King, King of England.

Montagu, Edward, Chief Justice of the Common Pleas, 293.

Montagu, Sir Henry, 293.

Montesquieu, the English constitution described by, was the post-Revolutionary constitution, 322; on the separation of powers, 322 sq.

Montfort, Simon de, 12, 15 sq.

More, Sir Thomas, on statutes contrary to the laws of the land, 72 and note; his dialogue with Sir R. Rich concerning statutes void because against the Law of God and the Church, 278 sq.; sufficiency of his indictment, 279.

Mort d'Ancestor, Assize of, 285.

Mostyn v. *Fabrigas*, 266 n.

"National" theory of the Norman conquest and régime in England, 8 sq., 11 sq., 14 sq.

Nationality, growth of the feeling of, in England, 52 sq., 56 sq.; under the Tudors, 336 sqq.

Nature, law of, 97 sqq., 105 sqq., 272.

Navarre, King of, his quarrel with the King of Castile, settled in the court of the King of England, 111 and note.

Nobility, effect of the Wars of the Roses upon, 131, 338 sqq.; decline of, under the Tudors, 338 sqq.

Nonclaim, statute of, 74 n.

Northampton, Assize of, 284.

Northington, Lord Chancellor, 96, 309 n., 366, 377.

Novel Disseisin, Assize of, 44, 262 sq.

Noy, William, on old and new laws, 74.

[404]

INDEX

Oath, councillors', 34 sq., 113 and note; of judges in Parliament, 138; of supremacy, 344; *ex officio*, abolished, 354.

O'Connell, Daniel, Case of, in 1844, 36.

Ordinance, 114, 313 sqq.; difference between statute and, 313 sqq.

Ordinances, of the Barons in 1310, 112; of 1311, 113 and note; of 1312, 252, 253; concerning wool in 1337, 332; concerning the staple in 1385, 332.

Organic state, the, under the Tudors, 336 sqq.

Otis, James, on void acts of Parliament, 309.

Papacy, mediaeval theories against the power of, 344; national opposition to, 345.

Parliament, 6, 7, 8, 15 sq., 17 sqq., 62, 109 sq.; awards of, 114, 205, 216 sqq.; its relation to the Council in early times, 17 sqq.

The King's power over, 380 sq.; according to Prynne, 155 sqq.

Knights summoned to, 21; burgesses summoned to, 21; its component parts under Edward I, 21 sq.

Its "judicial" functions, 25, 109 sqq., 197 sq., 317; in abeyance under the Tudors, 131 sq., 136, 291; judges in, 31 sqq., 137 sq.; opened by one of the judges in 1401, 36; of 1305, 48; a law-declaring body, 51.

Bound by acts of a preceding Parliament, 60; and by the fundamental law, 62 sqq.; definitely becomes a law-making organ, 93, 109 sq., 112, 120; as a court, 109 sqq., 137 sqq., 156 sqq., 248 sqq., 259; frequency of sessions, 113; its relation to the King's other courts, 113 n., 119 sq., 165 sq., 254, 290, 322; its relation to the Chancellor, 115 sq., 116 n., 250 sq., 254; held on legal term days, 114.

Its "acts," 114, 136 sq., 216 sqq.; their relation to the judges, 257 sqq.; "expository" acts, 257.

As a court of record, 139; order of, 159 sq.

Effect of dissolution of, on prisoners detained by order of, 160 sq.; on an impeachment, 187 sq.; its jealousy of the Council, 212 sq., 215 sq.; its jealousy of the Court of Chancery, 213 sq.; lawyers excluded from, 214 sqq.; Reformation Parliament, 104; Long Parliament, 85, 104, 154.

Privileges of, 139, 161, 230 sqq.; freedom of speech, 220 sqq., 229 sqq., 242 sqq.; abuses of privilege in the eighteenth century, 376; descended from the ancient *Curia*, 295; its struggle with the "prerogative courts" in the seventeenth century, 295; its inability to declare a new treason, 306; not exclusively legislative, 317; retained many of its feudal characteristics, 321 sq.; its relation to international law, 329; as an advisory council, 330 sq.; its legal demands and the King's, 342 sq.; its first definite assumption of sovereignty, 352; becomes permanent and regular, 353 sq.; effect of its permanency and regularity on the administration of law in the courts, 354.

Its sovereignty, 350, 353, 355 sqq., 378; a deduction from actual conditions in England after the Revolution, 357; the theory not suited for a universal political prin-

[405]

INDEX

ciple, 357 sq., 376; in the empire, 369; Lilburne on, 89 sq.; effect of civil wars of the seventeenth century upon, 93 sqq.; Milton on, 94; evil effects of, 377; assumed in 1642, 389 sq.

Its relations with the self-governing colonies, 366 sqq.; chooses auditors and treasurers, 372; election petitions in, 376 sq.; the Crown's power to dissolve, 380 sq.

See Legislative sovereignty, Sovereignty, Sovereign.

Parliament (the word), 27 (and note) sqq., 29 n., 197.

Parson, the King cannot be made a parson by act of Parliament, 277 sq.

Peers, excused from jury service, 114; trial of, 177.

Penn, William, the basis of his government of Delaware, 364.

Peter's Pence, the Act concerning, in 1533, 333.

Petition of Right, 82 sqq.

Petitions, 199 sqq., 219, 252; addressed to King or Council in early times, 184 and note; addressed to the Commons, 202 sq., 207, 213; relief asked for in, 205 sq.; character of those presenting, 206 sqq.; to the Lords, 206 sq.; from the Commons, 207; preferred in Parliament by attorneys, 208.

Receivers of, 208 sqq.; their relation to the Chancery, 210 and note; their relation to the Masters of Requests, 255 sq.

Conclude with a prayer, 212, 223; a commission created in 21 Ric. II empowered to hear and determine petitions, 332.

Triers of, in Parliament, 198 sqq., 251 sqq.; their relation to the Council, 201 sqq., 205 sqq.; their relation to the King's ordinary courts, 202.

Petyt, William, 154, 312 n.; on an award of Parliament, 216, 218 and note.

Piers the Plowman, 117, 209.

Pitt, William, Earl of Chatham, 360.

Playter's Case, 265 and note.

Political theories, the result of political conditions, 355.

Pollock, Sir Frederick, on the practice of judges in declaring statutes void, 271, 275, 276; on Tregor's Case, 287 sq.; on the character of early statutes, 326 sq.

Pope, the, 272, 278 sq.

Postnati, Case of the, 137, 171.

Praerogativa Regis, so called Statute of, 64 n.

Precedent, its effect on the English Constitution, 146, 154.

Precedents of the Tudor period variously interpreted in the seventeenth century, 351.

Prerogative, 299, 302, 304 n., 310, 313, 316 sq., 380, 381 and note; James I's statement of, 78 sqq., 347 sq.; Bracton's statement of, 101 sqq.; Fleta's statement of, 101; Prynne on, 154 sqq.; Bacon on, 335; Staunford on, 337 sq.; Bagehot on, 381 n.

Prescription, 131.

Primogeniture, 329.

Privy Council, 119, 317.

Proclamations, 312, 313 sqq., 317 and note, 333 sq.; Henry VIII's statute of, 333 sq.

Pronunciationes Parliamenti. *See* Speeches from the Throne.

Propositions of New Castle, 371.

Prorogation of Parliament, Prynne's interpretation of Magna Charta on, 154 sq.

[406]

INDEX

Provisions of Oxford, 250 sq.
Prynne, William, 158 n., 183 n., 235; his views concerning the powers of the judges in the early Council, 33; on Magna Charta, 65 sq.; on the fundamental law, 65 sq., 84 sq., 85 n.; his *Soveraigne Power of Parliaments and Kingdomes*, 154 sqq.; on the meaning of "jurisdiction," 169 sq.; on the jurisdiction of the Commons, 191 sqq.; on the exclusion of lawyers from Parliament, 215; on the relation of the receivers of petitions and the Masters of Requests, 255 sq.; on ordinances and statutes, 314, 334. [83.
Pym, John, on the fundamental law,

Q*uia Emptores*, Statute of, doubt of its being a real statute, 314.
Quominus, 213.
Quo Warranto, 217.

R<small>ALEIGH</small>, Sir Walter, his views of Parliament as merely a council advisory to the King, 330; on the decline of the power of the nobility, 338 sqq.; on the relation of the King and Parliament, 342 sq.
Reason, "artificial," 108; Coke's doctrine of, 80, 99; Hobbes on, 95 n.
  Law of, 264; in the *Doctor and Student*, 98 sq., 105 sqq., 300.
Redlich, Joseph, views of, concerning the judicial functions of Parliament and the Commons, 230 n.
Reformation, the, its influence in creating the theory of the Divine Right of Kings, 344 sqq.
Reformation Parliament, 104.
Regina v. *Keyn*, 329.
Republicans, their use of fundamental law, 88 sq., 90 sqq.
Revolution, English, 350; inevitable character of, 342, 343; not the result of illegal oppression, 364 sq., 366.
  American, 358 sqq.; the result of the break-down of the constitution, 358; not a struggle for legal rights, 364 sqq.; the sequel to the English Revolution, 377; attitude of the Opposition in Parliament toward, 377 sq.
Rex et Regina v. *Knollys*, 241 sq.
Rich, Sir Richard, his dialogue with Sir T. More on Church and State, 278 sq.
Richard II, his defiance of the fundamental laws, 68 sqq.; charged with creating an unlawful commission to determine petitions, 332.
Rikehyl, or Rickhill, Sir William, justice of the Court of Common Pleas, 40.
Rolle, Henry, Chief Justice, 307; on parliamentary sovereignty, 159 sq.

S<small>T</small>. J<small>OHN</small>, Henry, Viscount Bolingbroke, buys his way back from exile, 372.
St. John, Oliver, on common law and statute, 84; on the judicial character of Parliament, in the Ship-Money Case, 150 sqq., 305 n.; on Strafford's Attainder, 226 and note.
Scotland, disputed succession to the crown of, 112.
Seals, Abbey, Case of, in 27 H. VI, 273 sqq.
Selden, John, 193; his opinion concerning the Case of Michael de la Pole, 40; his comment on Bracton's garbling of the Digest, 102; on the changes in the meaning of words, 167.
Separation of powers, 319, 385; Montesquieu on, 322 sq.

INDEX

Septennial Act, 60.
Seven Bishops, Case of, 242.
Sheffield v. *Ratcliffe*, 260 sq.
Ship-Money, Case of, 149 sqq., 303 sq.
Skelton, Sir Thomas, 39.
Smith, Sir Thomas, 53, 347; his Discourse on the Commonwealth of England, 124 sqq.; on Parliament as a court, 124 sqq., 356.
Sovereign, location of, in a state, 379. *See* Parliament, Legislative sovereignty, Sovereignty.
Sovereignty, legal and political, as distinguished by Mr. Bryce and Professor Dicey, 144, 379 sqq., 382 sqq.
  As existing in the state rather than in its governor, 383.
  Of Parliament, 109; Lilburne on, 89 sq.; effect of civil wars of seventeenth century upon, 93 sqq.
  See Parliament; Legislative sovereignty, Sovereign.
Speeches from the Throne (*Pronunciationes Parliamenti*), 331.
Spelman, Sir Henry, 166, 243 and note.
Stamp Act, 309 n.
Staple, ordinance concerning, in 1385, 332.
Star Chamber, Court of, 293, 334; its abolition by the Long Parliament, 37; its relation to Parliament, 132, 134; its "legislative" powers, 135 sq., 319; Hudson's description of, 135; Coke on the statute of 3 H. VII organizing, 270 sq.
Statute of 11 H. VII for determination of cases on mere information, 301.
Statutes, 131, 169, 299; character of, under Edward I, 48; power of Parliament to alter, 60, 63 sq., 69 sqq.
  Their relation to customary law, as stated in the *Doctor and Student*, 72; as stated by Sir Thomas More, 72 and note; Coke on, 73 sq., 74 n.
  James I, on the authority of, 79; Milton on, 94; as a ground of the law of England, 106 sqq.; and ordinances, 114.
  Interpretation of, 257 sqq.; Ellesmere on, 261, 294.
  Declaratory of the common law, 268 sqq.; interpretation of, 269 sqq., 327; in the affirmative, 269 sq.
  Declared by the judges to be void, 270 sqq., 283 sqq., 297, 298 sqq., 326, 387.
  Against the Law of God and the Church, Sir T. More's view of, 278 sq.; view of some modern churchmen, 281 sq.; cases "excepted out of," 285 sq., 302, 311, 315 sq.; Herle's statement as to the makers of statutes not willing to put them into effect, 286 sqq., 296; drawn by the judges, 290, 324; brevity of, in early times, 315, 324; and international law, 329.
Staundeforde, Staunford, or Stanford, William, 73 n.; on prerogative, 337 sq.
Stauntons, Case of the, 326.
Stephen, King, his charters, 46 n., 53.
Stockdale v. *Hansard*, 241, 245.
Strafford, Thomas Wentworth, Earl of, on fundamental law, 83; attainder of, 151 sqq., 225 sq., 247, 269; on prerogative, 295 sq., 349; on "secondary" legislation, 335.
Streater, Captain John, Case of, 158 sqq., 238, 305 sq.
Strode, Richard, Case of, 220 sqq.
Stuart kings, their lack of caution, 341; the revolution not due entirely to their incapacity, 342.
Supremacy, Act of, in 1 Eliz., 172.

INDEX

Supreme, meaning of the word, 142 sqq., 144 n, 148, 161 sq., 344.
Supreme Court of the United States, 143, 165; De Tocqueville on, 3 sq.; its power to review legislation due only to the "rigid" constitution, 4 sq.; has reversed itself, 386.
Suspending power, as stated by James I, 79.

T*altarum's Case*, 267.
Taxation, the power of the King concerning, 316 sq.
Term days, Parliament held on, 114.
Thirning, William, Chief Justice of the Common Pleas, 40, 331.
Thomas v. Sorrell, 310 n., 311 n.
Thorp, Sir William, Chief Justice, 249; his case, 230.
Tonnage and poundage, 84, 316, 372.
Torts, not clearly distinguished from crimes in feudal times, 114.
Towns, representatives of, in Parliament, 185 sq.
Tractatus, 30 n.
Treason, 306; Edward III's Statute of, 116 sq., 247 sq.; in Strafford's trial, 151 sqq., 269.
Tregor's Case, 286 sqq.
Tresilian, Judge, Case of, 39 sq.
Trewynard's Case, 121.
Triennial Act, 60.
Tudors, England in their time as compared with the Stuart period, 351 sq.
Twysden, Roger, 153.

ULPIAN, 102.
Union with Scotland, Act of, intended to be permanent, 60.

United States, 355; citizens of the, a "litigious people," 3, 5, 6.

V*illatae*, 182 n.
Virginia, colonial charter of, granted in 1609, 361 sq.; conditions under, 363.

WASTE, Statute of, 220.
Wentworth, Thomas. *See* Strafford.
Westminster First, Statute of, 115 sq.
Westminster Second, Statute of, 213, 251, 297.
Weston, Justice, his opinion in the Ship-Money Case, 303 sq.
Whyte, Francis, on the power to amend the old law by statute, 74 n.
Wildman, Sir John, his views on fundamental law, 91.
William the Conqueror, 8, 53; laws of, 46 n.
Williams, Sir William, Case of, 242 sqq.
Wills, Statute of, 74 n.
Witenagemot, 7, 10; its continuance, 8, 9.
Woodfall's Case, 176 n.
Wool, ordinance for the exportation of, in 1337, 332.
Words, indefiniteness of the extent of the meaning of, in early times, 26 sqq.; evidence of, in the judicial history of Parliament, 166 sqq.; interpretation of, in statutes, 262.
Writs *in Consimili Casu*, 115 sq., 213, 251.
Writs, original, 200.
Writs of Summons, sent to knights and burgesses by Edward I, 21 sq.; form used for judges, 33 sq.

D. B. UPDIKE, THE MERRYMOUNT PRESS, BOSTON